The Complete Private Pilot

Seventh Edition

Bob Gardner

Aviation Supplies & Academics, Inc.
Renton, Washington

ASA-PPT

Aviation Supplies & Academics, Inc.
7005 132nd Place SE
Renton, Washington 98059-3153

Cover photo © James Lawrence

Printed in the United States of America

99 98 97 96 95   9 8 7 6 5 4 3 2

ISBN 1-56027-173-6
ASA-PPT

Library of Congress Cataloging-in-Publication data:

Gardner, Robert E., 1928–
    The complete private pilot / Robert E. Gardner. —7th ed.
        p.   cm.
    Includes index.
    ISBN 1-56027-173-6
    1. Private flying. I. Title
TL 721.4.G34 1994   94-5805
629.132'5217—dc20   CIP

Original illustration: Dick Bringloe and Don Szymanski
Photo credits: p.vi—Dora Muir; p. 2–4—(*courtesy NASA*);
p. 2–4—Robert Gardner; p. 2–11—(*courtesy General
Aviation News & Flyer*); p. 2–12—Robert Gardner; p. 2–18—
(*NASA*); p. 3–7—(*courtesy Sigma-Tek Aircraft Instruments*);
p. 3–8—(*courtesy Cessna Aircraft*); p. 3–9—Robert Gardner;
pp. 3–10, –11—(*Cessna Aircraft*); p. 4–1—Robert Gardner;
p. 4–3—(*Sigma-Tek Aircraft Instruments*); p. 4–4—(*courtesy
Safe Flight*); pp. 4–5, –7—(*Sigma-Tek Aircraft Instruments*);
p. 4–8—(*courtesy American Avionics*); p. 4–10—(*Cessna Aircraft*); pp. 4–11—(*American Avionics*); pp. 7–8—Robert
Gardner; p. 8–1—Henry Geijbeek; p. 8–2—(*American
Avionics*); pp. 8–8, –9, –11—(*courtesy NARCO*); p. 8–12—
(*courtesy ARNAV*); p. 9-2—(*American Avionics*); p. 9-6—
(*NARCO*); p. 10–5—Robert Gardner; p. 10–7—(*NASA*);
p. 11–26—(*courtesy Allied-Bendix*); p. 11–26—(*courtesy
3-M StormScope Weather Mapping System*); p. 12-1—(*ASA*);
pp. 16–8, –9, –11—(*courtesy Washington State Aeronautics
Commission*); p. 17–1—(*ASA*)

Contents

Continued

Introduction
by Richard Taylor

A new aviation book—one that plows new ground, one that develops material never before considered—is pretty hard to come by. And until there are some radical changes in the types of aircraft we fly and the techniques necessary to fly them, the situation is quite likely to stay that way.

But there are always better, if not "new," ways to communicate aviation information...that's what Bob Gardner has accomplished with *The Complete Private Pilot*.

A writer embarking on the task of creating a fundamental aviation text is faced with a formidable challenge; if prospective pilots are to reap the benefits of his work, the writing must be at once very readable and very comprehensive.

The Complete Private Pilot does both of those in spades, as Bob Gardner reaches into his own aeronautical experience and brings to the reader a clear exposition of the knowledge required by the budding private pilot.

It's not all here—you'll continue learning (we hope!) long after your initial study of regulations, weather, navigation, and so on—but *The Complete Private Pilot* is a great way to get started.

Your author has met the challenge well. *The Complete Private Pilot* is indeed readable, comprehensive, and perhaps more important than those, it's a book which will lead you to a greater understanding of flying's fundamentals.

I've always contended that a smart pilot is a safe pilot...you are to be commended for your choice of *The Complete Private Pilot* as a bedrock book in your aviation library.

About the Author

Robert Gardner has long been an ad- mired member of the aviation community. He began his flying career in Alaska in 1960 while in the U.S. Coast Guard. By 1966, Bob accomplished his Private land and sea, Commer- cial, instrument, Instructor, CFII and MEL. Over the next 16 years he was an instructor, charter pilot, desig- nated examiner, freight dog and Director of ASA Ground Schools.

Currently, Bob holds an Airline Transport Pilot Cer- tificate with single- and multi-engine land ratings; a CFI certificate with instrument and multi-engine rat- ings, and a Ground Instructor's Certificate with ad- vanced and instrument ratings. In addition, Bob is a Gold Seal Flight Instructor and has been instructing since 1968. He was recently awarded Flight Instructor of the Year in Washington State. To top off this impressive list of accomplishments, Bob is also a well- known author, journalist and airshow lecturer.

Books by Bob Gardner

The Complete Private Pilot, Seventh Edition

The Complete Private Pilot Syllabus

The Complete Private Pilot Workbook

The Complete Multi-engine Pilot

The Complete Advanced Pilot

Preface

Your mind is like a computer's memory bank. When you have a new experience or sensation, your mind compares it to what is in storage and either modifies what has been stored or adds the new data to the memory bank. Each flight will add new experiences and soon your mind will say, "That's not new—I've done this before!"... and flying high above the mountains or gliding quietly onto a grass strip will quickly become a part of you. This book is planned to build your aviation knowledge in the same way.

Chapters 1 and 2 will familiarize you with your airplane and the forces you will control to make it fly safely and efficiently. The airplane engine and the instruments you use to check its operation are discussed in Chapter 3, followed by a discussion of how flight instruments operate in Chapter 4. You must know how to safely load your airplane and predict its performance under varying conditions—Chapters 5 and 6 will cover those areas.

The bricks and mortar of navigation is pilotage—Chapter 7 tells you how. Electronics—radio navigation and communication are the subjects of Chapters 8 and 9. In Chapter 10 you will learn how to operate your airplane at both large airports with towers and jet traffic, and small country airports where you may be the only pilot for miles around.

Weather phenomena won't be so mysterious after you read Chapter 11 to learn how weather information is gathered and interpreted. Chapter 12 tells you which publications you should use to look up important information about flying in general and your trip in particular, and Chapter 13 warns of physiological effects of flight on your body. Chapters 14 and 15 explore the airspace system which we all must understand, and the regulations we all must adhere to. Winding it all up, Chapter 16 is a VFR cross-country flight which you will plan and fly, using all of the information and knowledge you will acquire as you read the book; and lastly, Chapter 17 is a step-by-step explanation of how to use an electronic flight computer.

Aviation Supplies & Academics, Inc., better known as ASA, has earned a worldwide reputation in aviation education with their test preparation books. That reputation for excellence is based in part on ASA's policy of going beyond test requirements into in-depth coverage of subject material. This book continues this policy by covering all of the subjects you can expect to be questioned on in the Private Pilot written examination but going beyond the test questions for a full understanding of each subject.

Aviation has a language of its own and you want to speak it fluently, so we have provided a glossary. Also included is the Pilot/Controller Glossary, reprinted from the AIM, for understanding of the terms used in the Air Traffic Control system. Each chapter includes review questions so that you can test your understanding of the material covered in that chapter. The questions are examples of questions from the FAA Private Pilot Test Book. The ASA *Private Pilot Workbook* exercises are intended to give you further insight into each subject. When you have completed this book and the accompanying workbook exercises you will be ready for the FAA written examination and the oral examination for your Private Pilot checkride.

Good luck!

Getting Acquainted with Your Airplane

1

In this book we are going to assume that your training airplane is all-metal, has one engine, a fixed-pitch propeller, and a non-retractable landing gear. A stroll along the ramp of your hometown airport will show you that there are many variables, however, and you may want to compare features on other airplanes with the one you fly. Here are some things to look for:

Fuselage Construction

The fuselages of almost all of the airplanes you see will be of aluminum construction with internal strengthening members. A close look will show that on some models more attention has been paid to reducing drag caused by rivet heads and other protrusions. Looking at non-metal airplanes will take you to both the past and the future. Fabric-covered airplanes with tubing structures (wood-framed airplanes are really classics!) are lovingly restored and flown by proud owners, but no less proud are the pilots of modern composite aircraft, formed of fiberglass or similar materials which offer great strength and minimal drag.

Wings

Almost all modern airplanes have a single wing, mounted either above or below the fuselage. Most, but not all, high wing airplanes have supporting struts. Low wing and strutless high wing airplanes are cantilevered: the internal structure is designed to support the load and there are no struts.

Wing fuel tanks are either "wet wings" with the wing structure serving as the fuel container, or are rubber bladders contained within the wing.

Ailerons

You won't find many airplanes that do not have ailerons, which are movable control surfaces at the outer trailing edge of the wings. Ailerons are used to bank the airplane. A control wheel or stick at the pilot station is moved in the direction of bank desired, and the ailerons are deflected through a system of cables, pulleys, and bellcranks or pushrods. When no control force is exerted, the ailerons are held flush with the wing surface by the airstream.

Flaps

The hinged portions of the trailing edges of the wings near the fuselage are called flaps, and are normally used to steepen the glide angle without increasing airspeed. As you walk along the ramp you will see many different types of flaps, some that simply hinge down and others that extend down and backward. Older airplanes may not have any flaps at all.

Empennage

The horizontal stabilizer, the rudder, the vertical fin, the elevator, or any combination thereof is referred to by pilots as the airplane's empennage or "tail feathers". These surfaces allow the pilot to change the airplane's attitude in relation to the horizon by moving the nose up and down or left and right as seen by the pilot. There may be a fixed horizontal stabilizer with a movable elevator, or the whole horizontal assembly may be movable. Fore-and-aft movement of the control wheel or stick is transmitted by cables and pulleys to these control surfaces, and left-right movement is controlled by the rudder, which is mounted at the rear of the vertical fin. The pilot depresses the rudder pedal in the desired direction of nose movement and a cable system moves the control surface. You will see V-tails, T-tails, and straight tails, and maybe a home-built airplane with no horizontal surfaces mounted on the tail.

Landing Gear

The two main landing wheels and their supporting structure are designed to withstand landing loads and to support the airplane on the ground. A third, smaller wheel mounted either forward (tricycle) or aft (conventional) is for ground steering control only. Nosewheels are usually close to or a part of the engine mount and are definitely not designed to absorb landing loads. (Your instructor will devote a lot of training time to making sure that you do not land on the nose wheel!)

The shiny cylinders on nose wheels and some main landing gear are called struts. They absorb the shock of landing and are filled with air and oil, just like your car's shock absorbers. When a strut is "flat" there is no cushioning effect and vibrations are transmitted to the entire airframe. You will see some airplanes which use a spring steel assembly on the main landing gear instead of a strut.

Wheel pants, or fairings, reduce aerodynamic drag and add a knot or two to airspeed. Landing gear which retracts into the wing or fuselage adds considerably to cruise speed.

Almost all airplanes use disc brakes on the main landing gear, and you can see the discs if there are no wheel pants. Checking brake condition is considerably easier to do on airplanes than it is on cars. If the nose wheel is not steerable with the rudder pedals and swivels freely, steering is accomplished by tapping the brake lightly on the side toward the turn.

Propeller

The propellers you see may be either fixed or variable in pitch, or blade angle. You will probably see some amphibians with pusher-type propellers, but most are mounted up front and pull the airplane through the air. The conical spinner is not only decorative but serves to direct air into the cooling air intakes.

Engine

Modern airplanes have four- or six-cylinder flat opposed engines: when you open the cowling you will see that the cylinders are on opposite sides of the engine, and that the flat profile allows maximum aerodynamic streamlining of the cowling. As you walk along the ramp you may see an older airplane with a radial engine, its cylinders arranged in a "star" pattern.

Lights

The lighting system on a modern airplane consists of position lights on the wing tips and tail (red on the left, green on the right and white on the tail), an anticollision light system which may be either red or white (or both) and one or more landing lights. Many airplanes also have bright flashing strobe lights to increases the chances of being seen during both day and night flights.

Aerodynamics

The subject of aerodynamics deals with the forces acting on bodies in motion through the air; in fact "aerodyne" means an aircraft deriving lift from its motion through the air. To oversimplify, an airplane flies because the pilot causes it to accelerate down the runway until its wings develop a lifting force greater than its weight, and it lands because the pilot causes the lifting force to be less than its weight. In flight, the pilot controls the magnitude and direction of lift through use of the flight controls.

To make the airplane go where you want it to go and do what you want it to do, you use the flight controls as tools and, like any artisan, you have to know what your tools are capable of and how they are used.

As a pilot you will be working with the forces of lift, drag, thrust, and weight. Of these, lift is the force that allows you to move in three dimensions. While it is true that *anything* can be made to "fly" if enough power is applied, an airplane features **airfoils**— shapes specifically designed to develop lift. The amount of lift generated by an airfoil is a function of the area of the lifting surface, the density of the air, the velocity of the airflow over the lifting surface, and the coefficient of lift. This is how these elements are related:

$$\text{Lift} = \text{Coefficient of Lift} \times \text{Area} \times \text{Velocity}^2 \times \text{Density}/2$$

Coefficient of Lift

Don't be intimidated by the words "coefficient of lift"—they apply to physical relationships that are easy to visualize. Before investigating just what coefficient of lift means, or how the other factors affect lift development, you should understand how an airfoil develops lift. Figure 2-1 shows a fluid (illustrated as ping-pong balls) moving through a tube with a restriction in it. If 1,000 units of fluid enter one end of the tube each second, and 1,000 units leave the tube each second, and there is not enough room at the restriction for 1,000 units of fluid to pass, something clearly has to change at the restriction. That "something" is velocity—fewer units must travel at a higher velocity if 1,000 units per second are going to pass the restriction.

Figure 2-1. *Bernoulli tube*

As the fluid moves through the tube, its total energy consists of forward movement (**kinetic energy**) and the static force it exerts against the walls of the tube. At the restriction, the energy of forward movement increases and, since total energy can neither increase nor decrease within the system, the static pressure has to decrease. A scientist named Daniel Bernoulli discovered this effect: when a fluid is accelerated the pressure it exerts is reduced. Bernoulli's Theorem accounts for most of the lift developed by an airfoil. You might consider an airfoil as a device designed to accelerate airflow.

If you are having difficulty relating tubes and fluids to airplane wings, the airfoil in Figure 2-2 represents the bottom half of Bernoulli's restricted tube, and the length of the arrows indicates the energy imparted to air molecules as they travel over it. They move most rapidly over the curved surface, which is the area of least pressure.

A second contributor to total lift is Newton's Third Law: for every action there is an equal and opposite reaction. As the airfoil moves through the air it pushes the air downward and, in accordance with Newton's Law, the air exerts an equal upward force.

Figure 2-2. *Bernoulli airfoil*

Because of differences in wing design and in operating conditions, it is impossible to say what percentage of total lift can be attributed to Bernoulli or to Newton at any time. In Figure 2-3, the dashed lines represent lift due to pressure difference and the solid lines indicate lift due to Newton's Law.

Figure 2-3. *Sources of lift*

Part of the explanation of coefficient of lift has to do with the curvature, or camber, of the upper surface of the wing and angle of incidence. A large curve, or **camber**, means greater acceleration of the air over the upper surface. Oncoming free air is drawn upward toward the low pressure area on top of the wing, accelerates over the curvature, and flows off the trailing edge (downwash). Most general aviation airplanes change camber and increase lift by moving the trailing edge up or down with control surfaces called ailerons and flaps. Changing lift development by changing wing camber is largely the province of the designer, and is only partially under the control of the pilot. **Angle of incidence**, *which is defined as the angle at which the wing is fastened to the fuselage*, is set by the designer at 1° to 3° in relation to the longitudinal axis and is beyond the control of the pilot.

Wing design is one element of the coefficient of lift, and the other is **angle of attack**—over which the pilot has direct control. An imaginary line drawn from the leading edge of the wing to the trailing edge is called the chord line, and *the angle between the chord line and the relative wind is called the angle of attack* (Figure 2-4A). If relative wind is an unfamiliar term, consider this: you are sitting in a convertible at a stop light with the wind blowing on the left side of your face; the wind that you feel is the true wind. When the light changes, and the car accelerates, the wind strikes you directly in the face—that is the relative wind, caused by motion.

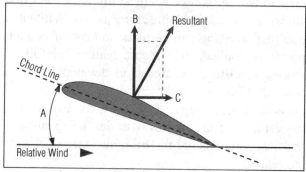

Figure 2-4. *Angle of attack*

In flight, *the relative wind is parallel and opposite to the flight path*. Figure 2-5 shows this relationship in level flight, climbing, and descending. To the wing of a military jet climbing almost vertically, the relative wind is coming straight down, while to the wing of an aerobatic airplane completing a loop, the relative wind is coming straight up. More importantly, when a pilot attempts to maintain altitude by using angle of attack alone, without adding power, the relative wind strikes the bottom of the wing as shown in Figure 2-6. This is called mushing flight, and if the pilot does not lower the nose to decrease the angle of attack, an aerodynamic stall is imminent.

Figure 2-5. *Relative wind is opposite to flight path*

Figure 2-6. *Mushing flight*

Lift developed by pressure difference (Bernoulli lift) depends on a smooth flow of air over the upper surface of the wing. As angle of attack is increased (Figure 2-7), the air being drawn over the top surface of the wing begins to tear away from the wing surface at the trailing edge, causing loss of lift. At high angles of attack the airflow near the trailing edge of the wing even reverses and begins to flow forward! Aerodynamicists devote considerable time and effort to designing wings that maintain a layer of smoothly flowing air over the maximum area of wing surface.

Figure 2-7. *Increasing angle of attack to the stall point*

A simple explanation of the aerodynamic stall is that the angle of attack can be increased until the oncoming air is unable to make the sharp turn necessary to follow the wing's surface, and begins to separate from it at the trailing edge. The separation point moves forward on the wing as the angle of attack is increased. The designer controls the progression of this process by twisting the wing slightly from the wing roots to the tips so that the inner sections of the wing lose lift first, and the outer sections (where the ailerons are located), continue to develop lift until the wing is fully stalled.

The NASA photographs (Figures 2-8 and 2-9) show how increasing the angle of attack causes the area of disturbed airflow to expand until total loss of lift occurs. With an angle of attack of 17°, there is still smooth airflow at the outer ends of the wings, while the inner sections are covered with disturbed airflow.

Figure 2-8. NASA Photo: 17° angle of attack

Figure 2-9. NASA Photo: 30° Angle of attack (modified wing)

The airflow in the vicinity of the ailerons on this experimental airfoil remains attached to the wing surface and the "pilot" of this wind-tunnel model would retain some roll control. The same wing at an angle of attack of 30° is fully stalled, with no smooth airflow remaining on the wing surface. Notice that air flowing through the gap between the aileron and the wing provides a small area of smooth airflow over the aileron itself. A normal (unmodified) wing stalls at an angle of attack of 18°- 20°.

To ensure that the wing root stalls first, some manufacturers install "stall strips" on the leading edge of the wing near the root. Some airplanes have slots in the leading edge near the wing tip which direct high pressure air from beneath the wing to the upper surface and ailerons, and thus retain controllability at high angles of attack (Figure 2-10). Short takeoff and landing (STOL) airplanes usually have some type of device on the leading edge of the wing which extends only at high angles of attack and which channels airflow in the same manner as the fixed slot in the illustration. Large jet aircraft also use leading edge lift devices.

Figure 2-10. Leading edge slots

Figure 2-7 also shows that the lift developed by the wing increases as angle of attack increases, until the angle of attack reaches a critical value (usually 18° - 20°) beyond which the air no longer flows smoothly over the wing surface and the wing stalls. The *only* thing that stalls the wing is exceeding the critical angle of attack. In training, most of your stall practice will be at slow speeds, with the nose of the airplane above the horizon, but you must realize that *the wing can be stalled at any airspeed and in any attitude*. The lift developed by the wing must support the weight of the airplane, and the pilot controls lift by varying the angle of attack. If the weight being supported by the wing is increased, either by overloading the airplane or by adding "G" (gravity) forces while maneuvering, the angle of attack must be increased to provide the necessary lift.

There is always the danger of exceeding the critical angle of attack and stalling the wing.

Velocity

Velocity of airflow over the lifting surface plays a major role in lift development. The effect of airspeed is dramatically evident because lift varies as the square of the airspeed: double the airspeed and the lift quadruples; cut the airspeed in half and the lift drops to 25% of the former value. Your control of lift through airspeed will play a major role in your ability to fly efficiently—flying "by the numbers" insures that you always have the proper angle of attack for the condition of flight (Figure 2-11).

Figure 2-11. *Angle of attack vs. attitude and speed*

Area

The pilot has very little control over the area of the lifting surface except when the flaps are designed to add area. The wing area of a jet airliner increases considerably as it approaches the runway, as its flaps are extended downward and backward. A wing with a large surface area is desirable at low speeds but would add unacceptable amounts of drag due to skin friction at high speeds.

Air Density

Changes in air density affect the creation of lift because it takes molecules of air flowing over the lifting surface to create lift, and as you climb there are fewer air molecules. High altitude means less lift, unless angle of attack or airspeed or both are increased. Water vapor in the air (high relative humidity) means that fewer air molecules are available for lift generation (it takes air, not water, to create lift),

so high moisture content also means less lift. Air density decreased by either high altitude or high moisture content will also decrease propeller efficiency (the propeller is an airfoil), and will decrease the power output of the engine which needs air, not moisture, to burn fuel efficiently. It isn't necessary to climb to high altitudes to encounter reductions in air density because air (a gas) expands when heated. At sea level on a hot day in July there will be fewer air molecules available to develop lift.

Drag

Lift is the first tool you will learn to control and use. The second tool you must understand is drag. There are two types of drag for you to be concerned about: **parasite drag** and **induced drag**. Parasite drag is largely beyond the control of the pilot because it comes from such things as struts, fixed landing gear, rivet heads, antennas, and the friction of air passing along the skin of the airplane. Engine cooling drag is 20% of total parasite drag—those air inlets behind the propeller channel a tremendous volume of air over and around the engine. Parasite drag increases as the square of the speed: double the airspeed and the drag quadruples. That is what limits top speed—when all of the available horsepower is being used to overcome drag, you can't go any faster. Figure 2-12 shows how parasite and induced drag vary with airspeed and how each contributes to total drag.

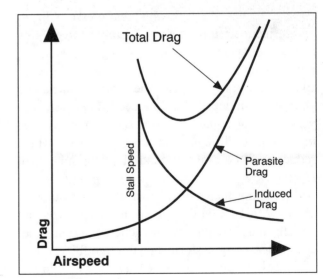

Figure 2-12. *Drag and speed graph*

Induced drag is the inevitable result of lift development. You know how Bernoulli's and Newton's effects in combination provide high pressure on the bottom of the wing and low pressure on the top—these forces are resolved at the wing tip as the high pressure air corkscrews up and around the wing tip toward the low pressure area. This meeting of high and low pressure air, with the rotational velocity imparted to the air, creates induced drag (Figure 2-13).

Figure 2-13. Wing-tip vortices

At large angles of attack with great pressure differences, induced drag is a considerable force; however, as airspeed increases and angle of attack is reduced, induced drag becomes less of a factor. Every time that you change the angle of attack, you change the induced drag. Induced drag varies inversely as the square of the airspeed. You will see many modern airplanes with winglets, devices which reduce induced drag by controlling the mixing of high and low pressure air at the tip of a lifting surface, and anything that reduces total drag adds to efficiency. Most recent design advances have been accomplished through drag reduction programs, because increasing performance through the addition of sheer horsepower has reached a practical limit.

Some airplanes can be equipped with spoilers, pilot-controlled flat plates that extend perpendicular to the top of the wing and destroy a large portion of the wing's lift. These after-market modifications allow the pilot to lose altitude rapidly without changing airspeed or thrust.

Thrust

Your third tool will be the thrust developed by the propeller as it is rotated by the engine and pulls the airplane through the air. Remember, the propeller is an airfoil, and all of the relationships of velocity, air density, and angle of attack apply. During the takeoff roll, thrust is at its maximum, and total drag is at a minimum. This imbalance of forces allows the airplane to accelerate. As airflow over the wing increases, lift begins to develop, and when the recommended takeoff speed has been attained the pilot helps the process by increasing the angle of attack. The airplane then becomes airborne (accelerates upward) as lift exceeds weight. The contribution of parasite drag, which increases with speed, will cause total drag to equal total thrust, and as airspeed stabilizes lift will equal weight. *In any steady state flight condition, whether climbing descending, or flying straight and level, the forces of lift and weight are equal and the forces of thrust and drag are equal).*

Figure 2-14. Relationship of forces acting on an airplane

Adding thrust will cause the airplane to accelerate (just as reducing power will cause it to decelerate) until the thrust/drag relationship has equalized and the airplane is stable at a new airspeed. You control the airplane's flight path by adjusting its attitude in relation to the horizon, and by changing thrust with the throttle. Attitude plus power equals performance.

Region of Reversed Command

If you haven't heard the terms "hanging on the prop" or "behind the power curve" yet, you will hear them from your instructor when you start work on short field takeoffs and landings. Induced drag is greatest at high angles of attack, and it is possible for you to fly at such an extreme angle of attack that it takes all of the available power just to equal induced drag and maintain altitude! Figure 2-15 shows seven airplanes, with the airspeed and power being used by each. Airplane 4 is operating at the speed and power setting for best endurance—using the least power to maintain altitude with an airspeed of 66 miles per hour. The airplanes to the right of airplane 4 are operating normally: with increased power each airplane achieves a higher airspeed. Look above airplane 4, however. Airplane 3 is using 15% more horsepower than airplane 4 but is going slower! Look at airplane 2—using almost twice as much power as airplane 4 to fly 10 knots slower. Finally, look at poor airplane 1. That is "hanging on the prop!" Airplane 1 is using every available ounce of power to maintain altitude while flying at only 46 miles per hour. Check each horsepower line and note that reducing the angle of attack (and thus reducing induced drag) at any power setting results in a speed increase.

Airplanes 1, 2, and 3 are all operating in the **region of reversed command** (behind the power curve), where it takes more power to fly more slowly. That's just the reverse of the normal power and airspeed relationship, and that's where the "region of reversed command" got its name.

You can tell by looking at the illustration that the pilots of airplanes 1, 2, and 3 probably can't see over the noses of their airplanes, and that is a good warning that speed is dangerously slow (additionally, the airspeed indicator is least accurate at high angles of attack!). If the pilot of an airplane operating in the region of reversed command reduces power or suddenly retracts the flaps, the only means of regaining the lost lift is to lower the nose, and there may not be enough altitude available for that.

You, the pilot, control both lift *and* drag. If you increase drag by operating at a high angle of attack you must add thrust (power) to overcome that drag, and you only have so much power available. Keep some power in reserve—don't operate at high angles of attack which put you behind the power curve.

1   100% AVAILABLE HORSEPOWER
46 MPH   120 MPH

2   70% AVAILABLE HORSEPOWER
55 MPH   105 MPH

3   55% AVAILABLE HORSEPOWER
60 MPH   87 MPH

4   40% AVAILABLE HORSEPOWER
66 MPH

Figure 2-15. Region of reversed command

Center of Pressure vs. Center of Gravity

All of the lift forces developed by the wing can be said to be concentrated in a single point called the **center of lift**, or the center of pressure, which you can visualize as a force pushing up on the bottom of the wing (the arrow in Figure 2-16). The center of pressure moves as the angle of attack changes. When you increase the angle of attack, the center of pressure moves forward on the bottom of the wing, and it moves aft as you decrease the angle of attack. If the airplane is properly loaded, the center of pressure will always be behind the **center of gravity**. If the center of pressure moves forward of the center of gravity, the nose of the airplane will pitch uncontrollably upward. With the center of pressure aft of the center of gravity, the tendency is for the airplane to be nose heavy. The designer counteracts this by having the horizontal stabilizer at a negative angle of attack, which creates a downward pressure at the tail (Figure 2-17). Chapter 5 discusses airplane loading in more detail.

Figure 2-17. How downforce on tail creates balance

Axes of Control

You control the airplane around three axes of rotation: lateral, longitudinal and vertical. All three pass through the center of gravity (note the CG symbols in Figure 2-18). The lateral axis of your airplane extends from wing tip to wing tip, and you control the pitch (nose up-nose down) attitude of the airplane by use of the elevator control. As you apply back pressure to the control wheel (or yoke) the elevator deflects upward and the air passing over it pushes the tail down.

You have effectively increased the camber or curvature of the horizontal stabilizer/elevator, and have developed a downward force. In the cockpit, you see this as the nose rising in relation to the horizon. Relaxing the back pressure, or exerting forward pressure, will lower the nose by reducing the downward force.

The throttle also contributes to control around the lateral axis: as you add throttle, the increased air flow from the propeller will push the tail down as it passes over the elevator ("blowing the tail down"). A power reduction will result in less downward pressure on the elevator, and the nose will move below the horizon (Figure 2-19). This is a built-in safety factor, insuring that the angle of attack will be reduced and the airplane will maintain flying speed if power is suddenly reduced.

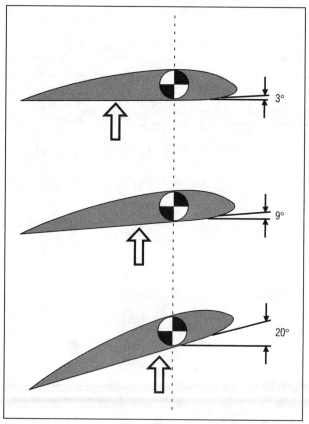

Figure 2-16. Movement of center of pressure with changes in angle of attack

Figure 2-18. *Axes of control around the center of gravity*

You control the airplane around the longitudinal or roll axis (which extends from nose to tail) with the ailerons, and the resultant movement is called "banking". Deflecting an aileron downward increases both the angle of attack and the camber of that portion of the wing, and the increased lift that results raises the wing. At the same time, the aileron on the other wing is being deflected upward, decreasing both angle of attack and camber and reducing the lift of that wing. One wing rises, the other lowers, and the airplane banks (Figure 2-20).

Figure 2-19. *Effect of throttle on altitude*

Figure 2-20. *Ailerons are used for roll control*

When you deflect one aileron down into the windstream, the other aileron "hides" behind the curvature of the wing. The wing on the side of the down aileron is dragged backward, which slows the turn. The slowing effect of the down aileron is called adverse aileron drag, and is overcome by the rudder. Designers have overcome this imbalance in some cases by equalizing the drag caused by both ailerons.

The rudder controls the airplane around the vertical, or yaw, axis. You use the rudder to offset any force which attempts to move the nose of the airplane from side to side (like adverse aileron drag). The rudder is a movable surface attached to the rear of the vertical fin which changes the camber and angle of attack and varies the lift force being exerted on either side of the tail surfaces. Because of the long lever arm between the cockpit and the tail surfaces, a very small rudder movement is seen as a large nose movement.

In Figure 2-21, a large yawing force to the right caused by a crosswind on takeoff or landing is offset by a small force applied to the rudder. Some airplanes are called "short coupled" because the tail is so close to the cockpit that very large rudder inputs are required for directional control, especially at low speeds.

Figure 2-21. *Small rudder deflection offsets large yawing tendency*

Control Effects and Stability

The three axes of control pass through the center of gravity. How the designer has related the centers of lift or pressure to the center of gravity affects the stability of the airplane. An inherently stable airplane requires little effort to control, but is slow to react to maneuvering forces; as stability is decreased, it will react more quickly but require constant attention. Aerobatic airplanes and airliners represent the extremes of stability.

Your airplane is designed to be stable around the yaw (vertical) axis by placing the tail surfaces away from the center of gravity. If you are in straight and level flight and depress the right rudder pedal, the nose will swing to the right, but will return very quickly to the original position when pressure is released. This is called "streamlining"—if no pressure is exerted on a control surface it will align itself with the airstream. (Do this experiment without passengers on board; it's unsettling for those in the back seat!)

Stability around the longitudinal axis is provided by dihedral, the upward slant of the wings from their roots to the wing tips (Figure 2-22). If the airplane is disturbed from straight and level flight by a wing being lowered, the descending wing will be at a greater angle of attack than the rising wing and the resulting increase in lift on the lowered wing will result in the wings leveling themselves. This built-in leveling effect makes small bank angles more difficult to sustain than larger bank angles. Almost all airplanes have good short-term lateral stability but poor long term lateral stability: in the absence of an autopilot don't expect hands-off, wings-level flight for long periods of time.

Figure 2-22. *Effect of dihedral*

Stability around the lateral (pitch) axis is determined by the relationship between the center of gravity and the position of the center of lift, which moves as the downward force on the horizontal stabilizer changes (Figure 2-23). If you disturb the airplane from straight-and-level by pulling back slightly on the control yoke and then releasing it, the airplane will climb briefly until airflow over the horizontal stabilizer diminishes, and then the reduced download on the stabilizer will allow the nose to drop below the horizon. The airspeed will then increase (momentarily) and the increasing download on the horizontal stabilizer created by the added airflow will raise the nose above the horizon. These oscillations will gradually diminish in amplitude until the airplane regains level flight.

The designer provides this stability when establishing the permissible limits of center of gravity movement. For every pitch attitude there is a power setting that creates just enough download on the horizontal stabilizer for the airplane to maintain level flight; an increase in power will cause the nose to pitch up, the speed to decrease, and the airplane to climb, and a reduction in power will have the opposite effect. Airplanes with the horizontal stabilizer mounted high on the vertical fin (T-tails) get little or no control effect from power changes because the control surface is above the propeller's discharge air (propwash). T-tailed airplanes (and all jets) must derive pitch control force solely from the relative wind.

An aerodynamic surface from the early days of flight is reappearing on modern aircraft. A canard (Figure 2-24) is a lifting surface mounted forward of the center of gravity which looks like a small wing. It has a slightly greater angle of attack than the main wing and thus will stall before the main wing. The lift developed by the canard is forward of the center of gravity, eliminating the need for a horizontal stabilizer. With the drag of the horizontal stabilizer and any elevator deflection eliminated, canards are faster and more fuel efficient than conventional airplanes.

Trimming Control Surfaces

Control surfaces are provided with trim tabs (Figure 2-25) so that the pilot can maintain a desired control position without exerting constant pressure.

Figure 2-24. Canard

Figure 2-23. Longitudinal stability

Figure 2-25. Trim tabs

Most trimming surfaces move in the opposite direction from desired control movement: if you want the elevator to be deflected upward the trim tab is deflected downward, and it exerts a force to hold the elevator in the desired position.

As you move up into more complicated, higher-powered airplanes, you will find that trim controls for all three axes are available in the cockpit. At the basic trainer level, some trim tabs are literally metal tabs to be adjusted on the ground and then test flown to assess the effect of the change. Airplanes with movable tail surfaces rotate the whole horizontal stabilizer/rudder assembly in reaction to trim wheel movement, and airplanes with stabilators (a movable stabilizer/elevator) move the stabilator with trim force. Three forms of elevator trim control are pictured (Figure 2-26): a horizontal stabilizer with elevator and elevator trim tab, a movable horizontal stabilizer, and (on Mooneys) an entire tail surface which moves with trim input. V-tailed airplanes use ruddervators which, as their name implies, are combination control surfaces.

Trim tabs are used *only* to relieve control pressures, and are not to be used by themselves to change the airplane's attitude. When the airspeed and altitude are at the desired values, any remaining control pressures should be trimmed off.

Flaps

Flaps are auxiliary control surfaces; that is, you do not use flaps to control the airplane around the three axes of control. *Flaps allow the pilot to descend at a steep angle without increasing airspeed*, which becomes very important during approaches to land (Figures 2-27 and 2-28). *Flaps are not speed brakes—*

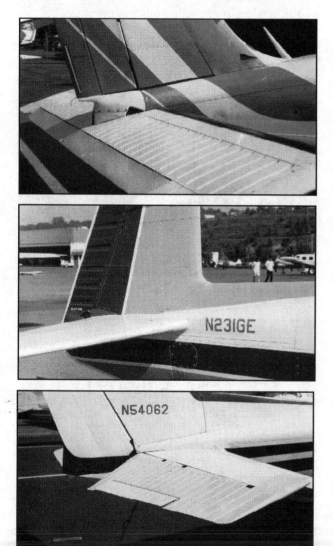

Figure 2-26. *Three forms of elevator trim control*

Figure 2-27. *Landing approach without flaps*

Figure 2-28. *Use of flaps allows a steeper descent angle*

in fact, the designer establishes maximum speeds for flap deflection to avoid structural overloads. Because flaps increase both the camber of the wing and the angle of attack by lowering the trailing edge, they allow the same amount of lift to be developed at a lower airspeed. You will experiment with this in training by maintaining altitude while extending flaps and gradually slowing the airplane.

Typically, the first increments of flap extension add more lift than drag, and so some airplanes use a takeoff flap setting of 15°-20°. Retracting the flaps when you do not have sufficient airspeed to support the airplane in the no-flaps configuration will cause loss of altitude—do not retract the flaps until you have sufficient airspeed. As you near full flap extension you get more drag than lift and these are the approach settings. Flap extension changes the location of the center of pressure on the wing and causes a pitch change. You should find out whether extending the flaps will cause your airplane to pitch nose up or nose down, and be ready to maintain a constant attitude as you apply flaps.

There are several types of flaps in general use (Figure 2-29). Plain flaps are hinged portions of the trailing edge of the wing: deflecting them increases wing camber and thereby increases lift. Fowler Flaps extend downward and also back, adding to wing area as well as camber. Split flaps extend downward from the trailing edge, while the upper wing surface is undisturbed. Designers also add high lift devices to the leading edge of the wing to channel high pressure air over the upper wing surface. These leading edge flaps are also referred to as slats, and you will see them on modern airline jets as well as short-takeoff-and-landing (STOL) airplanes.

Flaps can be extended electrically, hydraulically, or manually, and some leading edge devices are extended by decreasing aerodynamic pressure. Another means of increasing descent rate without increasing airspeed is the use of spoilers. Spoilers are vertical "fences" that may be extended from the top surface of the wing to disrupt airflow, killing lift. Spoilers have been used as flight controls on gliders for many years, and are now being used on powered airplanes.

Because the extension of flaps affects the angle of attack (by moving the chord line), or changes the wing area, flap use lowers the stall speed—with a greater angle of attack (or more area), less air has to flow over the wing to develop the same amount of lift. Figure 2-30 is a typical table of stall speed vs. flap extension related to bank angle. When referring

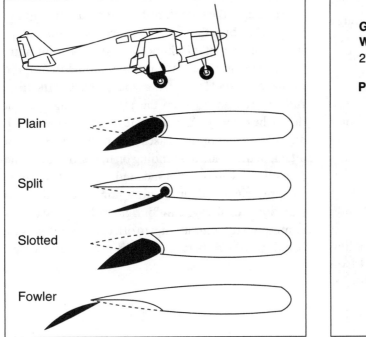

Figure 2-29. *Types of flaps*

Gross Weight 2750 Lbs		Angle of Bank			
		Level	30°	45°	60°
Power		**Gear and Flaps Up**			
On	MPH	62	67	74	88
	KTS	54	58	64	76
Off	MPH	75	81	89	106
	KTS	65	70	77	92
		Gear and Flaps Down			
On	MPH	54	58	64	76
	KTS	47	50	56	66
Off	MPH	66	71	78	93
	KTS	57	62	68	81

Figure 2-30. *Stall speed table*

to similar tables, you should be aware that airspeed indicator accuracy suffers at high angles of attack (low airspeeds).

Torque

Torque is really the result of four factors, although the end effect is the same: a tendency to yaw to the left in airplanes with propellers and engines that rotate clockwise as seen from the pilot's seat (Figure 2-31). One major factor is discharge air from the propeller corkscrewing around the fuselage as it moves aft, and striking the left side of the vertical tail surfaces. During the takeoff roll, the force it exerts to move the tail to the right is seen by the pilot as a movement of the nose to the left.

Figure 2-31. *Action/reaction*

Another factor is Newton's law of equal and opposite reactions: as the engine and propeller rotate clockwise, a counterclockwise force is transmitted through the engine mounts to the airframe. The designer may increase the angle of incidence of the left wing to offset this force, or mount the engine offset from the centerline to minimize the torque reaction.

A third major contributor is called **P-factor**, because the culprit is the propeller. As the blade on the right side of the propeller disc descends, it is exerting a force on the air (downwash effect, because the propeller is an airfoil), while the blade on the left side of the disc is at a low angle of attack and is exerting little or no force. The descending blade is also moving at a higher speed relative to the air than is the ascending blade, and this increased velocity creates more lift on the right side of the propeller disc, pulling the nose of the airplane to the left. The NASA wind-tunnel photographs (Figures 2-8 and 2-9) of disturbed air-flow also dramatically illustrate P-factor and the corkscrew flow of discharge air from the propeller at large angles of attack.

The last factor contributing to left-turning tendency is **gyroscopic precession,** and this is especially noticeable in airplanes with conventional landing gear (taildraggers). The propeller is a rotating mass, just like a solid disc of metal, and if a force is applied to a rotating mass it will act as though the force had been applied 90° in the direction of rotation (Figure 2-32). When the pilot of a taildragger lifts the tail during the takeoff run, the forward tilting of the propeller disc exerts a force at the right rear of the propeller disc which adds to the left-turning tendency. The illustration (Figure 2-32) shows P-factor and raising of the tail combining to create a left-turning force.

Figure 2-32. *Gyroscopic precession*

As you begin the takeoff roll, power is at a maximum and airflow over the control surfaces (with the exception of propeller discharge air) is at a minimum. Discharge air and P-factor will combine to turn the airplane to the left unless you provide offsetting rudder pressure to keep the plane moving straight down the runway. As you rotate the airplane to climb attitude, P-factor increases because the angle of attack of the blade descending on the right side of the propeller disc has increased, and you must continue to apply right rudder. A high power-low airspeed situation will always call for right rudder pressure. A common error is an attempt to offset torque effects by banking to the right rather than by use of right rudder.

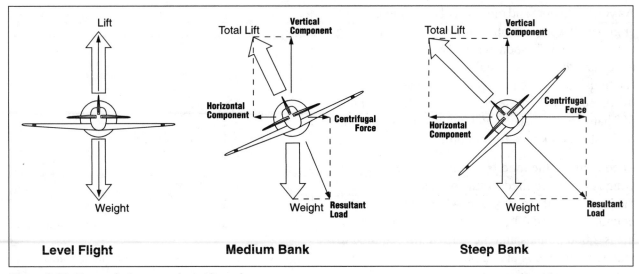

Figure 2-33. *Forces during normal coordinated turns*

Leveling off at cruise altitude, the forces of discharge air and P-factor still exist, although diminished because of reduced power, but now the airplane designer provides a corrective force. The left wing is rigged so that it develops slightly more lift at cruise speed than the right wing, offsetting the left-turning tendency. The vertical fin is also slightly offset, so that at cruise speeds the push of discharge air on the left side of the tail surfaces is corrected for. These corrections are exactly effective at only one airspeed: go faster or slower and aileron or rudder trim will be required.

Dynamics of The Turn

The lift developed by an airfoil acts perpendicular to the relative wind, and in level flight that force is vertical with no horizontal component. If you roll into a 90° bank, all of the lifting force will act horizontally, and with no vertical lift the airplane cannot maintain altitude (Figure 2-33). (The military demonstration teams do it but they have a tremendous power-to-weight ratio, and jet fighter fuselages are designed to provide some lift.)

In normal flying, you will not bank more than about 55° (60° of bank requires a parachute when dual), and as you bank the wings you will be varying the relationship between the vertical and horizontal components of lift. It is the horizontal component of lift that causes the airplane to turn. When a portion of the total lift developed by the wing acts horizontally, the remaining vertical component will be inadequate to support the weight of the airplane, and additional lift must be supplied by increasing the angle of attack, or the airspeed, or both to avoid loss of altitude. Increasing the angle of attack increases induced drag (remember that induced drag is the price you pay for lift), and, unless that drag is offset with thrust, you must inevitably lose airspeed in a level turn.

Note: The longitudinal component of lift is really called centripetal force, and centrifugal force, as in the diagram, really doesn't exist. However, the FAA still uses this diagram, and the theory of the horizontal component of lift opposing centrifugal force, on the written tests.

As you bank more and more steeply, and increase the angle of attack to maintain altitude (without adding power), you will soon reach the critical angle of attack and the wing will stall. Figure 2-34 shows the relationship between the bank angle in degrees and the percentage increase in stall speed. Note that in a 60° bank the stall speed will increase by 40%, from 60 knots to 84 knots, for example.

Load factor is the ratio between the weight that the wing is being required to support and the weight of the airplane. If an airplane which weighs 2,000 pounds is banked 60°, the horizontal component of lift is 2,000 pounds and the vertical lift required to maintain altitude is also 2,000 pounds: the wing is supporting 4,000 pounds and the load factor is 2.0. As Figure 2-35 shows, the horizontal component of lift is opposed by centrifugal force and the vertical component is opposed by weight, and as the bank steepens, the resultant load and the lift required to support it increase dramatically.

Figure 2-35. *Two forces cause load factor during turns*

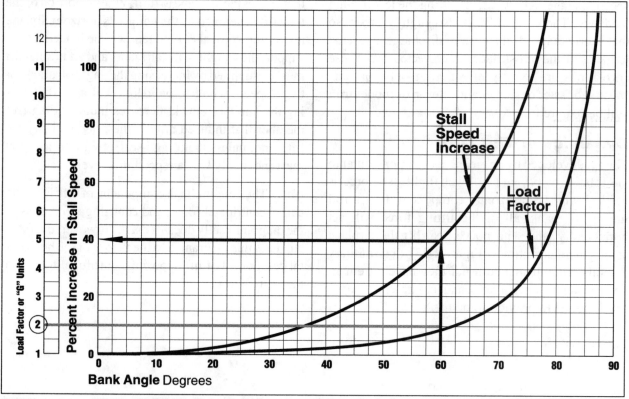

Figure 2-34. *Increase in stall speed and load factor*

From what has been said so far, you would assume that the rudder plays no part in turning an airplane, since it is the horizontal component of lift that supplies the turning force. This is true to the extent that no rudder pressure is required to sustain the turn itself, but rudder pressure *is* required to roll into and out of the turn because of adverse aileron drag, and may be required to overcome "torque" forces.

The rudder controls the airplane around the yaw (or vertical) axis. As an aileron is deflected downward to initiate a bank, that down aileron creates drag which opposes the turn. Rudder pressure is required to overcome this adverse aileron drag. The amount of rudder pressure required depends on the degree of aileron deflection. When the desired bank has been established, and the ailerons are neutralized, there is no aileron drag and therefore no rudder pressure is required to offset it. Rolling back to wings level flight requires aileron deflection, and rudder must be applied to offset the resulting drag. The slip and skid, or ball, instrument reflects your skill in providing just enough rudder pressure (coordinating aileron and rudder): if you use too much rudder you will force the ball to the outside of the turn, resulting in a skid. If you use too little rudder pressure the ball will fall to the inside of the turn and the airplane will be in a slip.

As discussed earlier, airplanes with propellers that turn clockwise as seen from the pilot's seat tend to turn left unless design features or pilot action counteract that tendency. When you are established in a turn to the left, then, no rudder pressure is required. It may take slight rudder pressure to hold your airplane in a right turn, however, since these forces act to roll it back to level flight. Again, the ball tells the tale.

One of the stock production numbers at an ice skating show has a line of skaters pivoting around a center, with the central skaters marking time and the outer skaters racing madly to keep up. When you bank your airplane's wings steeply, you re-create this situation aerodynamically: the inside, or lower wing is moving quite slowly, while the top, or outside wing has to cover a greater distance in exactly the same time and so must travel considerably faster. This results in more lift being developed by the outside wing, and the plane develops an overbanking tendency which may require opposite aileron to avoid a too-steep bank. Pilots who use rudder to maintain a turn while using opposite aileron to avoid overbanking risk a cross-control stall.

Stalls and Spins

Increasing the angle of attack until the air no longer flows smoothly over the wing surface will result in an aerodynamic stall as discussed earlier, and the designer's placement of the center of lift and the center of gravity make the stall self-correcting *if both wings stall simultaneously*. If one wing stalls before the other, the stalled wing will drop, the airplane will yaw toward the stalled wing, the nose of the airplane will drop below the horizon, and, if you don't stop the yaw with opposite rudder (not aileron!) and decrease the angle of attack by moving the control yoke forward, a spin will result. *An airplane must be stalled before it will spin.* In a well-developed spin, the lower or inside wing is fully stalled while the higher or outside wing is less stalled—the indicated airspeed in a spin will be quite low. Because a spin must be preceded by a stall, your flight instruction will emphasize stall recognition and recovery. Most airplanes are not approved for intentional spins, and before you or your instructor attempt an intentional spin you should check the Approved Flight Manual or Pilot's Operating Handbook. Most flight manuals include instructions on how to recover from an inadvertent spin, and you should become familiar with these instructions. An hour of dual instruction in an aerobatic airplane with a qualified instructor will erase any doubts about your ability to handle an inadvertent spin.

Figure 2-36 shows a test airplane on which NASA has installed experimental flow control devices on the outboard sections of the wings to improve spin recovery characteristics. Note the pilot's emergency escape door and the drag parachute.

Glide Ratio

If you are ever faced with an emergency landing because the engine stops, the airplane's ability to glide will suddenly become your top priority. An airplane's glide ratio is the number of feet forward that it will glide for each foot of altitude lost.

Figure 2-36. Experimental spin recovery flow control devices (black cuffs)

If an airplane with a ten-to-one glide ratio is one mile above sea level, it will be able to glide (in no-wind conditions) ten miles before reaching the surface. Gliding with the wind, of course, increases the range, while gliding into the wind reduces it.

Your Pilot's Operating Handbook should have the best glide speed at maximum gross weight listed in Section Three. Some manufacturers publish glide speeds for different weights. You probably won't be at max gross when you need to glide to safety (unless you have a problem immediately after takeoff with a full load), so you should know that the best glide speed varies directly with weight. That is, if the airplane is lighter than gross, the best glide speed is lower than the published speed. Just how much lower depends on the weight decrease, but in an emergency you're not going to be fooling with formulas. For most trainers, to get the speed much more than ten knots below the published figure, you and your instructor would have to jump out.

Summary

You won't find a better source of information on aerodynamics than the FAA's *Flight Training Handbook,* Advisory Circular 61-21A. You'll find it at pilot supply stores or Government Printing Office outlets.

Chapter 2
Aerodynamics Review Questions

1. When are the four aerodynamic forces that act on an airplane in equilibrium?

   A—When the aircraft is at rest on the ground.
   B—When the aircraft is accelerating.
   C—During unaccelerated flight.

2. The purpose of the rudder on an airplane is to

   A—control the yaw.
   B—control the overbanking tendency.
   C—maintain a crab angle to correct drift.

3. The term angle of attack is defined as the

   A—angle between the wing chord and the direction of the relative wind.
   B—angle between the airplane's climb angle and the horizon.
   C—angle formed by the longitudinal axis of the airplane and the chord line of the wing.

4. As altitude increases, the indicated airspeed at which a given airplane stalls in a particular configuration will

   A—decrease as the true airspeed increases.
   B—decrease as the true airspeed decreases.
   C—remain the same as at low altitude.

5. What causes an airplane (except a T-tail) to pitch nosedown when power is reduced and the controls are not adjusted?

   A—The CG shifts forward when thrust and drag are reduced.
   B—The downwash on the elevators from the propeller slipstream is reduced and elevator effectiveness is reduced.
   C—When thrust is reduced to less than weight, lift is also reduced and the wings can no longer support the weight.

6. What effect does an increased load factor have on an airplane during an approach to a stall?

   A—The airplane will stall at a higher air-speed.
   B—The airplane will have a tendency to spin.
   C—The airplane will have a tendency to yaw and roll as the stall is encountered.

7. What determines the longitudinal stability of an airplane?

   A—The location of the CG with respect to the center of lift.
   B—The effectiveness of the horizontal stabilizer, rudder, and rudder trim tab.
   C—The relationship of thrust and lift to weight and drag.

8. The left-turning tendency of an airplane caused by P-factor is the result of the

A—clockwise rotation of the engine and the propeller turning the airplane counter-clock-wise.
B—propeller blade descending on the right, producing more thrust than the ascending blade on the left.
C—gyroscopic forces applied to the rotating propeller blades acting 90° in advance of the point the force was applied.

9. The purpose of wing flaps is to

A—enable the pilot to make steeper approaches to a landing without increasing airspeed.
B—enable the pilot to reduce the airspeed for the approach to a landing.
C—create more drag in order to utilize power on the approach.

10. In what airspeed and power condition is torque effect the greatest in a single-engine airplane?

A—Low airspeed, high power.
B—Low airspeed, low power.
C—High airspeed, high power.

11. What makes an airplane turn?

A—Rudder and aileron.
B—Horizontal component of lift.
C—Rudder, aileron, and elevator.

12. As you maneuver an airplane you should realize that it can be stalled

A—only when the nose is high and the speed is low.
B—only when the airspeed decreases to the published stalling speed.
C—at any airspeed and in any attitude.

13. To counteract the effect of torque in a conventional single engine propeller-driven airplane, a pilot would normally add

A—left rudder pressure during the takeoff roll and while climbing with full power.
B—right rudder pressure when entering a glide from level cruising flight.
C—right rudder pressure during the takeoff roll and while climbing with full power.

14. To generate the same amount of lift as altitude is increased, an airplane must be flown at

A—the same true airspeed regardless of angle of attack.
B—a lower true airspeed and a greater angle of attack.
C—a higher true airspeed for any given angle of attack.

15. During a spin to the left, which wing(s) are stalled?

A—Both wings are stalled.
B—Neither wing is stalled.
C—Only the left wing is stalled.

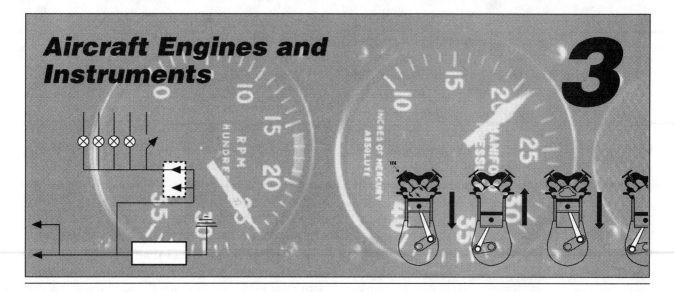

Aircraft Engines and Instruments 3

You don't have to be a mechanic to be a safe pilot, but a knowledge of how your engine works and what the engine instruments are telling you will make it easier to give your engine tender loving care and get long, reliable service from it.

There are many similarities between an automobile engine and an airplane engine. Both are **internal combustion engines,** both use spark plugs, and both use some type of fuel metering system related to throttle position. Many advances in modern automotive engines such as turbocharging and fuel injection are based on earlier aviation applications.

An aircraft engine is a four-cycle engine: Figure 3-1 illustrates the four cycles. The fuel-air mixture is drawn into the cylinder as the piston moves downward on the intake stroke; as the piston moves upward with the valves closed, the mixture is compressed during the compression stroke. The burning of the fuel-air mixture after ignition drives the piston downward during the power stroke, and as the piston rises again with the exhaust valve open the exhaust stroke ends the four stroke cycle. Because your aircraft engine has four or more cylinders, each igniting at a different time, there is always one piston on a power stroke, and the process is continuous.

A. Intake **B. Compression** **C. Power** **D. Exhaust**

A. Fuel mixture is drawn into cylinder by downward stroke.
B. Mixture is compressed by upward stroke.
C. Spark ignites mixture.
D. Burned gases are pushed out of cylinder by upward stroke.

Figure 3-1. Four strokes of an aircraft engine

Ignition

Your airplane engine uses a **magneto** as the source of ignition. Magneto may not be a familiar term to you, but your gas lawnmower, chain saw, or outboard motor all use magnetos. A magneto is a self-contained source of electrical impulses, using the physical motion of a coil and a fixed magnetic field to develop ignition voltage. To start the engine, you provide that physical motion by pulling a cord on your lawnmower, chain saw, or outboard. The starter motor does the job in the airplane, rotating the engine until the magneto-developed spark ignites the mixture. You have probably seen older airplanes without electrical systems (and newer airplanes with starter problems) being started manually—rotating the propeller by hand ("propping") causes the magneto to generate a voltage which goes to the spark plug to ignite the fuel/air mixture. Hand-propping an airplane is a hazardous undertaking which requires an experienced and knowledgeable person both in the cockpit and at the propeller. Once an airplane engine is started, the magnetos provide continuous ignition on their own—the airplane's electric system and the starter motor have done their jobs.

Each cylinder in your airplane engine has two spark plugs, each fired by a different magneto (*see* Figure 3-2). This has two advantages: better combustion efficiency, and safety. The engine will run on either magneto if one should develop a problem. *Magnetos are totally independent of the aircraft electrical system.*

When you turn the ignition off, with a key or with switches, you are connecting the electrical output of the magneto to the metal block of the engine where it is shorted to electrical ground and cannot fire the spark plugs. This "shorting out" is done through a wire called a P-lead, and if a P-lead is broken its associated magneto can fire the spark plugs even with the ignition in the OFF position. For this reason, you should treat all propellers with respect—moving the propeller might cause a magneto to start the engine unexpectedly if a P-lead has broken. During the preflight check of the airplane and its systems you will run the engine on each magneto separately. As you cut the ignition sources in half you will lose some power, reflected as a drop in revolutions per minute (RPM). If no drop occurs when one magneto is shut off, that magneto probably has a broken P-lead, and the flight should be delayed until a mechanic checks it. Some authorities recommend checking for a broken P-lead just before shutting the engine down after a flight, by turning the ignition switch to its "OFF" position momentarily while at idle power; if the engine continues to run, there is probably a broken P-lead.

Induction Systems

An airplane engine is a big air pump, taking in air through the induction system, mixing it with fuel, burning it, then pumping it overboard through the exhaust system. You will become familiar with two types of induction systems: **carburetor** and **fuel injection.** Figure 3-3 shows a float type carburetor similar to those in most light airplane installations.

Figure 3-2. Spark plugs and magnetos

Figure 3-3. Float type carburetor

Carburetor type induction systems are generally less expensive than fuel injection, and are easier to adjust. However, they do not deliver an equal fuel/air mixture to each cylinder, and are prone to induction system icing.

As air flows upward through the restriction called the venturi its speed increases and pressure drops, (remember Bernoulli's Theorem?). The air in the float chamber is vented to the outside, so the difference between outside air and the reduced pressure in the venturi forces fuel out of the float chamber, through the main discharge nozzle, and into the airstream. The amount of airflow through the carburetor is governed by the position of the throttle valve—you control that directly from the cockpit. The amount of fuel metered into the mixture is governed by the mixture control, and you control that in the cockpit as well. When you "step on the gas" in your automobile, or add power in your airplane, you are really controlling airflow directly and fuel flow indirectly. You really increase power by stepping on the air, not the gas.

As the fuel and air mixture expands in the carburetor throat it drops in temperature by 40° to 60°, due to both expansion of the air and evaporation of the fuel. If there is any moisture in the intake air, this sudden drop in temperature may cause the moisture to freeze on the carburetor walls and throttle valve, restricting airflow and reducing power just as surely as if you had retarded the throttle. Power loss due to carburetor ice is a possibility any time the outside air temperature is between 20°F and 70°F, with high relative humidity or visible moisture in the air.

To counter this threat, the manufacturer provides a carburetor heat control which takes heated air from a muff around the exhaust and directs it into the carburetor to melt the ice. Because the air gets its heat from the exhaust, carburetor heat must be used before the engine loses so much power that the heat from the exhaust is inadequate to do the job. This should be no problem if you keep an eye on your engine power instruments when operating in conditions where carburetor ice is possible.

As ice forms on the throttle valve and in the carburetor throat the reduction in power will be reflected in a reduction in RPM (with a fixed-pitch propeller). Application of FULL carburetor heat will result in a momentary further loss of RPM; then, as the ice melts and makes its way through the engine in the form of water, the RPMs will rise again (expect a moment or two of engine roughness!). The initial reduction in power experienced when the carburetor heat (Figure 3-4) is applied is due to hot air being less dense than cold air—this reduction in intake air density makes the fuel/air mixture ratio richer.

Figure 3-4. Carburetor heat

Carburetor heat should be either full ON, which causes a slight power loss, or full OFF while you watch for symptoms of icing. Partial heat is only used when you have additional instrumentation intended specifically for the detection of carburetor ice. The National Transportation Safety Board recommends that full carburetor heat be used whenever power is reduced below that required for cruise.

Fuel Injection

A fuel-injected induction system delivers an equal fuel/air mixture to each cylinder and requires careful adjustment. Because there is no carburetor, there can be no carburetor ice. Fuel injection systems are installed in more powerful airplanes, and virtually all **turbocharged** engines. Fuel injection systems (Figure 3-5) cannot develop carburetor ice, but induction system icing is not impossible. The intake air passes through a filter, and if that filter is clogged by wet snow or ice the air supply to the engine will be reduced and a power loss will result.

Figure 3-5. Fuel injection system

The primary power instrument in a fuel-injected engine installation is the **manifold pressure gauge.** Induction system icing will show up as a reduction in manifold pressure, and if you suspect that a loss of power is due to icing, there will always be some form of alternate air source so that the engine can breathe. When a controllable pitch (or constant speed) propeller is installed, the reduction in manifold pressure will be the only indication of induction system icing because the RPM will be held constant by a governor.

A manifold pressure gauge acts like a barometer, measuring the pressure in the intake manifold downstream (on the engine side) of the throttle butterfly. At power settings near idle, when the descending pistons are trying to pull air past the closed throttle butterfly, the manifold pressure is low. As you open the throttle to increase power, the pressure measured in the intake manifold increases as airflow increases. Without turbocharging, manifold pressure will approach but never equal the outside air pressure (unless you shut the engine down, something I don't recommend unless all three wheels are on the ground).

Fuel injected engines have a reputation of being hard to start when hot. This problem, when it exists, is usually caused by vapor lock, the result of fuel boiling into vapor in the fuel lines. When you shut down the engine at the completion of a flight the flow of cooling air no longer exists, and the engine must simply radiate its heat to its surroundings. It is inevitable that the fuel lines absorb some of this heat.

The manufacturer's approved flight manual will include a "hot start" procedure, and if it doesn't work you may simply have to wait until the fuel cools to a liquid state.

Fuel Systems

Some airplanes have very simple fuel systems, with the fuel flowing to the engine by gravity feed, and others have complex systems of main and auxiliary tanks with associated pumps and switches. You must understand your airplane's fuel system to be sure that fuel is available to the engine from startup to shutdown. Every year pilots make forced landings (or worse) due to fuel starvation, only to learn that fuel was available from another tank. Follow the manufacturer's starting instructions to the letter. A cold engine will require priming, either with a plunger-type manual primer, an electric fuel pump, or in some cases, pumping the throttle. Avoid overpriming—you may flood the engine or create a fire hazard. If your manufacturer's pilot's operating handbook requires that you take off and land with the fuel selector on the main tanks, or cautions you to use the auxiliary tanks only in straight-and-level flight, observe those restrictions—there may be interruptions in fuel flow if you don't.

Mixture Control

An airplane engine needs a mixture of approximately 15 parts of air for each part of fuel. If there is more air than 15:1 the mixture is called "lean", and when the ratio falls below 15:1 it is a "rich" mixture. There is a mixture control on your automobile carburetor or fuel injection system which is adjusted during tune-ups or when you move to the mountains from the flatlands. Airplanes make altitude changes of that magnitude in a matter of minutes, and you can't pull off the road to adjust the mixture, so the manufacturer provides a mixture control in the cockpit. Your engine needs additional cooling while supplying the power demands of takeoff and initial climb, and that additional cooling is provided by burning extra fuel or using a full rich mixture. Some carburetors have an enrichment valve which provides extra fuel when the throttle is full forward.

As the airplane climbs into air of diminishing density, the volume of air passing through the carburetor does not decrease but its weight does, and that upsets the 15:1 ratio toward the rich side: weight of fuel is unchanged, weight of air is decreased. Most manufacturer's operating handbooks require that the mixture control be full rich during climbs—check your handbook. When you arrive at cruise altitude, lean the mixture as recommended by the manufacturer. If you fail to lean at cruise altitude you are wasting fuel and are not operating the engine efficiently. Retarding the mixture control until the tachometer reaches a peak will do the trick in the absence of instrumentation for precise mixture adjustment. (See the section below on "Mixture Instrumentation.")

As you descend from cruise altitude, the reverse situation occurs: the mixture control has been leaned back to reduce the amount of fuel entering the mixture and, as the airplane descends into air of increasing density, the ratio swings to the lean side, with too much air for the amount of fuel. The recommended procedure is to enrich the mixture during the descent—but if you forget, the situation will be called to your attention by roughness as the engine tries to run on too little fuel. You will probably make several small mixture adjustments during the descent prior to going to full rich as a part of the pre-landing checklist. The best way to lean the mixture is to keep it at the leanest setting compatible with safe operating temperatures; too hot is better than too cold. You can't get the mixture too lean without the engine letting you know that it is unhappy.

Any time air of reduced density is introduced into the induction system, you can expect the symptoms of a too-rich mixture. If you are flying at 9,500 feet with the mixture properly leaned and add carburetor heat "just in case," the hot, less dense air will enrich the mixture and may cause rough running until the carburetor heat control is returned to the cold position. If you are operating at a high-altitude airport, the thin air may cause roughness during idle operation and taxiing, and the addition of carburetor heat during runup will make the roughness worse. Under those conditions, lean the mixture for the highest RPM during a *full-power* runup and leave it in that position for takeoff.

Mixture Instrumentation

Your airplane may be equipped with an **exhaust gas temperature gauge** (EGT) for precise mixture adjustment. These instruments read the highest temperature when the mixture is "just right": too much air or too much fuel and the exhaust temperature drops. There are also mixture settings to be used for best power and for best economy. Each engine manufacturer has guidelines on how the EGT instrument should be used, so before you use the EGT for mixture adjustment, familiarize yourself with the manufacturer's recommendations.

Airplanes with fuel injection systems will have a fuel flow gauge calibrated in gallons per hour or pounds per hour, and the performance tables will tell you the correct fuel flow for climb and for cruise power at different altitudes. Although these instruments are calibrated as flow meters, they actually measure fuel pressure, and a restriction in the fuel metering system may cause an incorrect high fuel flow indication. Solid state transducers are becoming available which actually measure fuel flow very accurately.

Fuel Grade and Contamination

An airplane engine is designed to operate most efficiently on one grade of fuel. There are three grades of aviation gasoline in use today: Grade 80 (which is dyed pink), Grade 100 Low-Lead (which is blue), and Grade 100 (green). The latter two differ only in lead content. Although many engines still in service specify Grade 80, it is being phased out by the petroleum industry. When the correct fuel for your airplane is not available, it is permissible to use a higher grade of fuel temporarily until the correct grade is available. If your engine specifications call for Grade 80 fuel, you can use a higher grade but check to see if the engine manufacturer has issued special operating procedures. NEVER use fuel of a lower grade than that specified for your engine. *Nonaviation diesel fuel is dyed a deep red; 80-octane users should look for a pink tint. If in doubt, drop some suspect fuel on a piece of paper. Aviation gasoline evaporates quickly, leaving a dye stain. Kerosine, diesel, or jet fuel spreads out and feel greasy.*

If the wrong grade of aviation gasoline has been pumped into your tanks (or, even worse, jet fuel), it will take only a few minutes of operation for destructive forces to be generated. It is always good practice to supervise the fueling of your airplane.

Note: Many airplane engines have received Supplemental Type Certificates (STCs) authorizing the use of automotive fuel. Make no assumptions: do not use automobile gas unless you are sure it is approved for your engine.

FAA tests indicate that engines using automobile fuel are more prone to induction system icing.

In addition to being sure that the fuel being pumped into your tanks is the correct grade, you must also guard against fuel contamination. The most common contaminant is water: airplane engines refuse to burn water, and your engine will let you know there is water in the fuel by running rough or stopping entirely. A common source of water in the tank is condensation. If you leave the fuel tanks less than full overnight, the cooling temperatures will cause the fuel to contract, drawing moist air into the tanks. This moisture will condense on the cold walls of the tank and sink to the bottom because water is heavier than gasoline.

One of your preflight duties is to drain fuel samples from low points in the fuel system; if any water shows up in the sample, continue to drain until no further contamination is apparent. The fuel pickup for the engine is at the low point in the tank, and water should show up there first, but it is possible for water to pool in the tank and not move toward the low point until the airplane moves. If the airplane has been parked in one place for an extended period, rock the wings vigorously and drain the sumps again after giving any trapped water time to move toward the low point of the fuel system. If the airplane has been parked on a slope, water may collect in the tank on the downhill side—drain the sumps with the airplane on a level surface.

You can practically eliminate condensation by being sure that the airplane's tanks are full at the end of each day's flying. While you are checking for water in the fuel, look for dirt or any other foreign matter which might cause a problem in the carburetor or fuel injectors. The fuel passes through many filters by the time it reaches your tanks from the refinery, and the odds against having a contaminant pumped into your tanks are high, but a moment's inattention during the fueling process can lead to disaster.

Any discussion of fuel contamination must address the question of running a tank dry. Never run a fuel tank dry, because you *may* introduce contaminants into the engine that would normally just float around in the bottom of the tank. A secondary consideration, especially true with fuel injection, is introducing air into the fuel lines when the tank runs dry. Fuel injected engines may be difficult to re-start even when you have switched to a full tank. Both electric and engine-driven fuel pumps work best with fluid, not with air, and it may take a few moments before the pumps are re-primed to deliver fuel to the engine. *Do not run a fuel tank dry.*

Detonation and Preignition

When driving your automobile, any unusual noise usually gets your attention. If you notice a pinging or knocking sound when adding power, you know that you may have to make a shop visit to have the timing checked. In flight, you can't hear the engine pinging, and must be sure to avoid conditions which might lead to **detonation**. Detonation occurs when the fuel/air mixture explodes instead of burning evenly. This develops stresses that can destroy the engine in a very short time. Factors which lead to detonation are fuel of too low a grade, high operating temperature, or a mixture which is too lean. To avoid detonation, you must use the specified fuel grade (or a higher grade), avoid operation with too lean a mixture, and keep a watchful eye on engine temperatures.

Preignition occurs when a "hot spot" within the cylinder causes the fuel/air mixture to ignite prematurely, and is usually caused by deposits on the spark plugs or valves. It usually has the same causes as detonation, and can be prevented in the same way. Your reaction, when detonation or preignition are suspected, must be directed toward cooling the engine. A richer mixture, a lower power setting, or a higher airspeed will help cool the engine and reduce any tendency toward detonation.

Engine Instrumentation

An airplane *must* have at least an oil temperature gauge and an oil pressure gauge, but may have additional instruments to give you a better picture of what is going on inside the cowling. A major consideration is avoiding overheating, and the engine manufacturer uses several methods to accomplish this.

Aircraft engines are air-cooled, and during preflight you will see the cooling fins on the cylinders. The excess fuel in a rich mixture is used as a cooling agent during takeoff and climb, while oil serves as a coolant at all times. The oil which circulates through and around the engine as a lubricant picks up heat as it travels. It passes through an oil cooler, where the heat is given up to the air, and the oil is cooled for another trip around. The oil temperature gauge will reflect how well the oil is able to perform this cooling task. If you have allowed the oil level to fall below recommended levels, the amount available may not be able to do the job adequately, and high oil temperature will result.

The oil pressure gauge is an indication of how well the oil is lubricating the engine. High oil temperature *and* low oil pressure would indicate a *major* problem and usually calls for a landing at the nearest airport. **The cylinder head temperature gauge**, when installed, is an excellent indicator of potentially damaging over-heating. When the CHT (Figure 3-6) starts rising toward the red line, enriching the mixture, reducing power, increasing airspeed, or opening the cowl flaps (if installed) will all contribute to temperature reduction. Excessively high temperatures will cause power loss, detonation, increased oil consumption, and possible internal engine damage.

Figure 3-6. *Cylinder head temperature gauge*

Electrical System

The airplane's electrical system consists of a battery and a generator or alternator with associated voltage regulators, current limiters or other protective devices. The primary function of the battery is to provide power to the starter motor—after the engine starts, the magnetos provide ignition, and the generator or alternator takes on the task of powering the radios, instruments, lights, electrical landing gear or flaps, and recharging the battery. Individual circuits are protected by circuit breakers or fuses.

Most modern airplanes use alternators rather than generators. Early electrical systems used generators (first wind-driven, then geared to the engine), because in their simplest form generators were self-energized with permanent magnets. They were large and heavy in relation to their output. The electrical output of an engine-driven generator is a function of engine speed, and generators became unable to handle the electrical demands of modern airplanes at taxiing and idle speeds. Airplane manufacturers switched to alternators because alternators are smaller and lighter for a given output and because the output voltage of an alternator is not dependent on engine speed. In combination with a voltage regulator, an alternator can provide a constant output voltage from idle RPM to full throttle.

Unlike a generator, however, an alternator requires current flow through its field windings in order to produce electricity. This current must come from the battery to the field windings through the solenoid (that's the click you hear when you turn on the master switch). If the airplane battery is totally discharged, the solenoid will not close (no click), so no current is available for the alternator field coils and the alternator is inoperative. If an external power source is available, use it, but follow the manufacturer's recommended procedure to the letter. Hand-propping will get the airplane back in the air, but the battery will not be recharged by the alternator. A new or recharged battery is the only answer. Alternator failure (which can be as simple as a broken or slipping drive belt) means that the battery must supply all required power until it is completely discharged, which may occur in a disconcertingly short time. Most airplanes with alternators have split electrical master switches (Figure 3-7) which allow the pilot to disconnect the alternator field coils from the battery after all non-essential electrical loads have been reduced. This will extend battery life for a few precious minutes.

Figure 3-7. *Alternator with split electrical master switches*

You will find an **ammeter** on your instrument panel with a zero center and + and - indications, or a **loadmeter** which reads from zero to some value such as 75 amperes and reflects the actual electrical load on the system. With the zero center ammeter, a reading on the minus side indicates that the alternator is not providing enough electricity to recharge the battery. With a loadmeter, a reading of zero indicates that there is no alternator output. During the preflight runup, turn on the landing light or pilot heat momentarily to see if the ammeter reflects a change in the electrical load. If system failure is indicated or suspected in flight, turn off unnecessary electrical equipment to reduce the load on the battery. A clue: almost all fuel gauges are electric, and if both fuel gauges begin to sink toward empty you may be out of electricity instead of gas.

On the ground, when you turn on the airplane's master switch, listen for the click of the solenoid being operated by battery current, and for the electric gyro instruments to begin spinning. The absence of these audible clues means a dead battery. Learn what your airplane has for an electrical supply and what the normal and abnormal indications are. You may find that a re-set function (or a second voltage regulator) has been provided so that you can overcome momentary electrical failure. In any case, an electrical failure will not affect engine operation.

If your airplane has a split master switch, leaving the "ALT" side off during engine start will reduce the load on the battery. Don't forget to turn it *on* after the engine starts.

Vacuum System

Certain flight instruments are powered by vacuum, just as windshield wipers on older cars were vacuum operated (Figure 3-8). The vacuum pump is mounted on the rear of the engine, together with other engine driven accessories such as fuel pumps and magnetos.

There is a vacuum indicator on the instrument panel so that you can keep tabs on the health of the vacuum system. Vacuum pump drive shafts are designed to shear (like an outboard motor shear pin) if internal mechanical failure occurs.

Figure 3-8. *Vacuum system*

Fixed Pitch Propellers

A fixed pitch propeller is a compromise between performance and speed. A propeller with a very flat blade angle (pitch) is called a climb prop. It takes very small bites of the air as it pulls itself and the airplane forward. The engine is able to develop takeoff power very quickly—you will notice in the specifications for your airplane a statement such as "150 horsepower at 2700 RPM"—and you will get good takeoff performance. When that flat pitch propeller which revved up to 2,700 RPM very rapidly at sea level gets to 10,000 feet, however, taking small bites of thin air won't give you much cruise airspeed. If high speed at cruise altitude is what you want, you need a propeller with a greater blade angle, which will take bigger bites of the thin air and improve cruise speed. When taking off and climbing with a cruise propeller, however, you will be amazed at how much runway you will leave behind before that propeller—now taking big bites of dense air—gets up to 2,700 RPM. You have sacrificed takeoff and climb performance for cruise speed. Any fixed-pitch propeller is, therefore, a performance compromise.

Controllable Pitch (Constant Speed) Propellers

The solution is a propeller that has a flat pitch (high RPM) for takeoff, and a coarse pitch (low RPM) for cruise: a **controllable pitch propeller** or constant speed propeller. These two names are used almost interchangeably. Although a controllable pitch propeller was at one time a ground-adjustable propeller, today's installations use a governor to change blade angle and thus maintain constant RPM.

Figure 3-9. Tachometer and manifold pressure gauge

You will have two power instruments with a constant speed propeller installation: the **tachometer**, and a **manifold pressure gauge** which is now your primary power instrument (Figure 3-9). The manifold pressure gauge reacts directly to throttle movement. For takeoff, the propeller control (linked to the governor to control RPM) is set full forward for high RPM. After the engine/propeller team have done their work and gotten you into the air in a hurry, you set climb power by first retarding the throttle, and then retarding the propeller control. During the climb, because barometric pressure decreases 1' per 1,000' of altitude, you must adjust the throttle setting to maintain climb power.

At cruise altitude, set cruise power according to the manufacturer's cruise chart for that altitude; a good thumb rule is the lowest RPM setting that allows smooth engine operation without vibration and a manifold pressure (throttle) setting that meets your requirements for either speed or economy. As you retard the prop control at altitude, the governor will increase the blade angle to take bigger bites of the air (low RPM): the characteristics of a cruise prop. Once you have set the propeller control to the desired RPM, the governor will change blade angle as required to maintain that RPM. If you have to add power to climb, or to increase airspeed, always advance the propeller control before the throttle; this will ensure that dangerously high pressures are not developed in the cylinders. Most pre-landing checklists include a reminder to move the propeller control to the high RPM position, to position it properly in case of an aborted landing. With the prop control full forward, you have completed the first half of the "increase power" procedure.

Turbocharging

We have discussed how the decrease in air density with altitude causes the manifold pressure to drop, requiring more throttle to maintain climb power. A turbocharger (Figure 3-10) allows sea level manifold pressure to be maintained to much higher altitudes by compressing air and packing it into the intake manifold. A turbine wheel is spun by exhaust gas, and a compressor on the same shaft compresses outside air and directs it into the induction system.

Figure 3-10. *Turbocharging system*

A "waste gate" controls the amount of exhaust that passes over the turbine. When no turbocharging is needed or desired, the waste gate is fully open and the exhaust gases bypass the turbine.

As manifold pressure drops off, and "boosting" is required, the waste gate is adjusted so that more of the exhaust gases pass through the turbine. When the waste gate is fully closed, all of the exhaust passes through the turbine before being discharged to the atmosphere, and further climb will cause manifold pressure to decrease. When full boost from the turbocharger is being used, and further climb will result in reduced power, the engine has reached its critical altitude.

Some turbocharger installations require that you control the manifold pressure manually, while others use automatic controllers. Where manual control is provided, the pilot must be sure that the waste gate is fully open prior to takeoff, except at high altitude airports where additional power may be required. Applying the full exhaust force to the turbine at a low altitude airport by having the waste gate closed will cause destructive pressures (overboosting). Automatic controllers adjust the waste gate position in accordance with power demands, and the possibility of overboosting is eliminated. Many turbocharger installations have a fixed orifice through which a minimum amount of exhaust gas always passes, bypassing the waste gate. This limits the maximum available power but reduces the possibility of overboosting.

Turbocharging allows you to get above most of the weather, but it has its drawbacks. The discharge air from the compressor to the induction system is very hot, and hot air is less dense than cool air. This raises the possibility of having to run an overly rich mixture to keep temperatures down. Many turbocharger installations include an intercooler, a heat exchanger which cools the air coming from the compressor before it enters the intake manifold.

Pilots of turbocharged airplanes must be very temperature conscious, keeping in mind that high temperatures can lead to preignition or detonation. They must also guard against sudden power reductions which will shock-cool the red-hot turbocharger. Turbocharger installations may have additional engine instrumentation, such as a **Compressor Discharge Temperature Gauge** (CDT), so that the pilot can get maximum utilization from the turbocharger without developing damaging internal engine temperatures.

Pressurization

A turbocharged airplane can take a pilot to altitudes where there is insufficient oxygen to sustain life, and a supplemental oxygen supply is mandatory to take full advantage of turbocharging unless the airplane is pressurized. Pressurization allows the pilot and passengers to enjoy near-sea level pressure in the cabin at flight altitudes above 10,000 feet, and cabin pressures in the order of 8,000 feet at altitudes up to 40,000 feet.

A pressurized airplane is very tightly sealed, and is much stronger structurally than an unpressurized airplane. As you walk around the ramp, you can identify pressurized airplanes by their rounded windows and doors. The pressurization system (Figure 3-11) takes compressed air (called "bleed air") from the turbocharger and, in effect, "inflates" the cabin to maintain a comfortable cabin pressure for passengers. Bleed air is also used for cabin heating and de-icing functions on jet aircraft.

Figure 3-11. Pressurization system

Every pressurized airplane has a maximum allowable differential between the pressure in the cabin and the outside atmosphere. This maximum is based on structural considerations, because it is possible to have too much cabin pressure. A pressurization controller operates an "outflow valve," which allows air to leak out of the cabin at a controlled rate to maintain a pressure differential well below the maximum allowable. The outflow valve is backed up by a safety valve that will release pressure before the maximum differential is reached. Air constantly leaks out of the cabin of a pressurized airplane through the outflow valve, and only a large opening such as a failed window would lower the cabin pressure enough to require that the occupants use an emergency oxygen system.

The operation of the pressurization system varies with different types and models of airplanes, and you should study the operation of any system thoroughly before using it. One of your major concerns should be that the pressurization system activate and deactivate without discomfort for yourself and your passengers. Pressurization "bumps," when the occupants feel sudden pressure changes in their ears, are usually caused by incorrect use of the pressurization controls.

Autopilots

You may buy, rent, or get checked out in an airplane with some type of autopilot, and it is important that you have a full understanding of the autopilot system. An autopilot simply gets roll, pitch, yaw, information from the flight instruments and moves the controls just as you would if you were in control. The most basic system is a wing leveler, which does nothing more than keep the wings level while you unfold maps or eat your lunch. The next step up in sophistication adds "heading hold," which allows you to command a turn to a heading and then holds that heading with the wings level.

For a few more dollars you get VOR tracking capability, which takes a signal from the VOR receiver/indicator and steers the airplane along a radial (see Chapter Eight for an explanation of VOR). You don't need any more than this as a non-instrument rated pilot.

If you are going to fly an autopilot-equipped airplane, insist on a thorough explanation and demonstration of all of its capabilities. There may be a pre-takeoff check of the autopilot in the Pilot Operating Handbook that does not appear on the airplane checklist. Seek it out and perform that check. Be sure that you are familiar with all available methods of disconnecting the autopilot—if there is an electrical or mechanical problem and the A/P decides to put the airplane into a dive or roll upside down, you need to know which switches to throw to put yourself back in charge.

Some instructors will tell you to just ignore the autopilot if one is installed. Don't accept that. You should know how to operate every item of equipment in the airplane, even if you don't intend to use it.

Chapter 3
Aircraft Engines and Instruments
Review Questions

1. What action can a pilot take to aid in cooling an engine that is overheating during a climb?

   A—Lean the mixture to best power condition.
   B—Increase RPM and reduce climb speed.
   C—Reduce rate of climb and increase airspeed.

2. How is engine operation controlled on an engine equipped with a constant-speed propeller?

   A—The throttle controls power output as registered on the manifold pressure gauge and the propeller control regulates engine RPM.
   B—The throttle controls power output as registered on the manifold pressure gauge and the propeller control regulates a constant blade angle.
   C—The throttle controls engine RPM as registered on the tachometer and the propeller control regulates the power output.

3. Is it necessary to preflight an aircraft that was hangared the night before in ready-to-fly condition?

   A—No, if the aircraft has not been handled since hangaring.
   B—Yes, because fuel contamination from condensation is possible.
   C—Yes, because the oil level should always be checked.

4. The presence of carburetor ice, in an airplane equipped with a fixed-pitch propeller can be verified by applying carburetor heat and noting

   A—a decrease in RPM and then a constant RPM indication.
   B—an immediate increase in RPM with no further change in RPM.
   C—a decrease in RPM and then a gradual increase in RPM.

5. The uncontrolled firing of the fuel/air charge in advance of normal spark ignition is known as

   A—combustion.
   B—preignition.
   C—detonation.

6. If the engine oil temperature and cylinder head temperature gauges have exceeded their normal operating range, the pilot may have been

   A—operating with the mixture set too rich.
   B—using fuel that has a higher-than-specified fuel rating.
   C—operating with too much power and with the mixture set too lean.

7. If an engine continues to run after the ignition switch is turned to the OFF position, the probable cause may be

   A—the mixture is too lean and this causes the engine to diesel.
   B—a broken magneto ground wire.
   C—fouled spark plugs.

8. Detonation occurs in a reciprocating aircraft engine when

A—hot spots in the combustion chamber ignite the fuel/air mixture in advance of normal ignition.
B—there is too rich a fuel/air mixture.
C—the unburned charge in the cylinders explodes instead of burning evenly.

9. For internal cooling, reciprocating aircraft engines are especially dependent on

A—a properly functioning thermostat.
B—air flowing over the exhaust manifold.
C—the circulation of lubricating oil.

10. If the grade of fuel used in an aircraft engine is lower than specified for the engine, it will most likely cause

A—a mixture of fuel and air that is not uniform in all cylinders.
B—an increase in power which could overstress internal engine components.
C—detonation.

11. In an aircraft equipped with a constant-speed propeller and a normally-aspirated engine, which procedure would be used to avoid placing undue stress on the engine components?

A—When power is being increased or decreased, the RPM should be adjusted before the manifold pressure.
B—When power is being decreased, reduce the RPM before reducing the manifold pressure.
C—When power is being increased, increase the RPM before increasing the manifold pressure.

12. The main purpose of the mixture control is to

A—adjust the fuel flow to obtain the proper air/fuel ratio.
B—increase the oxygen supplied to the engine.
C—decrease the oxygen supplied to the engine.

13. Which statement is true regarding the effect of the application of carburetor heat?

A—It reduces the density of air entering the carburetor, thus enriching the fuel/air mixture.
B—It reduces the density of air entering the carburetor, thus leaning the fuel/air mixture.
C—It reduces the volume of air entering the carburetor, thus enriching the fuel/air mixture.

14. What will occur if no leaning is made with the mixture control as the flight altitude increases?

A—The volume of air entering the carburetor remains constant and the amount of fuel decreases.
B—The volume of air entering the carburetor decreases and the amount of fuel decreases.
C—The density of air entering the carburetor decreases and the amount of fuel remains constant.

Flight Instruments

Figure 4-1. Flight instruments

Pitot-Static Instruments

The **pitot-static system** consists of a pitot (pressure-sensing) tube, a static (zero pressure) source and related plumbing and filters (Figure 4-1). The pitot-static instruments are the **airspeed indicator**, the **altimeter**, and the **vertical speed indicator**; they measure changes in air pressure caused by the airplane's vertical and horizontal movements in the atmosphere (Figure 4-2 on the next page).

The airspeed indicator requires input from both the pitot (pressure) and static (unchanging) sources (Figure 4-3). Air from the static port fills the airspeed instrument case, while air from the pitot tube is led to a diaphragm. As airspeed changes, the pressure exerted on the diaphragm also changes and the movement of the diaphragm in response to these changes is transmitted to the indicator needle. The designer tries to locate the pitot tube so that it registers pressure in free air and is not affected by local airflow around the supporting structure. The airspeed indicator is the only instrument which uses air pressure from the pitot tube.

Figure 4-2. *Pitot-static system*

Figure 4-3. *Pitot-static sources*

FLAPS UP												
KIAS	50	60	70	80	90	100	110	120	130	140	150	160
KCAS	55	63	71	80	89	99	108	118	128	138	147	157
FLAPS 10°												
KIAS	40	50	60	70	80	90	100	110	120	130	---	---
KCAS	50	54	62	71	81	91	100	110	120	130	---	---
FLAPS 30°												
KIAS	40	50	60	70	80	90	100	---	---	---	---	---
KCAS	47	54	62	71	81	90	101	---	---	---	---	---

Figure 4-4. *Airspeed correction table*

The static port is located where the airplane's motion through the air will create no pressure at all: on the side of the fuselage or on the back of the pitot tube. The airspeed indicator is calibrated to read the difference in pressure between impact air and still air—both inputs are required. If either the pitot tube or the static port is blocked, the system will be useless, much like trying to get electricity from only one side of an electrical outlet.

Blockage of the static system would disable the airspeed indicator, the altimeter, and the vertical speed indicator.

At the start of the takeoff roll, there is no difference in pressure between the pitot and static inputs, and the airspeed indicator reads zero. As the airplane accelerates, the pressure in the pitot tube increases and that pressure is transmitted to the airspeed indicator needle. The designer cannot completely isolate the pitot and static inputs from the effects of airflow around the wing or fuselage, so an airspeed correction table is provided (Figure 4-4). The needle on the airspeed indicator reads indicated airspeed (IAS); when corrected for installation or position error, it becomes calibrated (CAS). Note in Figure 4-4 that the greatest difference between indicated and calibrated airspeed occurs at low speeds which require high angles of attack, and that as the angle of attack is reduced and speed increases, the difference between IAS and CAS becomes negligible. The colored arcs on the airspeed indicator are usually based on calibrated airspeed; other operating speeds may be based on indicated airspeed. Check the operator's handbook to be sure.

It takes a pressure of about 34 pounds per square foot on the pitot side of the airspeed indicator's diaphragm to make the airspeed needle register 100 knots at sea level. As the airplane climbs to altitude, the air becomes less dense. The airplane will have to move much faster through the less dense air at altitude in order to develop a pressure of 34 psf in the pitot tube, so the true airspeed will be faster than 100 knots when the airspeed indicator shows 100 knots. Your flight computer will allow you to make accurate calculations of *true* airspeed using IAS, pressure altitude, and temperature, but a good rule of thumb is that *true airspeed increases by 2% per 1,000' of altitude.* At sea level under standard conditions, indicated and true air speed will be equal; at 10,000' MSL, an indicated 100 knots means a true airspeed of 120 knots. Your airplane may have an airspeed indicator similar to Figure 4-5, which allows you to enter pressure altitude and temperature and read true airspeed directly.

You will use true airspeed in flight planning, but most airspeeds that you will use in actual flight are indicated airspeeds. You will always use the same

Figure 4-5. Airspeed indicator

Airspeed Indicator Markings

The airspeed indicator has colored arcs to alert you to limiting airspeeds, and you should be aware of their significance (Figure 4-6). Most markings are based on calibrated airspeed. Check your airplane's Approved Flight Manual.

White Arc

The low speed end indicates the power-off stall speed in the landing configuration (V_{SO}), and the high speed end indicates the maximum allowable speed with flaps fully extended (V_{FE}).

Green Arc

The low speed end indicates the power-off stall speed in a specified configuration, usually gear and flaps ups (V_{S1}), and the high speed end indicates maximum structural cruising speed (V_{NO}) which should be exceeded only in smooth air.

Yellow Arc

The caution range: pilots should avoid operating at airspeeds in the caution range except when in smooth air.

Red Line

This is the never-exceed speed (V_{NE}). Destructive aerodynamic forces may result from flight at or above the red line.

indicated airspeeds, regardless of altitude. For example, if you are taking your flight training at a sea level airport and find that 70 knots indicated is the correct final approach speed, you will use 70 knots indicated airspeed on final when you fly to an airport at 5,000' above sea level. Your true airspeed will be 77 knots (2% times 5 = 10%, 1.1 times 70 = 77). Because the airplane approaching the airport at 5,000' is moving faster through the air in order to have an indicated airspeed of 70 knots, its ground speed will be higher and landing roll will be longer. A pilot who adds a few knots "just in case" while on final approach at a high altitude airport may have difficulty getting stopped on the available runway. Flying at the manufacturer's recommended airspeed will have predictable results.

Figure 4-6. Airspeed indicator markings

Speeds Not Marked On the Airspeed Indicator

Every airplane has a design maneuvering speed (V_A), which is the optimum speed in turbulence at maximum gross weight. *Maneuvering speed is reduced as weight is reduced.* Flight at maneuvering speed ensures that the airplane will stall before damaging aerodynamic loads are imposed on the wing structure.

Best angle of climb speed (V_X) is that speed which gives the most altitude in a given distance. You should fly at V_X to clear obstructions. Because flight at V_X requires a steep pitch attitude, engine cooling airflow and visibility are reduced. Climb at V_X only as long as necessary to clear the obstruction, then accelerate to V_Y. These speeds are for operation at maximum gross weight, and may be reduced by 1/2 of any weight decrease. That is, if the aircraft weighs 5 percent less than gross, V_X and V_Y can be reduced by 2-1/2 percent.

Best rate of climb speed (V_Y) will produce the greatest gain in altitude in a given time, better visibility over the nose, and better engine cooling. If getting to altitude quickly is your goal, use V_Y.

The manufacturer may designate other speeds, which you will find in the Pilot's Operating Handbook and possibly placarded on the instrument panel. Landing gear extension and retraction speeds, and speeds for partial flap extension will be found in the operating handbook and not on the airspeed indicator.

Angle of Attack Indicators

The airspeed indicator can be considered a form of angle of attack indicator, since indicated airspeed is dependent on angle of attack in addition to power setting. Several manufacturers provide actual angle of attack indicators, however, which are calibrated to measure the actual angle between the chord line and the relative wind and provide you with angle of attack information by some form of "safe-unsafe" instrument reading (Figure 4-7). One such instrument

Lift Sensor

Indicator

Figure 4-7. Angle of attack indicator

compares air pressure changes both vertically and horizontally and measures sink rate. In every case, you need only keep the instrument's needle in the "safe" area and no interpretation is required.

Altimeter

Aircraft altimeters are aneroid (dry) barometers calibrated to read in feet above sea level. The altimeter gets its input from the static port, which is unaffected by the airplane's movement through the air. An aneroid barometer contains several sealed wafers with a partial internal vacuum, so as the airplane moves vertically and the outside pressure changes, the wafers expand and contract much like an accordion. This expansion and contraction is transmitted through a linkage to the altimeter needles (Figure 4-8).

Figure 4-8. Altimeter/indicated altitudes

Encoding Altimeter

An encoding altimeter automatically reports pressure altitude to the radar scopes of air traffic controllers, and is required equipment in most controlled airspace (to be discussed in later chapters). As a pilot, you have no control over an encoder and cannot adjust it—you can't even turn it on and off.

Barometers provide a means of weighing the earth's atmosphere at a specific location. At a Flight Service Station or National Weather Service office, an actual mercury barometer may be used, and on a standard day the weight of the atmosphere will support a column of mercury (Hg) 29.92 inches high at sea level. Inches of mercury are the units of measure for barometric pressure and altimeter settings. The equivalent metric measure is 1013.2 millibars and since our weather is transmitted internationally, the Weather Service uses both inches and millibars in its reports.

Up to 18,000', altitude is measured above sea level, and sea level pressure may vary from 28.50" to 30.50" Hg (these are extremes). Your altimeter has an adjustment knob and an altimeter setting window (Figure 4-8), so that you can enter the sea level barometric pressure (altimeter setting) at your location as received from a nearby Flight Service Station or air traffic control facility. The altimeter will, when properly set, read altitude above mean sea level (MSL). As you increase the numbers in the altimeter setting window, the hands on the altimeter also show an increase: each .01 increase in the window is equal to 10 feet of altitude, each .1 is 100 feet, etc.

Above 18,000' (and after you get your instrument rating, since all operations above that altitude must be under instrument flight rules), you will set the window to 29.92" Hg and you will be reading your altitude above the standard datum plane. By international agreement, a standard day at sea level is defined as having a barometric pressure of 29.92 (with the temperature 15°C or 59°F), and by setting your altimeter to 29.92 it will read altitude above that standard level. Below 18,000', having the correct altimeter setting will keep you out of the trees, while above 18,000' (where there are no trees or mountains), the common altimeter setting of 29.92 provides altitude separation for IFR flights. There are several altitude terms with which you should become familiar:

Indicated altitude is simply what the hands on the altimeter point to. The long hand reads hundreds of feet (the calibrations are 20'), the next largest hand reads thousands of feet, and the third indicator reads in tens of thousands. The three-needle altimeter is easily misread, and many new airplanes are being equipped with a drum-pointer altimeter which has only one needle and a counter (Figure 4-9).

Figure 4-9. Drum-pointer altimeter

Figure 4-10. *Three-needle instrument indicators*

Refer to Figure 4-10.

Altimeter A's smallest (10,000') needle is just past one, the second largest (1,000') needle is between zero and one, and the largest (100') needle is on the five:

One 10,000
\+ No 0
\+ 500
———————
10,500

Altimeter B reads 9,500'—is that the answer you would get?

Absolute altitude is your actual height above the surface as read by a radar altimeter.

Pressure altitude is what the hands of the altimeter indicate when the altimeter setting window is set to 29.92" Hg. You will use pressure altitude in computations of density altitude, true airspeed and true altitude.

Density altitude is a critically important altitude; however, you can't read it on your altimeter but must calculate it, using pressure altitude and temperature. Density altitude is performance altitude—the airplane and engine perform as though they are at a different altitude than their true altitude. All performance charts are based on density altitude, and this book will deal with it in detail in Chapter Six.

True altitude is your height above sea level. When you set your altimeter setting window to the local altimeter setting, the altimeter should read field elevation (above sea level). If it doesn't, record the instrument error. Differences of over 75' indicate that the instrument needs overhaul or replacement. (Before you take any drastic steps, be sure that your airplane is not simply located at a point below the published field elevation.) The illustration in Figure 4-11 shows an airplane with its altitude above the ground (absolute altitude), above sea level (true altitude), and above the standard datum plane of 29.92" (pressure altitude).

Figure 4-11. *Altitude defenitions*

Any obstruction to the static port or static lines will make the altimeter unusable, so some aircraft have alternate static sources vented inside the cockpit. When using the alternate static source, there will be slight errors in the altimeter and airspeed indications.

The pressure inside the cockpit is lower than the outside pressure—with the alternate static source selected, the altimeter will read slightly high, the airspeed indicator will read high, and the vertical speed indicator will read correctly after momentarily indicating a climb.

Effects of Temperature and Pressure on Altimeters

When you fly into an area of lower barometric pressure (while maintaining a constant altimeter setting) your true altitude will be lower than your indicated altitude, and that can be dangerous. Avoid this by frequently checking with ground stations to keep the altimeter set to an altimeter setting received from a station within 100 miles. If you fly into an area of colder temperatures, where air density is increased, indicated altitude will again be higher than true altitude.

"From High to Low, Look Out Below" applies to both pressure and temperature. You have no means of adjusting for temperature changes, so remember that pressure levels rise on warm days and descend on cold days, and if you are flying a constant pressure level (altimeter setting), you may be dangerously low on a cold day.

Vertical Speed Indicator

The vertical speed indicator (Figure 4-12) is a static-pressure instrument which reflects rate of climb or descent by detecting rate of change in air pressure. Its internal construction is similar to that of the altimeter, but the aneroid wafer in the vertical speed indicator has a very small leak which allows its internal pressure to stabilize when altitude is not changing. During changes, there is a pressure differential between the air in the wafer and the air surrounding it, and the instrument indicates the change in this differential as climb or descent rate in feet per minute. The needle will lag actual changes in altitude until the rate of change stabilizes. However, if your instrument is marked "IVSI", this lag has been eliminated and it is an Instantaneous Vertical Speed Indicator. The VSI is not a required instrument for either VFR or IFR flight, but you won't find many airplanes without one. If the static port is clogged or frozen the VSI will be unusable—select the alternate static source if one is available.

Figure 4-12. *Vertical speed indicator*

Gyroscopic Instruments

The attitude indicator, the turn indicator, and the directional gyro or heading indicator operate on the principle of gyroscopic rigidity in space. A spinning body, such as a bicycle wheel, will maintain its position in space as long as a rotational force is applied—riding your bike "no hands" is an example of this. Precession, or turning, occurs when any external force is applied to the spinning body, which will react as though the force has been applied at a point 90° away in the direction of rotation. If you lean your bicycle to the right, the turning force is as though pressure has been applied to the left front of the wheel—90° in the direction of rotation. Actually turning the wheel to the right may cause the bicycle to topple over to the right, again the result of gyroscopic precession.

Turn and Slip Indicator

Your airplane may have either a turn needle or a turn coordinator, but in either case a ball instrument will be included. Both the turn needle and the turn coordinator (Figure 4-13 on the next page) indicate the rate of turn of the aircraft: when the turn needle is deflected one needle-width, or when the turn coordinator's airplane wing is on the index, the airplane is turning at the rate of 3° per second, and a complete circle will take 2 minutes. The turn and slip indicator shows rotation around the yaw axis (the ball), and around the roll axis (the miniature airplane or the needle).

Figure 4-13. Turn and slip indicator

Figure 4-14. Rate and radius of turn vs. speed

Unlike the turn needle, the turn coordinator is designed so that it reflects *roll* rate as well as turn rate. Neither instrument indicates bank angle. Bank angle, turn rate, and airspeed are interrelated, as shown in Figure 4-14. For a given bank angle, the rate of turn increases as the airspeed decreases. Consider a light trainer and a jet, both banked 20°: the trainer would complete a 360° turn in a much shorter time than the jet and with a much smaller radius. If both airplanes maintained a 3° per second turn rate, they would both complete the circle at the same time — but the jet would be at an extreme bank angle. The bank angle for a 3° per second turn is approximately 15 percent of the true airspeed, so the trainer at 80 knots would bank 12°, while the jet at 400 knots would have to bank 60°.

The ball indicates the *quality* of the turn, with respect to rudder-aileron coordination. The force that causes an airplane to turn is the horizontal component of lift (Figure 4-15), which is opposed by centrifugal force. If the rate of turn is too great for the angle of bank, centrifugal force is greater than the horizontal component of lift, and the ball rolls toward the outside of the turn. This is termed a "skidding" turn, and either a steeper bank angle (increasing horizontal component) or less rudder pressure on the inside of the turn (reduced centrifugal force) will return the ball to the center. The reverse situation has the ball falling to the inside of the turn in a "slip," caused by too little centrifugal force and too much horizontal component.

Figure 4-15. Forces during normal coordinated turns

Figure 4-16. *Interpreting the ball instrument*

Less bank angle or more inside rudder will return the ball to the center when slipping (Figure 4-16). A rule of thumb is to *"step on the ball"* — apply pressure to the rudder pedal on the side of the instrument that the ball is on.

Table 4-1 illustrates how various elements of a turn are affected if either bank angle or airspeed is kept constant. For example, with a constant bank angle, an increase in airspeed will decrease the rate of turn while increasing the turn radius; the load factor would not be affected.

Turn needles or turn coordinators are almost always electrically driven, but you may find a turn needle driven by vacuum from an engine-driven vacuum pump or a **venturi**. Be sure that you know what makes your turn indicator operate.

In most trainer-type airplanes, the gyro instruments (attitude and heading indicator) are vacuum operated. An engine-driven vacuum pump draws air into the instrument case and as the air passes over turbine wheels it imparts a rotational force (Figure 4-17 on the next page). When the gyroscope rotors are up to speed they become fixed in the plane of rotation, and the airplane moves around them. The instrument presentations are so designed that the pilot has an accurate representation of airplane attitude and heading. Not all gyro installations are entirely vacuum operated— you may find that your heading indicator is electric and the attitude indicator is vacuum, or both may be electrically operated. Check the power source for each instrument in your airplane so that you can better deal with failures.

CONSTANT BANK			
Airspeed	**Rate**	**Radius**	**Load Factor**
Increases	Decreases	Increases	Same
Decreases	Increases	Decreases	Same
CONSTANT AIRSPEED			
Angle of Bank	**Rate**	**Radius**	**Load Factor**
Increases	Increases	Decreases	Increases
Decreases	Decreases	Increases	Decreases

Table 4-1. *Constant bank and airspeed table*

Figure 4-17. Vacuum-operated gyro instruments

Attitude Indicator

The gyroscope and its linkage cause the horizon disc (Figure 4-18) to move in both pitch and roll behind the miniature airplane. If you compare the movement of the horizon line in the attitude indicator with the movement of the natural horizon, you will see that the instrument instantly and accurately reflects changes in the pitch and roll attitude of the airplane. It is this instantaneous representation that makes the attitude indicator the most valuable instrument on the panel when reference to the natural horizon is lost. The bank angle markings at the top of the instrument are 10°, 20°, 30°, 45° (the dot), 60° and 90°. For control of pitch attitude — nose up or nose down — keeping the miniature airplane's wings near the horizon line is the thing to do if you are caught unexpectedly in poor visibility, or while flying at night with a poorly defined horizon.

As part of your flight training, your instructor will have you control the airplane solely by reference to the flight instruments, and you will be expected to demonstrate your ability to maneuver the airplane by instruments on your private pilot checkride.

When you can't see the horizon and must maintain the airplane's attitude by instruments, don't bank any more than ten degrees (the first reference mark at the top of the attitude indicator).

Figure 4-18. *Attitude indicator*

Heading Indicator

You shouldn't always trust your heading indicator (directional gyro–*see* Figure 4-19) to tell you which way you are heading. The heading indicator is not a very smart instrument—it only repeats the heading that has been set into it. For that reason, it has an adjustment knob, and must be set to correspond to the magnetic compass (or to the runway heading) before it can be used for navigation.

Figure 4-19. *Heading indicator*

If you fail to set the heading indicator properly before takeoff, and do not notice that it disagrees with the **magnetic compass**, you can be many miles off course in a very short time.

Because the gyro's rotor spins at a velocity of about 18,000 RPM, its bearings must have a minimum of friction. As the bearings wear, or as dirt and contaminants (such as tobacco tar) collect at these critical points, the gyro will begin to slowly precess (drift) away from the heading you have set. You should check the heading indicator against the magnetic compass at least every 15 minutes, and more often if the instrument is showing signs of age such as grinding noises or rapid precession. Reset the heading indicator to the magnetic compass only when the airplane is in straight and level, unaccelerated flight. The magnetic compass develops errors during banks, climbs, and descents, and you do not want to set these errors into your heading indicator.

Magnetic Compass

The only instrument in your airplane that does not depend on some source of external power is the magnetic compass (Figure 4-20). All of your navigational procedures are based on magnetic information. Unfortunately, the magnetic compass is subject to more errors than any other instrument.

Figure 4-20. Magnetic compass

The magnetic compass consists of a card floating in a liquid, pivoted on a needle point, and having affixed to it small permanent magnets that align themselves (and therefore the card) with the earth's magnetic field. The card is marked so that you see your magnetic heading on the compass when the magnets are being attracted to the magnetic North Pole. The magnetic compass is subject to several errors: oscillation error, and **northerly turning error**, and **acceleration error**. Because of the single point suspension, the compass card swings in even the slightest turbulence, and you must average its swings to approximate a constant heading. If your compass does *not* swing when the air gets rough, check to be sure that the fluid hasn't leaked out!

Northerly turning error is caused by the fact that the lines of force of the earth's magnetic field are parallel to the earth's surface at the Equator, but bend downward toward the surface as latitude increases, and are essentially vertical at the magnetic poles. This force,

which pulls the ends of the compass magnets downward, is called "magnetic dip": When the airplane banks and the compass card tilts, the compass magnets, affected by dip, introduce a compass error. When you turn from a generally northerly heading, the compass will momentarily turn in the opposite direction, slow to a stop, and then follow the progress of the turn — but *lagging* the actual heading change. The amount of lag diminishes as the heading approaches east or west. Conversely, when you turn from a southerly heading the compass jumps out ahead of the turn, and *leads* the heading change, with the amount of lead again diminishing as east or west is approached. The amount of lead or lag which is attributable to northerly turning error is approximately equal to the airplane's latitude.

Acceleration error is evident on headings of east or west. If the airplane is accelerated, without changing heading, the compass will indicate a turn to the north, while deceleration on an east or west heading will cause the compass to indicate a turn to the south.

Use this memory aid: **A N D S** - *Accelerate North, Decelerate South. See* Figure 4-21.

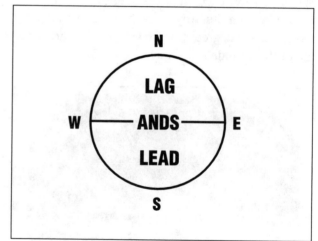

Figure 4-21. Compass errors

It is because of northerly turning error and acceleration error that you must set the heading indicator to agree with the magnetic compass *only* in straight and level, unaccelerated flight.

Magnetic deviation is an error which affects the accuracy of the magnetic compass but is caused by external forces. The magnetic influence of ferrous (steel) engine parts and electrical wiring cause deviation; Chapter Seven discusses the effect of deviation on navigation.

If you must rely solely on your magnetic compass for navigation, the most effective way to change heading is the timed turn. Note the magnetic compass heading, determine how many degrees you want to turn, and turn at 3° per second (using the index on the turn coordinator or turn needle) for the appropriate number of seconds. If you complete the turn within 5° or 10° of your target heading you are within acceptable limits.

Vertical Card Magnetic Compass

You may find an airplane with a vertical card magnetic compass. These relatively new devices contain no liquid, and have little or no oscillation error. Acceleration error and Northerly Turning Error are present but are quickly damped by internal electrical currents. They are considerably more expensive (but easier to use) than liquid-filled compasses.

Slaved Gyro Systems

If your airplane has a horizontal situation indicator (HSI) as a heading indicator, it may derive its directional information from a remote magnetic compass (or flux detector) mounted in the tail or wingtip, away from electrical influences. The weak electrical signals from the remote magnetic flux detector are amplified before being transmitted to the heading indicator, which then rotates or "slaves" into agreement with the directional information from the remote source. The system includes compensating devices to minimize or eliminate any deviation error.

The exact location of the amplifier and compensating devices varies between manufacturers, and the location of the magnetic flux detector is determined by the installer. Figure 4-22 illustrates a possible installation with optional flux detector locations.

In most installations, a "slaving switch" is provided so that you can rapidly adjust the heading indicator card to agree with the liquid-filled magnetic compass during the preflight checks, and in some installations you can select "free gyro" and adjust the heading indicator just as you do with simpler systems.

Figure 4-22. *Slaved gyro system*

Chapter 4
Flight Instrument Review Questions

1. The turn coordinator provides an indication of

   A—the movement of the airplane about the yaw and roll axes.
   B—the angle of bank to but not exceeding 30°.
   C—attitude of the airplane with reference to the longitudinal axis.

2. To receive accurate indications during flight from a heading indicator the instrument must be

   A—set prior to flight on a known heading.
   B—adequately powered so that it seeks the proper direction.
   C—periodically realigned with the magnetic compass as the gyro precesses.

3. In the Northern Hemisphere, a magnetic compass will normally indicate a turn toward the north if

   A—a left turn is entered from a west heading.
   B—an aircraft is decelerated while on an east or west heading.
   C—an aircraft is accelerated while on an east or west heading.

4. Deviation in a magnetic compass is caused by

   A—the difference in the location between true north and magnetic north.
   B—magnetic ore deposits in the Earth distorting the lines of magnetic force.
   C—magnetic fields within the airplane distorting the lines of magnetic force.

5. In the Northern Hemisphere, a magnetic compass will normally indicate initially a turn toward the east if

   A—an aircraft is accelerated while on a north heading.
   B—a right turn is entered from a north heading.
   C—a left turn is entered from a north heading.

6. How do variations in temperature affect the altimeter?

   A—Pressure levels are raised on warm days and the indicated altitude is lower than true altitude.
   B—Higher temperatures expand the pressure levels and the indicated altitude is higher than true altitude.
   C—Lower temperatures lower the pressure levels and the indicated altitude is lower than true altitude.

7. If it is necessary to set the altimeter from 29.15 to 29.85, what change is made on the indicated altitude?

   A—70-foot increase.
   B—700-foot increase.
   C—700-foot decrease.

8. The pitot system provides impact pressure for only the

A—airspeed indicator, altimeter, and vertical speed indicator.
B—altimeter and vertical speed indicator.
C—airspeed indicator.

9. What is an important airspeed limitation that is not color coded on airspeed indicators?

A—Never-exceed speed.
B—Maneuvering speed.
C—Maximum flaps-extended speed.

10. Refer to Figure 4-6 on Page 4-3. Which of the color coded markings on the airspeed indicator identifies the never-exceed speed?

A—Upper A/S limit of the white arc.
B—Upper A/S limit of the green arc.
C—The red radial line.

11. Refer to Figure 4-6 on Page 4-3. Which of the color coded markings identifies the power-off stalling speed with wing flaps and landing gear in the landing position?

A—Upper A/S limit of the white arc.
B—Lower A/S limit of the green arc.
C—Lower A/S limit of the white arc.

Weight and Balance

It would be nice to have an airplane in which we could fill all of the seats and all of the baggage area, fuel up to capacity, and take off safely without worrying about loading, but that is seldom (if ever) possible. The manufacturer dictates a maximum gross weight figure based on several factors including structural strength of the landing gear, power loading (weight per horsepower), wing loading (weight per square foot of wing area), strength of the wing structure, etc. *Overloading an airplane can have serious consequences! See* Figure 5-1—this pilot almost ran out of runway!

Airplanes are assigned to categories depending on the amount of weight the wing structure can sustain, and those categories dictate how the airplane can be used. The requirements are based on "G's"—one G is 1 x the force of gravity (or the weight of the airplane). A *Normal* category airplane can have a load of 3.8 Gs imposed on its wing, a *Utility* category airplane is stressed for 4.4 Gs, and an airplane in the

Aerobatic category is designed to withstand a load of 8 Gs. Aerobatic airplanes usually have G meters installed to record how many Gs the airplane experienced during an aerobatic maneuver, (some sadder but wiser pilots have said that a G meter gives you information you really don't want to know!). Many airplanes are certificated in both the Normal and Utility categories, but in the utility catagory are more limited in gross weight, in weight distribution, or in authorized maneuvers.

If you overload an airplane, the wing will have to be flown at a greater than normal angle of attack to develop enough lift to support the extra weight—this increases the stall speed, decreases the cruise speed, and limits the angle you can bank before reaching the critical angle of attack. Carrying more than the design maximum weight also means longer takeoff runs. If you combine overweight with a soft runway surface or a high density altitude, you are asking for trouble.

Figure 5-1. *Landing over an obstacle*

Loads applied to the wing during maneuvering can overstress the airplane's structure. Figure 5-2 shows the relationship between bank angle and load factor while maintaining attitude. You can see that for a normal category airplane 3.8 G will be reached at about a 75° bank angle, and for an airplane certificated in the Utility category, a bank of about 77° will bring the load factor to 4.4 G. If the wing is designed for a wings level load of 2,000 pounds and you load the airplane to 2,500 pounds, in a 60° bank you will be adding an additional 1,000 pounds to the load on the wing.

Figure 5-2. *Load factor chart*

A one-time overload may not cause problems, but repeatedly overstressing components may cause them to fail many flight hours later, while performing normal maneuvers.

Some airplanes are additionally limited to a "zero fuel" weight which usually shows up as a placard saying "All weight in excess of 3,500 pounds must be in the form of fuel" or something similar. The designer establishes this limitation to insure that not all of the weight is concentrated in the fuselage, where an overload can exert a damaging bending force on the wing structure.

Center of gravity (CG) location relates directly to longitudinal stability. You will recall from Chapter Two that the airplane is maneuvered around three axes which pass through the center of gravity, and that all lift forces are concentrated at the center of

pressure on the wing. The designer knows how the center of pressure will move as angle of attack changes, and limits the allowable movement of the center of gravity so that a properly loaded airplane will always be controllable.

Figure 5-3 shows how airflow over the horizontal stabilizer creates a downward pressure (download) which offsets the nose-down tendency caused by the center of pressure being aft of the center of gravity. As angle of attack is increased, the center of pressure moves forward; at the same time, airflow over the horizontal stabilizer is diminishing, reducing the downward pressure.

Figure 5-3. *Longitudinal stability*

At the critical angle of attack, the center of pressure is so close to the center of gravity, and the elevator has so little downward pressure, that the nose pitches down and the airplane reduces the angle of attack. This natural tendency to reduce the angle of attack and avoid stalling is a built-in safety factor available *only* when the airplane is loaded within design limits. *See* Figure 5-4.

If the airplane is loaded so that the center of gravity is forward of the designed forward limit, a greater than normal downward pressure on the horizontal stabilizer will be required, and the up elevator necessary to balance the weight up front will add drag. The wing will have to be flown at a greater angle of attack to develop enough lift to support the weight of the airplane *and* the download on the tail, which will slow the airplane and increase the stall speed. During the landing flare, the elevator may not have enough travel available to prevent landing on the nosewheel, especially if power has been reduced and airflow

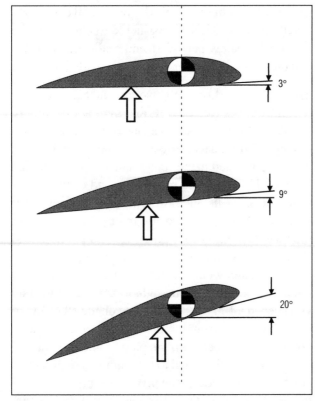

Figure 5-4. *Center of pressure movement*

Figure 5-5. *Forward CG loading*

Figure 5-6. *Aft CG loading*

over the tail surfaces diminished. On a takeoff attempt with a forward center of gravity, additional speed (and runway) will be required before the heavy nose can be rotated to climb attitude. *See* Figure 5-5.

Loading the airplane so that the center of gravity is at the aft limit has *some* advantages: less download on the horizontal stabilizer is required, so there is less drag and the airplane can fly at a smaller angle of attack. These factors pay off in cruise speed and fuel economy. Load the airplane so that the CG falls outside of the design limits, however, and you have a tiger by the tail. *See* Figure 5-6.

Stall speed will be lower, but if a stall does occur recovery will be difficulty, if not impossible. In cruise flight, the elevator control forces will be so light that you might inadvertently overstress the airplane, and during the landing flare you may have difficulty maintaining the proper attitude.

It is worthwhile to compute weight and center of gravity location for several typical loadings: for example, full fuel and a single pilot; full fuel, a 170 pound pilot and three 170 pound passengers; or half filled tanks, two persons on board and maximum authorized baggage. These calculations will provide benchmarks so that an unusual loading situation will be recognized, and a weight and balance calculated for that special situation.

Another effect of loading an airplane so that the center of gravity falls outside the aft limits of the envelope relates to rudder authority. You know that the rudder rotates the airplane around the vertical (yaw) axis, and that the vertical axis passes through the center of gravity. Let's design an imaginary airplane with the rudder 12 feet from the center of gravity location with the airplane properly loaded. On a day with gusty crosswind it might take full rudder deflection to keep the airplane pointing straight down the runway during the takeoff roll. Now, let's reload that airplane so that the center of gravity moves aft 12 inches, so that the distance from the rudder to the CG is only 11 feet. With the lever arm reduced by 1 foot, full rudder pressure may not be adequate to handle the crosswind! You will hear some airplanes referred to as "short coupled"—this means that the distance from the CG to the rudder is short even when the airplane is properly loaded, and it takes quick and assertive rudder use to maintain control on takeoff.

Improper (or unbalanced) distribution of weight outside of the fuselage can also have undesirable effects. In a typical single-engine airplane, if one wing tank is full and the other is empty, you will need aileron pressure to hold the wings level. The aileron drag will cause a yaw which must be overcome with rudder. The total effect is a reduction in speed and in fuel economy.

Twin-engine airplanes with baggage compartments in the wings offer ample opportunity for misloading and creating lateral imbalance.

Weight and Balance Calculations

One document which must be in the airplane at all times is the manufacturer's data required to compute the weight and center of gravity location under different loading conditions. You will find this information in the Approved Flight Manual (not the Owner's Handbook) for older airplanes, and in the Pilot's Operating Handbook for newer airplanes. The airplane's empty weight and center of gravity position have been furnished by the manufacturer and serve as a starting point. If equipment has been added or removed since the airplane was built, an FAA Form 337 will have been prepared by the mechanic who performed the work. This updates the empty weight and center of gravity location and that form will be with the weight and balance data (also check the airframe maintenance log).

The empty weight of the airplane includes unusable fuel and optional equipment; full oil *may* be included — check the data for your airplane. Gasoline weighs 6 pounds per gallon and oil weighs 7.5 pounds per

gallon, not per quart. Typically engine oil capacity is given in quarts — it's easy to include the weight of the oil at 7.5 pounds per quart and really mess up the calculations!

The balance portion of the weight and balance problem introduces two new terms: **arm** and **moment**. The easiest way to visualize these terms is to go back to your childhood teeter-totter. Assume that it was 12 feet long, pivoted in the center, and that you weighed 50 pounds. When you sat on one end of the teeter-totter the arm (distance from the pivot point to your seat) was 6 feet, making the moment (your weight times the arm) 300 foot-pounds. A 50-pound friend sitting on the other end of the board an equal distance from the center would balance the teeter-totter. Without a 50-pound friend, though, to have any fun at all you needed a 100 pound playmate on the other end of the board 3 feet from the pivot point, or maybe a 75 pound friend 4 feet from the pivot point. To balance, in other words, there had to be a moment of 300 foot-pounds on each side of the pivot. The airplane manufacturer provides data on distance (arm) from a datum point which you can multiply times the weight of fuel, baggage, or passengers to derive the moment. The manufacturer may provide moments for various weights without requiring the intermediate step of providing the distance (arm). You may have to interpolate between given weights if your passengers, baggage, or fuel load do not exactly match the tabulated values.

Figure 5-7 on Page 5-6 shows a graphic method of presenting the weight and balance information and determining the position of the center of gravity, and Figures 5-8 and 5-9 (on Pages 5-7 and 5-8) show a tabular method. To avoid large, confusing numbers, moments are presented as moment/1000. With the tabular method, the CG position is determined by dividing the total moments by the total weight. As weights are shifted around within the airplane by moving baggage from forward compartments to aft compartments, by moving passengers, or even by extending and retracting the landing gear, the center of gravity follows the weight—if the weight moves aft so does the CG.

Use Figure 5-7: Calculate the CG and determine the plotted position on the CG moment envelope chart.

	Weight	Mom/1000
Empty weight	1,350	51.5
Pilot and front passenger	380	—
Fuel 48 gal	288	—
Oil 8 qts	15	-0.2

1. CG 38.9, out of limits forward.
2. CG 39.9, utility category.
3. CG 38.9, normal category.
4. CG 39.9, normal category.

From the loading graph, find the moment/1000 for pilot and front seat passenger weight of 380 pounds: 14.0. Find the moment/1000 for 288 pounds of fuel: 13.8. Total weight = 2,033 pounds, total moment/1000 = 79.1. Center of gravity = total moment ÷ total weight = 79,100 ÷ 2,033 = 38.9. Plot on the center of gravity moment envelope a weight of 2,033 pounds and a moment/1,000 of 79.1; the plotted point falls in the normal category area (3).

Upon landing, the front passenger (180 pounds) departs the airplane. A rear passenger (204 pounds) moves to the front passenger position. What effect does this have on the CG if the airplane weighed 2,690 pounds and the moment/100 was 2,260 just prior to the passenger transfer?

Use Figures 5-8 and 5-9:

1. The weight changes but the CG is not affected.
2. The CG moves forward approximately 0.1".
3. The CG moves forward approximately 2.4".
4. The CG moves forward approximately 3.0".

Compute the CG before the passenger movement:

CG = total moment ÷ total weight
= 226,000 ÷ 2,690
= 84.01"

Front passenger	2,690		226,000 = 84.01"
departs:	−180 lbs		−15,300
	2,510		210,700 total mom.

Compute moment for 204 lb passenger in both rear and front seats:

204 x 121 = 24,684 moment before moving
204 x 85 = 17,340 moment after moving
          ————
          7,344 reduction

210,700 − 7,344 after passenger moves forward
          = 203,356 moment

CG = total moment ÷ total weight
203,356 ÷ 2,510 = 81.02 or 3" forward

Remember, the CG moved with the weight!

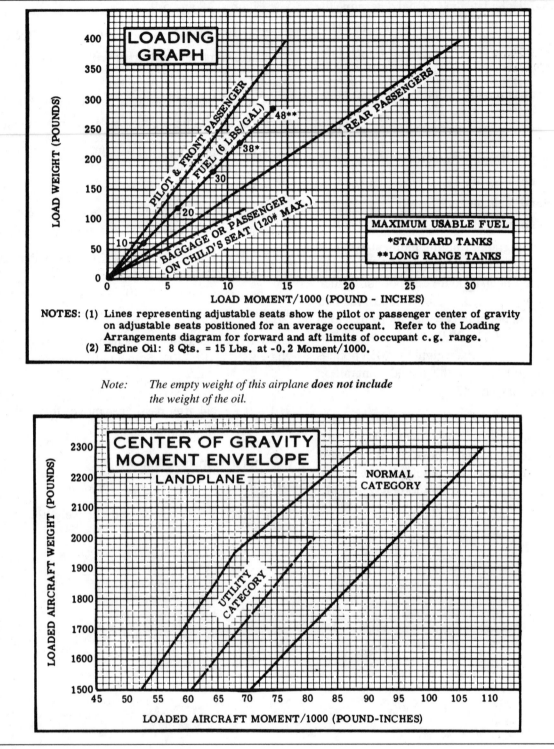

NOTES: (1) Lines representing adjustable seats show the pilot or passenger center of gravity on adjustable seats positioned for an average occupant. Refer to the Loading Arrangements diagram for forward and aft limits of occupant c.g. range.
(2) Engine Oil: 8 Qts. = 15 Lbs. at -0.2 Moment/1000.

Note: The empty weight of this airplane **does not include** the weight of the oil.

Figure 5-7. Loading graph

Occupants

Front Seats ARM 85		Rear Seats ARM 121	
Weight	Moment 100	Weight	Moment 100
120	102	120	145
130	110	130	157
140	119	140	169
150	128	150	182
160	136	160	194
170	144	170	206
180	153	180	218
190	162	190	230
200	170	200	242

Baggage or 5th Seat Occupant ARN 140

Weight	Moment 100
10	14
20	28
30	42
40	56
50	70
60	84
70	98
80	112
90	126
100	140
110	154
120	168
130	182
140	196
150	210
160	224
170	238
180	252
190	266
200	280
210	294
220	308
230	322
240	336
250	350
260	364
270	378

Usable Fuel

Main Wing Tanks ARM 75

Gallons	Weight	Moment 100
5	30	22
10	60	45
15	90	68
20	120	90
25	150	112
30	180	135
35	210	158
40	240	180
44	264	198

Auxiliary Wing Tanks ARM 94

Gallons	Weight	Moment 100
5	30	28
10	60	56
15	90	85
19	114	107

*Oil

Quarts	Weight	Moment 100
10	19	5

*Included in Basic Empty Weight

Empty Weight – 2015

MOM/100 – 155400

Moment Limits vs Weight

Moment limits are based on the following weight and center of gravity limit data (landing gear down).

Weight Condition	Forward CG Limit	AFT CG Limit
2950 lb. (take-off or landing)	82.1	84.7
2525 lb.	77.5	85.7
2475 lb. or less	77.0	85.7

Figure 5-8. Tabular method

Weight	Minimum Moment 100	Maximum Moment 100		Weight	Minimum Moment 100	Maximum Moment 100
2100	1617	1800		2600	2037	2224
2110	1625	1808		2610	2048	2232
2120	1632	1817		2620	2058	2239
2130	1640	1825		2630	2069	2247
2140	1648	1834		2640	2080	2255
2150	1656	1843		2650	2090	2263
2160	1663	1851		2660	2101	2271
2170	1671	1860		2670	2112	2279
2180	1679	1868		2680	2123	2287
2190	1686	1877		2690	2133	2295
2200	1694	1885		2700	2144	2303
2210	1702	1894		2710	2155	2311
2220	1709	1903		2720	2166	2319
2230	1717	1911		2730	2177	2326
2240	1725	1920		2740	2188	2334
2250	1733	1928		2750	2199	2342
2260	1740	1937		2760	2210	2350
2270	1748	1945		2770	2221	2358
2280	1756	1954		2780	2232	2366
2290	1763	1963		2790	2243	2374
2300	1771	1971				
2310	1779	1980		2800	2254	2381
2320	1786	1988		2810	2265	2389
2330	1794	1997		2820	2276	2397
2340	1802	2005		2830	2287	2405
2350	1810	2014		2840	2298	2413
2360	1817	2023		2850	2309	2421
2370	1825	2031		2860	2320	2428
2380	1833	2040		2870	2332	2436
2390	1840	2048		2880	2343	2444
				2890	2354	2452
2400	1848	2057		2900	2365	2460
2410	1856	2065		2910	2377	2468
2420	1863	2074		2920	2388	2475
2430	1871	2083		2930	2399	2483
2440	1879	2091		2940	2411	2491
2450	1887	2100		2950	2422	2499
2460	1894	2108				
2470	1902	2117				
2480	1911	2125				
2490	1921	2134				
2500	1932	2143				
2510	1942	2151				
2520	1953	2160				
2530	1963	2168				
2540	1974	2176				
2550	1984	2184				
2560	1995	2192				
2570	2005	2200				
2580	2016	2208				
2590	2026	2216				

Figure 5-9. Moment limits vs. weight

Chapter 5
Weight and Balance Review Questions

Use Figure 5-7 on Page 5-6 for review problems 1 through 4.

1. Determine the CG moment/1000 with the following data:

	Weight/lb.	/Moment/1000
Empty weight	1,350	51.5
Pilot and front passenger	340	—
Fuel (std. tanks)	Capacity	—
Oil 8 qts	15	-0.2

   A—69.9 lb./in.
   B—74.9 lb./in.
   C—77.0 lb./in.

2. What is the maximum amount of fuel that may be aboard the airplane on takeoff if it is loaded as follows?

	Weight/lb.	/Moment/1000
Empty weight	1,350	51.5
Pilot and front passenger	340	—
Rear passengers	310	—
Baggage	45	—
Oil 8 qts.	15	-0.2

   A—24 gal.
   B—34 gal.
   C—40 gal.

3. What is the maximum amount of baggage that may be loaded aboard the airplane for the CG to remain within the loading envelope?

	Weight/lb.	Moment/1000
Empty weight	1,350	51.5
Pilot and front passenger	250	—
Rear passengers	400	—
Baggage	—	—
Fuel 30 gal	—	—
Oil 8 qts	15	-0.2

   A—120 lb.
   B—105 lb.
   C—90 lb.

4. Calculate the CG and determine the plotted position on the CG moment envelope chart.

	Weight/ lb.	Moment/1000
Empty weight	1,350	51.5
Pilot and front passenger	380	—
Fuel 48 gal	288	—
Oil 8 qts	15	-0.2

   A—CG 38.9, out of limits forward.
   B—CG 39.9, utility category.
   C—CG 38.9, normal category.

Use Figure 5-8 on Page 5-7, and Figure 5-9 on Page 5-8 for review problems 5 and 6:

5. Determine if the airplane weight and balance are within limits.

   Front seat occupants .... 340 lb
   Rear seat occupants .... 295 lb
   Fuel .... 44 gal
   Baggage .... 56 lb

   A—Within limits.
   B—20 lb. overweight, CG within limits.
   C—Weight within limits, CG out of limits forward.

6. Which action can adjust the airplane's weight to maximum gross weight and the CG within limits for takeoffs?

   Front seat occupants .... 425 lb.
   Rear seat occupants .... 300 lb.
   Fuel, main tanks .... 44 gal.

   A—Drain 12 gal. of fuel.
   B—Drain 9 gal. of fuel.
   C—Transfer 12 gal. of fuel from the main tanks to the auxiliary tanks.

7. What effect does a 35-gal fuel burn have on the weight and balance if the airplane weighed 2,890 lb. and the MOM/100 was 2,452 at takeoff?

   A—Weight is reduced by 210 lb. and the CG is unaffected
   B—Weight is reduced to 2,680 lb. and the CG moves forward.
   C—Weight is reduced by 210 lb. and the CG is aft of limits.

Performance

Airplanes are manufactured and fly all over the world, and pilots everywhere rely on consistent performance in accordance with their airplane's Operating Handbook. Would you expect an airplane manufacturer to provide a different handbook to a Peruvian mountain pilot than is provided to a miner in Death Valley?

Obviously, the operating conditions vary widely in altitude and temperature. It is not necessary to have different manuals, and the reason lies in the term "International Standard Atmosphere (ISA)." At airplane manufacturing sites, engineering test flights go on in rain and in sunshine, in summer and in winter. All of the airspeeds, rates of climb, fuel burns, and takeoff and landing distances determined by test pilots are reduced to what they would be on a standard day at sea level.

By internationally accepted standards, a standard day has a barometric pressure of 29.92" Hg and a temperature of 15°C (59°F), and the standard atmospheric temperature lapse rate (decrease in temperature with increasing altitude) is assumed to be 2°C per 1,000' of altitude above sea level—the International Standard Atmosphere.

Engineers take the information from the test flights, reduce it to its equivalent under standard conditions, and furnish the pilot with charts and graphs to predict airplane performance under widely varying pressure and temperature conditions.

Density Altitude

The basis for predicting performance is density altitude—pressure altitude corrected for non-standard temperature. Your responsibilities as a pilot will include calculating the effect that existing or forecast weather conditions will have on your takeoff and climb performance from a departure airport. You must also consider the true airspeed and fuel consumption rate at your chosen cruise altitude, and compare the predicted landing distance to the amount of runway available at the destination airport (and any en route airports you might have to use in an emergency). You will have to compute the density altitude for the different airports, consult your airplane's performance charts, and get the numbers for the expected conditions.

In the discussion of the factors that produce lift, you learned that the density of the air has a direct effect on the amount of lift developed at a given airspeed or angle of attack, and you learned that high altitude, high temperature, and high humidity separately or in combination have the worst effect on performance.

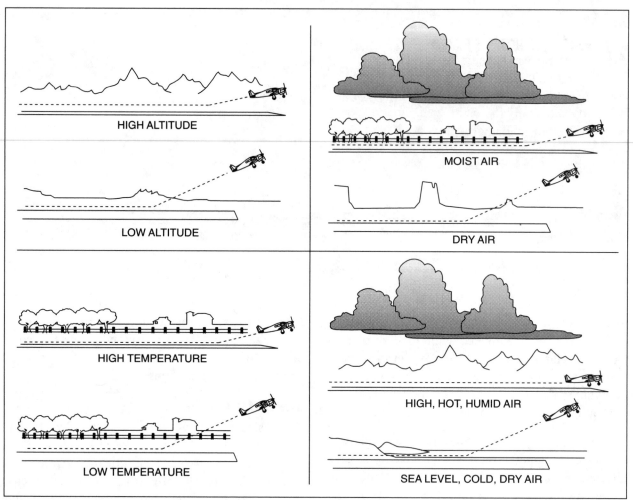

Figure 6-1. *Conditions affecting length of takeoff run*

All of the charts, tables, computers, etc., that will be used in the calculation of density altitude performance take into account only pressure altitude and temperature, no provision is made for the effects of humidity on performance (Figure 6-1). A conservative approach is to add 1,000' to any density altitude you arrive at by use of pressure altitude and temperature and then calculate the performance figures based on that altitude.

The quickest way to determine pressure altitude when you are in the airplane is to note the setting in the **Kollsman window** (the little window you use for entering altimeter setting), then set it to 29.92; the altimeter will indicate pressure altitude. (Return the altimeter setting to its previous setting before you forget it!) If you are determining density altitude for a distant airport and have gotten its temperature and altimeter setting from the hourly weather sequence reports, determine the difference between 29.92 and the reported altimeter setting and apply the difference to the field elevation:

Altimeter setting	30.20	Field elevation	2,348
	− 29.92		− 280
	.28	altitude =	2,068
= 280' Pressure			

(1.00" = 1.000', .1" = 100', .01" = 10')

To be sure that you apply the pressure difference correctly, ask yourself which way the altimeter needles will move as the altimeter setting is changed from 30.20 to 29.92. In the example, they will move counterclockwise, and the pressure difference must be subtracted from the field elevation to derive pressure altitude at that airport.

Figure 6-2 will be found in your Private Pilot Question Book and provides pressure difference factors for you to apply: determine the pressure altitude by applying the pressure difference factor from the columns on the right to the field elevation. Find the temperature on the bottom scale, draw a vertical line from the temperature to the pressure altitude (slanting) line, then draw a horizontal line to the left margin to read density altitude.

Another method is to use the slide rule side of your flight computer by setting the pressure altitude (29.92 reading of the altimeter) in the window opposite the temperature and read density altitude at the index. You can use the reading of your airplane's outside air temperature (OAT) gauge without correction.

Pressure altitude, density altitude, and true altitude are all equal at sea level on a standard day, a condition which does not often occur. Pressure altitude is equal to density altitude only when the temperature is standard for that pressure altitude. If the air mass is warmer than standard, density altitude will be higher than pressure altitude and if the air mass is colder than standard density altitude will be lower than pressure altitude. You will read performance figures for turbo-props and jets given as "ISA + 10°" or "ISA - 5°." These figures show performance at temperatures differing from the International Standard Atmosphere.

Because true altitude is the actual altitude above mean sea level, when you are on the ground your altimeter should read the published airport elevation when you set the altimeter to the current local altimeter setting.

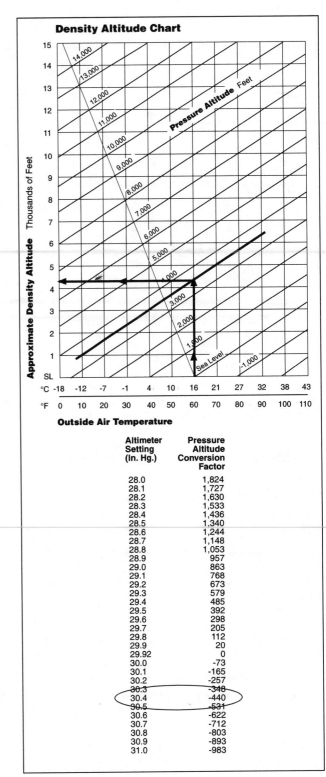

Figure 6-2. *Pressure altitude and density chart*

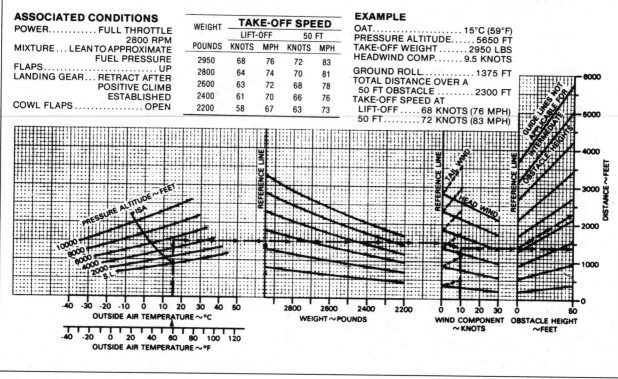

ASSOCIATED CONDITIONS

POWER.............FULL THROTTLE 2800 RPM
MIXTURE...LEAN TO APPROXIMATE FUEL PRESSURE
FLAPS...........................UP
LANDING GEAR...RETRACT AFTER POSITIVE CLIMB ESTABLISHED
COWL FLAPS.................OPEN

WEIGHT	TAKE-OFF SPEED			
	LIFT-OFF		50 FT	
POUNDS	KNOTS	MPH	KNOTS	MPH
2950	68	76	72	83
2800	64	74	70	81
2600	63	72	68	78
2400	61	70	66	76
2200	58	67	63	73

EXAMPLE

OAT.....................15°C (59°F)
PRESSURE ALTITUDE.....5650 FT
TAKE-OFF WEIGHT.......2950 LBS
HEADWIND COMP.......9.5 KNOTS

GROUND ROLL.........1375 FT
TOTAL DISTANCE OVER A
50 FT OBSTACLE.........2300 FT
TAKE-OFF SPEED AT
LIFT-OFF.....68 KNOTS (76 MPH)
50 FT........72 KNOTS (83 MPH)

Figure 6-3. Takeoff distance

Takeoff and Climb Performance

Figure 6-3 is a Takeoff Performance Chart. Note the line marked "ISA" which represents the standard temperature for each altitude shown. Also note how an increase in either temperature, pressure altitude, or weight will adversely affect takeoff distance.

Follow the example problem through to see how the takeoff distance was derived. Now try this one:

OAT .... Standard
Pressure altitude ....4,000 ft.
Takeoff weight............................2,800 lb.
Headwind component. .... 20 kts.

Determine total distance to clear a 50-foot obstacle.

1. 1,250 ft.
2. 1,500 ft.
3. 1,750 ft.
4. 1,900 ft.

Figure 6-4 is another table used to predict takeoff performance. It may be necessary to interpolate one or more of the values given. Be conservative; if your answer falls between two values, select the longer takeoff distance. Read the notes and be sure that you are duplicating the conditions under which the engineers arrived at the figures, remembering that factory pilots used a new airplane in top condition. Add a "fudge factor" for the effects of time on the airframe and engine. Factory performance figures assume normal pilot techniques—you do not have to be super-pilot.

Gross weight .... 1,700 lbs.
OAT .... 66°F
Pressure altitude ....5,000 ft.
Wind (headwind) .... .20 kts.

Distance to clear a 50-foot obstacle?

1. 575 ft.
2. 633 ft.
3. 518 ft.
4. 930 ft.

Takeoff Distance from Hard Surface Runway with Flaps Up

Gross Weight Pounds	IAS At 50 feet	Head Wind Knots	At Sea Level & 59°F		At 2500 FT & 50°F		At 5000 FT & 41°F		At 7500 FT & 32°F	
			Ground Run	Total to Clear 50 FT OBS	Ground Run	Total to Clear 50 FT OBS	Ground Run	Total to Clear 50 FT OBS	Ground Run	Total to Clear 50 FT OBS
2300	68	0	865	1525	1040	1910	1255	2480	1565	3855
		10	615	1170	750	1485	920	1955	1160	3110
		20	405	850	505	1100	630	1480	810	2425
2000	63	0	630	1095	755	1325	905	1625	1120	2155
		10	435	820	530	1005	645	1250	810	1685
		20	275	580	340	720	425	910	595	1255
1700	58	0	435	780	520	920	625	1095	765	1370
		10	290	570	355	680	430	820	535	1040
		20	175	385	215	470	270	575	345	745

Notes 1. Increase distance 10% for each 25°F above standard temperature for particular altitude.
2. For operation on a dry, grass runway, increase distances (both "Ground Run" and "Total to Clear 50 Foot Obstacle") by 7% of the "Total to Clear 50 Foot Obstacle" figure.

Figure 6-4. Take-off data

The manufacturer's takeoff performance tables or the operating procedures section of the approved flight manual will contain a recommended takeoff speed. This speed must be attained before you rotate the airplane to climb attitude—you can't force the airplane to lift off or climb at a slower speed. A good rule to follow is this: you should have accelerated to 75% of takeoff speed in the first half of the available runway. If the airplane has not reached that speed by the midway point you should stop, taxi back, and do some performance calculations.

Climb Performance

Figure 6-5 is used to predict rate-of-climb and fuel used during climb. Note how climb performance drops off with altitude, how indicated airspeed for maximum rate-of-climb decreases with altitude, and how much fuel is used during climb.

Pressure altitude .... Sea level
Temperature .... 89°F
Gross weight .... 2,000 lbs.
Indicated airspeed .... 79 MPH

Maximum Rate-of-Climb Data

Gross Weight Pounds	At Sea Level & 59°F			At 5000 FT & 41°F			At 10,000 FT & 23°F			At 15,000 FT & 5°F		
	IAS MPH	Rate of Climb FT/MIN	GAL of Fuel Used	IAS MPH	Rate of Climb FT/MIN	From S.L. Fuel Used	IAS MPH	Rate of Climb FT/MIN	From S.L. Fuel Used	IAS MPH	Rate of Climb FT/MIN	From S.L. Fuel Used
2300	82	645	1.0	81	435	2.6	79	230	4.8	78	22	11.5
2000	79	840	1.0	79	610	2.2	76	380	3.6	75	155	6.3
1700	77	1085	1.0	76	825	1.9	73	570	2.9	72	315	4.4

Notes 1. Flaps up, full throttle, mixture leaned for smooth operation above 3,000 feet.
2. Fuel used includes warm up and take-off allowance.
3. For hot weather, decrease rate-of-climb 20 feet/minute for each 10°F above standard day temperature for particular altitude.

Figure 6-5. Maximum rate-of-climb data

After climbing for five minutes your altimeter would read approximately:

1. 4,100 ft.
2. 4,000 ft.
3. 3,900 ft.
4. 4,260 ft.

Apply the following conditions to the above chart.

Pressure altitude .... 5,000'
Temperature .... 61°F
Gross weight .... 2,000 lbs.
Indicated airspeed .... 79 MPH

Assume you have climbed at a constant rate for 3 minutes. What would be the approximate gain in altitude?

1. 1,810 ft.
2. 1,790 ft.
3. 1,710 ft.
4. 1,830 ft.

Best Angle and Best Rate-of-Climb Speeds

Figure 6-6 plots the relationship between airspeed and climb rate in feet per minute for a typical light airplane. A line from the origin of the graph is tangent to the curve at the best angle of climb speed and the apex of the curve is the best rate of climb speed.

The best angle of climb speed (V_X) is safely above the stall and slightly slower than the best rate of climb speed (V_Y). You will use V_X for clearing obstacles after takeoff and will accelerate to V_Y as soon as the obstacles are cleared. Both forward visibility and engine cooling are adversely affected by the nose-high attitude at the best angle of climb speed (Figures 6-7 and 6-8).

It has nothing to do with design climb speeds, but it is a fact that you will gain more altitude per unit of distance when climbing into the wind than when climbing downwind. You are climbing x number of feet per minute and spending more minutes while climbing into the wind. If you climb at 60 knots into a 60 knot wind you will go straight up!

Figure 6-6. *Relationship between airspeed and climb rate*

Figure 6-7. *Best angle of climb speed*

Figure 6-8. *Best rate-of-climb speed*

Cruise Power Settings 75% Maximum Continuous Power (or Full Throttle) 2800 LBS

Pressure Altitude Feet	ISA -20°C (-36°F)								Standard Day (ISA)								ISA +20°C (+36°F)							
	IOAT °F	°C	Engine Speed RPM	Manifold Pressure IN HG	Fuel Flow Per Engine PSI	GPH	TAS KTS	MPH	IOAT °F	°C	Engine Speed RPM	Manifold Pressure IN HG	Fuel Flow Per Engine PSI	GPH	TAS KTS	MPH	IOAT °F	°C	Engine Speed RPM	Manifold Pressure IN HG	Fuel Flow Per Engine PSI	GPH	TAS KTS	MPH
Sea Level	27	-3	2450	23.1	8.2	13.6	156	180	63	17	2450	23.8	8.2	13.6	159	183	99	37	2450	24.4	8.2	13.6	162	186
2000	19	-7	2450	22.8	8.2	13.6	158	182	55	13	2450	23.5	8.2	13.6	162	186	93	34	2450	24.2	8.2	13.6	165	190
4000	12	-11	2450	22.6	8.2	13.6	161	185	50	10	2450	23.3	8.2	13.6	165	190	86	30	2450	23.9	8.2	13.6	168	193
6000	7	-14	2450	22.3	8.2	13.6	164	189	43	6	2450	23.0	8.2	13.6	167	192	79	26	2450	23.4	8.0	13.4	170	195
8000	0	-18	2450	21.8	8.0	13.3	166	191	36	2	2450	21.8	7.6	12.8	167	192	72	22	2450	21.8	7.2	12.3	168	193
10,000	-8	-22	2450	20.3	7.2	12.3	164	189	28	-2	2450	20.3	6.8	11.8	165	190	64	18	2450	20.3	6.5	11.4	166	191
12,000	-15	-26	2450	18.8	6.4	11.3	162	185	21	-6	2450	18.8	6.2	10.9	163	188	57	14	2450	18.8	5.9	10.6	163	186
14,000	-22	-30	2450	17.4	5.9	10.5	169	183	14	-10	2450	17.4	5.6	10.1	160	184	50	10	2450	17.4	5.3	9.8	160	184
16,000	-29	-34	2450	16.1	5.3	9.7	156	180	7	-14	2450	16.1	6.1	9.4	156	180	43	6	2450	16.1	4.9	9.1	155	178

Notes   1. Full throttle maifold pressure settings are approximate. 2. Shaded area represents operation with full throttle.

Figure 6-9. Cruise chart

Cruise Performance

Figure 6-9 is a cruise chart for a typical single engine airplane with a controllable pitch propeller.

This is the 75% power chart for this airplane; its approved flight manual will contain similar charts for 65%, 55% and possibly 45%. True airspeed and fuel consumption figures are given for standard conditions, and conditions much colder and warmer than standard. You must check the winds and temperatures forecast for your desired cruise altitude to estimate time enroute and fuel burn.

What is the expected fuel consumption for a 1000 mile flight under these conditions?

Pressure altitude ....8,000 ft.
Temperature ....-18°C
Manifold pressure .... 21.8" Hg
Wind .... Calm

1. 41.9 gal.
2. 69.6 gal.
3. 71.4 gal.
4. 73.8 gal.

If the manufacturer of your airplane provides a maximum rate of climb chart your figures can be further refined. Remember that for day VFR you must land with a 30 minute fuel reserve, and that 45 minutes in reserve is required for night VFR. In planning your flight, don't look for the altitude and power setting that will give maximum speed if the fuel consumption will force a fuel stop enroute. A slower speed that makes the fuel stop unnecessary will pay off in the long run because of the time lost on the ground and the fuel burned in climbing back to cruise altitude.

Descent Planning

The most efficient way to descend is to maintain cruise speed while descending at a comfortable rate, and in VFR conditions you are in complete command of where and when to start down. Add 1000' to the destination airport's field elevation for pattern altitude, and subtract that figure from your cruise altitude to determine how much altitude must be lost. Divide that figure by 300 and you will have the number of miles from your destination to begin your descent at 300 feet per mile.

Landing Distance

Your pre-flight planning must include familiarizing yourself with the runway length and condition at the destination airport. Be sure to ask the briefer what surface winds are forecast (if your destination has a

Landing Distance Flaps Lowered to 40°/Power Off/Hard Surface Runway/Zero Wind

Gross Weight Pounds	Approach Speed IAS, MPH	At Sea Level & 59° F		At 2500 FT & 50° F		At 5000 FT & 41° F		At 7500 FT & 32° F	
		Ground Roll	Total to Clear 50 FT OBS	Ground Roll	Total to Clear 50 FT OBS	Ground Roll	Total to Clear 50 FT OBS	Ground Roll	Total to Clear 50 FT OBS
1600	60	445	1075	470	1135	495	1195	520	1255

Notes 1. Decrease the distances shown by 10% for each 4 knots of headwind.
2. Increase the distance by 10% fojr each 60°F temperature increase above standard.
3. For operation on a dry grass runway, increase distances (both "Ground Roll" and "Total to Clear 50-Foot Obstacle" by 20% of the "Total to Clear 50-Foot Obstacle" figure.

Figure 6-10. Landing distance chart

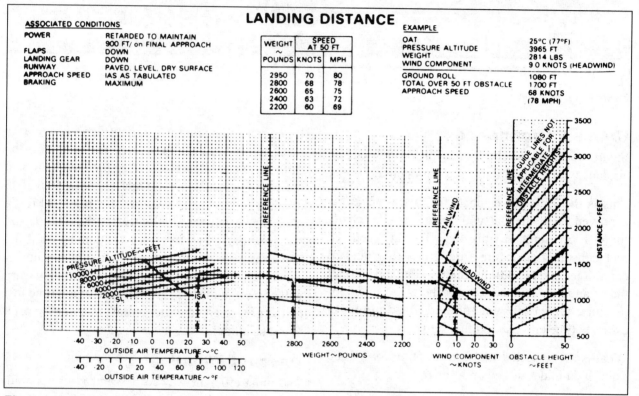

Figure 6-11. Landing distance graph

weather observer) in order to anticipate which runway will be in use. Figures 6-10 and 6-11 show two different types of landing distance charts, and you will notice again that altitude and temperature (density altitude) have a definite effect on landing performance. Notice the speeds recommended by the manufacturer: they provide a safe margin above the stall and should be adhered to.

Additional airspeed means more energy that must be dissipated and more runway left behind before the wing can no longer support the aircraft and the wheels touch down.

Use Figure 6-10:

Determine the total landing distance required to clear a 50-foot obstacle.

Pressure altitude .... 7,500 ft.
Headwind .... 8 kts.
Temperature .... Std.
Runway surface .... dry grass

1. 1,004 ft.

2. 1,255 ft.

3. 1,506 ft.

4. 1,757 ft.

Figure 6-12. Ground effect

Use Figure 6-11:

What is the approximate landing roll?

OAT .... 90°F
Pressure altitude .... 4,000 ft.
Weight .... 2,800 lbs.
Tailwind component .... 5 kts

1. 1,200 ft.
2. 1,575 ft.
3. 1,725 ft.
4. 1,950 ft.

Ground Effect

When induced drag was discussed in Chapter 2, it was associated with low speeds and high angles of attack—typically takeoff and landing conditions. When the wing is less than one-half the wingspan above the ground, induced drag is reduced by the interaction between the ground and the wingtip vortices and downwash. If you can get the wing within 3 feet of the ground, induced drag is reduced by 48%. This reduction in drag is called ground effect (Figure 6-12).

All airplanes experience **ground effect** but it is more noticeable in low wing airplanes. The reduction in induced drag causes "float" if excess airspeed is used on final, and downwash from the wing bouncing off of the surface reduces elevator effectiveness, causing the nose to pitch down slightly. On takeoff, ground effect will enable the airplane to lift off at a speed below normal stall speed. If the pilot stays in ground effect, and accelerates before climbing, this is a useful soft field or high altitude technique. If the pilot attempts to climb out of ground effect before gaining at least best angle of climb speed (V_X), the airplane may sink back to the surface.

Trim Speed

Trim speed is a concept that belongs to both aerodynamics and performance. In Chapter Two you were told that trim tabs provide a means of relieving control pressure, and you were warned to not use trim as a means of achieving a specific attitude or airspeed. The setting of the elevator trim tab determines the position of the horizontal stabilizer and thus the airplane's pitch attitude. When you check that the trim is in the takeoff range during your preflight runup, you insure that the airplane will lift off and climb normally when there is sufficient airflow over the control surfaces. If you fail to perform this check, the airplane will either hug the ground and resist your efforts to make it fly or it will pitch up into what you will recognize as an impossibly nose-high attitude and you will have to exert strong forward pressure to avoid a stall. (You can always overpower the trim, even when it is set outside of normal limits.) If you leave the elevator trim set in one position and never change it, the airplane will fly at its "trim speed." If you add power, it will climb at its trim speed (after a few oscillations up and down), and if you reduce power it will descend at trim speed. Of course, there will be an intermediate power setting where the airplane will maintain level flight at trim speed. Try this experiment during a training flight: with the airplane trimmed for level flight, apply back pressure to the yoke and then release it, keeping the wings level with rudder pressure. The airplane will climb and descend in gradually decreasing oscillations until it is once again in level flight at its trim speed. Change the power setting, re-trim for level flight, and try again. The airplane will always return to level flight at trim speed. Now trim the elevator so that the vertical speed indicator shows a zero rate of climb or descent at the speed you use when descending from the downwind leg onto base and final, noting the power setting and where the airplane's nose is in relation to the horizon. Without touching the trim, retard the throttle 500 RPM. With little or no effort on your part, the airplane should stabilize in a 500 foot per minute descent without changing airspeed (check the nose down attitude). When you have lost 500 feet of altitude, return the throttle to the setting you noted earlier; the airplane should level off and maintain trim speed. Now add 500 RPM and watch what happens to the airspeed and vertical speed. This is a very valuable tool for predictable performance: a known power setting and a known (trimmed) pitch attitude will always give you the same vertical speed and airspeed. Every time you reach for the trim wheel, you change the trim speed. Keep your airplane in trim at your desired speed. Then, when you get something in your eye or drop a chart on the floor, you know that the airplane won't immediately take off on its own.

Chapter 6
Performance Review Questions

1. After takeoff, which airspeed would permit the pilot to gain the most altitude in a given period of time?

   A—Cruising climb speed.
   B—Best rate-of-climb speed.
   C—Best angle-of-climb speed.

2. What effect does high density altitude have on aircraft performance?

   A—It increases engine performance.
   B—It reduces an aircraft's climb performance.
   C—It increases lift because the light air exerts less force on the airfoils.

3. How can pressure altitude be determined?

   A—Set the field elevation in the altimeter setting window and read the indicated altitude.
   B—Set the altimeter to zero and read the value in the altimeter setting window.
   C—Set 29.92 in the altimeter setting window and read the indicated altitude.

4. Determine the approximate fuel flow at 75% maximum continuous power at 6,500 feet with a temperature 36° higher than standard. (Use Figure 6-9 on Page 6-7.)

   A—12.4 gal/hr.
   B—12.7 gal/hr.
   C—13.1 gal/hr.

5. What effect does higher density altitude have on propeller efficiency?

   A—Increased efficiency due to less friction on the propeller blades.
   B—Reduced efficiency because the propeller exerts less force than at lower density altitudes.
   C—Increased efficiency because the propeller exerts less force on the thinner air.

6. An airplane is usually affected by ground effect at what height above the surface?

   A—Between 100 and 200 ft above the surface in calm wind conditions.
   B—Less than half of the airplane's wingspan above the surface.
   C—Twice the length of the airplane's wingspan above the surface.

7. Which adverse effect must a pilot be aware of as a result of the phenomenon of ground effect during takeoff?

   A—Difficulty in getting airborne even though airspeed is sufficient for normal takeoff.
   B—Becoming airborne before reaching recommended takeoff speed.
   C—Settling back to the surface immediately after becoming airborne.

8. If you plan to land at an airport where the elevation is 7,500 feet, the indicated approach airspeed should be

A—the same as that used at a sea level airport.
B—lower than that used at a sea level airport.
C—higher than that used at a sea level airport.

9. As altitude increases, the indicated airspeed at which a given airplane stalls in a particular configuration will

A—decrease as the true airspeed decreases.
B—decrease as the true airspeed increases.
C—remain the same as at low altitude.

10. Of what practical value is pressure altitude?

A—To use on all aircraft performance charts since the charts are based on pressure altitude.
B—To use for obstacle clearance at higher altitudes where accurate altimeter settings are not available.
C—To use for computer solutions to determine density altitude, true altitude, true airspeed, etc.

11. Determine the approximate ground roll distance for takeoff under the following conditions. *See* Figure 6-3 on Page 6-4.

OAT .... 90°F
Pressure altitude .... 2,000 ft.
Takeoff weight .... 2,500 lb.
Wind... 20 kts.

A—650 ft.
B—800 ft.
C—1,000 ft.

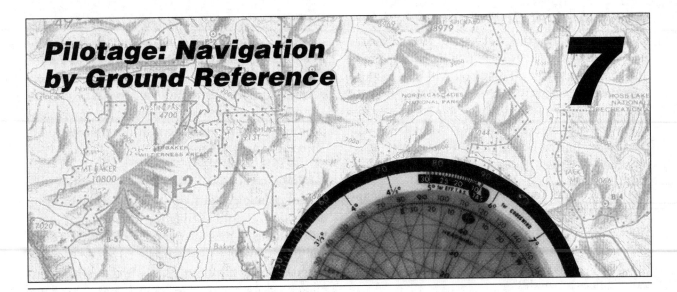

Pilotage: Navigation by Ground Reference

7

VFR pilots *navigate* by a system of *pilotage*; that is, they lay out a course on an aeronautical chart and direct the flight of their aircraft along that course by reference to the terrain. Pilots *plan* their flights by dead reckoning. That statement deserves some explanation: in the days of sail, mariners kept track of their position as accurately as they could by estimating their speed and the effects of wind and current and having a "deduced reckoning" of where they had traveled since their last known position. They logged the result as "ded. reckoning." The airplane pilot of today lays out a course line, allows for wind and magnetic errors, derives a heading and a groundspeed and estimates a time of arrival at the destination. That is dead reckoning—the planning phase. Unlike the sailor, the VFR pilot can maintain a visual track over the ground and pass over charted reference points. That is pilotage. From the early days, pilot has meant navigator.

Aeronautical Charts

You will use three types of charts as a VFR pilot. The World Aeronautical Chart (WAC) is printed on a scale of 1:1,000,000, or approximately 16 statute miles to the inch. The contiguous (48) United States are covered by just 11 WAC charts. Because each chart covers such a large area, WACs are usually used by pilots of relatively fast airplanes for long cross-country flights. They are not as detailed as sectional charts, they do not include all airports, and boundaries of controlled airspace are not shown. WAC charts are revised annually.

Sectional charts are used for most VFR local and medium-range cross-country navigation. With a scale of 1:500,000, or approximately 8 statute miles to the inch, it takes 34 charts to cover the continental U.S., 16 to cover Alaska, and 1 for the Hawaiian Islands. Sectionals are excellent for visual navigation: they show roads, freeways, railroads, power lines, lakes, rivers, terrain contours and populated areas. Military airfields, public, private and emergency airports are also shown. An excerpt from the Seattle Sectional Chart is included with this book and will be used in the flight planning, airspace, and regulations sections. Sectional charts are revised every six months.

Terminal Area Charts, with a scale of 4 miles to the inch, are published for those areas that have Class B airspace (see Chapter 14). Because VFR pilots must always know where they are in relation to the boundaries of the Class B airspace, Terminal Area charts are highly detailed and include VFR reporting points for easy reference. A "VFR Flyways Planning Chart" is printed on the back of each chart to aid you in navigating near the Class B airspace. Revised Terminal Area Charts are issued every six months.

The Jeppesen Company publishes a VFR Navservice chart series to aid pilots who fly in the congested airspace of southern California. Unlike FAA charts that tell VFR pilots where they shouldn't fly, these new charts show courses and altitude that will avoid class B and C airspace and uncomplicate flight in that area. Expect this service to be extended to other congested areas.

Geographical Coordinates

The sailor who "dead reckons" a voyage across untracked waters needs to be familiar with latitude and longitude—you do not. You will use latitude-longitude coordinates with some advanced radio navigation systems but lat-long coordinates do not play a part in practical VFR flying. You will be using the lat-long lines on your WAC or sectional chart, however, so a brief explanation is in order.

Figure 7-1 shows **parallels** of latitude marching upward from the Equator (0° latitude) to the Poles (90° North or South latitude). If you slice a globe along lines of latitude, the slices get progressively smaller toward the poles, so distance measurements along latitude lines are useless.

Lines of longitude are called **meridians**, and divide the earth from pole to pole, the 0° meridian passing through Greenwich, England. Meridians are numbered eastward across Europe and Asia and westward across the Atlantic Ocean and the Americas until the 180° meridian is reached in mid-Pacific. The continental United States lies roughly between 70° and 125° West longitude and between 26° and 49° North latitude. Meridians are **Great Circles**: if you slice a globe along meridians, all of the slices will be the same size. All meridians are the same length: 10,600 nautical miles from Pole to Pole, 60 nautical miles per degree.

Each degree is further divided into 60 minutes, and this makes it possible to measure distance accurately: one minute of latitude equals one **nautical mile** when measured along a line of longitude toward either pole.

As you look at your aeronautical chart, lines of longitude and latitude are at right angles. As you look at a globe, however, lines of longitude converge toward the poles. Because there is some unavoidable distortion of scale between the bottom and the top of an aeronautical chart, you should make course measurements as close as possible to the mid-latitude portion of the chart.

On the excerpt of the Seattle sectional chart, find the Easton State airport (**A**). Count up 15 minutes from the latitude line marked 47° to find the latitude of Easton State. Count left 11 minutes from the longitude line marked 121° to find the longitude of Easton State. Its geographic position is 47°15' 15" north, 121° 11' 15" west. You don't need to be any more accurate than the nearest minute in order to locate an airport using latitude and longitude. The geographic position of all airports is found in the Airport/Facility Directory (A/FD).

Time

The measurement of time is an integral part of air navigation. Before leaving the discussion of longitude and the 0° meridian, the subject of time zones and time conversions should be covered. The only rational way to have flight times and weather information apply across the country and around the world is to have a single time reference. That reference is the time at Greenwich, England (on the 0° line of longitude). *Once referred to as Greenwich Mean Time the time standard is now called Universal Coordinated Time (UTC).* Each 15° of longitude east or west of Greenwich marks a one hour time difference. Figure 7-2 shows the time differences across the United States with a legend for time conversion to and from Coordinated Universal Time or **ZULU time**. ZULU is the phonetic identifier for the letter Z; in the 24 hour clock system UCT is shown as 0800Z, 2200Z, etc. You should become familiar with time zone conversions for your area of operations. Here are two time conversion problems to illustrate:

Figure 7-1. *Meridians and parallels*

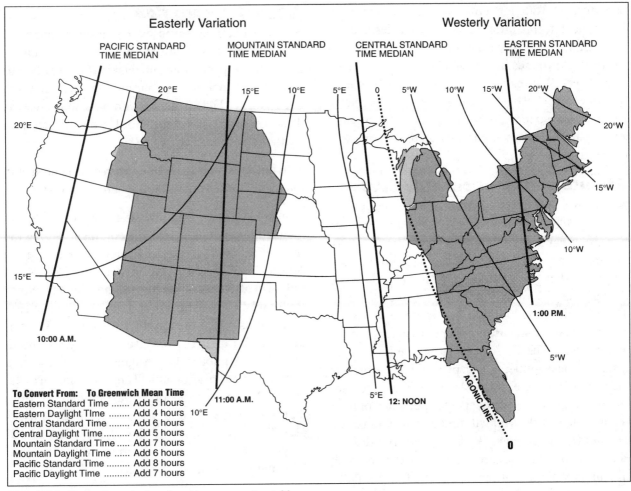

Easterly Variation | Westerly Variation

PACIFIC STANDARD TIME MEDIAN
MOUNTAIN STANDARD TIME MEDIAN
CENTRAL STANDARD TIME MEDIAN
EASTERN STANDARD TIME MEDIAN

To Convert From:	To Greenwich Mean Time
Eastern Standard Time	Add 5 hours
Eastern Daylight Time	Add 4 hours
Central Standard Time	Add 6 hours
Central Daylight Time	Add 5 hours
Mountain Standard Time	Add 7 hours
Mountain Daylight Time	Add 6 hours
Pacific Standard Time	Add 8 hours
Pacific Daylight Time	Add 7 hours

Figure 7-2. Magnetic variation chart/time conversion table

An aircraft departs an airport in the Central Standard time zone at 0930 CST for a 2-hour flight to an airport located in the mountain standard time zone. What should the landing time be?

1. 0930 MST.

2. 1030 MST.

3. 1130 MST.

4. 1230 MST.

There are two ways of approaching this problem. First, according to the time difference chart, at the departure time of 0930 CST it is 0830 MST, and a 2 hour flight should land at 1030 MST. The second method is to add 2 hours to 0930 CST to get the CST landing time at the destination (forget to set your watch back?). Subtract the one hour time difference to get 1030 MST.

An aircraft departs an airport in the Pacific Standard time zone at 1030 PST for a 4-hour flight to an airport located in the central time zone. At what ZULU time should the landing be?

1. 2030Z.

2. 2130Z.

3. 2230Z.

4. 2330Z.

What is ZULU time at departure? The chart says that to convert PST to UCT you must add 8 hours, so takeoff time is 1830Z. Arrival time after a 4-hour flight will be 2230Z.

Flight Service Station personnel and air traffic controllers use ZULU time, and will be reluctant to do time conversions for you. (Of course, you can buy a watch with dual time zones!) If you are planning a departure for 1800 local time and there is a forecast for thunderstorms after 2100Z at your destination, you will have to know time conversion to be able to relate that to your estimated time of arrival. As a new pilot, you will probably stay within one time zone or possibly travel between two time zones. Just remember that, for example, you live in the "plus 5" time zone (plus 4 in the summer), and conversions will come easily to you.

Statute and Nautical Mile Scale

Navigators on the sea or in the air find the use of nautical miles for distance measurement convenient because a nautical mile is 6,000 feet (really 6,080, but that complicates things) and is also one minute of latitude. When you counted up 15 minutes to locate the latitude of Easton State airport, you counted up 15 nautical miles. You will find mileage scales for both nautical and **statute miles** on aeronautical charts and plotters. The FAA uses nautical miles for all distance measurements except visibility, which is measured in statute miles. Airspeed indicators are calibrated in **knots** (nautical miles per hour) only or in knots and MPH; you will find a conversion scale on your flight computer. *Winds are always given in knots,* so you must be sure that you are dealing with like units when flight planning. The CX-1A Pathfinder electronic calculator contains conversion programs for knots/MPH and nautical miles/statute miles.

Magnetic Variation

For flight planning purposes you must recognize that although the lines of latitude and longitude on charts are neatly perpendicular and relate to the **True North Pole** there is nothing in your airplane that relates to True North. The magnetic compass indicates the direction to the magnetic North Pole, which is in northern Canada (Figure 7-3).

You must take the **variation** between true north and magnetic north into account when flight planning.

Figure 7-4 shows **isogonic lines**, or lines of equal magnetic variation, across the continent. Along the line which passes through Chicago and Key West, a pilot looking toward the North Star or the True North Pole will also be looking toward the magnetic North Pole, and there will be no variation. That line of zero variation is called the **agonic line.** East or West of that line, the angle between true and magnetic north increases. A pilot in Los Angeles who measures a course line on an aeronautical chart in relation to the longitude lines (or true north) must subtract 14° from that true course to get a magnetic course (*"East is least"*), while a pilot in Philadelphia will add 10° (*"West is best"*). You will determine the true course by using your navigation plotter.

Using the Navigation Plotter

A navigation plotter combines a protractor with mileage scales, and they are available in many forms. You use the protractor to measure the angle between a line of latitude or longitude and your course line.

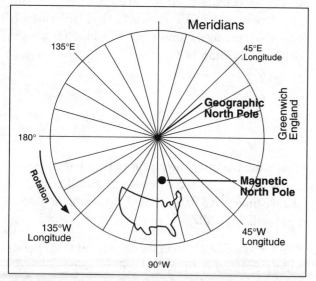

Figure 7-3. Magnetic and true north poles

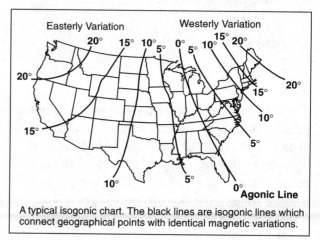

A typical isogonic chart. The black lines are isogonic lines which connect geographical points with identical magnetic variations.

Figure 7-4. Isogonic lines

Refer to the Seattle Sectional chart excerpt in the back of the book. Draw a line from the center of the airport symbol at Easton (**A**) to the center of the airport symbol at Wenatchee (**H**). Align the straight edge of your plotter with this course line and slide the plotter until the hole is over a vertical line of longitude; the angle should be approximately 78 degrees, indicating that the true course from Easton to Wenatchee is 078° and that the course for the return trip is 258°.

Deviation

A course, whether identified as true or magnetic, is only a line on a chart linking departure point and destination. For flight planning purposes, you must allow for magnetic influences in the airplane itself and for the effect of wind drift. Because your airplane has some iron and steel components which are affected by the earth's magnetic field, and because it contains wiring which creates a magnetic field within the airplane itself, the airplane's magnetic compass develops an error called **deviation** which varies with aircraft heading. Looking back at Figure 7-4 it is apparent that the heading of the airplane has nothing to do with magnetic variation—a pilot in Seattle must apply a -20° Easterly variation regardless of the direction of flight. Because magnetic deviation is unique to each airplane and is dependent on heading, a compass correction card (Figure 7-5) must be prepared by accurately lining up the airplane on known magnetic headings, checking the magnetic compass reading, and recording the deviation error for each heading. Small adjustment magnets are provided so that the error can be minimized.

This compass correction table is originally made at the factory but should be re-checked by a mechanic whenever cockpit equipment installations are made. When a pilot has applied variation and deviation to a measured true course, the result is the compass course:

True ± Variation = Magnetic ± Deviation = Compass

FOR (MH)	0	30	60	90	120	150	180	210	240	270	300	330
STEER (CH)	2	28	56	88	120	152	183	212	240	268	298	328

Figure 7-5. Compass correction card

Variation is shown on navigational charts to the nearest one-half degree. You will find that rounding off to the nearest whole degree will speed up your calculations without affecting accuracy. If you make long flights over water or featureless terrain, deviation and compass course will be very important to you, and an accurate compass correction card may be a lifesaver. Pilots who fly by reference to the surface (pilotage) will make little use of compass **heading** except to adjust their gyroscopic heading indicators.

Any difference between an airplane's planned **course** and its **track** over the ground is caused by wind drift—the difference between an airplane's course and its heading is caused by **wind drift**. Always compute the **wind correction angle** first, and then apply variation and deviation, as National Weather Service winds aloft forecasts are always referenced to True North.

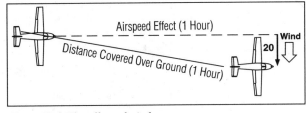

Figure 7-6. The effect of wind

Correcting for Wind Drift

Figure 7-6 shows the effect of wind drift on an airplane's flight path if no corrective action is taken. The wind correction angle necessary to offset the wind drift will allow the airplane's track over the ground to agree with the planned course. Determining wind correction angle with a known wind direction, wind velocity, true course and true airspeed is a trigonometry problem.

Solving the Wind Drift

The **wind triangle** consists of four known values and two unknowns. You know the angle between true north and your course (true course), and the angle between true north and the wind direction; you also know your true airspeed and the wind velocity. With these values, you can construct a triangle to solve for the unknowns: groundspeed and true heading. Refer to Figure 7-7 on Page 7-6.

Figure 7-7. Wind triangle

Wind direction: .... 320° true
Wind velocity: .... 30 knots
True course: ....060°
True airspeed: .... 100 knots

The vertical line represents true north. Line A-B represents the true wind, and is drawn downwind— a wind from 320° "blows" the line to 140°. The length of line A-B represents the wind velocity in convenient units. Using a protractor, draw a line of indefinite length from point A so that the angle represents the true course as measured on your chart. A line with a length representing the true airspeed (100 knots) is drawn from point B to intersect the true course line at point C. The distance from point A to point C is the groundspeed, (103 knots) and the angle that line B-C makes with the true north line (043°) is the true heading. The wind correction angle (17°) is the difference between the true course and the true heading. Magnetic variation must be applied to convert true heading to magnetic heading, and deviation applied to that to get compass heading. Very few pilots draw wind triangles, because the triangle can be solved mechanically and electronically much more quickly, but it's a great way to really teach yourself the fundamentals of aerial navigation.

Winds aloft forecasts are only available for selected altitudes: 3,000', 6,000', 9,000', etc. In most cases you will have to interpolate for your planned cruise altitude. Keep in mind that these are forecasts, and don't expect extreme accuracy.

Using The Slide-Type Computer

True course .... 230°
True airspeed .... 140 MPH
Wind .... 150° at 17 knots

(Convert wind or airspeed so that both are in the same units. 17 knots = 19.6 MPH)

Orient the rotatable disk so that the true wind direction (150°) is at the true index. From the center, count *up* the number of units representing wind velocity (19.6) (Figure 7-8). Rotate the disk so that the true course (230°) is aligned with the true index; note that the wind dot is now in the correct relationship to the course. Move the slide until the wind dot falls on the speed arc representing the true airspeed (140) (Figure 7-9). You have solved the wind triangle: the groundspeed (135 mph) is read directly under the center grommet and the wind correction angle (8° left) is read under the wind dot. A left wind correction angle is subtracted from the true course and a right wind correction angle is added to the true course to get true heading.

Figure 7-8

Figure 7-9

Using the Circular Computer

See Figure 7-10:

True course .... 115°
True airspeed .... 90 kts
Wind .... 240° at 38 kts

Make a wind dot where the wind direction line crosses the wind velocity arc. Rotate the disk with the wind dot to align the true course with the true index; rotate the outer disk to align the true airspeed with the true index. The position of the wind dot now shows you the number of knots of crosswind component and headwind/tailwind component. Find the number of knots of crosswind component on the outer scale; opposite it you will read the wind correction angle. If the crosswind component is more than 10% of the true airspeed use the larger of the two angles. Apply the headwind/tailwind component to the true airspeed to get groundspeed. If the wind correction angle exceeds 5° read the "effective true airspeed" to the left of the true index.

Right crosswind component = 31 kts.
Tailwind component = 21 knots
Wind correction angle is greater than 10°:

Opposite 20° on "Effective True Airspeed" scale read 84.5 knots. Add 21 knot tailwind to TAS to get groundspeed of 105.5.

Figure 7-10. *Plotting and finding groundspeed and wind correction angle*

Accuracy

Before relying too heavily on the results of wind problems, you must consider that the data you are working with is not precise. The National Weather Service wind direction forecasts are in 10° increments and can be off as much as 45° (for wind velocities forecast to be less than 25 knots) before a corrected forecast is issued. You can calculate headings to one-half of one degree but you cannot fly that accurately. Also, most pilots understand and accept deviation error in the magnetic compass but ignore it until their heading indicator fails. It is for these reasons that you must follow your progress over the ground visually.

The CX-1A Pathfinder Electronic Calculator

ASA's CX-1A Pathfinder electronic calculator offers a quick convenient means of solving wind and other navigation problems. Its use will be discussed in detail in Chapter 17.

Time-speed-distance problems can be solved with a four-function pocket calculator, and you will learn how in this chapter. Without a table of trigonometric functions, a four-function calculator cannot do wind triangle solutions.

Personal Computers

A pilot with a computer at home or office can buy any one of a myriad of programs designed to make flight planning quick, easy, and accurate. These programs vary from the inexpensive, which read out only heading, groundspeed, and time enroute, to the very costly programs which not only provide flight planning information for several airplanes (so you can decide which one is most cost-efficient for the trip) but what kind of fuel and food service is available at the destination. The best computer programs (regardless of cost) are those which print out a flight log for you to take along.

Subscribers to DUATS (*See* Chapter 11) and CompuServe have access to flight planning and weather information through their personal computers.

Groundspeed vs. Airspeed

When you drive your automobile for one hour at 60 miles per hour, you can be fairly certain that you will travel 60 miles during that hour. In flight, whether or not one hour at 60 miles per hour will actually cover 60 miles will be determined by the wind. If you somehow manage to get airborne under control and are flying into a 60 MPH headwind with an airspeed of 60 MPH, you aren't going to make it out of sight of the airport: your speed over the ground will be zero. This is an extreme example, although pilots in the Plains states have a fund of stories about airplanes "flying" in strong winds that prove that it can happen. You need to develop an understanding of the airspeed/groundspeed relationship on a more normal basis.

First, forget the comparison with the automobile and standardize all speed measurements in knots: the National Weather Service provides wind velocity information in knots and confusion will result if you mix units of measurement. The General Aviation Manufacturer's Association has standardized on knots for airspeed indicators. The same flight computer solution that you used to determine wind correction angle gave you a groundspeed figure. You entered true airspeed and true wind direction and velocity and the computer read out groundspeed. You determine true airspeed by reference to cruise performance charts (Chapter 6) or by applying the 2% per 1,000' rule to your indicated airspeed (Chapter 4).

No matter how you arrived at the groundspeed figure, you must use it in combination with the measured distance to the destination to determine time enroute.

It is important to make frequent groundspeed checks while enroute to ensure that your actual groundspeed agrees with your planned groundspeed. Remember, the winds you used in flight planning were *forecast* winds. In planning your flight you must be sure that upon arrival at your destination you have at least 30 minutes fuel left on board in the daytime and 45 minutes reserve fuel at night. Learn to think in terms of *time in your tanks* instead of distance. The Owner's Manual may say that you have a range of 450 miles, but if you are using 10 gallons per hour and have 35 gallons on board, you will only stay airborne for 3 ½ hours no matter how far you have managed to fly.

Rate Problems: Time-Speed Distance, Fuel Burn

Rate problems are solved on the slide rule side of your flight computer: the inner, rotatable disk represents time, and the outer, fixed disk represents miles or gallons. The numbers on both disks must be interpreted with common sense, because you must provide the decimal points. For instance, 30 on the computer might be 3 for one problem and 300 for another. As you try some sample problems, you will see how common sense is applied. The arrow at the 60 on the rotatable disk is the speed or rate arrow (some instructors call it the speedometer needle), and you will use it for all calculations of miles per hour, knots, or gallons per hour: read it as "something per hour". The computer lets you mechanically solve for any single unknown in these equations:

Distance = speed x time
Gallons = fuel burn rate x time

The computer presents the information in this form, with time on the inner, rotatable disc:

$$\frac{\text{Speed or GPH}}{60} = \frac{\text{Distance or Gallons}}{\text{Time}}$$

If you determine that the distance between two checkpoints is 23 nautical miles, and your elapsed time between the checkpoints is 14.3 minutes (14 minutes and 18 seconds), set 14.3 on the inner time scale opposite 23 on the outer distance scale and read 96.5 opposite the speed arrow: your groundspeed is 96.5 knots. It couldn't very well be 9.65 or 965 knots, could it? Finding 14.3 and 23 in this problem isn't too difficult because numbers between 1 and 99 are read directly. *See* Figure 7-11 on the next page.

In preflight planning you find that the distance to your destination is 248 NM and you learn from doing a wind problem that your predicted groundspeed is 114 knots. Put the speed arrow opposite 114 (now the 10 on the outside scale is read as 100, the 11 as 110, etc.) and find 248 on the outside scale. It is between 24 and 25, now read as 240 and 250. On the inner, rotatable (time) disk opposite 248, read the estimated time enroute as 132 minutes or 2:12. When elapsed time is the unknown, be careful not to confuse minutes with tenths of hours. *See* Figure 7-12.

Figure 7-11

Figure 7-12

The cruise charts tell you that your fuel consumption rate will be 8.2 gallons per hour—how much fuel will you burn on the 248 mile trip? Place the rate arrow opposite 8.2 (between 80 and 90) and find 2:12 on the inside, time scale. Across from 2:12 (or 132) you will find 18.0 on the outside scale which now represents gallons. Make sense? Just over 2 hours at 8 gallons an hour has to be just over 16 gallons, doesn't it? Always check computer problems "in your head" to make sure that you are in the ballpark. *See* Figure 7-13.

Time-speed-distance and fuel problems can be worked out using a typical four-function calculator by cross-multiplying and then dividing. Try the three problems above with your pocket calculator. First, remember that the speed/rate arrow represents 60 and is always at the lower left. Time is always at the lower right. Here is the first problem you did with the slide rule type computer set up for a four-function calculator:

$$\frac{?}{60} : \frac{23}{14.3}$$ Multiply two knowns diagonally across (60 x 23) and divide by the third known factor, 14.3.

$$? = \frac{23 \times 60}{14.3} = 96.5 \text{ knots}$$

This is the second problem above:

$$\frac{114}{60} : \frac{248}{?}$$ is the same as 60 x 248 ÷ 114 = 130.526.

$$\frac{248 \times 60}{114} = 130.526 \text{ minutes}$$

Figure 7-13

The third problem you did with the slide rule computer was a fuel problem. Set it up on your pocket calculator:

$$\frac{8.2}{60} : \frac{?}{130.5}$$ is the same as 8.2 x 130 ÷ 60 = 17.84.

$$? = \frac{8.2 \times 130.5}{60} = 17.84$$

Just set the problem up on your calculator as you would on the flight computer, cross-multiply and divide.

Don't throw your flight computer away—you need it for density altitude, true altitude, and true airspeed problems, plus conversions.

Miscellaneous Solutions

Around the edge of your flight computer you will find arrows with "naut" and "stat" for mileage conversion, and TAS for airspeed calculations. On the rotatable disk there are windows for calculations requiring input of pressure altitude and temperature. Some computers have a window for true altitude, others only provide for density altitude and airspeed calculations.

For mileage conversions, place the known value under the appropriate arrow, NAUT or STAT, and find the converted value under the other arrow. Statute miles nautical miles x 1.15 and statute mile x .87 = nautical miles (Figure 7-14).

Density altitude and airspeed problems use the same window (Figure 7-15). You need to know the air temperature and pressure altitude to compute density altitude. True airspeed calculations require air temperature, pressure altitude, and indicated airspeed. Convert temperature to Centigrade (C°) if it is in Fahrenheit (F°), and place the temperature opposite the pressure altitude in the window marked FOR AIRSPEED AND DENSITY ALTITUDE.

The markings are very small and extreme accuracy is difficult to achieve. When you have the temperature and pressure altitude properly set you will find the density altitude in the window marked for it. Opposite the indicated airspeed on the rotatable scale, you will find true airspeed on the outside scale. Figure 7-16 shows a solution for a temperature of -10° and a pressure altitude of 7,500'.

The density altitude window indicates 6,300'. If your indicated airspeed is 120 knots and you want to know true airspeed, don't move anything—just look opposite 120 on the inner scale and read 131.5 on the outer scale.

Do as many calculations as possible before takeoff—have distances between checkpoints written down and have an easy-to-use timer available. Your time for in-flight calculations will be limited, and thorough preflight preparation will make them easier.

Use common sense. Question wind correction angles of 30° to 40° or more and headwind/tailwind components that seem out of line. Use groundspeed checkpoints that are 10 miles or more apart so that a small

Figure 7-14. *220 nautical = 253 statute*

Figure 7-15. *Density altitude and true airspeed*

Figure 7-16. *Density altitude solution*

timing error will not have a major effect on your calculations, and choose checkpoints that allow accurate timing: roads, railroads, or shorelines make better checkpoints than city limits or tops of hills.

Refer to Chapter 17 to learn how the ASA CX-1A Pathfinder aids in quick accurate solutions to these problems.

Always orient a chart to your direction of flight, and learn to read charts upside down, so that visual checkpoints appear in correct relationship to the nose of your airplane. Finally, if you draw a line on your chart from departure point to destination, follow the line with your finger, and fly your airplane over every visual feature (road, drive-in theater, lake, etc.) along that line, you can't possibly get lost.

Chart Reading

In other chapters you will learn how to look at your aeronautical chart to determine radio frequencies and airspace designations. To fly by pilotage you must be able to quickly and accurately identify ground reference points visually. Refer to the Seattle sectional chart excerpt and the chart legend at the back of the book.

The importance of knowing the height of terrain and obstructions is obvious. Notice that in each rectangle formed by lines of latitude and longitude there is a large blue number with an adjacent smaller number. This represents the height above mean sea level of the highest terrain or man-made obstruction within that rectangle in thousands and hundreds of feet. 8^3, for instance, means that the highest obstruction is 8,300 feet above sea level. The heights of specific terrain features are indicated by a dot and the measured altitude; the altitude of the highest terrain within a latitude-longitude block is in large print.

You will notice that the highest obstacle is at least 100 feet below the 8^3 if man-made and at least 300 feet below the 8^3 if man-made and at least 300 feet below if a natural obstruction. This is for added safety. Man-made obstructions such as radio and television towers have two numbers adjacent to them. The top number (in bold italics) is the height of the top of the obstruction above mean sea level, and is the most meaningful number to you in choosing an altitude in that area. The number in parentheses is the actual height of the structure. Towers which are more than 1,000 feet in height (which usually require supporting guy wires that are virtually invisible) have a special symbol as shown in the chart legend.

Freeways, highways, and railroads are excellent references. Notice that major freeways are identified with their route numbers—Interstate 90 crosses the chart from Seattle to the lower right corner. You can often orient yourself by noticing an interchange or an obvious jog in a road, or by the relationship between a road and some other physical feature. Because they are centered in large right-of-way areas, power lines are just as useful as roads—you can see the cleared right-of-way much further than you can see the powerlines themselves.

Drive-in theaters and racetracks make good orientation points. Be wary of lakes—in a dry year the lake you are looking for might not be the same shape as indicated on the chart (or may not exist at all!).

Changes in elevation are depicted with contour lines. On the sectional chart excerpt you can see how tightly packed the contour lines are in the Cascade Mountains. Notice the interval between contour lines. The lines are every 500 feet on sectionals and every 1,000 feet on WAC charts.

Chapter 7

Pilotage: Navigation by Ground Reference
Review Questions

Figure Q7-1

1. What is the true course from Cedar Rapids (airport A in Figure Q7-1) to Fairfield (airport E)? The magnetic variation is 5°E.

   A—013°
   B—193°
   C—198°

2. While flying from Cedar Rapids to Fairfield, you cross Interstate 80 at 1015 and the highway west of Wellman at 1022. What is your estimated time of arrival at Fairfield if your ground-speed remains constant?

   A—1028
   B—1035
   C—1040

3. Your airplane uses 8.6 gallons of fuel per hour. You plan a 250 nautical mile flight at an average groundspeed of 115 knots. What is the minimum fuel required for the trip (allow a 30 minute reserve)?

   A—18.7 gallons.
   B—23.0 gallons.
   C—15.6 gallons.

4. Your groundspeed between Cedar Rapids and Fairfield (52 NM) is 111 knots. At an average fuel consumption rate of 7.2 gallons per hour, how much fuel will you use enroute?

   A—3.4 gallons.
   B—2.5 gallons.
   C—4.2 gallons.

Continued

5. Your true course is 270°, your true airspeed is 110 knots, the wind is from 330° at 18 knots, and the magnetic variation is 6° W. What is your groundspeed and magnetic heading?

A—119 knots; 278°
B—100 knots; 264°
C—101 knots; 284°

6. Upon refueling at your destination after a 345 nautical mile flight you take 32 gallons of fuel (tanks were full on departure). During the flight, your groundspeed averaged 136 knots. What was the fuel consumption rate for this flight?

A—11.0 gallons per hour.
B—14.0 gallons per hour.
C—12.6 gallons per hour.

Refer to the full-color Seattle sectional chart excerpt at the back of this book for questions 7 and 8.

7. What kind of lighting is available at the Cashmere-Dryden airport (47° 30' 45"N 120° 29' 15"W)?

A—No runway lighting is available.
B—Rotating beacon only.
C—Pilot-controlled runway lighting (or on request).

8. How tall is the antenna for radio station KPQ, 8 miles northwest of the Wenatchee airport, (**H**)?

A—560 feet.
B—943 feet.
C—313 feet.

9. Where would you look for information on how to activate pilot-controlled lighting?

A—Sectional chart legend.
B—Airman's Information Manual.
C—Airport/Facility Directory

10. How would you apply magnetic variation when planning a flight from Ellensburg (**I**) to Seattle (**C**)?

A—Subtract 47° 30' from the true course.
B—Add 19.5 degrees to the true course.
C—Subtract 19.5 degrees from the true course.

11. You are flying over Lake Kachess (near **A**) in the central Cascade Mountains. What sectional chart feature tells you the minimum safe altitude in that area?

A—Terrain with an elevation of 6,680' at the north end of the lake.
B—Maximum elevation number 7^9.
C—Contour lines on the mountains.

Radio Navigation

8

Figure 8-1. *VOR signal transmitter*

As a VFR pilot, you will probably use radio aids to navigation only as a backup to pilotage, rather than as a primary method of navigation. If, however, there is a radio airway going the same way you are, many flight planning problems will be minimized (if not eliminated) by using it.

The FAA has established the VHF omnidirectional range (VOR) system as the primary means of electronic navigation in federally controlled airspace, and you will find that most airplanes have at least one VOR receiver. The VOR system operates in the Very High Frequency range (108.0 MHz to 117.95 MHz), just above the FM broadcast band and below that band of frequencies designated for aircraft radio communication. VHF radio waves are subject to line-of-sight limitations (Figure 8-2) and you may find that at low altitudes you will be unable to receive a usable VOR signal.

VORs are classified as high altitude, low altitude, and terminal VORs. You should consult the Airport/Facility Directory to learn which class any VOR you propose to use falls into. It also lists altitudes and/or radials where the signal is unusable. *See* Figure 8-3 (on the next page).

Your aeronautical chart shows three symbols for VORs: VOR, VORTAC, and VOR-DME. There is no difference between these three types of stations as

Figure 8-2. *Line-of-sight limitations*

far as your cockpit course guidance indication is concerned. VORTAC and VOR-DME will be discussed under "Distance Measuring Equipment" in this chapter. *See* Figure 8-4.

All three types of transmitters broadcast a three-letter identifier in Morse Code, so that you can be sure that you have tuned the correct station and that the station is transmitting a usable signal. When the transmitter is undergoing maintenance or adjustment the FAA either removes the coded identification or changes the code to send T-E-S-T (- . .... -). You must check the Morse code against that shown on the sectional chart to be sure that the signal is usable.

The VOR ground station transmits a signal which is identifiable as 360 radials or lines of position to your airborne receiver-indicator, and these radials are oriented in relation to magnetic north. This not only eliminates consideration of magnetic variation from your flight planning calculations, but gives you a quick chart reference to magnetic directions. Selected radials are printed in blue on the navigational charts and identified as Victor (VOR) airways. Because the VOR airways are labeled with their magnetic direction, you can "eyeball" a course without precise measurement.

The VOR indicator in your cockpit provides the answers to three questions: (1) "Where is the station from me?", (2) "Where am I in relation to the station?", and (3) "In which direction must I fly to intercept the course to my destination?"

To answer these questions, the VOR uses three elements: (1) a Course Deviation Indicator (CDI) or needle, which tells you where you are in relation to a

Altitude Feet	Line of Sight Statute Miles
500	30
1,000	45
2,000	65
3,000	80
5,000	100
7,000	120
10,000	140
15,000	175

Figure 8-3. *Line-of-sight ranges*

Figure 8-4. *VOR symbols*

Figure 8-5. *VOR indicator*

selected radial, (2) an Omni Bearing Selector (OBS) which you use to select radials, and (3) a TO-FROM (or ambiguity) indicator (Figure 8-5).

Figure 8-6. *Two indications for same location*

When the OBS is rotated to center the CDI needle, the TO-FROM indicator will tell you where you are from the station and where the station is from you, simultaneously. In Figure 8-6 the pilot has rotated the OBS and the needle has centered with 265° selected; the TO-FROM indicator shows FROM, so the VOR is telling the pilot, "You are 265° FROM, or west of XYZ VOR, so the course TO XYZ must be 085°. Which way do you want to go?" Rotating the OBS to 085° causes the TO-FROM indicator to change to TO, although the airplane has not changed heading. *Because the VOR receiver tells the pilot the airplane's position in relation to the station, the heading of the airplane is not important.* To illustrate, in Figure 8-7 both cars are on North Main Street and both airplanes are located on the 360° radial—the fact that they are heading in different directions does not alter that. Changing the heading of the airplanes would not relocate them to the 180° radial, and turning the cars would not relocate them to South Main Street.

Figure 8-8 on Page 8-4 shows how the TO-FROM indicator is related to the VOR radial selected, and it also illustrates that heading has no effect on omni indications. All of the pilots in the illustration have selected the 010° radial with their omni bearing selectors: airplanes A and E both have indication W,

Figure 8-7. *TO/FROM indication is independent of heading*

while airplanes C, F, and H have indications U, T, and T respectively. Prove this to yourself by mentally turning all of the airplanes in the illustration to a heading of 010° to agree with the OBS—those south of the station will indicate TO, those north of the station will indicate FROM, and the CDI needle in each airplane shows the direction each must turn to intercept the 010° radial.

Note: Assume all omni bearings selectors are set to 010°

Figure 8-8. Relationship of TO/FROM indicator to selected radial

When you select an omni bearing (radial), you draw an electronic dividing line between the TO and FROM areas, and you can see the result of that division in the illustration. Airplanes B, D, G, and I are neither TO nor FROM, and their VOR indicators will show a neutral or OFF flag. You will also see an OFF flag when the transmitted signal is too weak for navigational use because of distance or low altitude.

Refer to the Seattle sectional chart excerpt at the back of the book. Notice that each VOR station has a magnetic compass rose centered on it and that each has a blue box adjacent to it with the frequency and Morse Code identifier. For convenience, all VOR, VORTAC and VOR-DME stations are called VORs in this text. A pilot on a cross-country flight enroute from over the Seattle VOR (**C**) to the Paine VOR (**B**) would have the VOR receiver tuned to 116.8 MHz and the CDI needle centered with the OBS set to 340°.

The TO-FROM indicator would show FROM, because the airplane is north of Seattle. Halfway to Paine VOR, the receiver is tuned to 114.2 MHz and the TO-FROM changes to TO because the airplane is south of Paine—the CDI remains centered. Passing over Paine, still northbound, the indicator changes to FROM, and the pilot selects the next VOR along the way when in range. If a wind from the west drifts the airplane off course, the CDI will move off center toward the wind (left), and the pilot must select a heading into the wind which will cause the needle to move back to the center. Retain a small wind drift correction that will keep the needle centered. This is how you will navigate along VOR airways, always

flying FROM the VOR behind you and then TO the VOR ahead of you, with the omni bearing differing from your heading by only the amount of wind drift correction. As long as the radial you have selected and the heading of the aircraft agree within +40° you will always change heading toward the needle to center it (Figure 8-9).

Orientation

If you are able to receive a good VOR signal, you can always orient yourself by simply turning the omnibearing selector until the needle centers. Combining the indications of the omnibearing selector and the TO-FROM flag will tell you at a glance where you are FROM the station or the direction TO the station. No math required, just read the numbers on the face of the indicator.

Occasionally, however, you will want to know your position in relation to a specific radial or airway and what heading to steer to intercept it. An easy method to accomplish this is to mentally superimpose the airplane's heading on the VOR indicator.

Let's assume that you have drawn a line from a VOR to a destination airport and determined that by following the 030 radial you will arrive over that airport. Just before takeoff, you have tuned your VOR receiver to the correct frequency and set the OBS to 030. After takeoff, departing the traffic pattern and avoiding some traffic take you away from the desired course. When you are able to concentrate on radio navigation, the airplane's heading is 190 degrees and the omni indication is what you see in Figure 8-9A.

Figure 8-9. *Always fly toward the needle*

First, mentally divide the indicator in half, perpendicular to the selected radial; this separates the TOs from the FROMS. In this example, we have a FROM indication; any airplane located from northwest around to southeast (300 clockwise to 120 in Figure 8-9B on Page 8-5) would have a FROM indication. (Next, imagine an arrow pointing to the station. Since we have 030 selected and are roughly north of the station, that arrow would point to the reciprocal of 030 or 210 as shown.)

The CDI needle is deflected to the left, toward numbers which extend from southwest through north. That tells you that a heading selected from that side of the omni indicator will intercept the 030 radial. Fly a heading from 211 through 299 and you will be headed back toward the VOR; fly a heading from 301 through 029 and when the needle centers you will be on your way to the destination airport.

Many VOR indicators have course deviation indicator needles that are not pivoted at the top but remain vertical as they move from one side of the indicator to the other. If your CDI needle is pivoted at the top, mentally break it loose and position it vertically. In Figure 8-9C, the dashed line represents the relocated needle. Now imagine your airplane located in the center of the VOR indicator, with its heading in agreement with the direction indicator (190, remember?). The combination of mental images allows you to visualize where your airplane is in relation to the radial. Although the needle is deflected to the left, a right turn to a heading of about 340 degrees will intercept the 030 radial so that you can proceed on course to your destination. A left turn would have been more than a 180 degree turn.

But let's now assume that as you turn north, the skies ahead are turning dark and stormy and you wisely decide to head back. A turn to any heading in the lower left quadrant (211 to 300) would take you toward your escape route. It looks as though a right turn to 250 would be a good choice. Of course, when you get around to 250, you should rotate the omnibearing selector to 210 and re-orient your imaginary airplane. Figure 8-9D shows how the real omni indicator and your imaginary additions would look as you set up to intercept the 030 radial and return to the departure airport.

You don't have to fly on Victor airways—you can make your own. Draw a line from the Paine VOR southwest to the Bremerton National Airport (**D**)—the bearing is about 190° from Paine to Bremerton. If you are flying north from a position over the Port Orchard airport (southeast of Bremerton National), and want to intercept the direct course between Bremerton and Paine, select 010° (the reciprocal of 190°) with your omni bearing selector. The TO-FROM will read TO because Paine is generally north of you, and the CDI needle will deflect to the left. It is telling you, "select a heading to the left of 010° to go TO Paine". You decide to turn to 340°, 30° to the left of 010° (you "take a 30° cut"). As you intercept the radial, the needle moves into the center, and you turn to 010° plus or minus a wind correction.

Could you find the Port Orchard airport if you were a stranger to the Pacific Northwest? Draw a line from the Seattle VOR to Port Orchard (**E**) to determine which radial of the Seattle VOR the Port Orchard airport is on, and draw another line from the Paine VOR to Port Orchard to identify the radial of the Paine VOR that crosses Port Orchard. Fly outbound on the Seattle 246° radial with the #1 radio's OBS on 246°, and the #2 radio tuned to Paine with its OBS on 184°. The needle on your #2 omni head will be deflected to the right as you fly across Puget Sound, and it will center when you are over Port Orchard.

Centering the OBS needles of two VOR indicators is a good method of locating yourself if you become disoriented. Be sure both TO-FROM flags read FROM, because you want to determine your position FROM both stations. If you are not sure whether or not you have crossed a selected radial, use this rule: if the needle is on the same side as the station, you're not there yet.

In the example above, as you fly west across Puget Sound toward Port Orchard the Paine Field VOR is to your right and the CDI needle is deflected to the right; it will center over the Port Orchard airport and deflect to the left if you go too far.

VOR needle sensitivity is a function of distance from the transmitting station. At a distance of 60 miles from the transmitter, one degree of needle deflection equals one nautical mile on the ground, or 100 feet per mile. The scale of your course deviation indicator is 20° wide (10° each side of center), so at a distance of 60 miles a half-scale needle deflection means that you are 5 miles off course. When you are 12 miles from the station, the same half-scale deflection means that you are only 1 mile off course. Figure 8-10 shows the distance represented by half-scale deflection at various distances from the VOR transmitter.

The VOR airways (the blue lines on the sectional chart) are checked regularly by the FAA for accuracy. When you fly a radial of your own choosing, there may be slight inaccuracies between your "needle centered" position on the radial and your visual position in relation to ground reference points. When the radial is considered to be totally unusable by the FAA it is listed in the Airport/Facility Directory. This is a good reason for you to check your position visually and to use the VOR only as a backup for VFR flight.

Your VOR receiver-indicator should be checked for accuracy at least every 30 days, even if you only use it as a backup to pilotage. The FAA has designated VOR checkpoints on the ground at many airports, and has also designated airborne checkpoints that can be overflown and the VOR indication checked. The Airport/Facility Directory is the place to look for information on VOR checkpoints (Figure 8-11). At some large airports (listed in the A/FD) a special VOR test transmitter called a VOT is installed. The VOT transmitter is designed to send a single 360° radial, so that you get a signal indicating that you are north of the station regardless of your actual location. then the VOTs frequency is selected the needle should center within ±4° of 180° TO or 360° FROM.

In many cases the transmitted VOR signal is interrupted or distorted by the terrain or similar conditions, making it inaccurate and unusable at some altitudes, or in certain directions, or both. The listing for the VOR station in the Airport/Facility Directory will list any such restrictions (Figure 8-12). You may also notice irregularities in the needle indication that are caused by the propeller interfering with the received signal at certain RPM settings—changing RPM will solve this problem.

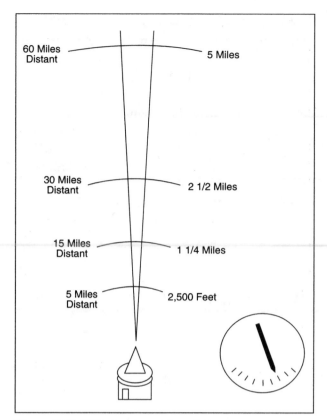

Figure 8-10. *VOR signal spread vs. distance*

VOR RECEIVER CHECK WASHINGTON					
VOR RECEIVER CHECK POINTS					
Facility Name (Arpt Name)	Freq/Ident	Type Check Pt. Gnd. AB/ALT	Azimuth from Fac. Mag.	Dist. from Fac. N.M.	Check Point Description
Ellensburg (Bowers Field)	117.9/ELN	A/2300	255	3.5	Over W end obwy 07-25.
Olympia (Olympia)	113.4/OLM	G	347		On ramp in front of admin building.
Paine (Snohomish Co. (Paine Field))	114.2/PAE	G	022	0.4	On twy H east of wy 11 threshold.
Seattle	116.8/SEA	A/2000	194	27	Over Nisqually River/I-5 bri
	116.8/SEA	A/1500	202	11.5	Over smelter stack.
	116.8/SEA	A/2500	307	19.5	Over NW end of bridge of st hwy 305.
Seattle (Crest Airpark)	116.8/SEA	A/200	106	10.3	Over centerline on aprch en runway 33.

VOR TEST FACILITIES (VOT)			
Facility Name (Airport Name)	Frequency	Type VOT Facility	Remarks
Seattle (Boeing Field King County Intl)	108.6	G	
Spokane Intl	109.6	G	

Figure 8-11. *VOR receiver checkpoints (from A/FD)*

ELLENSBURG 47°01'28"N 120°27'26"W   SEATTLE
(L) ABVORTAC 117.9   ELN   Chan 126   260° 2.5 NM to Bower Fld. 1766/21E **L-1C, 9A**
VORTAC unusable:
345°–005° beyond 10 NM below 8000'   005°–040° below 7000'
040°–080° below 5000'   080°–115° beyond 18 NM below 5000'
135°–190° beyond 25 NM below 5300'   190°–254° beyond 28 NM below 8000'
254°–265° beyond 30 NM below 7400'   300°–325° beyond 25 NM below 10,500'
325°–345° beyond 15 NM below 8000'
RCO 122.2 122.1R 117.9T (SEATTLE FSS)

Figure 8-12. *Restrictions to VOR signals (from A/FD)*

Distance Measuring Equipment

Many airplanes are equipped with **DME** which reads the distance from the transmitting station in nautical miles. Although the DME transmitter and receiver use Ultra High Frequencies (UHF), this is of no concern to the pilot. Just tuning the DME to the frequency of the associated VOR does the trick. Range information from the DME is slant range from the ground up to the airplane, not horizontal range on the ground. If you are 6,000' above the transmitting station, the DME readout will not go below 1.0 nautical mile; accuracy suffers when close to the station because of slant range considerations (Figure 8-13).

Figure 8-14. *Typical DME*

Figure 8-13. *Slant range considerations*

Distance information can be received from either VORTACs or VOR-DMEs—there is no practical difference to the user. The UHF range of frequencies is even more sensitive to line-of-sight limitations than the VHF range is—you may receive an adequate VOR signal when unable to receive the associated DME because of intervening terrain. In addition to distance information, some DME indicators also read out groundspeed and time to the station. Figure 8-14 shows a typical modern DME with its readouts. Groundspeed and time readouts are correct only when you are navigating directly toward or away from the transmitting station.

Automatic Direction Finder

The Automatic Direction Finder (ADF) receiver in your airplane (Figure 8-15) receives transmissions in the Low and Medium Frequency ranges, generally from 190 KHz to 1750 KHz. In the range from 190 KHz to 550 KHz it is used with non-directional beacons (NDBs) operated by the FAA or Coast Guard.

The ADF receiver will have a function switch with several positions. In the ANT or REC position it will provide no direction-finding capability, but will have good audio clarity for positive identification of the navigation station (or for listening to music, news, and sports). The TEST position will electronically deflect the ADF needle so that you can be sure that it is working, and that the signal from the navigation station is adequate for navigation.

When the switch is in the ADF position, the indicator needle will point directly to the transmitting station. In contrast to the VOR, when the airplane heading changes, the ADF needle moves. You read the angle between the needle and the nose of the airplane as a bearing *relative* to the nose. What you really want to know is the *magnetic* bearing to or from the transmitting station, because all of your navigation is based on magnetic north. It is possible to compute **magnetic bearing** when **relative bearing** and **magnetic heading** are known. *See* Figure 8-16 and 8-17.

Magnetic heading (MH): heading you are steering.

Relative bearing (RB): angle between the nose of the airplane and the ADF needle, measured *clockwise*.

Magnetic bearing to the station = MH + RB

035° + 225° = 260° to the station

Figure 8-15. *Automatic Direction Finder (ADF)*

Figure 8-16. *Relative bearing*

Most light airplanes with ADF receivers have a rotatable card on the indicator. The card can be set to agree with the magnetic heading on the heading indicator to eliminate the mathematics.

In the illustration (Figure 8-18) the magnetic heading is 035°. Can you match the ADF indicators with the correct magnetic bearing to the station?

R 2. 045°　　**S** 3. 305°　　**T** 1. 095°

225 + 035 = 260

Figure 8-17. *Bearing TO station*

Figure 8-18. *Magnetic compass with ADF indicators*

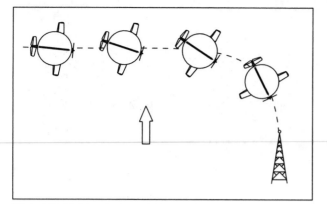

Figure 8-19. *Homing–no wind correction*

Figure 8-20. *Tracking—correcting for wind*

Using Your Automatic Direction Finder

If your airplane is equipped with an Automatic Direction Finder receiver you can use it to "home" directly to a low frequency radio station such as an FAA radiobeacon or a standard broadcast station. "Homing" means that you turn your airplane so that the ADF indicator needle points directly ahead (0° relative) and continue to turn the airplane as required to keep the needle in that position. The drawback of homing is that if there is any wind your airplane will follow a curved track arcing downwind from the straight-line track to the station. This is not only inefficient and time consuming, but you might be drifted close to terrain or obstacles at night (Figure 8-19).

The frequencies and antenna locations of broadcast stations are printed in blue on sectional charts. Broadcast stations are required to identify themselves only every 30 minutes, so you might be homing for quite a while on the wrong station!

To follow a straight track to a radio station using the ADF, you must establish a wind correction angle which will exactly offset wind drift. The first step in tracking is to place the needle at the 0° relative position by turning the airplane, just as in homing. As the wind blows the airplane downwind, the needle will move into the wind; when the needle has moved 5°, turn into the wind twice that amount (10°). This will make your heading 5° on the windward side of the direct course, with the ADF needle deflected 5° away from the wind. If the needle moves back toward the nose (into the wind), the wind drift correction is

too small—add another 5°. If the needle moves away from the wind, the correction is too great and should be cut in half. This fine-tuning will continue until you pass over the radio antenna (Figure 8-20).

Another practical use of the ADF is establishing off-course checkpoints while on a VFR flight. If there is a low frequency station on either side of your course line, you can get an approximate position fix by noting when the ADF needle points directly off your wingtip toward the station (Figure 8-21). With a little imagination you can orient yourself in relation to a broadcast station or radio beacon using the ADF. As stated earlier, the head of the needle points to the station—so your position must be indicated by the tail of the needle. When you have the ADF receiver tuned to a station, note the position of the tail of the needle on the ADF indicator and mentally move it to the heading indicator; it will approximate your magnetic bearing from the station (Figure 8-21).

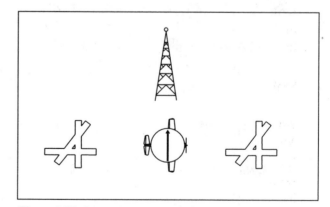

Figure 8-21. *Approximate position fix using ADF*

Figure 8-22. *Electronic RMI*

Radio Magnetic Indicator

Figure 8-22 shows a type of electronic **RMI** (Radio Magnetic Indicator) available in modern VOR receivers from many manufacturers. By selecting the frequency of the VOR station and TO or FROM, you get a direct digital readout of the radial on which you are located. This feature is also valuable in identifying radials which cross your course line and form intersections. Just watch the digital numbers click by until the desired radial shows up.

A radio magnetic indicator (RMI) combines an ADF needle, one or more VOR needles, and a compass card driven by the directional gyro or similar source of magnetic information. With an RMI, the needle selected (ADF or VOR) indicates the magnetic bearing to the station continuously, without pilot input. When reading an RMI, the arrow head represents the bearing TO the station, and the tail represents bearing FROM the station. You can use the RMI to determine your bearing from the transmitting station in the same way that you use the ADF's rotatable card, except that with an RMI the card is rotated for you by a gyro. Look at the four RMI indicators in Figure 8-23:

1. Indicator A shows that the airplane is 030° magnetic from the station, heading 330°. A left turn to 210° would take you to the station.

2. Indicator B shows the airplane crossing the 010° bearing from the station on a heading of 315°. To intercept the 180° bearing inbound to the station you would turn left to any heading between 191° and 269°.

3. Indicator C shows an airplane tracking to a station with a left crosswind from 245° The pilot has turned left (into the wind), and the needle has moved to the right of the nose.

Figure 8-23. *RMI indicators*

4. Indicator D shows an airplane tracking to a station with a right crosswind from 240°. The magnetic bearing to the station is 200°.

Area Navigation

Area navigation, or RNAV, provides a means of straightline navigation using VORTACs (or VOR-DMEs) without dog-legging from station to station. The equipment allows you to establish navigational fixes called "waypoints" along the straight line course which can be identified by the DME distance and VOR radial from the VORTAC. Steering to the waypoint is accomplished by the same left-right CDI needle used in VOR navigation, and distance to the waypoint is read out simultaneously. The RNAV equipment electronically "relocates" all of the enroute VORTACs so that they define the straight-line track. Several waypoints can be preset, and the pilot selects them in sequence as the flight progresses.

An example, using the Seattle sectional chart excerpt in the back of the book, would be an RNAV route between the Olympia airport (**F**) and Harvey Field (**G**), just east of Paine Field at the top of the chart.

The first en route waypoint would be the Seattle 273° radial at 7.3 nautical miles, and the second would be Harvey Field, using the Paine Field 064° radial at 7.8 nautical miles. These points define a straight line course between Olympia and Harvey Field. Using RNAV, you would have a continuous distance readout from Harvey Field. RNAV and Loran (below) give you the capability of accurately navigating to airports not served by any navigational aid.

Loran

The Loran system overcomes the major drawback of the VOR system (line-of-sight reception limitation) by using a frequency of 100 KHz, in the Very Low Frequency range. Radio waves in this range can be received 1,000 to 1,200 nautical miles from the transmitting station, and they are unaffected by terrain. Best (and most consistent) accuracy is achieved within 700 nautical miles of the transmitting stations and in a position equidistant from them.

A Loran chain consists of a master station and two or more secondary stations, all transmitting on 100 KHz—there is no need for the pilot to tune the Loran receiver. The receiver is able to distinguish between different chains because each chain has a specific "group repetition rate," the rate at which each station in the chain sends out pulsed transmissions, and it is by group repetition rate that the pilot selects the chain for the area of operation. For example, when the pilot selects group repetition rate 9940, the Loran receiver locks on to stations in Washington, California, and Nevada and provides navigational coverage along the entire West Coast.

Loran receivers are "user friendly" because no tuning is required and chain selection is virtually automatic.

In the airplane, the receiver determines the difference in time between the reception of the master's pulse and the pulse from each secondary station. These time differences are measured in tenths of millionths of a second. When lines of equal time difference between reception of the master pulse and that from each secondary station are plotted, they form curved lines called hyperbolas around the stations (Figure 8-25); Loran is called a hyperbolic means of navigation.

Each secondary station in a Loran chain waits until a pulse is received from the master station, adds a "coding delay," and then transmits a pulse of its own.

In Figure 8-26, the receiver in the airplane has received a pulse from the master station (M) and one secondary (X), and the receiver has determined that the airplane is located along a line of position between M and X.

Figure 8-27 shows the reception of the M signal and that from station Y, determining a line of position which crosses the M-X line and positively fixes the airplane's position. Most Loran receivers will use more than two secondaries for position fixing and, if one secondary signal is weak, will automatically reject it.

In the primary reception area, the signal has traveled directly from the transmitting antenna to the receiving antenna by what is called the ground wave. A portion of the transmitted signal travels upward and is reflected back to earth by the ionosphere; this "sky wave" arrives at the receiver at a later time than the ground wave, and this skywave contamination can affect accuracy at long distances. It is possible to enhance and make use of the skywave, however,

Figure 8-24. Loran

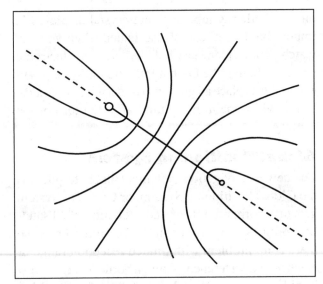

Figure 8-25. Hyperbolas around a station

and some manufacturers claim expanded range through its use.

The reception, calculation, and display of position information is continuous. How the position information is displayed and used varies between equipment manufacturers, but several features are commonly available, including:

Waypoint Designation: A pilot can designate a remote airport, a navigational aid, an airway intersec-tion, a favorite fishing hole, or any similar location as a "waypoint," and the Loran will indicate bearing and distance to the waypoint, the airplane's ground-speed, and the estimated time of arrival at the waypoint. All Loran equipment provides for waypoint designation using latitude and longitude, and other means such as radials from two VOR stations, or a VOR radial and DME distance are available from some manufacturers. A very useful feature is a "present position" input which allows a pilot to enter a position into the equipment s memory for future use—this might be the "best airport restaurant" waypoint.

Track: The Loran indicator will display the desired track over the ground, the actual track over the ground, and any off-track error in both miles and degrees (Figure 8-24).

Parallel Offset: If there is a thunderstorm or Class B airspace on the direct track to your destination, the Loran provides for offsetting your flight path several miles parallel to the direct track so that you can avoid the storm or Class B airspace while still receiving accurate course guidance.

Lat-Long: The airplane's position in latitude and longitude can be displayed to an accuracy of tenths of minutes (a tenth of a minute of latitude is 600 feet).

Figure 8-26. Pulses from stations M and X

Figure 8-27. Reception of M and Y signals

The accuracy of Loran position-fixing is affected by station geometry; that is, the angle formed by lines drawn between the master station and each secondary. Loran is most inaccurate "behind" a transmitting station, along the baseline extension. Almost all Loran equipment warns the pilot if accuracy is being affected by inadequate signal strength or poor station geometry.

Almost all manufacturers include a database as either standard equipment or as an option. A database contains pre-programmed waypoints which you can call up by scrolling through a list of identifiers. A small database may contain only(!) all of the VORs in the continental U.S., while a large database may contain (in addition to all of the VORs in North America), non directional beacons, airports with runways longer than 2,500 feet long, etc. You may be able to call an airport up on the Loran screen by using its 3-letter identifier (shown on Sectional and Terminal Control Area Charts) and have all of the appropriate radio frequencies displayed as well as the grades of fuel available and the names of some nearby motels. Many database-equipped sets have the ability to display the course and distance to the closest airport or even the closest six airports in an emergency. Databases can become outdated by changes in radio frequencies or airport data, so each manufacturer provides a method for the user to update the database.

A feature available in some newer Lorans is a warning when you are approaching special use airspace such as Class B or Class C airspace. Some sets have a vertical navigation feature, allowing you to intercept and follow a specific glide path from cruise altitude down to the pattern. And some Lorans can be interfaced with electronic wizardry to read out, among other things, how much fuel you will burn between your present position and your destination, how much you have on board, and whether you have enough fuel to make it! Wonderful stuff.

Another Loran-related aid to navigation is the "moving map" display. This can be a part of your Loran receiver-indicator or a separate installation (some are even portable and can be hand-held or mounted between the seats). With a moving map display, your Loran-determined position is shown in relation to airports, navigational aids, and special use airspace

on a cathode ray tube or liquid crystal display. It's impossible to get lost or disoriented when you can watch your airplane symbol "fly" over an electronic chart. Although the Global Positioning System will eventually replace all ground-based navigational aids, Loran will remain in use until after the turn of the century.

Global Positioning System

The newest navigation system available to pilots is the Global Positioning System, or GPS. The system gets its information from a constellation of 24 satellites orbiting the earth about 11,000 miles away, so there is no problem with limited reception range or electronic interference. Your airborne receiver must be able to "see" at least three satellites for a position fix and needs at least one more satellite to add altitude information.

Where Loran measures time difference, GPS measures distance. Yes, it measures the distance from your airplane to satellites thousands of miles away and uses this information to develop position and altitude information. The magic of microchips massages the data and comes up with groundspeed, track over the ground, bearing and distance to a waypoint, etc., just as Loran does. Several manufacturers cover their bets by providing both GPS and Loran in one box, with the best position for either source displayed.

As of mid-1995, the GPS system is being operated by the Department of Defense, which developed it and used it to great effect during the Gulf War. Although the FAA has no control over or input into the operations of the system at present, it is moving rapidly toward its acceptance for air navigation on a stand-alone basis. The Air Force can turn satellites on and off or take them out of service without notifying the FAA—this is unacceptable for navigation, but it is undergoing interagency review.

Also, the Air Force can degrade the precision of the GPS system through the use of Selective Availability (SA). With SA on, position accuracy is 300 meters; with SA off, you can establish your position within 100 meters. This is far more accurate than Loran position fixing. Again, the civil aviation industry has no control over when SA is used.

Differential GPS (DGPS) uses equipment in a known position on the ground to receive signals from the satellites, determine any position error by comparing where the satellites say it is to where it knows it is, and transmit corrections to airplanes (or boats) that increase fix accuracy to ten meters or less.

Although DGPS will be needed for instrument pilots to make precise approaches to airports, its range is limited and a DGPS installation will serve only one airport. A broader area will be served by the Wide Area Augmentation System, which will use a satellite in low orbit to transmit correction information to an area as large as several states. Testing of WAAS is now in progress using existing communications satellites.

A major problem with GPS is integrity—the ability of the system to warn its users that its positional information may be faulty. VORs have OFF flags, ADF needles freeze in position, Loran signals blink, but with GPS information coming from several of 24 satellites it is difficult to provide a warning of inaccuracy.

GPS equipment approved under TSO C129 has circuitry called Receiver Autonomous Integrity Monitoring (RAIM) that compares the position fixes provided by several satellites and throws out the data for any position that is not in agreement with the others. Your handheld GPS will not have this feature; in fact, pilots who buy panel-mounted TSO C129 equipment in 1995 are paying in excess of $5,000 for the privilege (including all peripherals and installation).

Even at the low-cost end of the scale (under $1,000 in 1995) it is possible to have a handheld GPS with an integral moving map and a database that includes all of the navaids in the United States together with airport information such as elevation, runway length, tower/ground frequency, and fuel availability. As the cost of microprocessors goes down you will get more bang for your buck.

You can get into trouble with some low-cost GPS units (and some Lorans) because the equipment will tell you the course to steer from your present position to your destination without regard for any intervening mountains or Special Use Airspace. As you go up in price, terrain and SUA warnings are included. Your best bet is to have a sectional on your lap so that you can follow your progress both with the electronic equipment and with your finger on the chart—that way you won't blow into Class B airspace or hit a mountain without warning.

Summary

To use VOR intelligently you have to understand how it works, with radials, needles, and TO-FROM flags. To use Automatic Direction Finder equipment intelligently you have to understand its limitations—atmospheric interference, short useful range, diurnal and shore effects—and you get involved with relative versus magnetic bearings which brings the magnetic compass into the picture. To use Loran intelligently you have to consider station geometry, skywave contamination, and area of useful signals. To use GPS all you do is turn it on and you are instantly flooded with a torrent of information and you don't have to understand how the system works in order to use the information.

Loran and GPS share one problem: Each manufacturer has its own way of doing things, and there is little relation between them. Some manufacturers that offer several models of Loran or GPS change the mode of operation from one model to another. Cost determines the number of features you will have available at the touch of a key or the turn of a knob. The variance is such that it would be impossible for a book such as this to attempt to teach you how to use either Loran or GPS.

1. Which pilot action is most likely to eliminate large fluctuations on the VOR course deviation indicator during flight?

   A—Recycle the ON-OFF switch.
   B—Disconnect the microphone.
   C—Change the engine RPM.

2. How can a pilot determine when a particular VOR is unreliable?

   A—A recorded voice stating "VOR shutdown for maintenance."
   B—A continuous series of dashes replacing the coded identification.
   C—An absence of the coded identification or T.E.S.T in Morse Code.

3. You want to track inbound on the 050° radial of a VOR station. The recommended procedure is to set the course selector to

   A—050° and make heading corrections toward the Course Deviation Indicator (CDI needle).
   B—050° and make heading corrections away from the Course Deviation Indicator (CDI needle).
   C—230° and make heading corrections toward the Course Deviation Indicator (CDI needle).

4. Your magnetic heading is 300° and the ADF needle is pointing to a station bearing 085° relative to the nose of the airplane. The magnetic bearing to the station is

   A—385°.
   B—025°.
   C—215°.

5. After selecting the frequency of a VOR station, you rotate the omni-bearing selector (OBS) until the needle centers. The OBS reads 120° and the TO-FROM indicator shows TO. The airplane heading is 270°).

   A—You are southeast of the station.
   B—You are northwest of the station.
   C—You are west of the station.

Refer to the full-color Seattle sectional chart excerpt at the back of the book for questions 6, 7, and 8.

6. You are flying from Seattle to Wenatchee on the V-120 airway, with your VOR receiver tuned to 116.8 MHz and the omnibearing selector on 069°. Directly over the north end of Kachess Lake you notice that the course deviation indicator needle is

   A—deflected to the right of center. You should change heading to the left to center the needle.
   B—deflected to the left of center. You should change heading to the left to center the needle.
   C—not centered. You should rotate the omnibearing selector until the TO-FROM indicator changes to TO and the needle centers.

7. Approaching Wenatchee you decide to use your Automatic Direction Finder as a backup means of radio navigation. You should

   A—tune the receiver to 1041 KHz.
   B—tune the receiver to 111.0 MHz.
   C—tune the receiver to 560 KHz.

8. You are over the city of Wenatchee (**H**) and the airport is straight ahead. The needle on your ADF indicator (tuned in accordance with question 7) is pointing

A—090° relative.
B—180° relative.
C—240° relative.

9. You have become disoriented and want to use your VOR to establish your general position. You tune and identify a VOR station and rotate the OBS until the needle centers with a TO indication. The OBS reads 285°.

A—You are northwest of the VOR and should turn to a heading of approximately 285° to fly to the station.
B—You are southeast of the VOR and should turn to a heading of approximately 285° to fly to the station.
C—You are southeast of the VOR and should turn to a heading of approximately 105° to fly to the station.

10. Distance Measuring Equipment (DME) is least accurate

A—at low altitude, far from the station.
B—at high altitude, close to the station.
C—when heading directly toward the station.

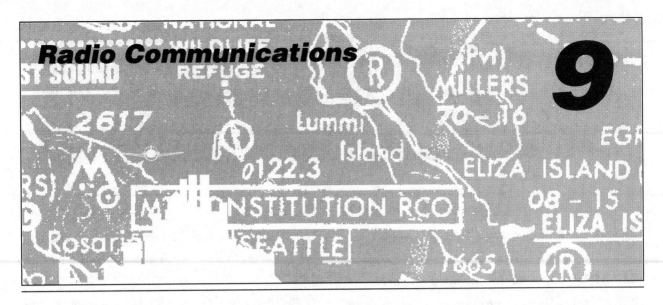

Radio Communications

9

When you listen to an AM radio at night, and tune down toward the lower end of the dial, you can pick up stations hundreds and even thousands of miles away. Low frequencies can be received at long distances even in the daytime, because they are not weakened or attenuated as they travel through the air and over the ground as much as higher frequencies are; however, atmospheric interference, or static, is a problem with low frequency transmissions. To avoid having critical aeronautical communications affected by static, frequencies in the Very High Frequency (VHF) range are used in aircraft radios. Radio transmissions in the VHF band are limited to line-of-sight (Figure 9-1) and that makes altitude an important factor—as you gain altitude the range of VHF is greatly increased.

Figure 9-1. *Line-of-sight limitations*

The FAA has assigned those frequencies between 118.0 MHz (Megahertz—millions of cycles per second) and 136.975 MHz for radio communication.

The table below shows how they are allocated. Most modern aircraft radios are capable of transmitting and receiving on at least 720 frequencies, or channels.

The FAA spaces assignments 25 KHz (thousands of cycles per second) apart (126.225, 126.275). If you are assigned a frequency which your radio cannot tune, just ask for an alternate frequency.

This is an all-inclusive list of frequency assignments, emphasizing those that you will probably be using most.

Voice Communication Frequencies

118.0 to 121.4 MHz - Air Traffic Control

121.5 MHz - Emergency Frequency, ELT signals

121.6 to 121.9 MHz - Airport Ground Control

121.95 MHz - Flight Schools

121.975 MHz - Private Aircraft Advisory (FSS)

122.0 MHz - FSS Enroute Flight Advisory Service ("Flight Watch")

122.025 to 122.075 MHz - FSS

122.1 MHz - FSS receive only

122.125 to 122.175 MHz - FSS

Continued

Figure 9-2. Typical VHF communications transceiver

122.2 MHz - FSS Common Enroute Simplex

122.225 to 122.675 MHz - FSS

122.7 MHz - Unicom, uncontrolled airports

122.725 MHz - Unicom, private airports not open to public

122.75 MHz - Unicom, air-to-air, private airports not open to public

122.775 MHz - Future Unicom or Multicom

122.8 MHz - Unicom, uncontrolled airports

122.825 MHz - Future Unicom or Multicom

122.85 MHz - Multicom

122.875 MHz - Future Unicom or Multicom

122.9 MHz - Multicom, airports with no tower, FSS or Unicom

122.925 MHz - Multicom, Natural Resources

122.95 MHz - Unicom, controlled airports

122.975 MHz - Unicom, high altitude

123.0 MHz - Unicom, uncontrolled airports

123.025 MHz - Future Unicom or Multicom

123.05 and 123.075 MHz - Unicom, heliports

123.1 MHz - Search and Rescue, temporary control towers

123.15 to 123.575 MHz - Flight Test

123.6 to 123.65 MHz - FSS or Air Traffic Control

123.675 to 128.8 MHz - Air Traffic Control

128.825 to 132.0 MHz - Aeronautical Enroute (ARINC)

132.05 to 136.975 MHz - Air Traffic Control

Figure 9-2 shows a typical modern aircraft radio with digital display of an active and a standby frequency, a popular feature in today's communication radios.

When you select the proper communication frequency, you will transmit and receive on that frequency. Modern radios have crystal-controlled frequency selection and require no tuning. While you have the push-to-talk switch on your microphone depressed, your receiver is blocked and you cannot hear any other transmissions—each party to the communication must finish transmitting before a reply can be received. This is called **simplexing**, and most of your radio communication will be simplex. Talking on one frequency and listening on another, as you do on the telephone, is called duplexing, a system that is rapidly being phased out by the FAA. It is still used in a few scattered locations to communicate with Flight Service Stations (FSS). In Figure 9-3, the St. Petersburg FSS receives on 122.1 MHz and transmits over the Lakeland VORTAC on 116.0 MHz.

Figure 9-3. Duplex communications

The table above gave general frequency assignments, but you need to know how to contact a specific tower, UNICOM, or Flight Service Station. The **Airport/Facility Directory (A/FD)** lists all of the radio frequencies available at any airport and also includes a listing of all Air Route Traffic Control Center frequencies—you will be using them for enroute radar services. A ready reference for most frequencies is your sectional aeronautical chart. Refer to the Seattle sectional chart and the sectional chart legend. Airports with control towers have a blue airport symbol, and very close to the symbol you will find a data block with "CT" such as that adjacent to the Seattle-Tacoma Airport where "CT 119.9" is the control tower frequency. If there is an asterisk (*) following the frequency, the tower does not operate continuously. If the chart says NFCT adjacent to the airport symbol it is a non-Federal control tower, operated by a private entity.

The letters **ATIS** mean Automatic Terminal Information Service, and when you listen to the ATIS frequency listed in the airport data block you receive a continuous taped broadcast of non-control information such as ceiling and visibility, altimeter setting, wind, runway in use, etc. If the ceiling is above 5,000 feet and the visibility is greater than 5 miles, that information might not be mentioned in the broadcast. Each time the ATIS is revised the phonetic designator is changed, and you should include in your initial call the fact that you have listened to the ATIS: "Portland Ground Control, Cessna 1234X on the ramp with information ALFA, taxi to 10R." The UNICOM (privately operated Aeronautical Advisory Service) frequency is listed at the end of the data block. Sectional charts also include a tabulation of all control tower and ATIS frequencies in the margin (Figure 9-4).

Figure 9-5 shows how Flight Service Station frequencies are presented. Note that some frequencies are not listed directly: the heavy line box means that 121.5 and 122.2 are available (but not shown).

CONTROL TOWER FREQUENCIES
ON SEATTLE SECTIONAL CHART

Airports which have control towers are indicated on this chart by the letters CT followed by the primary VHF local control frequency. Selected transmitting frequencies for each control tower are tabulated in the adjoining spaces, the low or medium transmitting frequency is listed first followed by a VHF local control frequency and the primary VHF and UHF military frequencies, when these frequencies are available. An asterisk (*) follows the part time tower frequency remoted to the collocated full time FSS for use as Airport Advisory Service (AAS) during hours tower is closed. Receiving frequencies are shown thus: 122.5R. Hours shown are local time.

Automatic Terminal Information Service (ATIS) frequencies, shown on the face of the chart are normal arriving frequencies, all ATIS frequencies available are tabulated below. ARS and/or PAR indicates Radar Instrument Approach available.

GRANT CO	Opr 0700-2300	118.1 124.2 247.8
GRAY AAF	126.2 248.2 ASR/PAR	
LEWISTON-NEZ PERCE CO	Opr 0500-2200	119.4 318.8
(Lewiston Twr)		
McCHORD AFB	ATIS 109.6 270.1	124.8 259.3 ASR/PAR
McNARY (Salem Twr)	Opr 0700-2300	119.1 257.2
OLYMPIA	Opr 0800-2000	124.4 233.2
PENDLETON	Opr 0600-2200	118.7 257.8
PORTLAND HILLSBORO	Opr 0700-2300	119.3* 239.3
(Hillsboro Twr)		
PORTLAND INTL	ATIS 126.9 354.0	118.7 247.8 ASR

Figure 9-4. *Tower and ATIS frequencies*

Figure 9-5. *Communications boxes*

All other frequencies are listed above the box. If a frequency which is normally standard such as 121.5 or 122.2 is not available, it will be listed above the box with a strike-through: ~~122.2~~.

When you call a Flight Service Station, you must advise them which remote communications outlet you are listening to: "Preston Radio, Ercoupe 345X, over Bisbee, listening 122.4." A thin blue line box indicates that the Flight Service Station has only those frequencies that are printed outside the box. Where an FSS has a remote control capability, you will see a box with RCO (Remote Communication Outlet), or LRCO (Limited RCO) or a navaid frequency box with the name of the controlling FSS beneath the box (Figure 9-6). Look northwest of the Seattle-Tacoma Airport for an RCO box. Each regional Airport/Facility Directory includes a complete listing of Flight Service Station remote outlets. When you use a remote outlet, be sure to include a statement of your position in your first transmission; the person on the other end is monitoring several speakers from remote outlets and needs to know where you are in order to select the correct transmitter to reply on.

Radio Procedures

The Airman's Information Manual (AIM) section on correct phraseology, the phonetic alphabet, and pronunciation of numbers is included as an appendix to this book. The appendix also contains the Pilot/Controller Glossary from the AIM which explains terms used in communication with air traffic controllers. You should become familiar with the contents of both. You will learn a lot just by listening on aircraft frequencies to hear how other pilots communicate with each other and with ground personnel. A visit to a Flight Service Station, control tower, or a radar facility will convince you that everyone on the ground is prepared to help you have a safe flight and that having "mike fright" will just keep you from taking advantage of the many services available.

Figure 9-6. RCO

Always listen before transmitting, so that you do not interfere with a communication in progress, and listen to what is being said—in many cases you may hear information that makes your call unnecessary. If your airplane's radio installation provides a switch so that you can transmit on either radio, be sure that you are using the correct radio before you transmit—this is a common mistake and you will hear it happen to the most grizzled old airline captains. Always begin your transmission with the name of the station that you are calling: "Logan Tower," "Orlando Ground," "Dallas Radio," "Podunk UNICOM," followed by your own identification (in full, if it is the initial contact): "Twin Cessna 2345X."

It is not necessary to wait for an acknowledgment that communication has been established if you are reasonably certain that your transmission has been received: "Seattle Tower, Piper 2345X 6 miles north with BRAVO, landing". Be as brief as practicable without omitting necessary information and always give your position when requesting a clearance from Air Traffic Control. Remember this sequence: WHO you are calling, WHO you are, WHERE you are, and WHAT your intentions are.

An airplane cockpit is a noisy place, and your microphone is designed to filter out engine noise if you use it properly. Hold the microphone close to your lips and speak directly into it. Holding the microphone away from your lips will allow engine noise to mask your transmission.

Radio Use at Non-Tower Airports

Unless an airport has an operating control tower, you do not even need to have a radio to use that airport. For safety's sake, however, you should have a radio—but do not expect all other airplanes in the area to have radios. Many airports have no radio facility. When operating in the vicinity of a non-radio airport use the Common Traffic Advisory Frequency (**CTAF**, shown as **ⓒ** on sectional charts) listed in the Airport/Facility Directory. In most cases this will be the multicom frequency 122.9 MHz, because you will be broadcasting your position and intentions in the blind (no specific addressee): "Podunk Traffic, Mooney 2345X 10 miles north landing." Don't use 122.9 MHz as an airborne "party line" to talk to your friends in flight—122.75 MHz may be used for that purpose.

At most airports with a UNICOM (Aeronautical Advisory Service), the UNICOM frequency will be the CTAF. Don't be surprised if you attempt to call UNICOM and get no reply—this is a non-governmental service provided by the local operator, and those busy people may not hear your call. UNICOM frequencies are shared by many uncontrolled airports, and some may be so close together that pilots at different airports will interfere with one another. To avoid confusion, always begin your transmission with the name of the airport at which you are operating: "Podunk traffic, Grumman 2345X left downwind runway 16, touch and go." UNICOM is used for many purposes and is quite informal, but you should not let this informality change your normal good communication habits. Be sure to use both your eyes and your radio at airports where you must taxi on the active runway to get into takeoff position or taxi back to an exit after landing.

Some uncontrolled airports have Flight Service Stations on the field, and 123.6 MHz (or the CTAF) should be used for airport advisory service. Call the FSS for the active runway when departing, and be sure to call about 15 miles out when arriving to get the local weather, runway in use, and any reported traffic in the pattern. Use other FSS frequencies for in-flight filing of flight plans and requests for other services. Where Enroute Flight Advisory Service (Flight Watch) is available on 122.0 MHz (0600 to 2200 local time), use that frequency to request weather reports and forecasts (122.0 MHz is used *only* for weather information).

Communication at Airports with Operating Towers

Airspace around an airport with an operating control tower is Class D airspace; it will usually extend vertically to 2,500 feet above airport elevation and horizontally a nominal 4.4 nautical miles (the boundaries may vary, but will be charted). If you need to enter Class D airspace, you must first communicate with the tower. If you are departing, you must first receive taxi instructions from the ground controller, who directs all activity on the ramps and taxiways. With few exceptions, ground control operates on 121.6, 121.7, 121.8, or 121.9 MHz. Controllers will frequently shorten this by eliminating the 121: "Contact ground point seven leaving the runway." The ground controller will give you clearance to the active runway, and that clearance authorizes you to use all taxiways and cross all runways enroute to the runup area. Figure 9-7 illustrates a situation where an airplane cleared from the ramp to runway 9 would be cleared to taxi across the approach end of runway 36L and 36R enroute. If you are in any doubt about taxiing across a runway, stop and clarify the situation with the controller.

Figure 9-7. *Taxiing to the active runway*

Figure 9-8. *Typical transponder*

If you are at a strange airport, ask for progressive taxi instructions and the controller will guide you.

When you are ready for takeoff, contact the tower controller for takeoff clearance. The tower (or "local") controller is responsible for all aircraft in the Class D airspace and on the active runway—don't taxi onto the runway without a clearance. You must maintain communication with the tower controllers while within their airspace (the Class D airspace). When you have departed the Class D airspace you are on your own (or you may request radar services). You do not have to ask the tower for permission to change frequencies after you have crossed the Class D airspace boundary.

On arrival, before you enter the Class D airspace you should listen to the ATIS (if there is one) and advise the tower controller on initial contact that you have the ATIS information. Where there is no ATIS, listen on the tower frequency and note the instructions given to other pilots. Once you are sure of the runway in use, wind, and altimeter setting you can say: "Miami Tower, Baron 2345X 10 miles west with the numbers." After landing, do not change to ground control until advised to do so by the tower. Some tower-controlled airports have UNICOM, but because you will be getting all of your weather information and clearances from the tower, your use of UNICOM at that tower-controlled airport will be limited to such things as calling for fuel, ordering rental cars, etc.

Transponder

Although the **transponder** has no microphone or speaker, it is a means of communication with ground radar facilities. Interrogation signals transmitted from the ground are received by your transponder, (Figure 9-8), and it replies with a coded signal which the controller can read on the radar scope. Each time the transponder reply light flickers, it has responded to an interrogation. In congested areas the transponder will be replying to interrogation from several radars, while in remote areas it may receive only an occasional interrogation. Always set the four numbers on your transponder to 1200 when flying VFR. Otherwise, enter a specific code as directed by a radar controller while receiving radar services. *The FARs require that all transponder equipped airplanes have them turned on while in flight.* Be careful when setting your transponder—some codes have special meanings. Code 7700, for instance, is the emergency transponder code, used only to alert ground personnel that you are in distress. Code 7500 is the hijacking code, and code 7600 is used by instrument pilots in case of communications failure. Code 7777 belongs to the military. If a controller asks you to change codes, always acknowledge by reading the new code back to the controller.

Push your transponder's IDENT button only when told to do so by the controller. This feature causes your radar return to intensify on the controller's scope for exact identification, and when pushed it will stay activated for about 20 seconds. IDENTing when not directed to do so might result in a misidentification by the controller. When the transponder function switch is ON, you are in Mode A (indicating your position) only, and with the function switch in the ALT (Mode C) position, the transponder will also transmit altitude information to the ground (if an encoding altimeter is installed in the airplane).

A transponder with Mode C capability is required for operation in Class B or C airspace or when flying in controlled airspace above 10,000 feet. You can request a waiver of these requirements if you give ATC one hour's notice. Additionally Mode C is required if you fly within 30 nautical miles of the Class B airspace's primary airport and from the surface to 10,000 feet MSL.

Almost all radar facilities require a transponder return for tracking. At those facilities with the most modern equipment, the controller does not see an actual target generated by your airplane but a computer generated target based on your transponder. That is the reason why you will occasionally see airplanes visually which have not been called to your attention by the controller—if they don't have a transponder (or if their transponder is off)—they don't show up on the radar.

Radar Services for VFR Pilots

There are two types of radar service available to you as a VFR pilot: radar traffic advisory service (**flight following**) and terminal radar service. Terminal Radar Service, presently provided as Basic Service, includes safety alerts, traffic advisories, limited vectoring, and sequencing when available.

Limited vectoring is an excellent way to fly more safely through a congested terminal area or to get to a strange airport. The radar controller will do everything possible for you, but keeping on the right side of the Federal Aviation Regulations is your responsibility. A heading which would take you into cloud or provide anything less than the required separation from clouds must be refused, and the controller advised of the reason. "Tomahawk 45X won't be able to maintain VFR on that heading." You are also required to see and avoid other aircraft. The radar is only an aid. The controller will give you traffic information using the clock in relation to your direction of movement. Each number on the clock represents 30°, and in no-wind conditions traffic at 2 o'clock would be 60° to the right of the nose. If you have established a 30° correction into a wind from the left, traffic reported at 2 o'clock would be directly off your right wing (Figure 9-9).

Figure 9-9. Traffic information using clock positions

TRSA service is provided in Terminal Radar Service Areas (**TRSA**s), which are outlined in black on your sectional chart (with their vertical limits), and identified in the Airport/Facility Directory. Participation is voluntary, but recommended. This service is *not* limited to "workload permitting", but is available at all times. You will be separated from all IFR and all participating VFR traffic, but you must remember that not all VFR pilots participate by requesting radar service and you may see airplanes that the radar controller has not called out to you as traffic. Generally, radar only sees those airplanes with transponders, although the capability to pick up targets by radar reflection alone can be selected. Again, the responsibility to remain clear of traffic and in VFR conditions rests with you.

You will find the frequencies for terminal radar service in the A/FD, listed under the airport served by the radar facility. In some cases the ATIS advises VFR pilots to contact Approach Control and gives the frequency. This is also true upon departure from an airport with terminal radar service—the ATIS may tell you to call on a certain frequency for a clearance before calling the ground controller for taxi instructions. In a TRSA, if you do not desire radar services you need only advise the controller

"Negative TRSA service," and you will be on your own—then you will be one of those non-participating aircraft that everyone else is looking out for.

Radar Traffic Advisory Service provides only traffic advice, and that is what you will get if you "request radar flight following." If you are being provided with radar service after departure, the radar controller will "hand you off" to the next controller (with a frequency change), and that controller will in turn pass you along. If you are enroute and want radar service, call the nearest FSS. They will give you the correct frequency for your present location. Radar controllers will always tell you when radar service is terminated instead of just "dropping" you. You should return the favor by always advising the radar controller when you no longer desire radar service—don't just change frequencies.

Class C airspace (Pages 10-11 and 14-9) is replacing most Terminal Radar Service Areas; where TSRAs still exist, they are shown on charts with a solid black outline. At this writing there are very few in the country.

VHF/DF (Direction Finding)

VHF/DF is used to aid lost or disoriented pilots. However, this subject is discussed under Radio Communications because all you need to get VHF Direction Finder service is a transmitter and a receiver. Many Flight Service Stations (listed in the A/FD) can take bearings on your radio transmissions, and after a series of bearings, give you headings to steer to a nearby airport. This is not nearly as quick or as accurate as radar, but if you are lost and have no transponder it is an excellent service. FSS specialists like to practice VHF/DF steers (in fact, each specialist must give a minimum number of "steers" to remain qualified), so don't hesitate to ask for one on some nice VFR day when you are not lost or disoriented.

Emergency Communications

The International Calling and Distress frequency for VHF is 121.5 MHz. *Memorize this frequency.* If you are not already in communication with some FAA facility and you become lost, disoriented or have any kind of emergency, do not hesitate to tune to 121.5

and call "MAYDAY, MAYDAY, MAYDAY STINSON 2345X calling any station!" You will get many answers—respond to the loudest one. Do not be reluctant to call for help for fear of embarrassment—the longer you delay in confessing your predicament, the less fuel you will have to carry out the instructions of an assisting agency. In an emergency, you should also set your transponder to 7700—this sets off bells and buzzers at radar facilities and will help the controllers pinpoint your position even if you are too busy with the situation at hand to call anyone on the radio.

Ground Controlled Approaches

If there is a military or a joint-use civil-military airport in your area, ask your instructor to take you there for a practice ground controlled approach. This is a procedure to be used only in an emergency when unforecast weather traps you on top of clouds (after you are licensed, of course—as a student you must maintain visual contact with the ground). All you have to do during a GCA is follow instructions from the controller.

Emergency Locator Transmitter

With very limited exceptions, every airplane must carry an emergency locator transmitter (**ELT**) which automatically transmits when it is turned on by a pilot in distress or by impact forces. ELTs transmit on both the VHF and UHF distress frequencies: 121.5 MHz and 243.0 MHz (used by the military). To be sure that your ELT will operate in an emergency, you are allowed to turn it on *briefly* during the first five minutes of each hour (while monitoring 121.5 on your communications receiver). Because ELTs have been activated by hard landings, many pilots monitor 121.5 MHz briefly before shutting down their engines, just to be sure that no signal is being transmitted. False ELT signals must be tracked down by search and rescue forces and verified as being false; so pilots must take every precaution against error. The battery in your ELT must be replaced when one-half of its useful life has expired (or if your brief tests have accumulated one hour of transmitting time), and the service technician will mark that date on the side of the transmitter case.

Radio Communication Phraseology and Technique

Always use the phonetic alphabet when identifying your aircraft and to spell out groups of letter or unusual words under difficult communications conditions. Do not make up your own phonetic equivalents; this alphabet was developed internationally to be understandable by non-English speaking pilots and ground personnel.

Phonetic Alphabet

A .... ALFA (ALFAH)
B .... BRAVO (BRAHVOH)
C .... CHARLIE (CHAR-LEE OR SHAR-LEE)
D .... DELTA (DELL-TA)
E .... ECHO (ECK-OH)
F ....FOXTROT (FOKS-TROT)
G ....GOLF (GOLF)
H .... HOTEL (HOH-TEL)
I .... INDIA (IN-DEE-AH)
J ....JULIETT (JOO-LEE-ETT)
K .... KILO (KEY-LOH)
L .... LIMA (LEE-MAH)
M .... MIKE (MIKE)
N ....NOVEMBER (NO-VEM-BER)
O .... OSCAR (OSS-CAH)
P................................... PAPA (PAH-PAH)
Q .... QUEBEC (KEH-BECK)
R .... ROMEO (ROW-ME-OH)
S .... SIERRA (SEE-AIR-AH)
T .... TANGO (TANG-GO)
U .... UNIFORM (YOU-NEE-FORM)
V ....VICTOR (VIK-TAH)
W .... WHISKEY (WISS-KEY)
X ....XRAY (ECKS-RAY)
Y .... YANKEE (YANG-KEY)
Z .... ZULU (ZOO-LOO)

1 .... ONE (WUN)
2 .... TWO (TOO)
3 .... THREE (TREE)
4 .... FOUR (FOW-ER)
5 .... FIVE (FIFE)
6 .... SIX (SIX)
7 .... SEVEN (SEVEN)
8 ....EIGHT (AIT)
9 .... NINE (NIN-ER)
0 .... ZERO (ZEE-RO)

Figures

Misunderstandings about altitude assignments can be hazardous. The examples below are taken from the Airman's Information Manual and demonstrate officially accepted techniques. However, as you monitor aviation frequencies you will hear pilots use a decimal system: TWO POINT FIVE for 2,500. The FAA has never commented on this practice and it is commonly accepted—don't try it in another country.

500 ....FIVE HUNDRED
10,000 .... TEN THOUSAND
13,500 .... ONE THREE THOUSAND FIVE HUNDRED

Pilots flying above 18,000 feet use flight levels when referring to altitude:

"CENTURION 45X LEAVING ONE SEVEN THOUSAND FOR FLIGHT LEVEL TWO THREE ZERO."

Bearings, courses, and radials are always spoken in three digits:

"CESSNA 38N TURN LEFT HEADING THREE ZERO ZERO, INTERCEPT THE DALLAS ZERO ONE FIVE RADIAL."

Address ground controllers as SEATTLE GROUND CONTROL, control towers as O'HARE TOWER, radar facilities as MIAMI APPROACH, MEMPHIS DEPARTURE, or ATLANTA CENTER. When calling a Flight Service Station, use RADIO: "PORTLAND RADIO, MOONEY FOUR VICTOR WHISKEY."

When making the initial contact with a controller, use your full callsign, without the initial NOVEMBER: "BOISE GROUND, PIPER THREE SIX NINE ECHO ROMEO AT THE RAMP WITH INFORMATION GOLF, TAXI FOR TAKEOFF."

Use of the last three digits is acceptable for subsequent transmissions: "ROGER, TAXI TWO EIGHT RIGHT, NINE ECHO ROMEO."

Many uncontrolled airports share Unicom frequencies, and if you do not identify the airport at which you are operating, your transmissions may serve to confuse other pilots monitoring the frequency. Don't say, "STINSON FOUR SIX WHISKEY DOWNWIND FOR RUNWAY SIX," say "ARLINGTON TRAFFIC, STINSON FOUR SIX WHISKEY DOWNWIND FOR RUNWAY SIX, ARLINGTON." That way, pilots at other airports sharing Arlington's Unicom frequency will not be nervously looking over their shoulders.

Chapter 9
Radio Communications Review Questions

Refer to the full-color Seattle sectional chart excerpt in the back of this book.

1. What UNICOM frequency, if any is indicated for Seattle-Tacoma International Airport?

   A—None is listed.
   B—119-9 MHz.
   C—122.95 MHz.

2. Approaching the Wenatchee Airport (east edge of chart excerpt), which frequency would you use to obtain an airport advisory of traffic in the pattern and runway in use?

   A—122.3 MHz.
   B—111.0 MHz.
   C—123.0 MHz.

3. What is the procedure for an approach and landing at the Auburn Municipal Airport just south-east of Seattle-Tacoma Airport?

   A—Obtain a clearance from Seattle-Tacoma tower on 119.9 MHz 10 miles from Auburn.
   B—Remain below 3,000' MSL and receive an airport advisory on 122.8 MHz.
   C—Request a clearance from Seattle Approach Control on 122.0 MHz.

4. Operational tests of the ELT (emergency locator transmitter) should be made only

   A—during the first 5 minutes of an hour.
   B—after one-half the shelf life of the battery.
   C—upon replacing the battery.

5. When are non-rechargeable batteries of an ELT to be replaced?

   A—Every 24 months.
   B—When 50 percent of their useful life expires or they were in use for a cumulative period of one hour.
   C—At the time of each 100-hour or annual inspection.

6. To use VHF/DF facilities for assistance in locating and aircraft's position, the aircraft must have

   A—a VHF transmitter and receiver.
   B—an IFF transponder.
   C—an ELT.

7. When making routine transponder code changes, pilots should avoid inadvertent selection of which codes?

   A—3100, 7600, 7700.
   B—7500, 7600, 7700.
   C—7000, 7600, 7700.

8. When landing at an airport that does not have a tower, FSS, or UNICOM, broadcast your intentions in the blind on

   A—123.0 MHz.
   B—123.6 MHz.
   C—The Common Traffic Advisory Frequency.

9. Below FL180, updated enroute weather advisories should be obtained from Flight Watch on

A—122.1 MHz.
B—122.0 MHz.
C—122.4 MHz.

10. ATIS is the continuous broadcast of recorded information

A—concerning nonessential information to relieve frequency congestion.
B—concerning noncontrol information in selected high-activity terminal areas.
C—concerning sky conditions limited to ceilings below 1,000 ft. and visibility's less than 3 mi.

11. The correct method for stating 4,500 ft. MSL to ATC is

A—"FORTY-FIVE HUNDRED FEET"
B—"FOUR POINT FIVE"
C—"FOUR THOUSAND FIVE HUNDRED"

12. When flying HAWK N666CB, the proper phraseology for initial contact with McAlester FSS is

A—"McALESTER RADIO, HAWK SIX SIX SIX CHARLIE BRAVO"
B—"McALESTER STATION, HAWK SIX SIX SIX CEEBEE"
C—"McALESTER RADIO, HAWK TRIPLE SIX CHARLIE BRAVO"

13. What frequency can be used to chat with a pilot in another airplane?

A—The Common Traffic Advisory Frequency.
B—122.75 MHz.
C—122.9 MHz.

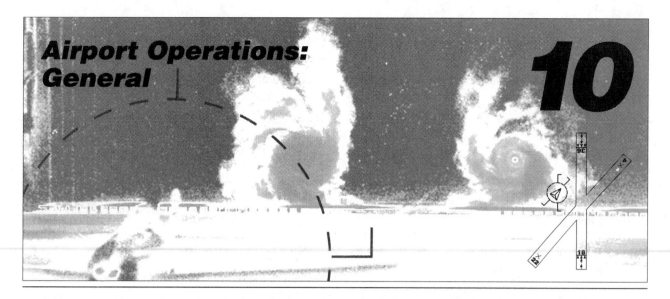

Airport Operations: General

10

At any airport, you will have to be able to identify the runway in use, taxi safely, be aware of wake turbulence hazards, deal with the line crew, know who (if anyone) controls your actions, interpret lights and markings, etc. This chapter will discuss general airport operations and then differentiate between tower and non-tower airports.

As your flying experience expands to include more airports, you will find some features that they all have in common. For instance, all runways are numbered according to their directions in relation to magnetic north, to the closest 10°. A runway laid out 078° from magnetic north would be numbered 8:

Figure 10-1. Runway numbering

Figure 10-2. Wind indicators

rounded off to 080° and the zeros dropped. The opposite end of the runway would be numbered 26 (the reciprocal) (Figure 10-1). Some large airports have parallel runways which are identified as left, right, or center: runway 27R, runway 6L, etc.

You will normally take off and land into the wind and the wind indicator tells the direction the wind is blowing from. Every airport should have some form of wind indicator or landing direction indicator. Figure 10-2 shows several types of landing direction indicators: the tetrahedron, the windsock, and the wind tee. All of the indicators in the illustration indicate a wind from the west.

At some airports, the tetrahedron or wind tee may be tied down to show the favored runway and will not accurately reflect wind conditions. Always observe

Figure 10-3. Landing strip and pattern indicators

what other pilots in the pattern are doing and conform with the pattern in use. Figures 10-3 and 10-4 show landing strip indicators and landing pattern indicators—the landing strip indicators parallel the runways and the landing pattern indicators show the direction that traffic flows to and from the runways. Your pattern should conform with the traffic flow indicated for the runway in use. *See* Figure 10-4.

Frequently, terrain or the presence of a congested area dictate the use of a right hand pattern. Figure 10-5 shows pattern indicators which keep traffic from overflying the area northwest of the water tank. Where there are no pattern indicators, the FARs require that all turns in the pattern be made to the left. When you fly over a strange airport and do not see a pattern indicator, you are safe in assuming a left-hand pattern.

Figure 10-6 shows the FAA recommended standard left hand traffic pattern with arrival and departure procedures. If the airport has an *FAA required* traffic pattern, you must use that pattern (few airports have such patterns—FAR Part 93 lists them).

Adjacent to every airport symbol on an aeronautical chart there is a data block with the airport name, its elevation above sea level, the length of the longest runway in hundred of feet, the airport's 3-letter identifier, a ⬤**R** if radar is available, the AWOS

frequency if that service is available, and information on lighting and radio services available. All of the information can be deciphered by use of the sectional chart legend, but you should be able to get the essential information at a glance.

For example, look at the data block for Seattle-Tacoma International Airport on the sectional chart excerpt. The airport is 429 feet above sea level, the longest runway is 11,900 feet long, and runway lighting is available from sunset to sunrise. Radio frequencies for the control tower, Automatic Terminal Information Service, and Aeronautical Advisory Service (UNICOM) are also listed.

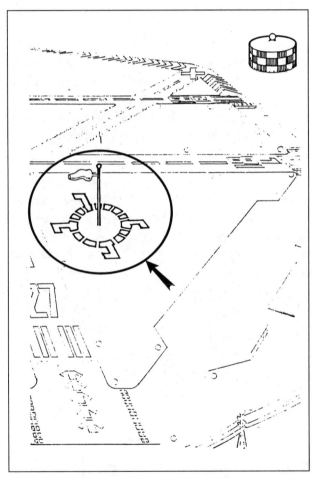

Figure 10-5. Tower and traffic pattern indicators

Figure 10-4. Pattern markings

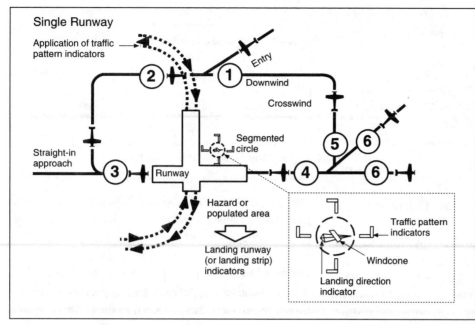

Figure 10-6. Diagram from AC90-66A

Where runway markings are provided, you will find centerline marking, a threshold marking where the landing surface begins, and a "hold line" which separates the active runway from the taxiway. Runways used for instrument approaches have additional markings. If there are obstacles in the approach path, the threshold may be displaced; arrows will lead to the displaced threshold. Note that in the illustration (Figure 10-7) the threshold of runway 27 has been displaced because of the power lines. Any paved area which appears to be usable, but which is not usable for normal operations, is marked with yellow chevrons. Such areas may be used as overruns at the end of a runway. In Figure 10-7, the taxiway beyond the threshold of runway 18R is marked as unusable.

On the sectional chart you will notice many airports without runway symbols: these airports have unpaved runways or paved runways less than 1500' in length. Airport symbols with little protrusions around their edges indicate that services (usually fuel) are available. You will also find airports with no radio service and airports without lighting. You should never be surprised by what you find at the end of a flight—you should know all about your destination airport before you take off. Charts and the Airport/Facility Directory are the government's means of providing airport information; there are also several private publishers of booklets with VFR airport information.

Airports can be divided into two categories: those with control towers and those without. On the sectional chart excerpt, you will see that airport symbols printed in blue are those airports with towers and those printed in magenta have no towers. When the tower is not in operation, the airports with blue symbols are to be treated as non-tower airports. Part-time towers are indicated by an asterisk next to the control tower frequency. Check the data blocks for the Tacoma Industrial and Olympia airports as examples of part-time towers. The Airport/Facility Directory also contains information on hours of operation.

Figure 10-7. Displaced threshold

For night operations, taxiways are marked with **omnidirectional** blue lights and the active runway is marked with omnidirectional white lights. Green lights mark the threshold, and red lights alert you to the end of the landing surface—these are directional lights, showing green in one direction and red in the other. Hazards, such as the water tank in Figure 10-5 on Page 10-2, are marked with red lights.

At many airports the lighting is controlled by the pilot, who transmits on a specified frequency (Usually the Common Traffic Advisory Frequency), and keys the microphone briefly to turn on the lights. At most airports with pilot controlled lighting the pilot can control the intensity of the lighting by varying the number of "clicks" on the microphone button. The lights turn off automatically after fifteen minutes. On aeronautical charts, airports with pilot-controlled lighting are indicated by *L; details on the frequency and keying code are found in the Airport/Facility Directory.

Rotating beacons are installed at all airports with towers and at many non-tower airports, and as they rotate the pilot sees a white flash followed by a single green flash. Military airports are identified at night by two white flashes between each green flash. When the rotating beacon is lighted in the daytime, it means that the weather is below the minimums required for visual flight. You should check the actual weather and not rely on the light, however, since many rotating beacons are turned on by timers or photoelectric cells.

VASI

Visual Approach Slope Indicators (**VASI**) are installed at both tower-controlled and non-tower

Figure 10-8. *Two- and three- bar VASI*

airports, and provide a visual means for the pilot to maintain a constant glide angle (usually 3 degrees) on final approach. Information on the type of VASI and the glide path angle can be found in the Airport/Facility Directory listing for the desired airport. A VASI installation defines the approach slope by providing light boxes adjacent to the runway—each box contains a light source and filters so arranged that when the pilot is on the desired glide path the box closest to the threshold (downwind) will show a white light, and the box furthest from the threshold (upwind) will show a red light. To the pilot on the correct glide path this appears as red over white: "red over white is right." Two white lights indicate a position too high on the glide path: "white over white, you're high as a kite." If a pilot is below the desired glide path both light boxes will show a red light: "red over red-you're dead" (a little morbid, but it rhymes and conveys a strong warning). Where a Visual Approach Slope Indicator is provided, you are required to use it by flying on or above the visual glide path until descent is required for landing. Figure 10-8 shows 2- and 3-bar VASI.

The eyes of the pilot of a long-bodied jet are about 50 feet above the surface when the landing gear touches down, so three sets of VASI boxes are provided on runways where such jets operate. The two sets of boxes closest to the threshold define the glide path for light aircraft and the two furthest define the glide path for jets.

Figure 10-9. *PAPI*

Figure 10-10. POMOLA

The FAA is installing the Precision Approach Path Indicator (PAPI) shown in Figure 10-9 at many airports because it gives a more accurate indication of off-glidepath flight than a VASI installation.

The FAA has approved use of other types of visual approach aids, such as a single-source amber-green-red indicator. This VASI shows a green light when you are on the glide path, an amber light when you are high, and a red light when you are dangerously low. Other approved lighting systems include a single line of lights which show red or white depending on your position on the glide path.

Providing the pilot with accurate descent path information is so important that some small airports have a visual aid consisting of painted boards installed beside the runway 50-100 feet apart. The pilot aligns the boards visually to stay on the glide path. This is called a "POMOLA", for Poor Man's Optical Landing Aid (Figure 10-10).

Taxiing

Strong gusty winds can make taxiing a chore, and mishandling the controls might result in loss of control. You must understand how to use the controls so that the wind cannot get beneath the wing or tail surfaces and cause you to drag a wing tip or have the propeller strike the ground.

When the wind is coming from a direction in front of the airplane, from wing tip to wing tip, hold the ailerons as though you are banking into the wind. The up-aileron on the windward side will depress the wing as the wind strikes it—the down-aileron on the opposite wing will create enough lift to oppose any

Figure 10-11. Taxiing diagram

overturning tendency. The elevator should be in a neutral position unless you are flying a taildragger, in which case full back elevator control will pin the tailwheel to the ground for steering control.

A quartering tailwind is most hazardous for a tricycle gear airplane, because a gust can lift the wing and tail and upset the airplane. To counter this tendency, when the wind is coming from any direction behind the airplane, the ailerons should be held away from the wind, and the elevator held in neutral or slightly forward (well forward in a taildragger). The down-aileron will now be on the windward side, and the wind from behind the wing will hold it down. Figure 10-11 illustrates this.

Crosswind Operations

Although airport designers try to align runways with the prevailing winds, there is always the possibility that the wind may not be blowing directly down the runway you intend to use. The manufacturer of your airplane has designated a maximum allowable crosswind component for your airplane, and you will find it either placarded in the cockpit or in the pilot's Operating Handbook. It is called "maximum *demonstrated* crosswind component" if the factory test pilot demonstrated that the airplane was controllable with a crosswind component at the published figure. You offset the crosswind component by using ailerons to control sideways drift and rudder to keep the

Figure 10-12. *Crosswind component*

longitudinal axis (and the airplane's direction of motion) aligned with the runway. When the crosswind component exceeds the published maximum, these aerodynamic controls may not be able to overcome the sideways drift and the tendency of the airplane to yaw or weathercock into the wind. You will "run out of rudder." *See* Figure 10-12 .

The difference between airplanes with conventional landing gear ("taildraggers") and those with tricycle landing gear becomes most obvious in crosswind takeoffs and landings. The center of gravity of a taildragger is behind the landing gear, and if a swerve begins (due to a crosswind or misuse of the rudders and/or brakes), the airplane will want to "swap ends." Quick and proper use of the rudders and/or brakes will stop this tendency. Taildragger pilots are justly proud of their abilities, and will tell you that a landing in a taildragger is not complete until the airplane is safely tied down.

The center of gravity of a tricycle gear airplane is forward of the landing gear, and upon landing the tendency is for the airplane to continue moving in the direction that it was moving at touchdown. It is your job as the pilot to be sure that at the moment of touchdown the airplane's motion is straight down the runway and that the longitudinal axis of the airplane is also aligned with the runway. If the airplane is pointed across the runway at touchdown, that is the direction it will go until you get on the rudders and straighten it out. If it is drifting sideways at touchdown due to inadequate crosswind correction, the landing gear will be subjected to side loads it was not designed to handle.

Wind Components

Demonstrated Crosswind Component is 17 Knots

Example:

Wind Speed	20 kts
Angle Between Wind Direction and Flight Path	50°
Headwind Component	13 Knots
Crosswind Component	15 Knots

Figure 10-13. *Crosswind diagram*

There are several techniques for crosswind takeoffs and landings and they all have one common thread: *the airplane must be pointing and moving parallel to the runway heading at liftoff or touchdown.* Some tricycle-gear airplanes have free-swiveling nose gear which aligns itself with the direction of travel as soon as it touches the runway, while on other airplanes the nose gear reacts to rudder input. If your trainer is one of the latter, any rudder input at touchdown may result in a swerve. The crosswind diagram (Figure 10-13) is one method of determining crosswind component.

Find the angle between the reported wind direction and the runway heading, and follow the line representing that angle to its intersection with the arc representing the reported wind velocity. A line drawn

Figure 10-14. Wing-tip vortices

downward from the point of intersection to the bottom scale will give you the crosswind component, and a horizontal line will give the headwind component:

Reported wind .... 270 at 20 knots
Runway in use .... Runway 30
Wind angle.. 30 degrees
Crosswind component .... 10 knots
Headwind component .... 17 knots

If you don't have a diagram available, use these rules of thumb to compute crosswind component; for wind angles of less than 20 degrees, ignore the crosswind component; for wind angles of 20-40 degrees multiply the reported wind velocity by .5, for angles of 40-60 degrees multiply by .7, and for angles of 60 degrees or more, consider the full wind velocity to be the crosswind component.

Wake Turbulence

An important consideration for pilots at any airport is the avoidance of wake turbulence. Every airplane leaves behind it two twin tornadoes corkscrewing aft from the wing tips. As the high pressure air below the wing tries to travel around the wing tip to the low pressure area on the top surface and the airplane moves forward, the circulation is clockwise from the left wing tip and counterclockwise from the right wing tip as seen from behind. In the NASA photo-

graph above (Figure 10-14), the airplane has flown between two smoke generators and the vortices are clearly seen. Because these wing-tip vortices are a product of lift development, they are strongest and most hazardous behind airplanes that are heavy, slow, and with landing gear and flaps retracted: a takeoff situation. Second most hazardous is the heavy slow airplane in the landing configuration.

Any lifting surface creates tip vortices. How severely they affect an airplane that encounters them depends on the relative weights and wingspans. A very light airplane encountering a vortex from a heavy jet may be thrown out of control, while a medium jet in the same position might experience only momentary turbulence. Research has shown that the wing-tip vortices descend 900 to 1,000' behind the generating airplane and then slowly dissipate. Crossing behind a heavy airplane and encountering both vortices can create destructive forces. An airplane with a wingspan smaller than the vortex can be rolled at a rate faster than its pilot can control (Figure 10-15).

When preparing to take off, if a heavy airplane is landing you should note the point at which it touched down—*vortices are only generated when the wings are developing lift.* You should plan your takeoff roll so that you lift off beyond the point at which the head airplane touched down. If you are preparing to take

Figure 10-15. *Wind indicators*

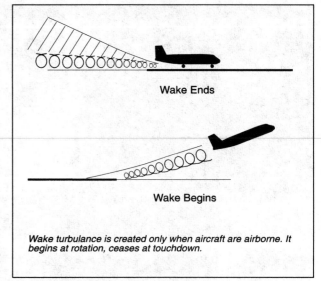

Wake turbulence is created only when aircraft are airborne. It begins at rotation, ceases at touchdown.

Figure 10-16. *Touchdown—rotations*

off and a heavy airplane has just departed, you should wait at least 3 minutes for its wake turbulence to dissipate (at airports with control towers the tower controller will probably delay your takeoff clearance). You can avoid its wake turbulence by lifting off at a point on the runway before its liftoff point and then climbing to windward above the heavy airplane's flight path. (Light airplanes can climb more steeply than a jet's flight path for a short distance.) You should be aware that wake vortices drift downwind and wait a few moments longer if you suspect they will drift into your path.

If you are landing behind an airplane which is generating hazardous wing-tip vortices, note its touchdown point and overfly its landing roll so that you land beyond its touchdown point (Figure 10-16). Heavy jets use up a lot more runway than you need. When landing after a heavy jet has just taken off, land on the runway numbers. Its vortices do not begin until it rotates for takeoff and begins generating lift.

Operating at an airport with crossing runways requires special care. Avoid being airborne when crossing a runway where a heavy airplane has just taken off or landed, and land short of the intersection if possible. *Remember that the heavy airplane creates vortices only when creating lift.*

Line Signals

An aspect of airport operations which is the same at all airports is the set of standardized hand and arm signals used by line personnel to direct ground operations. Figure 10-17 is self explanatory. When no line personnel are available to guide you, it is usually more prudent to shut down the airplane and push it into a parking space than to attempt to gauge clearances visually. Miscalculations are sure to be expensive.

Operations at Non-Tower Airports

Unless you learn to fly at a tower-controlled airport and never venture far from the comforting sound of a controller's voice, you will spend most of your time flying at non-tower airports. There are approximately 12,900 airports and only 691 towers. Some non-tower airports have on-field Flight Service Stations, a larger number have UNICOM, and many have no radio facility at all. Your airplane does not have to be radio-equipped to operate at these airports. Remember, even a tower-controlled airport becomes Class E or G airspace when the controller goes home. Figure 10-18 on Page 10-10 shows a control tower and traffic pattern indicators around the windsock. When the tower is closed at night, only one of the parallel runways will be lighted and the traffic pattern indicators will dictate traffic flow. If the wind direction changes during the night, the lighted runway may not be aligned with the wind; check the windsock.

Figure 10-17. *Hand signals*

In preparing to depart a non-tower airport, it is your responsibility to be sure that VFR conditions exist and are expected to continue or improve during your flight. You must also check the wind direction and velocity and the runway in use, and taxi safely to the runway area.

If there is a Flight Service Station on the field its personnel can provide you with weather, runway, and known traffic information. Flight Service Station briefers are trained specialists, with access to National Weather Service information on local, enroute, and destination weather conditions. FSS personnel are not air traffic controllers—they cannot give you clearance to taxi or to take off or land. UNICOM (Aeronautical Advisory Service) is even less formal, because the radio station is not operated by the government but by a private business as a service to the flying public. The operator has many other duties, and may not always be able to answer your call. Information on runway in use received from an FSS

Figure 10-18. Airport panoramic view

Figure 10-19. Runway markings

or UNICOM is advisory only—at a non-tower airport *you* decide which runway to use (but be ready to defend your decision if you decide not to go with the flow!). If you are unable to communicate with UNICOM, or if the FSS is closed, the Airman's Information Manual suggests that you broadcast in the blind (no specific addressee: "Podunk traffic, Chieftain 4125 GOLF departing runway 16 at Podunk") on the Common Traffic Advisory Frequency for that airport.

You will occasionally find runways at non-tower airports marked off with a large X at each end or in the center. An X-ed off *runway* is closed (Figure 10-18), and an X in the center of an airport indicates that the *airport* is closed. Some runways have displaced thresholds (Figure 10-19), usually because of obstructions in the approach path, and you must land beyond the displaced threshold markings. You can taxi on or begin your takeoff run from that area of the runway between the end of the paved surface and the displaced threshold unless chevron markings indicate that it is unusable. Figure 10-18 includes a closed runway, an unusable taxiway, displaced thresholds, and parallel runway markings.

When approaching a non-tower airport to land, you should begin planning your pattern entry about 10 miles out. Every airport has a Common Traffic Advisory Frequency, even though there may be no radio facility on the airport. Where there is a UNICOM,

listen briefly to learn which runway other pilots are using so that you can plan your entry. The presence of a Flight Service Station on the airport creates an Airport Advisory Area, and you should call on 123.6 MHz when 10 miles out for an airport advisory.

Because no clearance is required to enter the traffic pattern and land at a non-tower airport, it is not required that you maintain continuous radio contact with the ground station. The AIM does recommend that you announce your position and intentions when 10 miles out and when on downwind, base, and final so that other pilots in the area can coordinate their moments with yours. Also, because the CTAF may be shared by several airports, your transmissions should include the name of the airport at which you intend to land. "Podunk Traffic, Duke 2345X on left downwind for runway 23." Keep your transmissions brief and to the point so that others may use the frequency.

Operations at Airports with Control Towers

A controlled airport is one with an operating control tower. Control towers are commissioned at airports because the volume of traffic demands a high degree of coordination, so when you operate into or depart from such an airport you should expect your movements to be controlled by the tower. You can ask the **tower controller** for a runway other than the active, and if safety and traffic permits, you may get it. With that exception, there is no opportunity for a pilot to make his or her own decision on where to taxi or which runway to use.

At many airports with control towers there is an Automatic Terminal Information Service (ATIS) which continuously broadcasts non-control information on existing weather conditions, runway in use, and applicable Notices to Airmen. Non-control means that the ATIS gives you the information necessary to plan your arrival but you still need a clearance from the tower or approach control to operate in Class B, C or D airspace. Your first action, whether arriving or departing, should be to monitor the ATIS broadcast. Each ATIS tape is identified with a letter of the phonetic alphabet (see Appendix B). When contacting ground control, the tower controller, or an approach control facility, you should state in your initial contact that you have the ATIS information: "Bay Approach, Comanche 587 Sierra, 10 miles southeast with DELTA." Federal Aviation Regulations Part 91 requires that you establish communications with an air traffic control tower before entering Class B, C or D airspace, but if your radio fails in flight (or if you have no radio and have made prior arrangements with the tower) you can still enter the pattern and receive clearance to land through light gun signals (Table 10-1).

Some towers are equipped with BRITE (visible in daylight) radar display, to aid controllers. If you are disoriented at an unfamiliar airport, or because the visibility is restricted by haze or smoke, these towers can suggest headings for you to fly to get to the airport traffic pattern.

Color and Type of Signal	On the Ground	In Flight
STEADY GREEN	Cleared for takeoff	Cleared to land
FLASHING GREEN	Cleared to taxi	Return for landing (to be followed by steady green at proper time)
STEADY RED	Stop	Give way to other aircraft and continue circling
FLASHING RED	Taxi clear of landing area (runway) in use	Airport unsafe — do not land
FLASHING WHITE	Return to starting point on airport	
ALTERNATING RED & GREEN	General Warning Signal — Exercise Extreme Caution	

Table 10-1. Light gun signals

Class C Airspace

Hundreds of tower-controlled airports are protected by Class C airspace and more are being designated every year. Use current charts and check for NOTAMs. Chapter 14 discusses Class C airspace in detail. What you need to know in the context of operations at airports with control towers is that the controller at the radar facility that governs the airspace surrounding the airport serves as a sort of perimeter guard for the tower controller. You can't enter Class C airspace (shown on sectional charts with a solid magenta line) until you have established two-way communication with that controller, who is usually called "Podunk Approach Control".

The controller wants to know who you are, where you are, and your intentions. "Spokane Approach Control, Cessna 4836G is 15 miles northeast, landing at Felts Field." If the controller says to remain clear of the Class C airspace, you must do just that. The regulations do not require that you receive a clearance, just that communications be established; but if the airspace is busy the effect is the same—you can't enter until the controller says you can. The approach controller will sequence you for landing and then hand you off to the tower controller. Keep a sharper than usual lookout, because if the area wasn't congested, there would be no need to designate it as Class C airspace.

Class D Airspace

Class D airspace is shown by a dashed blue line on charts. Because it is always associated with an operating control tower, Class D airspace imposes a communication requirement on all pilots desiring to land, take off, or just pass through. It also imposes a weather restriction.

As a VFR pilot you cannot fly through Class B, C, D or E airspace unless the flight visibility is at least three statute miles and you can stay 500 feet below, 1,000 feet above, and 2,000 feet horizontally from any cloud; you can't take off or land under basic visual flight rules if the reported ceiling is less than 1,000 feet above the ground or the *ground* visibility is less than three statute miles.

You can, however, ask the tower controller for a Special VFR clearance. This authorizes you to take off and operate within the Class B, C, D, or E airspace if the ground visibility is at least one statute mile and you can remain clear of all clouds, and to enter the airspace and land if the flight visibility is at least one statute mile and you can stay clear of clouds. Special VFR is useful when bad weather is localized and you know that you will be in good visual conditions once you leave the immediate area of the airport; the authorization can be a trap if you will be dodging clouds, buildings, and antennas after you cross the boundary of the Class B, C, D, or E airspace.

Occasionally, your first clue that things are not very good at your destination airport will be when you call the controller and hear "Podunk Airport weather is below basic VFR minimums—what are your intentions?" Your response, of course, is that you want a Special VFR clearance. Don't be surprised if you are told to just fly around in visual conditions (and well clear of the Class D airspace) while the tower takes care of some instrument-rated pilots.

You cannot operate under Special VFR at night until you earn an instrument rating.

When the tower controller goes home, most Class D airspace becomes Class E airspace. The communication requirement goes away but the visibility and cloud clearance requirements stay. Of course, there is no one to report ground visibility when this happens and it is your responsibility to ensure that the flight visibility is at least three statute miles.

Ground Operations

When the **ground controller** clears you to the active runway, that clearance authorizes you to cross any intersecting runways on the way to the runway area, but does not include clearance onto the active runway. In Figure 10-18 on Page 10-10, a pilot cleared to runway 9 would have a clearance to taxi across the thresholds of runways 27, 36R, and 36L unless directed to hold short. So that there is no misunderstanding, you are required to read back to the controller any instructions to hold short of the runway.

At night, the ground controller will not direct you to taxi onto the runway into takeoff position to hold awaiting takeoff clearance, and will not authorize takeoff from an intersection if the controller cannot see that intersection clearly.

The ground controller's area of responsibility ends at the yellow hold lines, and the tower controller "owns" the runway and the Class D airspace associated with the airport. After landing, remain on the tower controller's frequency until directed to contact ground control.

Class E Airspace

There are airports with the same weather restrictions but no control tower; at those airports, controlled airspace (Class E) extends down to the airport surface. They are shown with a dashed magenta line on sectional charts (two examples on the sectional chart excerpt are Bremerton National and Fairchild International). You can still get a Special VFR authorization to take off or land, but you must get it through a Flight Service Station. The FSS must check with air traffic controllers to be sure that no instrument approaches or departures are taking place before issuing a clearance to you.

When an airport has either Class B, C, D, or E airspace, the lighting of the rotating beacon during daylight hours is intended to indicate that the weather is below basic VFR minimums (1,000-foot ceiling and three statute miles visibility). In many cases these beacons are controlled by automatic devices and your decision on whether or not basic VFR minimums exist should not depend on the beacon alone.

Chapter 10
Airport Operations Review Questions

1. An air traffic control clearance provides

    A—priority over all other traffic.
    B—adequate separation from all traffic.
    C—authorization to proceed under specified traffic conditions in controlled airspace.

2. A flashing green air traffic control signal directed to an aircraft on the surface is a signal that the pilot

    A—is cleared to taxi.
    B—should exercise extreme caution.
    C—should taxi clear of the runway in use.

3. Which is the correct traffic pattern departure to use at an airport without a control tower?

    A—Depart in any direction consistent with safety, after crossing the airport boundary.
    B—Make all turns to the left.
    C—Comply with any FAA traffic pattern established for the airport.

4. If instructed by ground control to taxi to runway 9, the pilot may proceed

    A—via taxiways and across runways to, but not onto, runway 9.
    B—to the next intersecting runway where further clearance is required.
    C—via any route at the pilot's discretion onto runway 9 and hold until cleared for takeoff.

5. Prior to entering an airport advisory area, a pilot

    A—must obtain a clearance from air traffic control.
    B—should monitor ATIS for weather and traffic advisories.
    C—should contact the local FSS for airport and traffic advisories.

6. The numbers 9 and 27 on a runway indicate that the runway is oriented approximately

    A—090° and 270° magnetic.
    B—090° and 270° true.
    C—009° and 027° magnetic.

7. An airport's rotating beacon operated during the daylight hours indicates

    A—that there are obstructions on the airport.
    B—that weather in the Class B, C, D, E airspace is below basic VFR weather minimums.
    C—the airport is temporarily closed.

8. Airport taxiways are identified at night by

    A—alternating red and green edge lights.
    B—white directional edge lights.
    C—blue omnidirectional edge lights.

9. A below glideslope indication from a tri-color VASI is

   A—a pink light signal.
   B—an amber light signal.
   C—a red light signal.

10. How is a runway recognized as being closed?

    A—Red lights are placed at the approach end of tile runway.
    B—Yellow chevrons are painted on the runway beyond the threshold.
    C—X is displayed on the runway.

11. According to the diagram in Figure Q10-1,

    A—takeoffs and landings are permissible at position C since this is 1 short takeoff and landing runway.
    B—Runway 30 is equipped at position E with emergency arresting gear to provide a means of stopping military aircraft.
    C—takeoffs may be started at position A on runway 12, and the landing portion of this runway begins at position B.

12. That portion of the runway identified by the letter A in Figure Q10-1

    A—may be used for taxiing but should not be used for takeoffs or landings.
    B—may be used for taxiing or takeoffs but not for landings.
    C—may not be used except in an emergency.

13. What is the crosswind component for landing on runway 18 if the tower reports the wind as 220° at 30 knots? See Figure 10-13 on Page 10-6 .

    A—19 knots
    B—23 knots.
    C—30 knots.

14. How should the controls be held while taxing a tricycle-gear equipped airplane into a left quartering headwind?

    A—Left aileron up, neutral elevator.
    B—Left aileron down, neutral elevator.
    C—Left aileron up, down elevator.

15. Of the following conditions, which is the most critical when taxiing a nosewheel equipped high-wing airplane?

    A—Direct crosswind.
    B—Quartering tailwind.
    C—Quartering headwind.

16. Wing-tip vortices, the dangerous turbulence that might be encountered behind a large aircraft, are created only when that aircraft is

    A—operating at high airspeeds.
    B—heavily loaded.
    C—developing lift.

Figure Q10-1. *Airport diagram*

17. Wing-tip vortices created by large aircraft tend to

 A—sink below the aircraft generating the turbulence.
 B—rise into the takeoff pattern.
 C—rise into the takeoff or landing path of a crossing runway.

18. The segmented circle shown in Figure 10-3 on Page 10-1 indicates that the airport traffic is

 A—left-hand for Rwy 17 and right-hand for Rwy 35.
 B—right-hand for Rwy 9 and left-hand for Rwy 27.
 C—left-hand for Rwy 35 and right-hand for Rwy 17.

19. Which runway and traffic pattern should be used as indicated by the wind cone in the segmented circle depicted in Figure 10-3 on Page 10-1?

 A—Right-hand traffic on Rwy 35.
 B—Left-hand traffic on Rwy 35 or right-hand traffic on Rwy 27.
 C—Left-hand traffic on Rwy 27 or Rwy 35.

20. When approaching to land on a runway served by a VASI, the pilot shall

 A—intercept and remain on the glideslope until touchdown only if the aircraft is operating on an instrument flight plan.
 B—maintain an altitude at or above the glideslope.
 C—remain on the glideslope and land between the light bars.

21. You are on final approach to a runway equipped with a Precision Approach Path Indicator (PAPI), and see three white lights and one red light. You are

 A—low on the glide path.
 B—slightly high on the glide path.
 C—slightly low on the glide path.

22. You are approaching an airport within Class C airspace. Which of these statements is true?

 A—You must have a clearance from ATC before entering the Class C airspace.
 B—You must be in two-way communication with ATC before entering the Class C airspace.
 C—Your airplane must be equipped with a transponder, two-way radio, and VOR to enter Class C airspace.

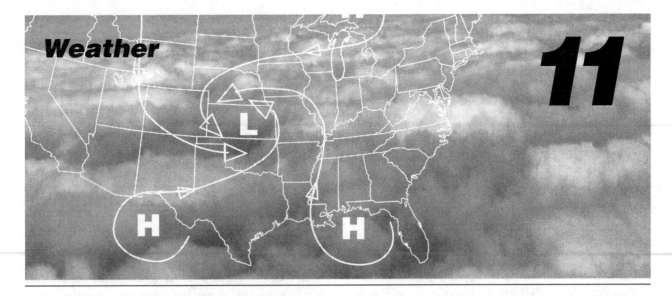

Weather

11

As a pilot limited to flight under Visual Flight Rules, your primary interest in weather and weather changes should be "How will that weather condition affect visibility for departure, enroute, and at my destination?" Your second area of concern will be clouds, because you must maintain separation from clouds at all times. You need to know whether clouds might form where none now exist or if scattered clouds might merge into an impenetrable overcast. You will want to avoid thunderstorms and other severe weather for safety reasons. Flying is fun, but fighting the weather is not. Every pilot should be a student of the weather, and as the hours in your flight log accumulate you should develop a weather "sense" to keep the fun in flying.

The primary source of all weather changes is the sun. It heats the surface of the earth at varying rates, depending not only on cloud cover and the angle at which the sun's rays strike the earth but on the type of surface being heated. For instance, land changes temperature far more rapidly than water, deserts and barren areas change temperature more rapidly than forested areas, and cloud cover affects the rate at which any surface gains and loses heat. Heated air, being less dense than cool air, rises and creates low pressure areas. When the rising air has cooled, it descends and creates areas of high pressure. Air heated at the Equator rises, cools, and moves toward the North and South Poles. Meteorologists have identified three loops of rising and descending air, as

illustrated, with a net flow toward the poles at high altitude (Figure 11-1). The relatively weak cell over the mid-latitudes (including the United States) flows south-to-north. The moisture content of an air mass depends on its temperature and affects its density, and it is these variations in pressure, density, temperature, and moisture content that define air masses and weather systems. The earth of course, rotates beneath these weather systems and their effects are felt many miles distant from where the sun's heat began the process. If the earth did not rotate, air descending from the Poles would flow directly south to the Equator, to be heated again to repeat the cycle.

Figure 11-1. *3-cell circulation pattern and prevailing winds*

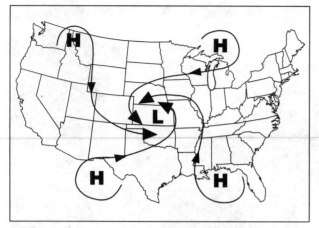

Figure 11-2. *Circulation around pressure centers*

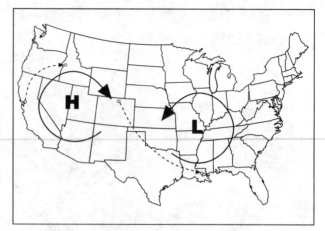

Figure 11-3. *Taking advantage of pressure systems*

Because of the earth's rotation, a phenomenon known as **Coriolis Force** deflects the moving air, so that in the latitudes of the United States the prevailing upper level winds are westerly. This causes weather systems to move across the country from west to east.

Air rising in a low pressure area draws air from outside the low into the center, and the general circulation pattern is counterclockwise. An extreme example of this is the tornado or cyclone which, as it

rotates, draws air, houses, trees, and other debris into its center and up, depositing them many miles away (Figure 11-2).

Air descending in a high pressure system circulates clockwise, and as the air reaches the surface it travels away from the center. Pilots on long cross-country trips can take advantage of these circulation patterns to get favorable winds (Figure 11-3).

Figure 11-4. *Surface weather map*

Figure 11-5. Coriolis effect

On a surface weather analysis chart (Figure 11-4), you can see high and low pressure areas. These are defined by meteorologists who take barometric pressure readings at airports and National Weather Service offices across the country and plot their findings on a chart. By connecting the points of equal pressure (called **isobars**) they define pressure patterns. Where the isobars are tightly packed, pressure is changing rapidly, and strong winds should be expected. Isobars which are widely spaced indicate less force to drive the wind. As the air from high pressure areas rushes to fill in the low pressure areas, you would expect the wind to blow downhill; that is, directly outward from the center of a high to the center of a low.

The air tries to do exactly that, and the driving force is called the **gradient** force. Coriolis Force deflects the wind so that in fact the direction of air motion crosses the isobars at an angle (Figure 11-5).

On the surface analysis chart you will see wind arrows that do not seem to agree with any rule, because of the effects of local conditions or surface friction. Mountain ranges, passes, valleys—all have local influence on the direction of air movement up to about 2,000' above ground level.

As a general rule, winds above 2,000' AGL come from a direction several degrees clockwise from the surface wind: with a surface wind of 180°, the wind at 2,000' AGL might be from 220° and the wind at 4,000' AGL from 240°.

To understand and anticipate weather changes, you must be aware of pressure systems and their movement. To know what might happen with cloud formations and obstructions to visibility you must consider the moisture content of the air. All air contains moisture in the form of water vapor; *the amount of water a given volume of air can hold is dependent on the temperature of the air.* As a volume of air is heated, the amount of moisture it can hold in invisible form increases: a temperature increase of 20°F doubles the air's capacity to hold moisture. Conversely, cooling the air reduces the amount of water vapor that can be hidden from sight, and when the air contains 100% of the moisture it can hold invisibly it becomes visible in the form of clouds, fog, or precipitation. The moisture condenses into droplets which can be seen, and which restrict your ability to see.

The temperature at which the air becomes saturated with moisture and can contain no more without that moisture getting you wet is called the **dew point**. You have heard the television weather person report "The temperature is 65°, the dewpoint is 48°"— under those conditions, if the air suddenly cools 17° it will be saturated and any further cooling or addition of moisture to the air will result in fog or rain. What the weather reporter calls **relative humidity** is simply how close the air is to being saturated. The illustration (Figure 11-6 on the next page.) uses a cup of liquid (representing the atmosphere) at different temperatures to show how the percentage of moisture content increases from 50% to 100%. A good example of high relative humidity is a hot July day when the air is full of moisture but there isn't a cloud in the sky. You feel uncomfortable because perspiration on your body cannot evaporate into air already full of moisture (Figure 11-6). Take a cold can out of a soft drink dispenser on a clear July day and watch beads of water form on its sides. Where does the water come from, if not from the air?

Figure 11-6. *Temperature vs. saturation*

The measure of relative humidity is the spread between temperature and dew point. If that spread is reported to be less than 5°F, you should investigate further to determine the potential for a reduction in visibility. Is the sun rising, or setting? The answer can help you predict the temperature trend and whether the temperature/dew point spread will increase or decrease. Is the wind blowing from over water or from over land? Moisture can be added to the air by evaporation from rain or bodies of water. Moisture being added to the air can tip the balance toward saturation. If your investigation shows the potential for a decrease in the difference between temperature and dew point for any reason, you must consider the possibility that you will not be able to complete the trip under visual conditions.

Knowledge of the temperature/dew point relationship is valuable in estimating the height of cloud bases. When rising air currents are evidenced by the formation of cumulus clouds, the air is cooling at the rate of approximately 4.4°F per 1,000'. For example, if the temperature at the surface is 78°F and the dewpoint is 62°F, the difference is 16° ÷ 4.4 x 1,000 = 3,600' above the surface. This is where you would expect cloud bases to be under the conditions stated. For height of cloud bases above sea level, you must add the elevation of the station at which the observations were made.

Fronts

A weather front exists where air masses with different properties meet. The terms warm and cold are relative: 30°F air is warmer than 10°F air, but that "warm" air doesn't call for bathing suits. Cold air is more dense than warm air, so where two dissimilar masses meet the cold air stays near the surface. Figure 11-7 shows a cold front: cold air advancing from west to east and displacing warm air. Because the cold air is dense and relatively heavy, it moves rapidly across the surface, pushing the warm air up.

Friction slows the cold air movement at the surface, so that the front is quite vertical in cross-section and the band of frontal weather is narrow. Cold fronts can move as fast as 30 knots. Your awareness of this rapid movement, together with facts you already know about temperature and dew point will allow you to make the following generalizations about cold front weather.

Visibility: Good behind the front. Warm air and pollutants rise rapidly because warm air is less dense than cold air.

Flight conditions: Bumpy as thermal currents rise.

Precipitation: Showery in the frontal area as the warm air is forced aloft and its moisture condenses. The ability of the air to hold moisture decreases as the air cools, and as the moisture contained in each column of rising air condenses into water droplets, showers result.

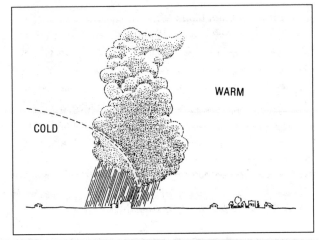

Figure 11-7. Cross-section of typical cold front

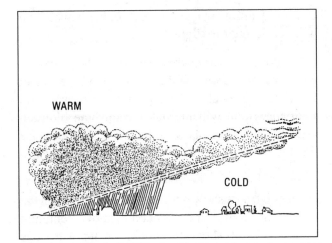

Figure 11-8. Cross-section of typical warm front

Cloud Type: Cumulus, due to air being raised rapidly to the condensation level. Cumulus clouds are a sign of unstable air; the rising air columns are warmer than the surrounding air and continue to rise under their own power.

Icing possibility: Clear ice. Cumulus clouds develop large water droplets which freeze into clear sheets of ice when they strike an airplane.

A warm front exists when a warm air mass overtakes a slow-moving cold air mass; the lighter warm air cannot displace the heavier cold air, and the warm air is forced to rise as it moves forward (Figure 11-8). This slow upward movement combined with the slow forward movement characteristic of warm fronts, allows the warm air to cool slowly and, as it reaches the condensation level, stratiform clouds develop. While cold frontal conditions exist over a very short distance, warm fronts slope upward for many miles, and warm frontal weather may be extensive.

You may encounter warm front clouds 50 to 100 miles from where the front is depicted on the surface analysis chart. The following are the characteristics of warm frontal weather:

Visibility: Poor; pollutants trapped by warm air aloft. Air warmed at the surface can only rise until it reaches air at its own temperature.

Flight conditions: Smooth, no thermal activity.

Precipitation: Drizzle or continuous rain as moist air is slowly raised to the condensation level.

Cloud Type: Stratus or layered, the result of slow cooling.

Icing possibility: Rime ice; small water droplets which freeze instantaneously upon contacting an airplane and form a rough, milky coating.

Occasionally, a fast moving cold front will overtake a warm front (Figure 11-9) and lift the warm air away from the surface. This is called an *occlusion*, and occluded frontal weather contains the worst features of both warm and cold fronts: turbulent flying conditions, showers and/or continuous precipitation, poor visibility in precipitation, and broad geographic extent of frontal weather conditions.

Air masses can maintain their warm/cold identity and yet not exert any displacement force. When this happens, the front becomes stationary, and the associated weather covers a large geographic area.

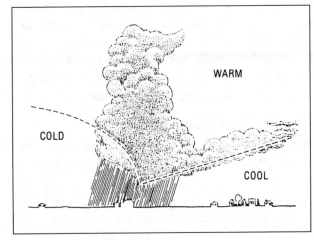

Figure 11-9. Occluded fronts

In your planning, what you see is probably what you will get during the flight.

When you look at a weather map which shows frontal positions, cold fronts will be marked in blue, warm fronts in red, occluded fronts will be purple, and stationary fronts will alternate red and blue. You can identify fronts on black-and-white charts because the cold front symbols look like icicles and warm front symbols appear as blisters (Figure 11-10).

Occluded fronts show both icicles and blisters on the side of the front in the direction of movement, and stationary fronts show the symbols on opposite sides of the frontal line, indicating opposing forces.

Stability

You need a general understanding of air mass stability in order to anticipate weather changes which might affect your flight. The amount of moisture in the air influences the rate at which the air cools with increasing altitude. The standard "lapse rate," or rate at which cooling takes place, is 2°C per 1,000' of altitude. An air mass which cools more rapidly than 2°/1,000' is considered to be unstable. Any situation that has cool or cold air overlying warm air is a potentially unstable situation because the warm air, being lighter, will rise and will cool more slowly than the surrounding air. The column of rising air then has the impetus to continue to rise; this is the basis on which thunderstorms develop.

An air mass with warm air overlying cold air is stable, because the heavy cold air cannot rise to displace the lighter warm air. *When the temperature rises abruptly with altitude, a* **temperature inversion** *exists*—this condition is marked by poor visibility because warm polluted air cannot rise above the inversion level. This is the familiar smog or haze layer, and it usually takes the passage of a major system to clean it out. The possibility of turbulence always exists at the top of an inversion layer.

Cloud Families

What you have learned about air movement and the relationship of temperature to moisture content leads right into the study of cloud formation, and by "reading" the clouds you will be able to anticipate the effects of weather changes on your flight.

Figure 11-10. Surface analysis symbols

Meteorologists divide clouds into four families: high clouds, middle clouds, low clouds, and clouds with extensive vertical development. The latter group signals the presence of strong columns of rising air (called convective air currents) which at the very least mean a rough ride, and may herald the onset of precipitation or a developing thunderstorm (Figure 11-11).

Nice fluffy-looking clouds marking the tops of columns of rising air are called cumulus clouds, because they are in a building or accumulating stage as the air rises to the condensation level—you can expect a bumpy ride beneath them and a smooth ride above (Figure 11-12). Stratocumulus clouds are in the low family, altocumulus in the middle altitudes, and cirrocumulus is the word for fluffy clouds at high altitudes. Cumulus clouds are a sign of instability in the air mass because stable air has no tendency to move vertically.

Figure 11-12. Thermal turbulence

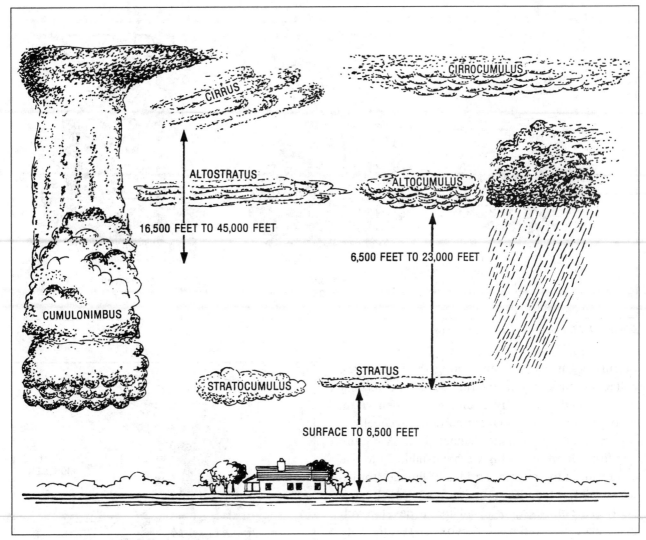

Figure 11-11. Typical cloud formations

Stratus or layered clouds indicate a stable air mass; they have little vertical development—fog is defined as a stratus cloud at the surface. A stratus cloud deck may make the day dark and gloomy, but the smooth ride will make up for it. Altostratus clouds are found in the mid-altitudes and cirrostratus are very high thin layers of ice crystals. Cloud names can be combinations: stratocumulus is a good example. Clouds with "nimbo" or "nimbus" in their names indicate the presence of precipitation. "Virga" is the name for moisture that falls from a cloud but evaporates before reaching the surface. It is a visible indication of a downdraft and possible wind shear. Do not fly beneath or through virga.

Thunderstorms

Thunderstorms deserve special treatment, and they even have a special cloud name: cumulonimbus, abbreviated as CB or CU. When you hear pilots on the radio talking about "towering cues to the north-west" or "several CBs to the east" they aren't talking about pool halls or CB radio but about clouds indicating threatening weather. Three elements must be present for thunderstorm development: warm air, moisture, and an unstable airmass. With all three present, it takes very little to begin the process: the sun heating a parking lot or a plowed field, wind blowing up a mountain slope—these are typical of the things that can start a column of rising air.

Figure 11-13. *Life cycle of a thunderstorm*

Storms begun by the sun heating the surface are called air mass thunderstorms. They are usually localized and you can fly around them. When warm, moist air moves up a mountain and a storm develops, it is called an orographic thunderstorm. A rapidly moving cold front forcing warm unstable air to rise can result in the most hazardous of thunderstorms, the squall line thunderstorm. It is not unusual, especially in the midwest, for squall lines to develop well in advance of a cold front. As you can see, the only variable is the force that starts the lifting process—after that, the storm grows on its own.

Figure 11-13 shows the life cycle of a thunderstorm, beginning with the cumulus or building stage as the warm moist air rises. The instability of the air allows this process to feed on itself as the air column, even though cooling with altitude, is warmer than the surrounding air. The moisture in the air condenses into water droplets, adding more heat to the rising air. The droplets do not fall out of the cloud initially, but are carried to higher altitudes as they grow even larger through collision with other droplets in the turbulent air. These growing water droplets can even freeze into hail at the top of the cloud and be blown downwind to create a hazard to aircraft well outside the cloud mass.

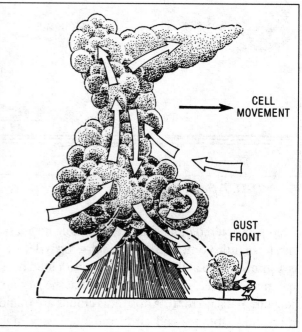

Figure 11-14. *Mature stage of a steady state thunderstorm cell*

A thunderstorm has reached maturity when the water droplets are big enough to overcome the upward air currents and precipitation reaches the ground (Figure 11-14). The falling rain creates downdrafts in opposition to the updrafts which began the whole process. This updraft/downdraft combination within a short distance makes penetrating a thunderstorm hazardous to the structural integrity of *any* size aircraft.

Figure 11-15. Turbulence near buildings

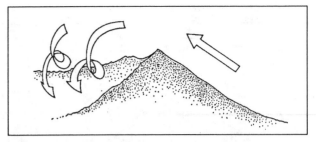

Figure 11-16. Turbulence near mountains

The downdrafts soon overpower the updrafts and the storm cell dissipates into heavy rain. The process just described is continuous as long as the conditions of warm, moist air, instability, and lifting force are present and as far as the pilot is concerned, the birth and death of individual cells is not apparent. The rapid vertical movement of air up and down in close proximity develops electrical charges, and lightning from cloud to cloud or from cloud to ground is a part of all thunderstorm activity.

The external appearance of cumulus clouds should never be used as an indicator of what might be found inside. Gleaming white, puffy, clouds with all the outward menace of a pile of marshmallows might contain destructive forces, while a threatening greyblack area might contain only heavy rain and a few bumps. As a VFR pilot you must not fly into *any* cloud, but a knowledge of thunderstorms may save you from encountering hail in clear air downwind from a cumulonimbus cloud or from being punished by turbulence as you fly through conflicting air currents beneath one. Severe turbulence should be expected up to 20 miles from a severe thunderstorm, and up to 10 miles from lesser storms. Thunderstorm clouds may be embedded in a continuous layer of other clouds, creating an unseen hazard for the pilot attempting to fly visually in marginal conditions.

Pilots may also experience gusty winds and turbulence near the surface many miles around the actual location of a thunderstorm cell as the downdrafts strike the ground and move outward (Figure 11-14).

"Microbursts" have recently been identified as small shafts of descending air associated with thunderstorms. Because of their small diameter, microbursts are not easily detected by weather instruments, making it even more important that pilots stay away from areas where thunderstorms are existing or forecast.

Wind Shear

Wind shear is defined as a change in direction or speed of air movement, either horizontal or vertical, that takes place within a short distance. It can be the result of mechanical forces such as turbulence around buildings adjacent to the runway, or may be encountered when flying into the wind on the lee (downwind) side of a mountain ridge (Figures 11-15 and 11-16). Wind shear is most frequently related to a weather phenomena such as thunderstorms. A rapid wind shift from a headwind to a tailwind can cause an unexpected loss of altitude and airspeed, and, if a storm cell is within 15 miles of the airport you should delay your takeoff to avoid such a shift.

You are already aware of the vertical shear forces present when an aircraft enters a mature thunderstorm and encounters updrafts and downdrafts in rapid succession—a pilot attempting to fight these forces could quickly exceed the load limit on the aircraft structure. The pilot's only recourse is to keep the wings level, maintain attitude (not altitude), and go along for the ride until clear of the cell. Other types of wind shear encounters will require that you keep

Figure 11-17. *Turbulence*

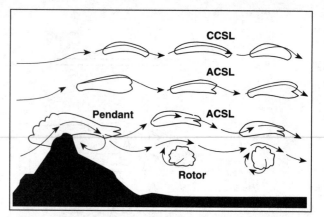

Figure 11-18. *"Standing" or "Mountain" wave pattern*

Figure 11-19. *Radiation (ground) fog*

the aircraft under control but should not endanger its safety. An example is flying through a front: the wind always shifts as you fly through a front, and this is a form of wind shear. If you are departing an airport which is under the influence of a temperature inversion, with little or no air movement near the surface, you may be surprised by wind shear turbulence as you climb through the inversion layer if the winds 2,000' to 4,000' above the surface are at least 25 knots.

The gust front associated with thunderstorm-generated downdrafts can create wind shear hazards 15 to 25 miles from the storm itself, and unless its presence is revealed by blowing dust, there will be no warning. Winds aloft blowing at 50 knots or more can create severe turbulence downwind from mountain ranges (Figure 11-17).

If there is sufficient moisture in the air for cloud formation, a lens-shaped cloud will form which remains stationary in relation to the ground. This "standing lenticular" (called an altocumulus standing lenticular or ACSL) is a signpost warning of turbulence (Figure 11-18). In your flight planning, be sure to check into the possibility of thunderstorm activity on or near your route and of strong winds aloft if you will be flying in mountainous terrain wind shear and turbulence are uncomfortable at best.

Fog

Fog is probably the most deceptive hazard to safe flight that a VFR pilot has to consider in flight planning. Fog can form or dissipate virtually instantaneously, and it can form under conditions that appear to be ideal for flight. Still, with your knowledge of the movement of air masses and of the temperature/dew point relationship, you can guard against unpleasant surprises.

Radiation fog catches many pilots off guard. Calm winds and clear skies would seem to be the answers to a pilot's prayers, but when these conditions occur and the temperature/dew point spread is small, radiation fog is a good possibility. The clear skies allow the land to radiate heat, cooling the air near the surface to the dewpoint and causing fog to form (Figure 11-19). This is a night or early morning phenomenon, and a few hours of sunlight will raise the air temperature above the dew point, "burning off" the fog. From cruise altitude, a thin ground fog layer (ground fog is a type of radiation fog) may seem fairly harmless to a pilot who can see runways and buildings as though through a veil.

Figure 11-20. *Advection fog*

On a landing approach, however, what looked thin from altitude obscures everything because the pilot is now looking at the fog layer horizontally. When ground fog is predicted (or any time the T/DP spread is less than 3°), include a fog-free alternate airport in your planning.

Advection fog results when moist air moves, and to anticipate it you must consider where the moist air is coming from and what it is moving toward. Typically, the moist air is moving from over water to over colder land; the moist air condenses into fog when cooled by the land (Figure 11-20). The process can be reversed when warm moist air from land moves over cold water.

Your key for planning purposes is knowing the wind direction, surface temperatures, and dew points, and whether the wind is coming from over land or water. What is the relative humidity at a reporting station upwind from you? Because advection fog is created by moving air, wind will not blow it away, and it will not burn off as readily as radiation fog; advection fog can be persistent and can form at any time.

Upslope fog's name gives away its origin. As moist, stable air is moved toward higher terrain, it cools to its dewpoint and condenses as fog. While flying you will see it first in valleys, filling them and obscuring as much of the high ground as the moisture content of the air allows and lasting as long as the upward force exists. Contrast this with the upward movement of moist *unstable* air which can lead to thunderstorm formation.

We don't stop flying just because it's raining, but what starts out as a simple rainy day flight can end up quite differently. When rain falls into cool, almost saturated air, the moisture it adds can result in what is called precipitation-induced fog and lower visibilities well below the minimums required for flight. Occluded fronts, warm fronts, slow moving cold fronts and stationary fronts all have the ingredients necessary for the onset of precipitation-induced fog. When any of these conditions are forecast for your time or route of flight (or if you encounter precipitation), you must consider the possibility of reduced visibility due to fog.

Condensation Nuclei

In industrial areas, or anywhere that pollutants might be found in the air, fog will form more readily and dissipate more slowly. When the water vapor has something to condense on, such as a pollutant particle, fog will be more persistent than when such nuclei are not present.

Sources of Weather Information

The Federal Aviation Regulations require that a pilot planning a flight not in the vicinity of an airport become familiar with weather reports and forecasts for the route of flight. As of 1995, The FAA has contracted with two providers of computerized weather to give pilots free access to the Direct User Access Terminal (DUAT) service, discussed in detail on Page 11-24. Many FBOs provide computer briefing stations; some are supported by state aeronautical divisions. Computer briefings eliminate being placed on "hold" for long periods and can provide charts for you to interpret at your leisure. Congress has extended DUATS funding through 1995; the future of DUATS is uncertain—it may become a 900-number service if it loses government support.

The ideal briefing is "in person" at the FSS, where you can look at the reports, forecasts, and charts from the NS, and ask questions of the briefer before filing your flight plan. This is becoming more difficult as the FAA consolidates the FSS system into a small number of Automated Flight Service Stations (AFSS). Next best is a telephone briefing by an FSS specialist who refers to the weather data to help you plan your flight; however, you must know the right questions to ask in this situation.

Three types of preflight briefings are available: standard, abbreviated, and outlook. If you have not collected any weather information before calling the FSS, ask for the standard briefing—then you can be sure that nothing will be left out. Ask for an abbreviated briefing if you want to update an earlier briefing or add to information you have already received from another source. In this situation, tell the briefer where you got the original information so that he or she can fill in any gaps.

Request an outlook briefing when your proposed departure time will be more than six hours after the briefing and then back it up with a standard briefing closer to takeoff time.

The Airman's Information Manual and the Airport/Facility Directory contain telephone numbers for pilot weather briefings that are not available to the public for general weather information, and when you call you should *identify yourself as a pilot*. The briefer will need to know your destination and planned route of flight, and the type of airplane you will be flying.

You can also listen to Transcribed Weather Broadcasts (TWEBS) and the Hazardous Inflight Weather Advisory Service (HIWAS) on selected radio navigational aids (VORs and NDBs) for weather updates. Check your chart legend or the A/FD to identify navaids that broadcast weather information. In flight, the En route Flight Advisory Service (EFAS), or Flight Watch, can be contacted on 122.0 MHz between 0600 and 2200 local time for direct contact with a weather briefer. If you have a radio in your airplane you will always have access to up-to-date weather information and must not rely solely on a pre-takeoff briefing.

The weather information during the morning news on national network television gives a broad overview of national weather, and for pilots with access to cable The Weather Channel is helpful. TWC may carry forecasts specifically aimed at pilots in the near future.

The National Oceanographic and Atmospheric Administration (NOAA) broadcasts weather continuously on UHF frequencies in the 162 MHz range. These frequencies cannot be tuned by your aircraft radio. Radios designed specifically for receiving these broadcasts are available at electronics stores.

Pilot reports (PIREPs) provide the most current information for any given route. Pilots are encouraged to contact Flight Watch and report the actual conditions they are encountering. These PIREPs will be passed on to pilots inquiring about flying the same route and will provide better information about those areas between weather reporting stations.

Weather Reports

During operating hours every reporting station issues an hourly sequence report (SA or METAR) that includes cloud cover and visibility, wind direction and velocity, barometric pressure and altimeter setting, and remarks, and may include applicable Notices to Airmen. Figure 11-21 is the key to interpreting hourly sequences; however, it will become invalid on January 1, 1996 and the National Weather Service has not yet made a replacement available.

Note: this key will not be available to you on your FAA written examination, so learn to read and understand the information without the key.

Figure 11-22 contains hourly sequences for five widely separated stations: Wink, TX (INK), Boise, ID (BOI), Los Angeles, CA (LAX), Chicago, IL (MDW), and New York NY (JFK).

KEY TO MANUAL AVIATION WEATHER OBSERVATIONS

LOCATION IDENTIFIER, TYPE AND TIME OF REPORT	SKY CONDITION AND CEILING	VISIBILITY, WEATHER, AND OBSTRUCTIONS TO VISION	SEA-LEVEL PRESSURE	TEMPERATURE AND DEW POINT	WIND DIRECTION, SPEED AND CHARACTER	ALTIMETER SETTING	REMARKS AND CODED DATA
MCI SA 0758	15 SCT M15 OVC	1R — F	132	/58/56	/1807	/993/	R01VR20V40

LOCATION IDENTIFIER:
3 or 4 alphanumeric characters (airport identifier).
TYPE OF REPORT:
SA = Scheduled record (hourly) observation.
SP = Special observation indicating a significant change in one or more of the observed elements.
RS = SA that also qualifies as an SP.
USP = Urgent special observation (tornado).
TIME OF REPORT:
Coordinated Universal Time (UTC or Z) using 24-hour clock. Example: 2255 = 10:55 pm.
SKY CONDITION AND CEILING:
Sky condition contractions are for each layer in ascending order. Numbers preceding contractions are base height in hundreds of feet above ground level (AGL). Sky condition contractions are: (— = Thin).
CLR = Clear: Less than 0.1 sky cover.
SCT = Scattered: 0.1 to 0.5 sky cover.
BKN = Broken: 0.6 to 0.9 sky cover.
OVC = Overcast: More than 0.9 sky cover.
— X = Partially obscured. 0.9 or less of sky hidden by precipitation or obstruction to vision (cloud bases at the surface).
X = Obscured: entire sky hidden.
A letter preceding height of a layer identifies a ceiling and indicates how ceiling was obtained.
E = Estimated.   **M** = Measured.
W = Vertical visibility into obscured sky.
V following height = variable ceiling.

VISIBILITY:
Reported in statute miles and fractions.
V = Variable.
WEATHER & OBSTRUCTIONS TO VISION:

A	Hail	**GF**	Ground fog
D	Dust	**ZR**	Freezing rain
R	Rain	**BD**	Blowing dust
F	Fog	**SP**	Snow pellets
S	Snow	**BN**	Blowing sand
H	Haze	**SW**	Snow showers
K	Smoke	**BS**	Blowing snow
IF	Ice fog	**T**	Thunderstorm
L	Drizzle	**T+**	Severe thunderstorm
IP	Ice pellets	**RW**	Rain showers
IC	Ice crystals	**IPW**	Ice pellet showers
SG	Snow grains	**ZL**	Freezing drizzle

— = Light.   (no sign) = Moderate.   + = Heavy.
SEA-LEVEL PRESSURE:
Pressure in hectopascals (millibars): Shown as 3 digits. Leading 9 or 10 and decimal point is omitted. Examples: 150 = 1015.0   950 = 995.0
TEMPERATURE AND DEW POINT:
Reported in Degrees Fahrenheit (°F).
WIND DIRECTION SPEED & CHARACTER:
Direction in tens of degrees from true north, speed in knots. 0000 = calm.   **G** = gusty.
Q = squall. Peak speed of gusts in the past ten minutes follows G or Q. WSHFT in Remarks = windshift occurred at time indicated. Example: 3627G40 = 360° at 27 peak gusts 40 knots.

ALTIMETER SETTING:
Actual altimeter setting with first digit omitted.
Examples: 005 = 30.05"   992 = 29.92"
RUNWAY VISUAL RANGE (RVR):
RVR is reported for some stations. Value(s) during 10 minutes prior to observation are given in hundreds of feet. Runway number precedes RVR report.   V = Variable.
DECODED REPORT:
Kansas City Int'l Airport: Record observation completed at 0758Z. 1500 feet scattered clouds, measured ceiling 2500 feet overcast, visibility 1 mile, light rain, fog, sea level pressure 1013.2 hectopascals, temperature 58° F, dewpoint 56° F, wind 180°, 7 knots, altimeter setting 29.93". Runway 01 visual range varying from 2000 to 4000 feet in the past 10 minutes.
PILOT REPORTS (PIREPS):
A PIREP describes actual in-flight conditions. Pilots are encouraged to provide PIREPS to an FAA facility.   Example: UA /OV FRR 275045 /TM 1745 /FL330 /TP B727 /SK 185 BKN 220 280 BKN 310 /TA-53 /WV 290120 /TB LGT-MDT CAT ABV 310.   **Decoded:** Pilot report, Front Royal VORTAC, 275 radial 45nm, at 1745Z, flight level 330; Boeing 727; cloud base 18500 broken, tops 22000, second layer 28000 broken, tops 31000; air temperature minus 53 degrees Celsius; wind 290 degrees 120 knots; light to moderate clear air turbulence above 31000.

NOAA/PA 93055

U.S. DEPARTMENT OF COMMERCE — NATIONAL OCEANIC AND ATMOSPHERIC ADMINISTRATION — NATIONAL WEATHER SERVICE   4/14/83

KEY TO AVIATION WEATHER FORECASTS

TERMINAL FORECASTS (FT) contain information for specific airports. They are issued 3 times a day, amended as needed, and are valid for a 24 hour period. The last six hours of each period is covered by a categorical forecast indicating when VFR, MVFR, IFR, or LIFR conditions are expected. Terminal forecasts are written in the following form:
Airport Identifier: 3 or 4 alphanumeric characters.
Date And Valid Time Period Of Forecast: Z or UTC.
Message Type: RTD (Delayed), COR (Corrected), or AMD (Amended).
Ceiling: identified by the letter "C" prefix.
Cloud Heights: In hundreds of feet above the airport (AGL).
Cloud Amount: CLR (Clear), SCT (Scattered), BKN (Broken), OVC (Overcast), or X (Obscured).
Visibility: In statute miles (6+ indicates unrestricted).
Weather & Obstruction To Visibility: Standard weather / visibility symbols used.
Surface Wind: In tens of degrees and knots. Omitted when less than 6 knots. Gusts indicated by a G followed by maximum speed.
Ceiling And Visibility Categories:

Category	Ceiling (feet)		Visibility (miles)
LIFR	less than 500	and / or	less than 1
IFR	500 to 1000	and / or	1 to 3
MVFR	1000 thru 3000	and / or	3 thru 5
VFR	more than 3000	and	more than 5

Example Of Terminal Forecast:
DCA 221010 10 SCT C18 BKN 5SW — 3415G25 OCNL C8 X 1/2 SW.
12Z C50 BKN 3312G22.
04Z MVFR CIG...
Decoded Example: Washington National Airport for the 22nd of the month valid from 10Z to 10Z. Scattered clouds at 1000 feet, ceiling 1800 feet broken, visibility 5 miles in light snow showers, surface wind 340 degrees at 15 knots, gusts to 25 knots. Occasional ceiling 800 feet, sky obscured, visibility one-half mile in moderate snow showers. By 12Z becoming ceiling 5000 feet broken, surface wind 330 degrees at 12 knots, gusts to 22 knots. The categorical outlook for the last 6 hours beginning at 04Z calls for marginal VFR conditions due to ceiling.

AREA FORECASTS (FA) provide an 18-hour synopsis of expected weather patterns; a 12-hour forecast of VFR cloud cover, weather and visibility; and a 6-hour categorical outlook. FAs are prepared 3 times a day (4 times a day in Alaska and Hawaii) and are supplemented and updated by SIGMETs, AIRMETs, and by FA amendments. Heights in the FA are above mean sea level (MSL) unless stated as above ground level (AGL). Ceilings (CIG) are always AGL.

WIND and TEMPERATURE ALOFT FORECASTS (FD) are 6, 12, and 24-hour forecasts of wind direction, speed, and temperatures for selected altitudes to 53,000 feet MSL at specified locations. Direction is relative to true north rounded to the nearest 10 degrees. Speed is in knots. Temperatures aloft (in degrees Celsius) are specified with wind data for all but the 3000-foot MSL level and those levels within 2500 feet of the ground. Temperatures above 24,000 feet MSL are always negative. Winds at other locations and intermediate altitudes can be obtained by interpolation.
Example of Winds Aloft Forecast:

FT	3000	6000	9000	
ACY	2925	2833 + 02	2930 — 03	etc.

Decoded example: For Atlantic City, N.J., at 6000 feet MSL wind from 280 degrees true at 33 knots, temperature 2 degrees Celsius.

IN-FLIGHT ADVISORIES of potentially hazardous weather and include SIGMETs, CONVECTIVE SIGMETs, AIRMETs, and Center Weather Advisories (CWA). SIGMETs warn of hazardous conditions of importance to all aircraft i.e., severe icing or turbulence, duststorms, sandstorms, and volcanic ash. AIRMETs warn of less severe conditions which may be hazardous to some aircraft or pilots. SIGMETs are issued as needed, AIRMET bulletins are issued routinely and supplement the Area Forecast (FA). CONVECTIVE SIGMETs are issued hourly for thunderstorms in the conterminous U.S. Center Weather Advisories, issued as needed, are detailed advisories of conditions which meet or approach SIGMET or AIRMET criteria.
Example Of Sigmet:
SIGMET OSCAR 2 VALID UNTIL 052100
KS NE
FROM PWE TO OSW TO LBL TO PWE
SVR TURBC BLO 60 XPCD DUE TO STG NWLY FLOW BHD CDFNT.
CONDS CONTG BYD 2100Z.
Decoded Example: SIGMET OSCAR 2 is valid until 2100Z on the 5th day of the month. For Kansas and Nebraska from Pawnee City VORTAC to Oswego VORTAC to Liberal VORTAC to Pawnee City VORTAC. Severe turbulence below 6000 feet expected due to strong northwesterly flow behind a coldfront. Conditions continuing beyond 2100Z.

TRANSCRIBED WEATHER BROADCASTS (TWEB) are continuous broadcasts of recorded NOTAM and weather information prepared for a 50-nautical mile wide zone along a route and for selected terminal areas. TWEBs are broadcast over selected NDB and VOR facilities and generally contain a weather synopsis, in-flight advisories, route and/or local vicinity forecasts, Winds Aloft Forecasts, current weather reports, NOTAMs, and special notices.

U.S. DEPARTMENT OF COMMERCE — NATIONAL OCEANIC AND ATMOSPHERIC ADMINISTRATION — NATIONAL WEATHER SERVICE   4/14/83

Figure 11-21

```
INK  SA  1854  CLR 15 106/77/73/63/1112G18/000
BOI  SA  1854  150 SCT 30 181/62/42/1204/015
LAX  SA  1852  7 SCT 250 SCT 6HK 129/60/59/2504/991
MDW  RS  1856  -X M7 OVC 11/2R+F 990/63/61/3205/980/RF2 RB12
JFK  RS  1853  W5 X 1/2F 180/68/64/1804/006/R04RV22V30 TWR
               VSBY 1/4
```

Figure 11-22. Hourly sequences for selected stations

Each report begins with the three-letter identifier for the airport where the observation was made. INK, BOI, and LAX are record observations (SA), while MDW and JFK are making both a record and a special observation (RS). The four numbers following the type of observation are the time of observation using Coordinated Universal Time (UCT).

To operate legally under Visual Flight Rules you must know what the reported ceiling is, and the next data group gives you that information. Ceilings may be measured (lowest cloud report prefixed with M), by an instrument called a ceilometer which bounces a light off of the cloud base, estimated (prefix E) by an observer, or reported by an aircraft (prefix A). To constitute a ceiling, the lowest cloud layer must be reported as broken (BKN) or overcast (OVC); a layer of scattered clouds (SCT) or a thin layer (-SCT, -BKN, -OVC) does not constitute a ceiling but may restrict your flying when cloud clearance requirements are considered.

Cloud heights are measured above the ground and are reported in hundreds of feet, so INK, BOI, and LAX do not have legal ceilings. MDW's ceiling of 700' overcast would keep you on the ground; and JFK is reporting "ceiling indefinite 500', sky obscured." That means that the observer estimates that he or she can see 500 feet up into the clouds but cannot see the horizon in any direction. That report would make even an instrument pilot think twice. The cloud layers are reported in order of height, with the highest layer last: at LAX two layers are reported; one at 700' and one at 25,000'. Because ceiling is reported as height above ground level; you must add the field elevation to the ceiling report to learn the height of the clouds above sea level.

After the sky and cloud report, the prevailing visibility is shown . The National Weather Service defines prevailing visibility as the greatest visibility that exists through at least 180° of the horizon—note that it need not be 180° continuous degrees. INK and BOI are reporting visibilities of 15 and 30 miles respectively, LAX has 6 miles in haze and smoke, MDW is reporting 1-1/2 miles (watch those fractions!) in heavy rain and fog, and JFK has 1/2 mile visibility in fog (in the Remarks section, the JFK tower reports only 1/4 mile visibility at its location).

Separated from the visibility report by a space is a series of five data blocks: the first is sea level pressure in millibars, a metric measure of pressure used on weather charts. The next two numbers are the temperature and dewpoint in Fahrenheit; note the T/DP spread at INK and BOI, where it is clear, and the spreads at the three reporting stations with restricted visibility. Next, the wind is reported as a four-digit group—the first two digits indicate wind direction in relation to true north in tens of degrees, and the last two digits indicate wind velocity in knots. At INK the wind is from 110° at 12 knots, gusting to 18—the other four stations are reporting only 4 or 5 knots. The last three digit group is the altimeter setting. Standard sea level pressure is 29.92" Hg, so the first digit of the altimeter setting is either a 2 or a 3 and is omitted. You supply whichever brings the altimeter setting closest to 30.00. INK is interpreted as 30.00', BOI 30.15', LAX 29.91," etc. Everything after the altimeter setting is "remarks." You must always look for them because they may explain or expand upon information in the body of the report. At MDW, for instance, the body of the report says the prevailing visibility is 1 1/2 miles, and the remarks say that the rain and fog obscure only 2/10 of the horizon.

Note that the time of the report at MDW is 1856, and there is a remark noting that the rain began at 1812. At JFK the visibility report is expanded for instrument pilots—it tells them that for runway 04R the visual range is 2,200 feet, variable to 3,000 feet. You can worry about that when you are instrument rated— with an indefinite ceiling and 1/2 mile of visibility you will not be flying at JFK under VFR! A full explanation of the criteria used in these reports is contained in *Aviation Weather Services*, (Advisory Circular 00-45C).

An important part of your flight planning is to look at or ask for the most recent hourly sequence report for your destination airport and several enroute airports, so that you can see whether the weather is good enough for VFR operations at your destination. You also should be sure that you can make an en route stop if you have to. Check the previous hour's sequences (if they are available) to see what weather trends you can detect. Is the T/DP spread increasing, or decreasing? Pressure rising, or falling (check the altimeter setting)? Cloud layers rising or lowering? Wind picking up? Shifting? What runway will probably be in use at the destination? Any Notices to Airmen? Remember, you are required to be informed about anything that can affect the safety of your flight.

A program that will be completed January 1, 1996, will change the format in which hourly sequences are presented. You will find the METAR format easier to interpret than the format in Figure 11-22. (There is a full explanation of the METAR format in Appendix C.) You will be able to identify the new format because each report will begin with "METAR."

For several years, when you receive textual weather by any means it will be a mixture of old and new. You will be able to identify the new format because each report will begin with METAR.

Automated Weather Reporting Stations

When you read the hourly sequences during a personal visit to the Flight Service Station, download them with your personal computer, or have them read to you during a telephone briefing, you should be aware that some of the weather information included in those sequences comes from devices that automatically measure different elements of the weather situation and transmit their findings to the National Weather Service. The Automatic Weather Observing Station (AWOS), designed by the FAA, and the Automatic Surface Observing Stations (ASOS), designed by the NWS, are the most common. *See* Figures 11-23 and 11-24. The NWS will have 1,700 ASOS installations in operation across the country by 1995.

The ASOS has many advantages over the AWOS, but both measure cloud cover, visibility, barometric pressure, precipitation and wind. The difference lies in how these measurements are made and how the results are transmitted to the NWS. At those locations where a computerized voice transmits the readings over aviation radio frequencies, the necessary information will be on sectional charts. Where the ASOS can be contacted by telephone, the number will be printed in the Airport/Facility Directory.

The measurements sent to the NWS by these automatic stations help the meteorologists develop the "big picture" on how weather systems are forming and moving. While ceilings and visibility measurements from an ASOS are accepted by the FAA as a legal basis for making pilot decisions, if the data from a specific station goes against the local trend you want to think long and hard before accepting it at face value.

For example, if the area forecast calls for ceilings below 1,000 feet AGL with visibilities less than 3 miles and the ASOS at your destination says that the weather is clear and the visibility is greater than ten miles, you should investigate what other reporting stations in the vicinity have to say; the ASOS might be looking straight up through a hole in the cloud cover or checking visibility in the only direction not affected by a fog bank. Similarly, if the weather in the area is supposed to be VFR and the automated station reports instrument meteorological conditions you should look for a reason. The ASOS is much better at avoiding this kind of problem than is the AWOS.

During the development of the ASOS its measurements were compared with those made by human observers and the correlation was quite close. As a pilot, you must remember that a weather observer spends only a few minutes each hour looking at the weather and spends the rest of the time on the telephone or radio and doing paperwork; the ASOS takes measurements constantly and transmits them to the NWS where they are integrated by computer with other reports from other facilities. This provides a better picture of a changing weather situation than hourly observations.

```
HTM  SA 1755 A02A M19V OVC 1R-F 125/36/34/2116G24/990 TWR VSBY 2
PWT  SA 1755 AWOS M20 OVC 1V 36/34/2015G25/977 PRESFR
ABC  RS 1755 AO2 M26V OVC 2-R 133/39/36/1214/012 R29LVR10V50
AST  SA 1755 A02A 12 SCT M25 BKN 4 128/42/38/2516/000
```

Figure 11-23. Automated observations

KEY TO AWOS (AUTOMATED WEATHER OBSERVING SYSTEM) OBSERVATIONS

LOCATION IDENTIFIER TYPE OF REPORT TIME OF REPORT STATION TYPE	SKY CONDITION AND CEILING BELOW 12,000'	VISIBILITY	TEMPERATURE / DEW POINT / WIND DIRECTION, SPEED AND CHARACTER / ALTIMETER SETTING /	REMARKS: AUTOMATED REMARKS GENERATED AUTOMATICALLY IF CONDITIONS EXIST. AUGMENTED REMARKS ADDED IF CONDITIONS EXIST AND CERTIFIED WEATHER OBSERVER IS ATTENDING THE SYSTEM
HTM SA 1755 AWOS	M20 OVC	1V	36/34/2015G25/990/	P010/VSBY 1/2V2 WND 17V23/WEA: R — F

LOCATION IDENTIFIER: 3 or 4 alphanumeric characters (usually the airport identifier).

TYPE OF REPORT: SA = Scheduled record (routine) observation. All observations identified as SA. Most are transmitted at 20-minute intervals (approximately 15, 35 and 55 minutes past each hour).

TIME OF REPORT: Coordinated Universal Time (UTC or Z) using 24-hour clock.

STATION TYPE: AWOS = Automated Weather Observing System site. **Note:** In the future, some systems will use " AO " designators.

SKY CONDITION AND CEILING: Sky condition contractions are for each layer in ascending order. Numbers preceding contractions are base heights in hundreds of feet above ground level (AGL).

CLR BLO 120 = No clouds below 12,000 ft.
SCT = Scattered: 0.1 to 0.5 sky cover.
BKN = Broken: 0.6 to 0.9 sky cover.
OVC = Overcast: More than 0.9 sky cover.
X = Obscured sky —**X** = Partially obscured
A letter preceding the height of a base identifies a ceiling layer and indicates how ceiling height was determined.
M = Measured   **W** = Indefinite

VISIBILITY: Reported in statute miles and fractions. Visibility greater than 10 not reported. V= variable: see Automated Remarks

TEMPERATURE AND DEW POINT: Reported in degrees Fahrenheit.

WIND DIRECTION, SPEED & CHARACTER: Direction in tens of degrees from true north, except voice broadcast is in degrees magnetic. Speed in knots. **0000** = calm. **G** = gusts. See Automated Remarks for variable direction.

ALTIMETER SETTING: Hundredths of inches of mercury. Shown as last 3 digits only without decimal point (e.g., 30.05 inches = 005).

PRESENT WEATHER/OBSTRUCTIONS TO VISION: Reported only when observer is available. See Augmented Remarks. In the future, some systems will report precipitation, fog, and haze in the body of the observation.

AUTOMATED REMARKS: Precipitation accumulation reported in hundredth of inches (e.g., P110 = 1.10 inches; P010 = 0.10 inch). **WND V** = variable wind direction. **VSBY V** = variable visibility. **DENSITY ALTITUDE** is included in the voice broadcast when more than 1000 feet above airport elevation.

MISSING DATA: Reported as " M ".

AUGMENTED REMARKS: " **WEA:** " indicates manual observer data. Remarks include operationally significant weather conditions within a five mile radius of the airport (e.g., thunderstorms, precipitation, obstructions to vision when visibility is 3 miles or less, fog banks). Standard weather observation contractions are used.

DECODED REPORT: Hometown Municipal Airport, observation at 1755 UTC, AWOS report. Measured ceiling 2000 feet overcast. Visibility 1 mile variable. Temperature 36 degrees (F), dew point 34 degrees (F), wind from 200 degrees true at 15 knots gusting to 25 knots, altimeter setting 29.90 inches. Precipitation accumulation during past hour 0.10 inch. Visibility variable between 1/2 and 2 miles. Wind direction variable from 170 degrees to 230 degrees true. Observer reports light rain (R—) and fog (F).

NOTE: Refer to the *Airman's Information Manual* for more information. Refer to the *Airport/Facility Directory*, aeronautical charts, and related publications for broadcast, telephone and location data. Check *Notices to Airmen* for AWOS system status.

U.S. DEPARTMENT OF TRANSPORTATION – FEDERAL AVIATION ADMINISTRATION   *U.S. G.P.O.: 1993—350-770   4/14/93

KEY TO ASOS (AUTOMATED SURFACE OBSERVING SYSTEM) WEATHER OBSERVATIONS

LOCATION IDENTIFIER TYPE OF REPORT TIME OF REPORT STATION TYPE	SKY CONDITION AND CEILING BELOW 12,000'	VISIBILITY, WEATHER, AND OBSTRUCTIONS TO VISION	SEA-LEVEL PRESSURE / TEMPERATURE / DEW POINT / WIND DIRECTION, SPEED AND CHARACTER / ALTIMETER SETTING /	REMARKS AUTOMATED REMARKS GENERATED AUTOMATICALLY IF CONDITIONS EXIST. AUGMENTED REMARKS ADDED IF CONDITIONS EXIST AND CERTIFIED WEATHER OBSERVER IS ATTENDING THE SYSTEM	STATUS REMARKS SYSTEM GENERATED
HTM RS 1755 AO2A	M19V OVC	1R — F	125/36/34/2116G24/990/	R29LVR10V50 CIG 16V22 TWR VSBY 2 PK WND 2032/1732 PRESFR	ZRNO $

LOCATION IDENTIFIER:
3 or 4 alphanumeric characters (usually airport identifier).

TYPE OF REPORT:
SA = Scheduled record (hourly) observation.
SP = Special observation indicating a significant change in one or more of the observed elements.
RS = SA that also qualifies as an SP.
USP = Urgent special observation to report tornado.

TIME OF REPORT:
Coordinated Universal Time (UTC or Z) using 24-hr clock.

STATION TYPE:
AO2 = Unattended (no observer) ASOS.
AO2A = Attended (observer present) ASOS.

SKY CONDITION AND CEILING BELOW 12,000' AGL:
Sky condition contractions are for each layer in ascending order. Numbers preceding contractions are base height in hundreds of feet above ground level (AGL).
CLR BLO 120 = Less than 0.1 sky cover below 12,000'
SCT = Scattered: 0.1 to 0.5 sky cover.
BKN = Broken: 0.6 to 0.9 sky cover.
OVC = Overcast: More than 0.9 sky cover.
A letter preceding the height of a base identifies a ceiling layer and indicates how ceiling height was determined.
M = Measured   **W** = Indefinite
E = Estimated   **X** = Obscured sky
The letter **V** is added immediately following the height of a base to indicate a variable ceiling: see Remarks.

VISIBILITY:
Reported in statute miles and fractions from <1/4 through 10+. **V** = variable: see Remarks.

PRESENT WEATHER:
TORNADO (when augmented).
T = Thunder (when augmented): see Status Remarks.
R = Liquid precipitation that does not freeze (e.g., rain).
P — = Light precipitation in unknown form.
ZR = Liquid precipitation that freezes on impact (e.g., freezing rain): see Status Remarks.
A = Hail (when augmented).
S = Frozen precipitation other than hail (e.g., snow).
+ = Heavy.   No sign = Moderate.   **—** = Light.

OBSTRUCTIONS TO VISION:
Reported only when visibility is less than 7 statute miles.
F = Fog   **H** = Haze
VOLCANIC ASH (when augmented).

SEA-LEVEL PRESSURE:
Tenths of Hectopascals (millibars). Shown as last 3 digits only without decimal point (e.g., 950 = 995.0).

TEMPERATURE AND DEW POINT:
Degrees Fahrenheit.

WIND DIRECTION, SPEED AND CHARACTER:
Direction in tens of degrees from **true** north. Voice broadcast in degrees from **magnetic**. Speed in knots. **0000** = calm. **E** = estimated. **G** = gusts. **Q** = squalls. Variable wind, peak wind, wind shift: see Remarks.

ALTIMETER SETTING:
Hundredths of inches of mercury. Shown as last 3 digits only without decimal point (e.g., 005 = 30.05 inches).

MISSING DATA: Reported as **M**.

DENSITY ALTITUDE: Included on voice broadcast only when 1000 or more feet above airport elevation.

REMARKS: Can Include:
RVR (Runway Visual Range), **VOLCANIC ASH, VIRGA, TWR VSBY** (Tower visibility), **SFC VSBY** (Surface visibility), **VSBY V** (Variable visibility), **CIG V** (Variable ceiling), **WSHFT** (Windshift), **PK WND** (Peak wind), **WND V** (Variable wind direction), **PCPN** (Precipitation amount), **PRESRR** (Pressure rising rapidly), **PRESFR** (Pressure falling rapidly), **PRJMP** (Pressure jump), **B** (Time weather began), **E** (Time weather ended).

STATUS REMARKS:
PWINO = Present weather information not available.
ZRNO = Freezing rain information not available.
TNO = Thunderstorm information not available.
$ = Maintenance check indicator.

DECODED REPORT: Hometown Municipal Airport, record special observation at 1755 UTC. ASOS with observer. Measured ceiling 1900 feet variable, overcast. Visibility 1 mile, light rain, fog. Sea-level pressure 1012.5 hectopascals, temperature 36°F, dew point 34°F, wind from 210° true at 16 knots gusting to 24 knots, altimeter 29.90 inches. Runway 29L visual range 1000 variable to 5000 feet. Ceiling 1600 variable to 2200 feet, tower visibility 2 miles, peak wind 200° true at 32 knots at 1732 UTC, pressure falling rapidly. Freezing rain information not available, maintenance check indicator.

NOTE: Refer to *ASOS Guide for Pilots* and the *Airman's Information Manual* for more information. Refer to the *Airport/Facility Directory*, aeronautical charts, and related publications for broadcast, telephone and location data. Check *Notices to Airmen* for ASOS system status.

U.S. DEPARTMENT OF COMMERCE – NATIONAL OCEANIC AND ATMOSPHERIC ADMINISTRATION – NATIONAL WEATHER SERVICE   4/14/93

Figure 11-24

Terminal Forecast

Terminal forecasts (FTs) are prepared three times daily for selected reporting stations, predicting conditions for a 5 mile area surrounding the airport. Each forecast is valid for 24 hours and contains a categorical outlook for the final 6 hours of the period. Figure 11-25 contains terminal forecasts for several stations, all of them in Oklahoma.

Those stations which prepare terminal forecasts issue their first report of the day only after two hourly observations have been made. This means that you could be well on your way before an FT for your destination airport is available.

The date-time-group 011447 indicates a transmission time on the teletype circuit of 1447Z on the first day of the month; the date-time-groups in the body of the forecast (all 011515) mean something quite different: the valid period is from 1500Z on the first day of the month until 1500Z on the second day. In reading FTs you will find that the abbreviations VFR, MVFR, IFR, and LIFR define weather conditions differently than FAR Part 91 does: VFR means a ceiling higher than 3,000' AGL and visibility greater than 5 miles; MVFR indicates a forecast ceiling between 1,000 and 3,000 feet and/or visibility forecast to be 3 to 5 miles. IFR in the categorical outlook for the final six hours of the FT means a ceiling of less than 1,000 feet and/or visibility less than 3 miles, agreeing with the Part 91 definition, while LIFR (low IFR) will be mentioned when ceilings are expected to be below 500 feet and the visibility is expected to be less than 1 mile. You want to see at least MVFR if your flight is to take place within the 18 to 24 hour outlook period.

Because they are issued every 8 hours, you should keep checking the terminal forecasts right up to departure time. If forecast ceilings and/or visibilities are dropping with each new FT, investigate further. You can also check hourly sequences against terminal forecasts to see if the actual weather is better or worse than forecast. When reading an FT, note that

```
OKC FT 011515 C12 BKN 140 BKN 1815G28 LWR BKN V SCT
    18Z C30 BKN 250 BKN 2315G25 LWR BKN OCNL SCT CHC
        C7X1/2TRW+G40
    21Z CFP 100 SCT C250 BKN 3315G26 CHC C30 BKN 5TRW-
    02Z 100 SCT 250 SCT 3315G25.
    09Z VFR WIND.
```

Figure 11-25. Terminal forecast

visibility is only given if it is expected to be less than 10 miles, and wind is only mentioned if forecast to be greater than 10 knots. You will be familiar with the abbreviations used from using the key in Figure 11-21 on Page 11-13.

Note in the FT for OKC that at 1800Z in addition to strong winds there is a chance of a ceiling of 700' with sky obscured and visibility of 1/2 mile in heavy thundershowers. At 2100Z the ceiling is forecast to rise to 10,000' scattered with visibility greater than 10 miles. CFP, then, means "cold front passage". In the outlook section, when MVFR, IFR, or LIFR are noted the reason will be given, as in CIG TRW (ceiling and thundershowers) at MLC. When WIND is noted in the categorical outlook, expect winds in excess of 25 knots, and look for "LLWS" as a low level wind shear warning in the categorical outlook section.

The change in reporting formats discussed under hourly sequences will affect Terminal Forecasts as well. Beginning with the major international airports and being gradually phased in over the next several years is the TAF format; you have probably seen it in reports from military airports. Disregard the discussion of TAF codes in *Aviation Weather Services* (Advisory Circular 00-45C), because the format now being used is considerably easier to interpret. There is a full discussion of the TAF format in Appendix C.

Area Forecast (FA)

The Area Forecast is your only direct source of information on expected turbulence, icing, and heights of cloud tops. It contains a synopsis of the weather to help you evaluate the potential for change. It also includes forecasts of potentially hazardous weather as "flight precautions." Area forecasts are issued three times daily and are amended as required. The "Significant Clouds and Weather" portion is valid for 12 hours and contains an additional 6-hour outlook.

An area forecast covers several states and coastal waters; do not expect an area forecast to be as specific as a terminal forecast.

You will use the area forecast to fill in the gaps between reporting stations. Learning to decipher the abbreviations used in area forecasts is a study in itself—the Flight Service Station briefer will help you with them. *Aviation Weather Services* contains a list of commonly used abbreviations.

Because the area covered by an area forecast is so extensive, cloud heights are almost always given in feet above sea level, and you must be aware of terrain heights along your route to evaluate the effect of forecast clouds on your flight. Where "ceiling" (abbreviated as CIG) is used in an area forecast, the cloud height given is above ground level. The section headed "ICG AND FRZLVL" is your best source of forecast icing conditions.

"Thunderstorms imply possible severe or greater turbulence, severe icing, and low level wind shear." This warning, near the top of the area forecast in Figure 11-26, applies to Washington, Oregon, California, and coastal waters. This forecast is for a fairly benign May day on the West Coast.

This area forecast continues with predicted clouds and weather for small areas such as Northern California, Central California, coastal waters of Washington, Oregon and Northern California, etc. This format, broken down into a synopsis (SFOS), icing forecast (SFOI), turbulence forecast (SFOT), and a localized clouds and weather forecast (SFOC) allows the National Weather Service greater latitude in amending portions of the total area forecast (FA) without having to amend the entire forecast.

You can see the positions of fronts and pressure systems on a surface weather analysis chart (Figure 11-27, Page 11-20), keeping in mind that the information is several hours old by the time you see it.

Winds Aloft Forecast (FD)

These forecasts (Figure 11-28) are issued twice daily and include a "valid time." Heights are above sea level, and no forecast is available within 1500' of the reporting station's elevation. Wind direction and velocity are read just as they are in an hourly sequence, except that no gusts are forecast. The last two digits are forecast temperature in degrees Centigrade. Above 24,000', all temperatures are negative, so no + or - signs are used.

Wind direction is in relation to true north, and velocity is forecast in knots. Look for rapid changes in wind direction or velocity with altitude as a warning of turbulence. The winds aloft forecast will be the first thing you check in choosing a cruising altitude for favorable winds. The code for calm is 0000, and for "light and variable" it is 9900. When wind velocities are forecast to exceed 100 knots, the weather service still codes the direction, velocity, and temperature using six digits. This is accomplished by adding 50 to the wind direction, and subtracting 100 from the wind velocity. 731624 means wind from 230° (23 + 50 = 73) at 116 knots, temperature -24° above 24,000 feet.

```
SFOC FA 221045

SYNOPSIS AND VFR CLDS/WX SYNOPSIS VALID UNTIL 230500 CLDS/WX VALID UNTIL 222300...OTLK VALID
222300-230500

14
WA OR CA AND CSTL WTRS . SEE AIRMET SIERRA FOR IFR CONDS AND MTN OBSCN.

TSTMS IMPLY SVR OR GTR TURBC SVR ICG LLWS AND IFR CONDS. NON MSL HGTS NOTED BY AGL OR CIG.

SYNOPSIS...WLY FLOW ALF OVER NRN PTN OF AREA WILL GRDLY WKN DURG PD AS UPR LVL RIDGE OFFSHR
MOVS INLAND.

WA CASCDS WWD 30 BKN 60 BKN/OVC. WDLY SCT RW-. TOPS 180. AFT 21Z 30-50 SCT/BKN. TOPS 120.
OTLK...VFR. .

WA E OF CASCDS 80 SCT 120 BKN. AFT 15Z 80-100 BKN. ISOLD RW-. TOPS 180. OTLK...VFR.

OR CASCDS WWD NRN HALF...30-50 BKN 80 BKN. ISOLD RW-. TOPS 150. AFT 20Z 50 SCT/BKN. OTLK...VFR.

SRN HALF...50 BKN. OCNL 10 SCT/BKN CSTLN. AFT 20Z 60 SCT. OTLK...VFR.

OR E OF CASCDS 80-100 SCT/BKN. TOPS 150. ISOLD RW- NERN PTN AFT 16Z. OTLK...VFR.

NRN AND CNTRL CA CSTL SXNS...CLR. OCNL 10-15 SCT/BKN CSTLN TIL 18Z. TOPS 20. OTLK...VFR.

SACRAMENTO AND SAN JOAQUIN VLYS...CLR. OTLK...VFR.INTR MTNS...CLR. AFT 20Z 120 SCT. OTLK...VFR.

SRN CA..VBG-NID-60NNW BIH LN SWD NRN CSTL SXNS...CLR. OCNL 50 SCT MTNS. OTLK...VFR.

SRN CSTL SXNS...20 BKN. TOPS 40. AFT 18Z 30 SCT. OTLK...VFR.

INTR MTNS AND DESERTS...CLR. OTLK...VFR.

CSTL WTRS WA OR...15-30 BKN. TOPS 100. OTLK...VFR. CA...10-15 SCT. OCNL 10-15 BKN SRN CA. TOPS 30.
OTLK...MVFR CIG
```

Figure 11-26. *Area forecast*

Inflight Advisories

Weather information is available to a pilot in flight through listening to a Transcribed Weather Broadcast (TWEB) or the Hazardous Inflight Weather Advisory Service (HIWAS) on selected VORs and NDBs. A navaid with a TWEB will be identified on charts with a white T on a dark background in the frequency box for the navaid; the availability of the HIWAS is indicated by a square in the lower right corner of the frequency box. TWEBs contain forecasts for specific routes. If the taped information is not adequate, call Flight Watch on 122.0 MHz between 0600 and 2200 local time.

When weather hazardous to aircraft is forecast, a **SIGMET** or **AIRMET** will be issued and will be noted on the TWEB: "San Francisco AIRMET Charlie Two is current; contact the Flight Service Station for details." The Flight Watch specialist will have all applicable inflight warnings available when you call. An AIRMET concerns light aircraft only, and is issued when one or more of these conditions is forecast:

1. Moderate icing.

2. Moderate turbulence

3. Sustained winds of more than 30 knots at the surface.

4. Widespread areas of visibility less than 3 miles and/or ceilings less than 1000 feet.

5. Extensive mountain obscurement.

Figure 11-27. Surface weather

FDUS SWBC 011644
DATA BASED ON 011200Z

VALID 0220000Z   FOR USE 2100-0600Z.   TEMPS NEG ABV 24000

FT	3000	6000	9000	12000	18000	24000	30000	34000	39000
ABI		2512+14	2519+09	2426+-2	2438-14	2345-26	234840	234546	254152
ABQ			3115+02	3125-04	2934-18	2944-31	285240	285145	295151
AMA		3013	3120+03	2823-03	2536-16	2447-30	245642	255447	265351
ATL	1510	1811+13	1909+08	2107+02	2708-12	2710-24	271339	271648	252057
BNA	1920	2220+13	2220+08	2319+02	2421-12	2426-24	243240	243449	243659
BRO	1811	1917+17	2015+11	2214+05	2517-09	2626-21	273937	274845	276155
DAL	2115	2322+15	2325+09	2328+02	2335-13	2342-25	234940	244946	254754

Figure 11-28. Winds aloft forecast

A SIGMET advises of weather potentially hazardous to all aircraft:

1. Severe icing.
2. Severe or extreme turbulence.
3. Widespread sand or dust storms lowering visibilities to less than 3 miles.

Convective SIGMETs are issued in the continental United States when tornadoes, lines of thunderstorms, embedded thunderstorms, or hail 3/4" or more in diameter are forecast. These SIGMETS are issued at 55 minutes past the hour and alerts will be broadcast on all FSS and ATC frequencies except 121.5 MHz.

The FAA has begun implementation of a Hazardous In-Flight Weather Advisory Service (HIWAS) which is a continuous broadcast of SIGMETs, Convective SIGMETs, AIRMETs and urgent PIREPS on selected VORs. Where HIWAS has been implemented, all other broadcasts of hazardous weather have been eliminated. The publication Class II Notices to Airmen is your source of information on where HIWAS is in effect.

Your preflight weather briefing should equip you to make a go-no go decision, and while enroute you can re-evaluate that decision with the many in-flight weather services that are available. Because weather information is so readily available enroute, the FAA will not accept changed weather conditions as an excuse if you have a problem. On any flight away from the vicinity of an airport, you are required to have an alternative plan in mind in case you cannot carry out your planned flight.

Weather Depiction Chart

Figure 11-29 (on the next page) is a weather depiction chart which gives you a quick picture of where IFR and VER weather was located at the valid time given on the chart, This is not forecast information but allows you to determine general weather conditions on which to base flight planning decisions. The legend is on the chart.

The numbers below the station symbols represent the lowest cloud layer in hundreds of feet where no ceiling exists (25,000' in Arkansas and Alabama, for example), and the ceiling in hundreds of feet where

a ceiling is present (200' to 300' at the Oregon-California border). The numbers and symbols to the left of the station report visibility and the type of obstruction to visibility, if any (fog, in east Texas). Just as in a Terminal Forecast visibilities are not given if they are more than 6 miles. Also shown on the weather depiction chart is the location of any frontal activity, using the same symbols as the surface analysis map.

Radar Summary Chart

Radar will show only precipitation, not clouds or fog. The radar summary chart (Figure 11-30) shows the location of radar echoes from precipitation, and the direction and speed of movement of lines of cells and individual cells. The tops of precipitation as measured by radar are shown, as are any severe weather watch areas. The legend to decipher the chart is contained on the chart itself. You can safely assume that turbulence will be associated with areas of heavy precipitation, and plan to avoid flight near those areas. Remember, weather radar does not indicate the presence of clouds or fog, only precipitation. Never rely on ground-based radar to steer you through an area of thunderstorms, and rely on airborne weather radar for storm avoidance only if you are trained in its interpretation.

Low-Level Significant Weather Prognostic Charts

This panel of four charts (Figure 11-31 on Page 11-23) is an important planning tool for all pilots. Using the forecast freezing level positions and cloud cover, instrument pilots can see where icing conditions might exist. VFR pilots can avoid turbulence and marginal ceilings and visibilities.

The "low level" means that the data is for those altitudes between the surface and 24,000' MSL. "Prognostic" means that this is forecast information, not data based on actual observations, as is the case with the Radar Summary Chart, the Weather Depiction Chart, and the surface analysis map. The two panels on the left are a 12-hour forecast and the two right hand panels are a 24-hour forecast: the valid times are given on the charts. The top panels show the predicted position of the freezing level both at the surface (dotted line) and at altitude (identified by dashed lines), areas of forecast turbulence ("witches'

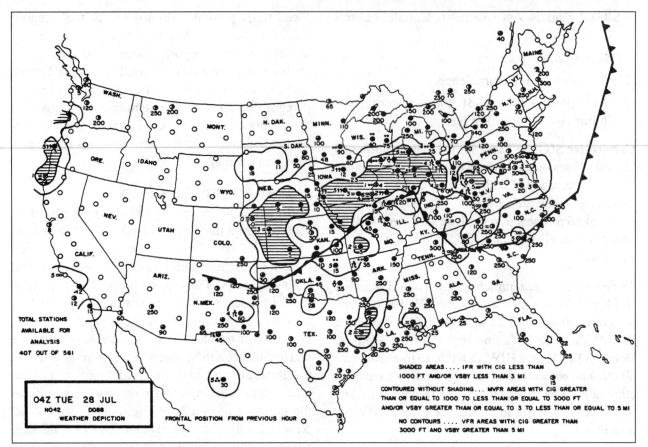

Figure 11-29. *Weather Depiction Chart*

Figure 11-30. *Radar Summary Chart*

Figure 11-31. Low-Level Significant Weather Prognostic chart

hats"), and areas of IFR and MVFR weather. The bottom panels show predicted frontal positions, location of pressure systems, and type and extent of expected precipitation. The significant weather prognostic charts give you a larger view of tomorrow's weather than does the area forecast.

Miscellaneous Sources

The Flight Service Station briefer (and the Flight Watch specialist) have satellite pictures of cloud cover available to supplement the printed weather data. National Weather Service meteorologists are stationed at FAA radar facilities to evaluate weather radar information and make it available to pilots on a current basis. Your local TV weather broadcaster is an excellent source of weather information, and will probably also have satellite pictures available.

Flight Service Stations nationwide can be accessed by dialing 1-800-WX-BRIEF. Through the magic of electronics and computers, the system will recognize the area code from which you are calling and direct your call to the correct Flight Service Station. If you are using a touchtone phone, you are given instructions on how to get route forecasts or local observations, or how to contact a live briefer. Rotary phone users are connected to a specialist.

If you are a personal computer user, or if your local fixed base operator has the proper equipment, the FAA has been sponsoring a free weather service known as the Direct User Access Terminal (DUAT). Budgetary constraints may cause this service to become either a 900-number (you pay) in 1996 or kill it off entirely. For the immediate future, the phone numbers in Figure 11-32 are valid. Jeppeson's JeppLink has been a fee-based service all along, and will not be affected by government cutbacks. The basic information and service available from all three vendors includes but is not limited to:

Severe Weather Forecasts and Alerts
Tropical Depression/Hurricane Advisories
Sigmets and Urgent Sigmets
Airmets
Center Weather Advisories
Area Forecasts

Surface Observations and Trends
Terminal Forecasts
Pilot Reports
Radar Summaries
NOTAMs
Winds and Temperature Aloft Forecasts
FDC NOTAMs (for instrument pilots)
Flight Plan Filing

DTC and GTE offer extra-value services such as weather maps and flight planning for a fee; Jeppeson provides similar services for its basic per-minute charge.

A new entry in the commercial aviation weather arena is facsimile. FAX weather vendors advertise in aviation magazines and newspapers; what they provide, how they provide it, and the cost of the service varies widely.

GTE DUAT
1-800-345-DUAT
Basic service free
Weather maps $1.50 to $2.50 each
Flight planning $5.00

Data Transformation Corp. (DTC)
1-800-AID-DUAT
Basic service free
Weather maps $1.00 per minute
Flight planning .65 per minute

JeppLink
1-800-553-7750
.30 per minute for all services
$3.50 monthly minimum when used

Figure 11-32. DUAT vendors

Pilot Reports

The best resource available to the weather briefers is an observation made by a pilot in flight—a pilot report, or PIREP.

There is no better way for the National Weather Service to fill in the gaps between reporting stations than by PIREPs, and they solicit your cooperation. Figure 11-33 is a PIREP form, available in pads from your local FSS. You don't need a form to make a report, however. Just call Flight Watch on 122.0 or contact a Flight Service Station on its published frequency (you can't go wrong by using 122.2). If you have the form available it will help you organize your report, but if not, the briefer knows what questions to ask.

Pilot reports are disseminated throughout the weather distribution network, and they have a surprising impact. Control towers use PIREPs for hazardous weather avoidance procedures, the FSS uses PIREPs to brief other pilots and provide in-flight advisories, the Air Route Traffic Control Centers use them to expedite the flow of enroute traffic and to determine most favorable altitudes, and the National Weather Service uses the reports to verify or amend conditions contained in aviation forecasts. Your report is important!

A PIREP shows up on the computer screen or teletype at the Flight Service Station looking like this:

UA/ OV OKC-TUL / TM 1800 / FL 120 / TP BE90 / SK 012 BKN 055 / 072 OVC O89 / CLR ABV / TA -9 / WV 0921 / TB MDT 055-072 / ICG LGT-MDT CLR 072-089

The pilot of this BE90 reported enroute from Oklahoma City to Tulsa at 1800 UTC while at 12,000 feet. Two layers of clouds had been encountered, a broken layer with its base at 1,200 feet and its top at 5,500 feet, and a second, overcast layer beginning at 7,200 feet and extending to 8,900 feet, with clear skies above.

The temperature at 12,000 feet was -9°C, and the wind was reported to be from 090 degrees at 21 knots. Moderate turbulence was being experienced

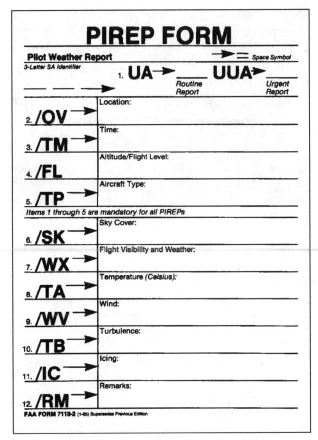

Figure 11-33. PIREP form

between 5,500 feet and 7,200 feet, and light to moderate clear icing was encountered while climbing between 7,200 feet and 8,900 feet.

If you had checked the weather for a trip along that route and had been told that the tops were forecast to be at 18,000 feet, you would be grateful to the anonymous BE90 pilot. On the other hand, if you had planned a VFR flight at 6,500 feet you would be making other arrangements.

In-Flight Weather Detection Devices

As a VFR pilot you cannot fly into the clouds, but sometimes hazardous weather exists in or above a cloud mass that you are flying beneath. It is also possible to inadvertently encounter hazardous weather at night when it cannot be seen to be avoided. You can equip your airplane with devices to ensure that you are able to stay well clear of hazardous weather, day or night.

Figure 11-34. *Airborne weather radar*

Airborne weather radar transmits pulses of radio frequency energy which reflect from precipitation. The reflected energy is amplified in the radar receiver and displayed on a cathode ray tube in the cockpit, providing information on the bearing and distance of the precipitation from the airplane. Both monochrome and color displays offer means of determining the relative strength of the reflected energy and therefore the intensity of the precipitation. Because heavy precipitation implies the presence of turbulence, you should use the radar information to stay well clear of any radar echoes. Because the return from a nearby heavy precipitation return may mask the existence of other echoes further away from your airplane, the interpretation of radar echoes requires training in the proper use of the equipment (Figure 11-34).

Weather detection systems such as the 3M Stormscope and the Strike Finder include passive receivers that detect and display electrical activity instead of precipitation. Because lightning is a part of every thunderstorm, these displays can show you where the storms are so that you can avoid them.

You should not consider weather radar or a weather detection system as a means of finding your way through a line of thunderstorms, since destructive turbulence that cannot be detected by either device may exist in an area where no echoes or returns are visible. Use these devices as weather avoidance aids (Figure 11-35).

Structural Icing and Frost

Structural icing and frost adversely affect airplane performance. For an airplane without deicing equipment, an encounter with inflight airframe icing is

Figure 11-35. *StormScope weather mapping system*

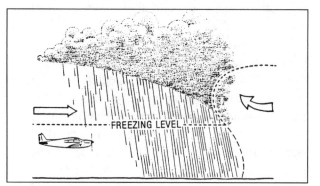

Figure 11-36. *Freezing rain*

viewed as an emergency—to be avoided at all costs. As a VFR pilot (if you are following the rules), the only way you can encounter hazardous structural icing is to fly into an area of freezing rain. It takes both visible moisture and temperatures below freezing to produce ice on your airplane, and while you can comfortably fly in the rain and will enjoy flying in crisp, clear, cold air, you never want to mix the two. Freezing rain will coat your entire airplane (not just the leading edges of the wings and tail surfaces) with ice almost instantaneously, resulting in an immediate, unplanned descent.

The presence of ice pellets at the surface indicates that there is freezing rain at a higher altitude and you definitely should not be flying. The bright side of freezing rain is that conditions conducive to it are readily forecast (Figure 11-36).

Frost presents more of a hazard to the VFR pilot than does freezing rain, because frost looks so harmless. When the surface temperature is below freezing, and the relative humidity is high, frost will form all over your airplane in a process called sublimation: the direct change from water vapor to solid form. Frost does not fall on your airplane, it forms on it. Frost does not weigh much, and it does not change the basic aerodynamic shape of the lifting surfaces; it does, however, create so much drag that it may be impossible to develop enough airspeed to become airborne. Airplanes that do manage to get airborne with a coat of frost find that stall speed has increased dramatically and/or they cannot climb.

Although it is time consuming and delays your flight, all frost must be removed from the airplane or at least polished smooth before flight is attempted. Do not attempt to remove frost (or snow, or ice) with water, either hot or cold. It can run back into control hinges, balanced control surfaces, or gear retraction mechanisms and freeze after takeoff. Use a de-icing fluid diluted as recommended by the manufacturer.

Frost can also be an in-flight hazard if the surface temperature of the airplane is below freezing and you fly into moist air. A layer of frost can form all over the airplane, including the windshield, and turn you into an unprepared, unsuspecting instrument pilot. The only answer is the defroster and/or a descent into warmer air.

Taxiing through puddles on a very cold day can also lead to complications. If you are flying a retractable gear airplane, cycle the gear once or twice after takeoff to be sure that water doesn't freeze the mechanism.

Using Your Weather Knowledge

The greatest hazard you face as a pilot limited to flight under Visual Flight Rules is loss of visual contact with the terrain and the resulting potential for becoming disoriented. Armed with the information in this chapter and a little common sense, you can avoid this hazard.

Obstructions to vision are related to moisture in the air. That moisture might take the form of a cloud, a rain shower, snow, or fog. Look at the big picture:

Is the wind coming from over a body of water toward rising terrain? (It doesn't have to be a lake or ocean. Rain-soaked ground can provide plenty of moisture.) Are you flying toward an area where the air mass is cooler? Is the temperature-dewpoint spread decreasing? Will the air in your vicinity be cooled enough by the approach of nightfall that any moisture it contains will condense into clouds?

If the natural horizon becomes obscured, consider a 180 degree turn toward safety. Don't assume that the horizon is where the base of the clouds meets the mountains, and reverse your vertical speed if climbing or descending—that can be a trap. Don't fly on top of a scattered cloud layer unless you are prepared to reverse course when they begin to thicken beneath you. Never fly on top of a broken or overcast layer. Always fly toward improving weather.

Attempting visual flight into weather conditions that require an instrument rating is the leading cause of accidents for non-instrument rated pilots with less than 400 hours of flight experience. If your flight will only be completed safely if the tailwind forecast holds up, or if the scattered thunderstorms don't occur on your flight path, or any similar "if," don't go.

When looking at a marginal weather situation and contemplating whether or not to go and take a look, remember the old pilot's motto: It is better to be on the ground wishing you were flying than to be up in the air wishing you were on the ground.

Chapter 11
Weather Review Questions

1. The conditions necessary for the formation of cumulonimbus clouds are a lifting action and

    A—unstable air containing an excess of condensation nuclei.
    B—unstable, moist air.
    C—either stable or unstable air.

2. The wind at 5,000 feet AGL is southwesterly while the surface wind is southerly. This difference in direction is primarily due to

    A—stronger pressure gradient at higher altitudes.
    B—friction between the wind and the surface.
    C—stronger Coriolis force at the surface.

3. Clouds, fog, or dew will always form when

    A—water vapor condenses.
    B—water vapor is present.
    C—relative humidity reaches 100 percent.

4. Steady precipitation preceding a front is an indication of

    A—stratiform clouds with moderate turbulence.
    B—cumuliform clouds with little or no turbulence.
    C—stratiform clouds with little or no turbulence.

5. How does frost affect the lifting surfaces of an airplane on takeoff?

    A—Frost may prevent the airplane from becoming airborne at normal takeoff speed.
    B—Frost will change the camber of the wing, increasing lift during takeoff.
    C—Frost may cause the airplane to become airborne with a lower angle of attack at a lower indicated airspeed.

6. What types of fog depend upon wind in order to exist?

    A—Radiation fog and ice fog.
    B—Steam fog and ground fog.
    C—Advection fog and upslope fog.

7. What conditions are necessary for the formation of thunderstorms?

    A—High humidity, lifting force, and unstable conditions.
    B—High humidity, high temperature, and cumulus clouds.
    C—Lifting force, moist air, and extensive cloud cover.

8. If there is thunderstorm activity in the vicinity of an airport at which you plan to land, which hazardous atmospheric phenomenon might be expected on the landing approach?

    A—Precipitation static.
    B—Wind-shear turbulence.
    C—Steady rain.

9. An almond or lens-shaped cloud which appears stationary, but which may contain winds of 50 knots or more, is referred to as

    A—an inactive frontal cloud.
    B—a funnel cloud.
    C—a lenticular cloud.

10. Every physical process of weather is accompanied by, or is the result of, a

A—movement of air.
B—pressure differential.
C—heat exchange.

11. What causes variations in altimeter settings between weather reporting points?

A—Unequal heating of the Earth's surface.
B—Variation of terrain elevation.
C—Coriolis force.

12. What are the standard pressure and temperature values for sea level?

A—15°C and 29.92" Hg.
B—59°C and 1013.2 millibars.
C—59°F and 29.92 millibars.

13. Radar weather reports are of special interest to pilots because they indicate

A—large areas of low ceilings and fog.
B—location of precipitation along with type, intensity, and trend.
C—location of broken to overcast clouds.

14. Ceiling is defined as the height above the Earth's surface of the

A—lowest reported obscuration and the highest layer of clouds reported as overcast.
B—lowest layer of clouds or obscuring phenomena reported as broken, overcast, and not classified as thin or partial.
C—lowest layer of clouds reported as scattered, broken, or thin.

15. From which primary source should information be obtained regarding expected weather at your destination and estimated time of arrival?

A—Low Level Prog Chart.
B—Weather Depiction Chart.
C—Terminal Forecast.

16. Upon encountering severe turbulence, which flight condition should the pilot attempt to maintain?

A—Constant altitude and airspeed.
B—Constant angle of attack.
C—Level flight attitude.

17. In which situation is advection fog most likely to form?

A—A warm, moist air mass on the windward side of mountains.
B—An air mass moving inland from the coast in winter.
C—A light breeze blowing colder air out to sea.

18. The base and tops of the overcast layer reported by a pilot in this PIREP are

UA / OV ICT / TM 1230 / FL 140 /TP M2OK / SK020 BKN 045 / O76 OVC 092 / TA-10 / WV2135 / TB LCT / ICG LGT

A—2,000 ft. MSL and 4,500 ft. MSL.
B—7,600 ft. AGL and 9,200 ft. AGL.
C—7,600 ft. MSL and 9,200 ft. MSL.

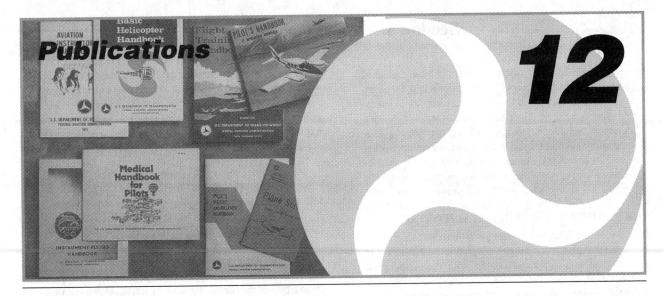

Publications

As you progress with your pilot training, your instructor will give you what will seem to be a never-ending series of instructions, procedures, methods, restrictions and advisories, and you will wonder how you will be able to remember it all. You don't have to. The Government Printing Office distributes hundreds of publications on aviation subjects and you should become familiar with what is available. All government publications are available from the Government Printing Office (GPO) in Washington, D.C. and GPO bookstores in major cities, but you will find that your local pilot supply store carries many of them. Private publishers have reprints which are more convenient to use and considerably less expensive than the government publication (but no less official). The ASA editions of the Federal Aviation Regulations and Airman's information Manual are excellent examples.

Airman's Information Manual

This is the basic reference for procedures, although it contains invaluable information on a host of aviation subjects. This list of chapter headings will give you some idea of the extent of coverage:

1. Navigation Aids
2. Aeronautical Lighting and Airport Marking Aids
3. Airspace
4. Air Traffic Control
5. Emergency Procedures
6. Safety of Flight
7. Medical Facts for Pilots
8. Aeronautical charts and Related Publications

Figure 12-1 on Page 12-2 is an example of the type of detailed information on procedures available in the Airmans information Manual. The **AIM** also includes a Pilot/Controller Glossary, so that you will know exactly what the controller means when instructions are given, and it is reprinted in the Appendix for your convenience. The AIM is updated every 16 weeks and is available by subscription from the Government Printing Office. You will also find it for sale by itself or combined with the Federal Aviation Regulations by ASA at your pilot supply store. ASA provides free update sheets with each volume to keep pilots current on changes in regulations and procedures.

Federal Aviation Regulations

Every pilot should have a copy of the **FARs**, and you will find the ASA combination FAR/AIM, which are updated yearly, books at the pilot supply store (Figure 12-2). The FAA does not change the regulations very often, and proposed changes are well publicized in aviation newspapers and magazines. The FARs are available from the Government Printing Office by subscription; subscribers are sent Notices of Proposed Rule Making when regulatory changes are being considered. In this book, the FARs will be discussed as they apply in discussing each subject. In Chapter 14 there is a discussion of FARs requiring explanation or illustration.

Airport/Facility Directory

Before setting off on a cross-country flight, you are required to become familiar with all available information regarding the flight, and the Airport/Facility

Section 3. Airport Operations

4-51. GENERAL

Increased traffic congestion, aircraft in climb and descent attitudes, and pilots preoccupation with cockpit duties are some factors that increase the hazardous accident potential near the airport. The situation is further compounded when the weather is marginal-that is, just meeting VFR requirements. Pilots must be particularly alert when operating in the vicinity of an airport. This section defines some rules, practices and procedures that pilots should be familiar with and adhere to for safe airport operations.

4-52. TOWER CONTROLLED AIRPORTS

a. When operating at an airport where traffic control is being exercised by a control tower, pilots are required to maintain two-way radio contact with the tower while operating within the CLASS, B, C, AND D SURFACE AREA unless the tower authorizes otherwise. Initial callup should be made about 15 miles from the airport. Unless there is good reason to leave the tower frequency before exiting the CLASS B, C, AND D SURFACE AREA, it is a good operating practice to remain on the tower frequency for the purpose of receiving traffic information. In the interest of reducing tower frequency congestion, pilots are reminded that it is not necessary to request permission to leave the tower frequency once outside of the CLASS B, C, AND D SURFACE AREA.

b. When necessary, the tower controller will issue clearances or other information for aircraft to generally follow the desired flight path (traffic patterns) when flying in the CLASS B, C, AND D SURFACE AREA and the proper taxi routes when operating on the ground. If not otherwise authorized or directed by the tower, pilots of fixed-wing aircraft approaching to land must circle the airport to the left. Pilots approaching to land in a helicopter must avoid the flow of fixed-wing traffic. However, in all instances, an appropriate clearance must be received from the tower before landing.

Figure 4—52[1]

NOTE – This diagram is intended only to illustrate terminology used in identifying various components of a traffic pattern. It should not be used as a reference or guide on how to enter a traffic pattern.

NOTE—This diagram is intended only to illustrate terminology used in identifying various components of a traffic pattern.

It should not be used as a reference or guide on how to enter a traffic pattern.

c. The following terminology for the various components of a traffic pattern has been adopted as standard for use by control towers and pilots (See Figure 4-52[1]):

1. Upwind leg—A flight path parallel to the landing runway in the direction of landing.

2. Crosswind leg—A flight path at right angles to the landing runway off its takeoff end.

3. Downwind leg—A flight path parallel to the landing runway in the opposite direction of landing.

4. Base leg—A flight path at right angles to the landing runway off its approach end and extending from the downwind leg to the intersection of the extended runway centerline.

Figure 12-1. Example of detailed information on procedures in AIM

Figure 12-2. FAR/AIM Series

Directory (A/FD) is your source of information on the destination airport and any others along the route you may decide to visit. Aeronautical charts show the elevation, runway length, and limited radio frequency information for an airport, but only in the Airport/Facility Directory will you learn that the runway is gravel, 75 feet wide, with trees on the west, and that it slopes upward to the north. The legend for individual airport listings is provided in Appendix D, Pages D-1 through D-7. You will also find pertinent excerpts in Chapter 16 (Flight Planning). In addition to the individual airport listings, the A/FD contains:

Special notices in regard to airports listed
FSS and National Weather Service telephone numbers
Frequencies of Air Route Traffic Control Centers
FAA General Aviation District Office telephone numbers
VOR receiver check points
Parachute jumping areas
Aeronautical Chart Bulletin

Location of Enroute Flight Advisory Stations (Flight Watch)

The Airport/Facility Directory is published in seven volumes depending on geographic location and is revised every 56 days.

Advisory Circulars

The Federal Aviation Regulations are brief and concise, written by and for lawyers, not pilots. There are many situations where a regulation or a procedure needs to be explained in detail so that the flying public can understand exactly what is required. This is the function of Advisory Circulars. ACs are non-regulatory in nature, serving only to explain the actual regulation or provide additional useful information to aid in compliance; however, the government expects every pilot to be aware of information published only in Advisory Circulars! Unfortunately, many pilots are unaware of their existence. Your instructor or flight school should have a copy of Advisory Circular 00, which is a complete listing of all current Advisory Circulars.

AC NO: 91-43

DATE: 6/26/75

ADVISORY CIRCULAR

DEPARTMENT OF TRANSPORTATION
FEDERAL AVIATION ADMINISTRATION

SUBJECT: UNRELIABLE AIRSPEED INDICATIONS

1. **PURPOSE.** The purpose of this Advisory Circular is to alert pilots to the possibility of erroneous airspeed/Mach indications that may be caused by blocking or freezing of the pitot system, and corrective action to be taken.

2. **BACKGROUND.** Unreliable airspeed/Mach indications may have contributed to one recent serious incident and a fatal accident. A frozen or blocked pitot system may have caused the unreliable indications. These erroneous readings can be so subtle, that a pilot may not detect the problem until it is too late for adequate corrective action. Many pilots may associate a frozen pitot head with symptoms of a rapidly decreasing or zero airspeed indication. This is not always the case, especially when operating high performance aircraft at high altitudes.

3. **DESCRIPTION.** When blocking or freezing of the pitot system occurs, two situations can develop as follows:

   a. If the ram air input to the pitot head is blocked, the indicated airspeed may drop to zero; and

   b. If the ram air input plus the drain hole is blocked, the pressure is trapped in the system and the airspeed indicator may react as an altimeter; e.g.:

      (1) During level flight, airspeed indication will not change even when actual airspeed is varied by large power changes;

      (2) During climb, airspeed indication will increase; and

      (3) During descent, airspeed indication will decrease.

4. **RECOMMENDATIONS.** Due to the critical nature of this in-flight problem, pilots should be aware of indications symptomatic of a frozen or blocked pitot system and take the following corrective action:

   a. Emphasis should be on attitude flying when these symptoms are recognized.

   b. Check position of pitot heat switches and associated circuit breakers.

   c. If conditions during or shortly after takeoff are conducive to pitot system icing, pitot heat should be on prior to flight.

R. P. SKULLY, Director
Flight Standards Service

Figure 12-3. Typical Advisory Circular

Advisory Circulars are numbered to correspond with the FARs—here are two examples: FAR Part 61 deals with airman and flight instructor certification, while Advisory Circular 61-65 explains flight instructor duties and responsibilities; FAR Part 91 is General Operating Rules, and Advisory Circular 91-23 is "the book" on weight and balance. Most pilots are only aware of those Advisory Circulars which are published in book form, such as *Aviation Weather* (AC 00-6A) or the *Flight Training Handbook* (AC 61-21A), but you should investigate whether the FAA publishes an AC on any subject you may be curious about. You can order Advisory Circulars (most are free, but some are for sale) from the Superintendent of Documents at the Government Printing Office in Washington, D. C. Figure 12-3 is a typical Advisory Circular.

Notices to Airmen

Information that might affect the safety of a flight, such as a runway closure, navaid outage, lighting system change, etc., is available from your Flight Service Station briefer.

Your briefer has ready access to local (L) NOTAMs, which concern airports within approximately 400 miles of the FSS. Items considered to be of local interest only are such things as taxiway closures, workers and equipment on the runways, rotating beacon outages, etc. If you want local NOTAM information for an airport in another FSS's area you will have to specifically request it. For long cross-country trips it is sometimes valuable to call one of the operators at your destination airport for last-minute information like "the gas pump is broken!!"

Distant (D) NOTAMs report things that might affect your decision to make a flight, such as VOR outages, runway closures, etc. Distant NOTAMs show up on the briefer's computer screen along with the hourly sequences.

Every two weeks the FAA publishes a book of what they call Class II NOTAMs, which involve long-term (but not permanent) changes. When a NOTAM is published in this book it no longer shows up on the briefer's screen; if you don't ask the briefer for any published NOTAMs that will affect your flight you will never find out about them.

Aviation Media

All pilots are expected to stay abreast of changes in regulations and procedures, but advancing technology is teaching new ways of navigating and of solving some of the mysteries of weather, and pilots cannot expect today's methods to apply forever. The aviation press is the best source of information on the changing world of flight, and we recommend that you read aviation newspapers and magazines.

Personal computer users will find that online services offer a wealth of information. The Aviation Special Interest Group Forum on CompuServe is where I hang out (my number is 72247,2617), but America Online and Prodigy also have areas where pilots can get together to exchange information. Internet users will find the rec.aviation newsgroup to be another good place to surf (I'm bobmrg@halcyon.com).

Refer to Notices to Airmen (Figure Q12-1) for questions 1 and 2.

1. What is the status of the runway lights for a landing at New Smyrna Beach Muni 1 on Rwy 15 after 2400?

A—For runway lights, key the transmitter the proper number of times on 122.8 MHz.
B—The lights on this runway are not operated at night.
C—The runway lights operate from dark to dawn.

2. The traffic pattern for light airplanes and gyroplanes at Ft. Lauderdale-Hollywood International Airport is changed to

A—800 ft.
B—1,000 ft.
C—1,300 ft.

3. FAA Advisory Circulars (some free, others at cost) are available to all pilots and are obtained by

A—distribution from the nearest FAA district office.
B—ordering those desired.
C—subscribing to the Federal Register.

4. information concerning parachute jumping sites maybe found in the

A—Graphic Notices and Supplemental Data.
B—Airport/Facility Directory.
C—NOTAMs.

```
                    FLORIDA
FT LAUDERDALE EXECUTIVE ARPT:  TPA  800  ft.
 TPA  for  jets  1300  ft. 4 Box VASI cmsnd
 left side Rwy 26. 2 Box VASI cmsnd  left
 side Rwy 13.  (3/81)
FT LAUDERDALE-HOLLYWOOD INTL ARPT: TPA 1000
 ft.  Thr Rwy 27L dsplcd 401 ft.  Thr  Rwy
 09L dsplcd 609 ft.  Thr Rwy 27R dsplcd 599
 ft. (3/81)
FT  MYERS  PAGE  FIELD ARPT:  Unicom  Freq
 123.05. (3/81)
MIAMI INTL ARPT: Wide Body & DC-8 acft  lndg
 Rwy 09L  & desiring to taxi west on Twy M
 are advised to use Twys M-8, M-9, M-10, M-
 11 or the end. Twys are numbered W to  E.
 (3/81) RVR Rwy 27L OTS UFN. (3/81)
NEW SMYRNA BEACH MUNI ARPT: Rwy 15/33 Rwy
 lgts oper dusk-dawn. Rwy  11/29  Rwy  lgts
 oper  dusk-2400.  For VASI and Rwy 11/29
 Rwy lgts after 2400 key 122.8 3 times  for
 low,  5  times  for  med,  and 7 times for
 high. (1/81)
```

Figure Q12-1. Notices to Airmen

Physical Effects

13

Medical Factors for Pilots

Chapter 3 discussed how to determine the health of the engine, and Chapter 6 discussed airplane performance under different conditions. This chapter will discuss the human element: how the performance of the pilot is affected by health and environmental factors. Many physical conditions which have minimal effect on the body's performance at ground level can have severe consequences "at altitude," which includes the upper limit operating levels of even small, single-engine airplanes. You should be aware of these conditions so that you can avoid problems with your own physical state during flight, and help your passengers have a safe and comfortable experience.

Drugs and Alcohol

The effects of drugs and alcohol on performance are intensified by altitude, and pilots are prohibited from flying within 8 hours of ingesting *any* alcoholic beverage and from flying while under the influence of any drug or medication. Even over-the-counter medications as seemingly innocuous as cough suppressants can affect judgment, memory, and alertness at altitude; pilots should check with an Aviation Medical Examiner for advice if in doubt about any medication. Pilots are required to ground themselves if they have any medical condition which affects their abilities as flight crewmembers.

Figure 13-2. Effects of alcohol are intensified by altitude.

Figure 13-1. Self-grounding is required when a pilot is feeling ill.

Hypoxia

Our bodies are acclimated to life on the ground where the atmosphere contains approximately 21 percent oxygen, and they require that same *amount* of oxygen in order to operate efficiently at altitude, where the atmosphere is thinner. A small pressure differential is required in your lungs to allow oxygen to be transferred to your bloodstream. As you climb to altitudes where pressure is reduced, the exchange of oxygen is inhibited, and the symptoms of hypoxia (oxygen sickness) begin to occur unless *supplemental* oxygen is used. These symptoms usually do not affect healthy, non-smoking pilots at altitudes below 12,000 feet in the daytime; deterioration in night vision can occur as low as 5,000 feet. *The body has no built-in alarm system to warn of hypoxia!* Symptoms of hypoxia include impaired judgment, memory, alertness, coordination, and the loss of ability to make calculations, and are followed by headache and drowsiness. The most insidious symptom is a state of euphoria or well-being: "I feel great! I just can't seem to figure out this VOR."

The agent in the blood which absorbs oxygen is called **hemoglobin**, and the ability of the hemoglobin to utilize oxygen can be reduced by carbon monoxide from smoking or exhaust fumes. Heavy smokers may experience the symptoms of hypoxia at much lower altitudes than non-smokers.

You can experience the symptoms of hypoxia under controlled conditions in an altitude chamber at a military facility. The local office of the Federal Aviation Administration has details on how to apply for this valuable physiology training. You may say "it can't happen to me," but when you find that you can't write your name or add a column of figures when deprived of oxygen in an altitude chamber, you will be convinced of the value of supplemental oxygen. The regulations governing use of oxygen are discussed in Chapter 15.

Hyperventilation

Rapid breathing under stress can reduce the amount of carbon dioxide in the lungs, leading to lightheadedness, drowsiness, tingling in the fingers, and eventual unconsciousness. The body requires a certain level of carbon dioxide in order to trigger the breathing reflex.

Figure 13-4. Supplementary oxygen is recommended at altitudes above 10,000' MSL.

Figure 13-3. Euphoria is a symptom of hypoxia.

Figure 13-5. Hyperventilation causes dizziness and may lead to loss of consciousness.

Flight situations which seem quite normal to a pilot may create stress in passengers, and hyperventilation is usually a passenger problem. A conscious slowing of the breathing rate will relieve symptoms of hyperventilation, and breathing into cupped hands or a paper bag to increase intake of carbon dioxide will also help. It is usually difficult to get children to control their breathing rate, and the cupped hands or bag method is most effective with them.

It is possible to experience the symptoms of hypoxia and hyperventilation simultaneously (if you are above 14,000 feet without oxygen you will surely be under stress!). If oxygen *is* available it should be set to deliver full flow immediately. As is the case in many other precarious flight situations, the best preventive is not getting into the situation in the first place.

Carbon Monoxide Poisoning

Even small amounts of carbon monoxide in the lungs inhibit the ability of the blood's hemoglobin to use oxygen efficiently, and the most common source of carbon monoxide in flight is the airplane's heater system. Carbon monoxide is tasteless and odorless, and the smell of exhaust gas cannot be relied on to warn of its presence. Chemical detectors which darken in the presence of carbon monoxide are available at pilot supply stores. If the smell of exhaust *is* noticed, of course, the heater should be shut off, all air vents opened, and a landing made at the nearest airport. If carbon monoxide does get into your bloodstream, it may take several days to dissipate—you can't get the heater fixed and take off again the same day without the possibility of experiencing hypoxia.

Flying and Diving

Many pilots enjoy both flying and scuba diving, and if you are in this group you should be aware that the two do not mix. Diving immediately after landing should cause no problems. Flying immediately after diving will cause problems, because the nitrogen forced into your joints while underwater may cause the "bends" in flight due to the reduced pressure at altitude. An extra day on the beach will probably eliminate that possibility.

Ear Problems

The changing pressures of flight can cause painful ear problems if the pilot or passenger is unable to equalize the pressure in the middle ear. When the airplane is climbing, air trapped in the middle ear expands and exits through the Eustachian tubes into the mouth, causing no problems. During descent, however, the pilot or passenger must attempt to equalize the pressure in the middle ear by yawning, swallowing, or tensing the throat muscles. Chewing gum can help. Holding the nose and "blowing gently" with the head held back can open the Eustachian tubes this is called the "valsalva" maneuver. *Caution:* don't ever "valsalva" when you have a head cold, as serious sinus infection may result.

If a passenger is experiencing ear blockage during descent, it may be necessary to climb until the pain is relieved, and then descend at a reduced rate. Because the potential for ear problems is always present when flying, pilots should not fly with any upper respiratory infection, such as a cold or sore throat. Be very wary of accepting passenger's assurances that, although they have a cold, they will not be bothered by flying. Remember, the problem becomes apparent on the way *down*, after it is too late to avoid it!

Vertigo

There are several illusions in flight which can lead to vertigo, which is best described as a disagreement between what your eyes and your body report to your brain. Almost everyone has had the experience of sitting in an automobile when an adjacent automobile begins to move slowly—the natural reaction is to step on your brakes, because for an instant your brain isn't sure which vehicle is moving. That is one form of vertigo, or spatial disorientation.

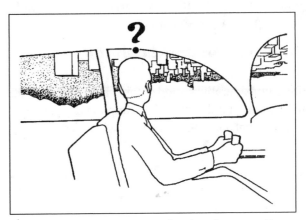

Figure 13-6. Disorientation results when the senses disagree.

There are many situations which can lead to spatial disorientation in flight, but the most common is loss of visual reference to the horizon. Non-instrument rated pilots, or pilots who have not learned to use the flight instruments when visual reference is lost, react to bodily sensations and may lose control of the airplane. It is not possible to "fly by the seat of your pants."

Your middle ear contains three tubes filled with liquid, and the inner surfaces of these tubes are lined with thousands of tiny hairs which sense movement of the liquid. It is the messages that these tiny hairs send to your brain that provide your sense of balance. When a turn begins, your brain gets the correct message, but if the maneuver is protracted the liquid stops moving, and the information to the brain is that the turn has stopped. If you then actually stop the turn, the liquid begins to flow the other way, and your middle ear tells your brain that the turn has reversed! During your training for the private pilot certificate, you will be taught how to use the flight instruments to keep the airplane under control while returning to visual conditions.

The most valuable of the five senses in flight is vision: believe the instruments, and avoid head movement. *See* Figure 13-6.

Another source of illusion and the potential for vertigo is flight on a clear, starlit night with scattered lights on the ground. With no horizon to separate the lights on the ground from the stars, it is possible to become disoriented and lose control of the airplane. Again, training in the use of the flight instruments will keep you right side up.

Night Vision and Scanning

Your eyes will adapt to dim light conditions, but only after a considerable period of time. It takes at least 30 minutes in total darkness for complete dark adaptation, and that adaptation can be lost by a few seconds exposure to a bright light. The use of red lights for cockpit lighting at night causes difficulty in reading aeronautical charts, and dim white lighting is standard. You should make every effort to become dark adapted, however, because other airplanes can only be detected at night by their lights and you want to detect them as far away as possible.

When landing at night, do not fly any differently than you do in daytime VFR conditions; visual illusions at night can lead you to dive for the runway or level off too high. Check your flight instruments to ensure that your attitude and airspeed are within normal limits.

Scanning the sky for other aircraft is just as important as maintaining control of your airplane, and deserves equal attention. You should not limit your scan to those areas ahead of the airplane at your altitude, but should scan systematically from over your left shoulder to as far to the right as you can see, looking both below and above your altitude. A constant sweep of the eyes will not be effective, because your eyes need time to focus on objects, so momentarily stopping for at least a second will enhance your ability to detect other airplanes. At night, because of the way your eyes work, you will see only those objects which are slightly out of your direct line of sight, and your scan will have to be slower and more deliberate.

Hazy conditions are especially difficult for pilots. With nothing specific to focus on, your eyes relax and "coast," seeking a comfortable focusing distance 10 to 30 feet in front of the aircraft. You are looking but not seeing. Because of the lack of contrast, terrain and obstacles appear to be further away than their actual distance. Choose any distant object that presents itself, even the top of a distant cloud, to keep your eyes working.

Chapter 13
Physical Effects Review Questions

1. A state of temporary confusion resulting from misleading information being sent to the brain by various sensory organs is defined as

    A—spatial disorientation.
    B—hyperventilation.
    C—hypoxia.

2. To preclude the effects of hypoxia, you should

    A—avoid flying above 10,000 ft. MSL for prolonged periods without breathing supplemental oxygen.
    B—rely on your body's built-in alarm system to warn when you are not getting enough oxygen.
    C—avoid hyperventilation which is caused by rapid heavy breathing and results in excessive carbon dioxide in the bloodstream.

3. Hypoxia is caused by

    A—nitrogen bubbles forming in the blood at high altitudes.
    B—trapped gasses in the body.
    C—reduced atmospheric pressure.

4. What is the most effective way to use the eyes during night flight?

    A—Look only at far away, dim lights.
    B—Scan slowly to permit off center viewing.
    C—Concentrate directly on each object for a few seconds.

5. The danger of spatial disorientation during flight in poor visual conditions may be reduced by

    A—shifting the eyes quickly between the exterior visual field and the instrument panel.
    B—having faith in the instruments rather than taking a chance on the sensory organs.
    C—leaning the body in the opposite direction of the motion of the aircraft.

6. What effect does haze have on the ability to see traffic or terrain features during flight?

    A—Haze causes the eyes to focus at infinity.
    B—Contrasting colors become less distinct making objects easier to see.
    C—All traffic or terrain features appear to be farther away than their actual distance.

Answers:
1—A, 2—A, 3—C, 4—B, 5—B, 6—C

As you plan a cross-country flight, you know that the ability to maneuver in three dimensions makes you responsible for being aware at all times of your position, both geographic and vertical. You must insure that you are always in compliance with the airspace regulations of the FARs. These regulations are intended to keep airplanes safely separated and, in the case of VFR pilots, to provide minimum visibility and cloud clearance distances so that conflicting traffic can be seen in time for corrective action to be taken. "See and be seen" is the basis of safe operations in the National Airspace System.

Controlled vs. Class G (Uncontrolled) Airspace

You will encounter the terms controlled and uncontrolled airspace frequently, and you must not assume that flight in controlled airspace means that Big Brother will be watching you to detect violations, or that uncontrolled airspace is a no-man's land for flight. For your purposes as a VFR pilot, controlled and uncontrolled airspace refer to visibility and cloud clearance standards, nothing more. Controlled airspace is "controlled" to protect pilots flying under instrument flight rules from conflicts with pilots flying under visual flight rules; when a pilot operating under IFR pops out of a cloud, there should be enough visibility and cloud clearance to see and avoid a VFR flight. For that reason, you should accept the restrictions discussed in this chapter as *minimums* and allow more leeway whenever possible.

Controlled Airspace includes Class A, B, C, D, and E airspace (Figure 14-1 on Page 14-2). Look at the sectional chart excerpt and notice the blue and magenta tints—they represent the horizontal boundaries of controlled airspace (Class A airspace begins at 18,000' MSL, and that is as high as a Sectional goes). Blue is only used where it abuts Class G airspace, however.

At airports with instrument approach procedures, controlled airspace can start at the surface—each of these situations will be covered in detail later. Figure 14-1 will give you an idea of what to expect. As you can see, most controlled airspace is Class E.

Follow the 069 radial of the Seattle VORTAC eastward (it's the V-120 airway). Until you fly past TAGOR intersection and cross the magenta line, you are in Class E airspace if your airplane is at least 700 feet above the ground; the fact that the magenta tint fades in the direction of Seattle indicates that this floor applies in the entire area surrounded by the tint.

After you pass the magenta line flying eastward along the 069 degree radial, the floor of Class E airspace becomes 1,200 feet above the ground (no shading) and that situation remains until you get to the magenta dashed line around the Wenatchee VORTAC.

Now look north and south of the 069 degree radial. If you turn to the north, you will cross a blue line that looks like a zipper into airspace labeled "9,500

Airspace Reclassification at a Glance

FL 600
18,000 MSL

Class A

Class E

14,500 AGL

Class B

Class C

Class D

Class G

Nontowered Airport

700 AGL

Class G

Class G

1,200 AGL

Class G

AGL – above ground level   FL – flight level   MSL – mean sea level

Figure 14-1. Airspace Classification

MSL." Because the elevation of the terrain varies so rapidly in mountainous terrain, it would be impossible for you to know whether or not you were flying 1,200 feet above the surface; accordingly, the notation tells you that the floor of Class E airspace is 9,500 feet MSL, not 1,200 feet AGL, in the area bounded by the zipper lines.

If you look south of V-120 you will see a triangle of airspace bounded by the hard edge of blue tint. Blue tint is charted only when it abuts Class G (uncontrolled) airspace, and that is the situation here: that triangle represents Class G airspace that starts at the surface and goes all the way up to 14,500 feet MSL. This type of airspace is an endangered species, existing almost exclusively in the mountains of the West.

Note that blue exists on either side of V-2-298, the 085 degree radial of SEA. That tells you that, in the absence of other labeling, the floor of controlled airspace along airways is 1,200 feet AGL and abuts Class G airspace up to 14,500 feet MSL.

As you fly across the country, then, you will spend almost all of your time in controlled airspace; you will have to have at least 3 miles flight visibility, stay 500 feet below clouds and/or 1,000 feet above them, and maintain a horizontal distance from clouds of at least 2,000 feet. If you follow these simple rules you will not become a victim of general aviation's greatest killer, visual flight into deteriorating weather.

Unless you are taking your flight training at an airport in the mountains, you will spend most of your time at altitudes below 10,000 feet MSL and the visibility and cloud clearance values above will apply. When you fly higher than 10,000 feet MSL, however, new rules apply. You will have no difficulty in remembering them if you keep in mind that there is no speed limit above that altitude. A cloud 2,000 feet away might hide a 240-knot turboprop or a 500-knot jet, so horizontal cloud clearance increases to 1 mile; these airplanes climb and descend at steep angles, so you must fly at least 1,000 feet above or below any clouds. Because of unrestricted speed, required flight visibility increases to 5 miles.

Class A Airspace

Class A airspace exists from 18,000 feet MSL to Flight Level 600 (all altitudes above 18,000 feet are called Flight Levels; FL230 is 23,000 feet, more or less). To fly in Class A airspace you must be instrument rated and operating on an instrument clearance; there is no VFR flying in Class A airspace. If you have to climb higher than 18,000 feet to stay out of the clouds (got that oxygen handy?) you must call Air Traffic Control and declare an emergency to avoid getting a violation.

Class B Airspace

The most important thing for you to remember about Class B airspace is that you cannot operate within its boundaries unless you have a specific clearance from

ATC to do so. Class B airspace (Figure 14-2) is shown on Sectional and WAC charts by solid blue circles or arcs; each segment within the airspace is identified with what looks like a fraction. On the Seattle Sectional chart excerpt the top of the fraction is 100, indicating that the top of Seattle's Class B airspace is 10,000 feet MSL; you can fly over the airspace at 10,500 feet without a clearance.

The bottom of the fraction is the floor of the airspace in thousands of feet; east of Bremerton National Airport (left edge of the excerpt) you can fly beneath the Class B airspace at 5,500 feet and west of Bremerton the Class B airspace does not exist. Note that the floor of Class B airspace over Seattle-Tacoma Airport is the surface of the airport itself.

Class B airspace is controlled airspace, of course, and you must have at least 3 miles flight visibility when flying in it. Cloud clearance is a special case, however; because a controller is keeping you away from other traffic by assigning heading and altitudes, you need not observe the cloud clearance requirements of other types of controlled airspace. "Clear of clouds" is the standard.

If you want to land at or depart from the primary airport in Class B airspace when the weather is marginal and you need a Special VFR clearance, look for the notation NO SVFR above the airport data block (see Seattle-Tacoma International Airport). Where you see that notation you are out of luck unless you are flying a helicopter.

Chapter 15 discusses the equipment requirements in Class B airspace, so they won't be covered here. You do need to know that the distances that define the airspace are measured horizontally on the ground, while your distance measuring equipment (DME) in the airplane reads slant range from the transmitting antenna. When your DME reads 10.0 miles, then, your horizontal distance from the antenna may be something like 9.8 miles, depending on your altitude. Moral: stay at least 1 mile outside of a charted boundary to be safe.

The next concern is altitude. I said earlier that you can legally fly 500 feet above the top of Class B airspace, but do you think that would be a safe thing to do when jets are climbing out at 4,000 to 6,000 feet

Figure 14-2. *Class B airspace*

per minute? Flight 500 feet below a shelf in the airspace, like the 5,500 feet east of Bremerton suggested earlier, might be a tad safer, but why take a chance? Unless you are going to ask for a clearance and enter Class B airspace, give it a wide berth.

As a VFR pilot, should you avoid Class B airspace entirely? What if you wanted to fly from Bremerton to an airport on the east edge of the chart excerpt. Would you fly all the way around just to keep from asking for a clearance? That doesn't make sense to me. You should have a Terminal Area Chart for the Class B airspace, and if you are a student you need specific instruction and a logbook endorsement from an instructor. In the Seattle area, with those requirements met all you need to do is call the radar facility that owns the airspace (shown on the Terminal Area Chart) and say "Seattle Approach, Whizbang 2345X at 2,000 feet over Bremerton, request clearance through your airspace, destination is Ellensburg." Almost always, you will hear "Cleared to operate in the Seattle Class B airspace, maintain 2,500 feet and squawk 4566." Occasionally, however, the controller will say "unable," and you will have to fly all the way around. Student pilots are prohibited from operating to or from the following airports within Class B airspace:

Atlanta	Newark
Boston	Kennedy
Chicago	La Guardia
Dallas	San Francisco
Los Angeles	Washington National
Miami	Andrews AFB

Class C Airspace

The portion of the Seattle Sectional Chart that has been excerpted for your use does not contain any Class C airspace. A little further north you would encounter some that surrounds the Whidbey Island Naval Air Station, quite a bit south you would find Class C airspace around the Portland International Airport, and off the chart to the east is the Spokane International Airport Class C airspace. In each case, the horizontal boundaries are shown by solid magenta circles.

What do the Whidbey Island, Portland, and Spokane have in common? Lots of jet traffic, but not enough to qualify for designation as Class B airspace. The controllers do not need to guide your every move, as they do in Seattle, but they do need to know who you are and what you intend to do in their airspace. Note that a clearance is not required to operate in Class C airspace, just two-way communication between you and the radar controller whose airspace you want to use.

Class C airspace is shown on Sectional and WAC charts by solid magenta circles or arcs; each segment within the airspace is identified with what looks like a fraction. In Figure 14-3 the top fraction is 40, indicating that the top of Whidbey Island's Class C airspace is 4,000 feet MSL; you can fly over the airspace at 4,500 feet without a clearance. The bottom of the fraction is the floor of the airspace in thousands of feet; i.e., 1,300 or 2,000. Note that the floor of Class C airspace over Whidbey Island Naval Air Station is the surface of the airport itself.

Extending a further 10 miles from the primary airport is the outer area; note that when you are at the edge of the outer area you are still 10 miles from the Class C airspace. The floor of the outer area is the lowest altitude at which radar coverage is available, and its ceiling is the top of the radar facility's airspace. The purpose of the outer area is to give pilots an opportunity to contact ATC in plenty of time. If you do not intend to land at the primary airspace you can fly through the outer area without saying anything to anyone, although it helps other pilots if you tell the radar facility your position and intentions.

Figure 14-3. *Whidbey Island Class C airspace*

What is the official definition of "communication?" Of course, if you call ATC and get a specific response that includes your airplane's N-number, you are home free. If the radar controller replies with your N-number and says "stand by," that too constitutes two-way communication and you can continue into the Class C airspace. But what if the controller says "Aircraft calling, stand by." That surely isn't communication because the controller might mean someone else, not you. Wait until you hear your number. Of course, if the controller says "remain clear of the Class C airspace" you must stay outside until the controller is able to handle your flight.

A special note for departures: You must be in communication with ATC while you are within the Class C airspace itself as you depart, of course, but the controller is required to provide radar service to you until you have left the outer area, ten miles beyond the outer circle. Give the busy controller a break and say "Terminate my radar service and thank you for your help" as soon as you are more than 10 miles from the primary airport.

Equipment requirements for Class C airspace are covered in Chapter 15.

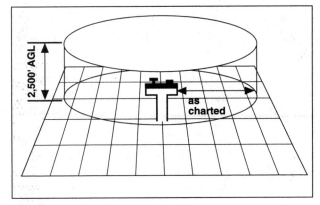

Figure 14-4. Class D airspace

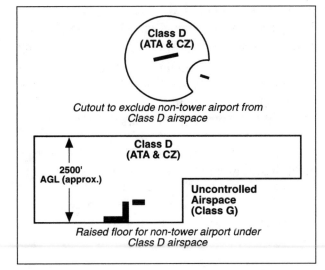

Figure 14-5. Class D airspace

Class D Airspace

Class D airspace exists wherever a control tower is in operation, and it imposes two obligations: First, there is a communication requirement. You can't take off from or land at a tower-controlled airport without a clearance from the tower controller. You can't even fly through Class D airspace without permission. Second is a weather requirement. For you to operate in Class D airspace under basic visual flight rules, the ground visibility must be at least three miles and the ceiling must be at least 1,000 feet above the ground.

What are the dimensions of Class D airspace? The horizontal boundary is shown on charts with a blue dashed line (the airport symbol is blue when there is a tower at the airport); the vertical extent is from the airport elevation to 2,500 feet above the airport. Figure 14-4 shows a nice cylindrical shape for clarity, but actual dimensions will vary widely. The elevation of the top of the airspace to the next highest hundred feet is shown in a little square box near the airport symbol. (Look at any tower-controlled airport except Seattle-Tacoma to check this. Sea-Tac shows -20 because it sits on a plateau above Puget Sound and the top of its Class D airspace is the 2,000-foot floor of the associated Class B airspace.)

It is possible to operate in Class D airspace without a radio. If your airplane simply doesn't have a radio, the best thing to do is call the tower on the telephone and tell the controller the type and color of your airplane, your estimated time of arrival, and the direction from which you will be coming. Expect a light gun signal. If your radio fails in flight a landing at a non-tower airport and a phone call is still the best

solution, but if that is impossible just fly to the tower airport, observe the direction of flight in the pattern, and join the pattern while wiggling your wings furiously and/or flipping your landing light on and off. Once again, expect light gun signals.

When the weather observer reports that the ground visibility is less than 3 miles or the ceiling is less than 1,000 feet, you cannot land in or take off from Class D airspace under basic visual flight rules (when you are inbound, this sounds like "the weather at Podunk is below basic VFR; what are your intentions?" Don't say "I want to come in and land"). You must ask for and receive a Special VFR clearance; you can't even do that if the ground visibility is less than 1 mile and you can't remain clear of clouds. Further, unless you hold an instrument rating you cannot operate under SVFR at night. At some airports (see Class B discussion) you can't get SVFR at all.

The shape of Class D airspace varies with local conditions. There will be extensions to provide protected airspace for incoming instrument flights, cutouts to exempt satellite airports from the communication and weather requirements, or shelves to allow pilots to fly into and out of airports beneath the edges of the airspace (Figure 14-5). If an extension is 2 miles or less (still shown with blue dashed lines), you need tower permission to fly in that airspace; if the extension is more than 2 miles (shown with magenta dashed lines) the communication requirement does not apply to the extension.

Look at Martha Lake Airport, located in the Snohomish County (Paine Field) Class D airspace near the left top corner of the chart excerpt. A pilot taking off from or landing at Martha Lake must communicate with Paine Tower and advise the controller of his or her intentions. There are no examples of cutouts or shelves on the chart excerpt.

The existence of Class D airspace is dependent on an operating control tower. There are hundreds of control towers that operate part-time, and when the controller goes home the Class D airspace requirements usually go, too—the airspace then becomes Class E airspace that extends all the way to the surface (Figure 14-1 "non-towered airport").

You have to look at the A/FD to be absolutely sure which classification of airspace is left behind when the tower operator goes home. There is a weather observer at the Olympia airport 24 hours a day; so when the tower shuts down, the Class D airspace becomes Class E all the way to the surface, and you still need VFR minimums or a Special VFR clearance to operate at Olympia in the middle of the night.

At Tacoma Narrows (**J** on Seattle sectional chart at back of book), when the tower operator locks the door there is no weather observer at the airport. That means that the bottom 700 feet of the airspace over the airport turns into Class G. There is no substitute for the Airport/Facility Directory for this purpose.

Class E Airspace

This class of airspace has already been fairly well defined; it exists above the floors defined by magenta dashed lines (the surface), the blue and magenta tints (700 or 1,200 AGL), and the MSL figures in mountainous areas (or 14,500 feet MSL), and extends up to the floor of the overlying airspace (either Class A, B, or C).

Victor airways, the blue lines identified with VOR radials, are eight miles wide. Airways extend from 1,200 feet AGL to 18,000 feet MSL but may exist in Class B, C, D, or E airspace. Above 18,000 feet the airways are jet routes: J-1, J-5, etc. If you are flying on an airway under Visual Flight Rules, you are expected to stay on the centerline except when climb-

ing or descending. Move off to the right when climbing or descending because IFR pilots maintain the centerline at all times.

Look at the airport data block for Paine Field, Tacoma Narrows, or Olympia. See the asterisk next to the tower frequency? That means that these are part-time towers, and you can find the actual operating hours on the back of the sectional chart or in the Airport/Facility Directory. When the tower is not in operation the airspace reverts to Class E; the communication requirement goes away but the visibility and cloud clearance requirements of Class E airspace are the same. That is, if you want to land or take off in marginal weather you must call a Flight Service Station for a Special VFR clearance.

Look at the Bremerton National airport at the left edge of the chart excerpt or Wenatchee airport at the right edge. The magenta dashed line indicates that Class E airspace extends from the floor of the overlying controlled airspace down to the surface. At Bremerton, the overlying airspace begins at either 18,000 MSL or 6,000 feet MSL if within the Seattle Class B airspace boundary. At Wenatchee (Pangborn Memorial) Class E airspace starts at the surface within the dashed, magenta line, begins at 700 feet AGL within the magenta rectangle and starts at 1,200 feet AGL in the blue shaded areas surrounding V-120 and V-25. In all three areas the top of Class E airspace is 18,000 feet MSL (Class A airspace).

Now look at the Ellensburg airport at the right edge of the excerpt. No dashed line, but Ellensburg does have an instrument approach, although you can't tell that from the chart. An inbound instrument pilot's protection stops at 700 feet AGL at Ellensburg; below that altitude the pilot is in Class G (uncontrolled) airspace and must mix in with the VFR traffic.

Class G Airspace

An easy definition of Class G airspace is that it exists wherever other classes do not. Most of the Class G airspace lies beneath floors at 700 or 1,200 feet above the ground. In this thin sliver of airspace you can fly (in the daytime) with only 1 mile flight visibility and the ability to remain clear of clouds. Most pilots call this "scud running," because it usually means trying to stay below a ragged cloud layer in poor visibility. At night, the cloud clearance and visibility requirements in Class G airspace are the same as daytime requirements in Class E airspace—flight visibility of at least 3 miles and lots of cloud clearance. You say that you can't see the clouds at night? Then why are you scud running? (As I write this, rescue teams are removing three bodies from a Cessna 172 that hit a mountain 1,400 feet up. VFR pilot, 80 hours flight time).

Special case: If you want to practice takeoffs and landings in Class G airspace at night with visibility less than 3 miles but more than 1 mile, you can do so if you stay within one-half mile of the runway.

Look again at the triangle of uncontrolled airspace just west of Wenatchee and Ellensburg. Remember, it goes from the surface to 14,500 feet MSL? If you are flying more than 1,200 feet above the ground in that triangle, you can get away with 1 mile visibility in the daytime, but cloud clearance standards are the same as Class E. So here you are, flying around at 6,500 feet or so, with only 1 mile visibility, perfectly legally! Of course, you have to stay in that little triangle, which might cramp your plans to go somewhere for lunch.

Visibility: Ground Vs. Flight

In discussing the regulations for flight in various kinds of airspace the terms "flight visibility" and "ground visibility" were used without comment. If you are departing an airport where ground visibility is reported by an observer, you are governed by that report. If you are landing at an airport where ground visibility is reported and you determine that the flight visibility meets the legal requirements of the airspace, your decision governs. Of course, if the tower is calling the ground visibility one mile and you decide that the flight visibility is three miles you can go ahead and land—but expect to be quizzed by the FAA. If you are operating at an airport where visibility is not reported, the decision is yours—if you say that the visibility is three miles no one can argue with you. However, newspaper reports of the accident will say "witnesses told investigators that the visibility was less than one-half mile when the airplane disappeared."

Sermon: The reputation of general aviation pilots goes right down the tube when someone who absolutely has to get home or to a destination crashes and kills a few people. You want to become a general aviation pilot or you wouldn't be reading this—please remember this: no job, no trip, no birthday, no wedding, nothing is important enough to kill yourself for. Do not push the limits of your ability, and don't overestimate what those limits are.

Terminal Radar Service Area

A type of airspace that is rapidly disappearing is the Terminal Radar Service Area (TRSA, Figure 14-6). Indicated on charts by a solid black circle, a TRSA is a kind of voluntary Class C airspace. That is, radar service is available if you want it, but you don't have to use it.

Because TRSAs are usually at joint military/civil fields, though, it is to your advantage to call in and get traffic advisories. When departing from an airport in a TRSA you will be told "Call ground control for your clearance." If you don't want radar service, all you have to say is "Negative radar." You will not be surrounded by armed MPs but will be allowed to taxi out and take off just like any other kind of Class D airspace.

Figure 14-6. *Terminal Radar Service Area*

Figure 14-7. Prohibited Area

PROHIBITED, RESTRICTED, WARNING, AND ALERT AREAS ON SEATTLE SECTIONAL CHART				
NO.	NAME	ALTITUDE	TIME	APPROPRIATE AUTHORITY
R-6701	Admiralty Inlet, Wash.	to 5,000	Sunrise to sunset Mon. Thru Fri. Sat & Sun by NOTAM 24 hr. in advance	†FAA Seattle ARTC Center *Area FSS Comdr., Medium Attack Tactical Electronic Warfare Wing NAS Whidbey Island, Wash.

Figure 14-8. Restricted Area

Special Use Airspace

There are several types of special use airspace, but they are almost all indicated on charts with blue hatching. Look just to the right of the Olympia airport at the lower left corner of the chart excerpt. The most restrictive is a Prohibited Area, such as that above the White House (Figure 14-7 is an example). There is no way to get permission to fly in a Prohibited Area and getting caught in one is painful for both your pocketbook and pilot certificate.

The next step down is a Restricted Area (Figure 14-8). They are designated and controlled by the military and usually involve firing ranges, etc. A table on each Sectional chart gives the operating hours and altitudes for each Restricted Area. The operating hours are not engraved in stone, however. During your preflight briefing, as the FSS if a Restricted

Figure 14-9. Warning Area

632 Corpus Christi, Texas	From 6000 to but not incl. 11,000	SR-2400 Mon. Fri. 1400-2400 Sun	Chief Naval Air Training

Figure 14-10. Alert Area

Area along your route is "hot," or give the controlling agency a call (at Navy Whidbey, the status of their Restricted Area is on the ATIS). Do not just blunder into the area, however, because the hazards you are being protected from are invisible.

Warning Areas and Alert Areas (Figures 14-9 and 14-10) also involve the military. Warning Areas have the same kinds of hazards as Restricted Areas, but are offshore in International waters. No clearance required, but keep your eyes open. Check their status with the Flight Service Station. Alert Areas involve a high volume of military training activity; again, no clearance is required but extreme vigilance (or avoidance) is.

Military Operating Areas (MOAs, Figure 14-11) are shown on charts with magenta hatching; again, look at the areas surrounding R-6703A, B, C, and D east of Olympia (that's the Army's Fort Lewis firing range, if you're curious). You do not need a clearance to fly in a MOA, but military airplanes operate in them without restriction—the FARs don't apply to them while flying in a MOA. Your FSS can tell you

Figure 14-11. *Military Operating Area*

the status of a MOA, of course. They can be overflown if too big to circumnavigate; the ceiling of each MOA is given in a table on the back of the Sectional.

Military Training Routes (MTRs) create the most hazard for general aviation airplanes. The good news is that they are charted: see the gray lines that run from the top to the bottom of the chart excerpt west of Ellensburg? IR and VR mean instrument and visual routes, of course, but there is more to it than that. Routes with 4 digit numbers are flown at or below 1,500 feet AGL, while routes with 3-number identifiers are flown above 1,500 feet AGL. Nothing like flying along at 2,500 feet and seeing a flight of C-130s go under you.

"Hot" times for MTRs are available from the FSS, and you are foolish if you do not check on the status of any MTR that will cross your flight path. The military might schedule a route for several hours and only use it for a portion of that time, but you can't afford to gamble. Military jet pilots fly very fast, with their heads in their cockpits, and they are painted with camouflage colors for a reason. Never fly parallel to an MTR—the military is allowed to be as much as eight miles off the centerline. Cross military training routes at right angles to reduce your time of exposure to a minimum.

Air Defense Identification Zones

Air Defense Identification Zones exist along the Pacific, Gulf, and Atlantic coasts, and aircraft inbound to the United States from outside of the ADIZ whose place and time of arrival within the zone are unknown will be intercepted by armed military aircraft. If you will be returning to the United States (from the Bahamas, for example) and will penetrate an ADIZ you must have a DVFR flight plan on file giving your point of penetration and estimated time of penetration. If you are simply operating within 10 miles of the coast you are exempt from this requirement.

Wildlife Refuge Area

Along the bottom edge of the Sectional chart excerpt you will see Mount Rainier National Park. Note the line of dots that marks the boundary. Wherever you see those dots they surround a wildlife refuge area, and you are asked, not required, to stay at least 2,000 feet above the terrain to minimize the effect of aircraft noise on wildlife. If you are a seaplane pilot, check with local authorities before you fly into a state or national park; seaplane operations are severely restricted in parks.

1. Under what conditions, if any, may civil pilots enter a restricted area?

   A—With the controlling agency's authorization.
   B—On airways with ATC clearance.
   C—Under no condition.

2. Under what condition may an aircraft operate from a satellite airport within Class C airspace?

   A—The pilot must monitor ATC until clear of the Class C airspace.
   B—The pilot must contact ATC as soon as practicable after takeoff.
   C—The pilot must secure prior approval from ATC before takeoff from the satellite airport.

3. What is the upper limit of Class D airspace?

   A—18,500 MSL.
   B—The base of the Continental Control Area.
   C—Usually 2,500 feet above the surface.

4. What are the horizontal limits of Class D airspace?

   A—5 NM from the airport boundary.
   B—As indicated with blue dashed lines.
   C—As indicated with magenta dashed lines.

5. Class D airspace is automatically in effect when

   A—its associated control tower is in operation.
   B—the weather is below VFR minimums.
   C—radar service is available.

6. What is the purpose of Class D airspace?

   A—To provide for the control of aircraft landing and taking off from an airport with an operating control tower.
   B—To provide for the control of all aircraft operating in the vicinity of an airport with an operating control tower.
   C—To restrict aircraft without radios from operating in the vicinity of an airport with an operating control tower.

7. Unless otherwise specified, Federal airways extend from

   A—1,200 ft. above the surface upward to 14,500 ft. MSL and are 16 NM wide.
   B—1,200 ft. above the surface upward to 18,000 ft. MSL and are 8 NM wide.
   C—the surface upward to 18,000 ft. MSL and are 4 NM wide.

8. What type airspace is associated with VOR Federal airways?

   A—Class B, C, D, or E airspace.
   B—Class E airspace.
   C—Class D airspace.

9. Class E airspace in the conterminous United States extends to, but not including

   A—the base of the continental control area.
   B—3,000 ft. MSL.
   C—18,000 ft. MSL.

10. What is the minimum weather condition required for airplanes operating under special VFR in Class B, C, D or E airspace?

A—1 mi. flight visibility.
B—1 mi. flight visibility and 1,000 ft. ceiling.
C—3 mi. flight visibility and 1,000 ft. ceiling.

11. For VFR flight operations above 10,000 ft. MSL and more than 1,200 ft. AGL, the minimum horizontal distance from clouds required is

A—1,000 ft.
B—2,000 ft.
C—1 mile.

12. No person may operate an airplane within Class B, C, D or E airspace associated with an airport at night under special VFR unless

A—the flight can be conducted 500 ft. below the clouds.
B—the airplane is equipped for instrument flight.
C—the flight visibility is at least 3 mi.

13. The minimum ceiling and visibility required to operate under basic visual flight rules in Class C, D or E airspace are

A—500 ft. and 1 mi.
B—1,000 ft. and 3 mi.
C—1,400 ft. and 2 mi.

14. In which type of airspace is VFR flight prohibited?

A—Class B.
B—Class D.
C—Class A.

15. What minimum pilot certification is required for operating to or from the airports within the 12 restricted Class B airspaces?

A—Student pilot certificate with appropriate logbook endorsements.
B—Private pilot certificate.
C—Private pilot certificate with an instrument rating.

16. What procedure is recommended when climbing or descending VFR on an airway?

A—Offset 4 mi. or more from centerline of the airway before changing altitude.
B—Advise the nearest FSS of the desired altitude change.
C—Climb or descend on the right side of the airway centerline.

Refer to Figure Q14-1 (on the next page) for questions 17 and 18.

17. You plan to fly under VFR from Airport A to Airport B. Regarding this flight, which of the following statements is true?

A—Flights below 7,000 feet must be operating on IFR flight plans.
B—Extreme caution should be exercised while flying through this area.
C—VFR flights are not permitted above 7,000 feet MSL.

18. Which statement is true regarding the Chippewa MOA?

A—The military services conduct low altitude navigation flights at or below 1,500 feet AGL at speed exceeding 250 knots within this area.
B—Some training activities may necessitate acrobatic maneuvers by military aircraft within this area.
C—VFR flights between 7,000 feet and Flight Level 180 are prohibited within this area.

Figure Q14-1. Excerpt from Chicago Sectional Aeronautical Chart

MOA NAME	ALTITUDE OF USE	TIME OF USE	CONTROLLING AGENCY
CHIPPEWA	7000	0930-1130 AND 1330-1530 TUE-SAT	ZMP CNTR
FALLS 1	500 ABL TO BUT NOT INCL 10,000 MSL	2 HRS IN ADVANCE BY NOTAM	ZMP CNTR
HILL TOP	12,000	0800-1900	SID CNTR
HOWARD EAST	9000	0700-2200 TUE-SUN	ZKKC CNTR
HOWARD WEST	10,000	0700-2200 TUE-SUN	ZKC CNTR
MINNOW	10,000	INTERMITTENT BY NOTAM NORMALLY DAYLIGHT HOURS	ZAU CNTR
TWELVE MILE	500 AGL TO BUT NOT INCL 9000	0900 TO 30 MIN AFTER SS TUE-SAT	ZID CNTR
VOLK EAST A	500 AGL TO BUT NOT INCL 11,000	0930-1100 AND 1330-1500 TUE-SAT	ZAU CNTR
VOLK EAST B	11,000	0930-1100 AND 1330-1100 TUE-SAT	ZAI CNTR

19. All operations within Class C airspace must

A—be conducted under instrument flight rules.

B—be in compliance with ATC clearances and instructions.

C—be in an aircraft equipped with a 4096 transponder with Mode C capability.

20. What are the visibility and cloud clearance requirements for VFR flight in Class G airspace below 10,000 feet at night?

A—One mile visibility and remain clear of clouds.

B—One mile visibility, 500 feet below, 1,000 feet above, and 2,000 horizontally from all clouds.

C—Three miles visibility, 500 feet below, 1,000 feet above, 2,000 feet horizontally from all clouds.

Regulations

15

The FAA expects you to be familiar with all of the Federal Aviation Regulations which apply to your flight operations, but as you read through the FARs you should be able to distinguish between those that are nice to know but do not affect your day-to-day flying (carriage of candidates in Federal elections, for example), and those which you simply *must* know (basic visual flight rules or right-of-way rules). This chapter will discuss those regulations which require explanation or illustration for full understanding.

Part 61

Certification: Pilots and Flight Instructors

61.3: Requirements for certificates, ratings, authorizations. If you are going to act as pilot-in-command or as a required flight crewmember you must have in your possession your pilot certificate and medical certificate. You must present these documents for inspection upon request by an official of the FAA, the NTSB, or any law enforcement officer.

61.5: Certificates and ratings. There are six pilot certificates: student, recreational, private, commercial, airline transport pilot, and flight instructor.

Recreational pilot: Can carry only one passenger. Must stay within 50 NM of the airport at which the pilot has received flight and ground instruction.

Limited to a single engine of less than 180 hp and fixed landing gear. Cannot fly where radio communication is required. Cannot fly at night or internationally.

Student Pilot: Limited to solo or dual (instructional) flights only.

Private Pilot: May carry passengers or cargo, day or night, as long as no charge is made. Is permitted to share expenses with passengers. May fly in conjunction with employment if flying is only incidental to the employment.

Commercial Pilot: May fly for compensation or hire. Must also meet requirements of FAR Part 135 to fly as air taxi pilot.

Airline Transport Pilot: May fly as pilot-in-command on an airline flight or on a multiengine scheduled commuter flight.

A certificated flight instructor can give both flight and ground instruction under the conditions stated in 61.193 and 61.195. A flight instructor certificate must be renewed every 24 calander months.

Your certificate will carry a category and class rating such as Airplane: Single Engine Land (Figure 15-1 on the next page). You cannot carry passengers unless you hold the appropriate category and class ratings, and an instrument rating is required for IFR whether you are carrying passengers or not. Figure 15-1 shows the categories and the applicable class ratings.

61.19: Duration of pilot certificates. Your student pilot certificate and flight instructor expires at the end of the 24th calendar month after it was issued. *All other pilot certificates have no expiration date* and are kept active by having a current medical certificate and a current biennial flight review.

61.23: Duration of medical certificates. The type of medical certificate you hold determines the privileges you can exercise as a pilot according to the certificate you hold. Figure 15-2 lists the classes of medical certificates, their durations, and the privileges authorized during the valid period. Medical certificates expire at the end of the *calendar* month; for example, a physical taken on the 15th of the month will expire at the *end* of the 6th, 12th, or 24th month, depending on the class of physical.

61.31: General limitations. Type ratings are required for airplanes weighing over 12,500 pounds or those powered by turbojets. A commercial pilot cannot operate an aircraft for compensation or hire without holding an appropriate category and class rating for that aircraft. No person may operate an airplane with more than 200 horsepower, or one that has retractable landing gear, flaps, and a controllable propeller, without having received flight instruction in that airplane, with a logbook endorsement to that effect made by the instructor. To act as pilot-in-command of a tailwheel airplane, you need a logbook endorsement from an instructor who has given you instruction in a tailwheel airplane. To act as PIC of an airplane with a service ceiling or maximum operating altitude of 25,000 feet (whichever is lower), you need both ground and flight training in high altitude operations.

61.51: Pilot logbooks. As a student pilot, you can log only solo and dual instruction time. After you receive your private pilot certificate you will be able to log pilot-in-command time. You can log as second-in-command time only that flight time when you act as SIC of an airplane requiring more than one pilot or when operating under regulations that require more than one pilot. You can log as instrument flight time only that time during which you operate the airplane solely by reference to instruments, under actual or simulated conditions. As a student pilot you must

Catagory/Class	Type
Airplane	ex. B-727
single-engine land	
multi-engine land	
single-engine sea	
multi-engine sea	
Rotocraft	ex. S-61
helicopter	
gyroplane	
Lighter-Than-Air	n.a.
airship	
free balloon	
Glider	
n.a.	

Figure 15-1. *Categories and class ratings*

carry your logbook on all solo cross-country flights as evidence of the required instructor clearances and endorsements.

Acting as pilot-in-command and logging PIC time are two different things. The pilot with responsibility for the safety of flight *acts* as PIC under Part 1 of the FARs, but need not ever touch the controls. As a certificated private or commercial pilot you can log as PIC all of the time during which you are the sole manipulator of the controls of an airplane for which you are rated.

61.56: Flight review. To act as pilot-in-command you must have satisfactorily accomplished a flight review within the past 24 calendar months (biennial flight review or BFR). You can take the review with any instructor, FAA operations inspector, or U. S. Armed Forces check pilot. The flight review must include at least one hour of ground instruction including a review of Part 91 and one hour of flight time performing maneuvers of the instructor/check pilot's choice. If you participate in a pilot proficiency award program such as the FAA's Wings Program, satisfactory completion is a substitute for a BFR. Also, if you take a checkride for a new certificate or rating that flight constitutes a BFR—make sure that the examiner endorses your logbook accordingly.

Figure 15-2. *Medical certificates*

To Exercise Privileges	Valid Months
Third Class Medical Certificate	
Private Pilot	24
Second Class Medical Certificate	
Commercial Pilot	12
Private Pilot	24
First Class Medical Certificate	
Airline Transport Pilot	6
Commercial Pilot	12
Private Pilot	24

To exercise the privileges of their pilot certificates, ATPs must get new medicals every 6 months, commercial pilots every 12 months, and private pilots every 24 months.

Medical certificates expire the last day of the 6th, 12th, or 24th month after they are issued, depending on the class of certificate.

You can take the review in any aircraft for which you are rated. That is, if you hold certificates for airplanes, gliders, and hot air balloons a BFR in any of those aircraft meets the requirements of the regulation.

Note that you cannot even fly solo unless you have a current biennial flight review.

61.57: Recent flight experience pilot-in-command. You may not carry passengers unless you have current experience, and that means 3 takeoffs and landings within the preceding 90 days in an aircraft of the same category and class as that in which you plan to carry passengers. You may fly solo to make those three takeoffs and landings, of course. If you are going to carry passengers in a tailwheel airplane, your 3 takeoffs and landings must have been in a taildragger, and to a full stop—no touch-and-goes permitted. Touch-and-goes are approved for tricycle gear airplanes. To carry passengers at night you must, within the preceding 90 days, have made 3 takeoffs and landings to a full stop *in an aircraft of the same category and class* during the period from one hour after sunset to one hour before sunrise. That means that if you are current at night in single engine landplanes, for instance, your night currency does not extend to multiengine landplanes, and you must do the 3 full-stop landings at night before carrying passengers in a twin at night.

A current pilot is one who meets the requirement for 3 takeoffs and landings within 90 days, and who also has accomplished a satisfactory current biennial flight review.

61.60: Change of address. If you change your permanent mailing address and do not advise the FAA within 30 days you cannot exercise the privileges of your pilot certificate. Just as soon as you have notified them you are back in the air again.

61.63: Additional aircraft ratings. If you want to add a category or class rating to your certificate (rotorcraft might be a new category, multiengine land a new class rating), you must take a checkride, but no written examination is required for powered aircraft. You must present a logbook record that you have received instruction and are competent in the category or class for which the addition is sought.

61.89-61.93: Student pilot general limitations cross-country requirements. Student pilots may not carry passengers, act as pilot-in-command on an international flight, fly for compensation or hire, or fly in furtherance of a business. A student pilot must have his or her solo endorsement renewed every 90 days by a flight instructor, and must be specifically signed off for each cross-country flight with very narrowly limited exceptions.

Student pilots are not permitted to fly solo when the visibility is less than 3 miles in daylight and 5 miles at night. Also, student pilots must be in visual contact with the ground at all times; flight above a cloud layer is prohibited.

61.87: Solo flight requirements for student pilots. This regulation provides an extensive list of procedures and maneuvers at which you must demonstrate acceptable proficiency before your instructor can sign you off for solo. Your logbook should be endorsed to show that you have received training in each item listed. It also requires that your instructor administer and grade a written examination on the appropriate portions of Parts 61 and 91 before you can solo.

Reading 61.87 will give you an excellent insight into how your initial training will be conducted and what you must learn.

61.95: Operations in Class B airspace and at airports located within Class B airspace. This regulation says that student pilot must receive both flight and ground instruction regarding operations in specific Class B airspace and to or from an airport lying within its surface area. Your instructor must endorse your logbook accordingly and renew the endorsement every 90 days until you receive your private pilot certificate. If you plan a cross-country trip that will take you into another Class B airspace, you can't go until you and your instructor have gone through the same procedure for that location.

61.118: Private pilot privileges and limitations; pilot-in-command. Private pilots may not accept compensation for flying; they are allowed to share the operating expenses of the flight with their passengers, but the FARs do not go into detail on just what is allowable as expenses (your insurance might not cover a flight for which a charge is made). Private pilots are allowed to fly in connection with their employment if they are not being paid solely for their piloting activities. For instance, you can fly some clients over some property they are considering as a part of your duties in real estate, but you cannot be asked by your employer to transport customers on flights unrelated to real estate if your employer reimburses you. You, as a private pilot, may carry paying passengers on a flight for a charitable organization if the passengers have contributed to the organization. Approved charities are very narrowly defined, and the airplane must meet commercial maintenance requirements. You may demonstrate airplanes as an airplane salesperson after you have logged 200 hours of flight time.

The question of sharing expenses has resulted in some legal decisions. If you are flying somewhere and want to take someone along to share expenses but would go anyway if no passenger could be found, that is acceptable. If the only reason you are taking a trip is that someone will share expenses with you, that is considered compensation. If you rent airplanes to take your friends on trips just to build time, trips that you would not take without their financial contribution, you are flirting with a violation of this regulation.

Part 91
Air Traffic and General
Operating Rules

91.3: Responsibility and authority, pilot-in-command. You, as the pilot-in-command, are the final authority as to the operation of your aircraft. In an emergency, you can take any action required to meet the emergency, even though that action might violate the FARs. If, however, you do deviate from the rules in an emergency, you may be *requested* to send a written report to the FAA. This regulation is your authority to tell a controlling agency that you cannot follow a directive because in your estimation to do so would be unsafe.

91.13: Careless or reckless operation. This is a catch-all regulation. If you have any type of accident or incident, the assumption is that you must have been either careless or reckless. Your responsibility is to leave nothing to chance: use written checklists rather than rely on memory. As pilot-in-command, do not let anyone interfere with your control of the airplane (see 91.17 below).

91.17: Liquor and drugs. You cannot act as a crewmember of a civil aircraft within 8 hours of consuming alcoholic beverages. This is the "bottle to throttle" rule. Also, you may not allow a passenger under the influence of alcohol or drugs on your aircraft unless that person is under the care of medical personnel. Also, when you accept your pilot certificate you agree to submit to a breathalyzer or blood test at the request of any law officer or FAA official if you operate or attempt to operate an aircraft. If your blood alcohol content exceeds .04 percent you may face certificate action.

91.21: Portable electronic devices. Some portable electronic devices interfere with the airplane's radio navigation systems, and may not be used on air carrier airplanes or when operating IFR. You, as pilot-in-command, should ensure that any such device in use in your airplane will not affect the operation of your radios.

Figure 15-3. Right-of-way priority

91.103: Preflight action. Before beginning any flight, you are required to familiarize yourself with *all* information concerning the flight. You can't say, "I didn't know." The information must always include runway lengths at airports you intend to use, and the takeoff and landing performance figures for your airplane under the conditions to be expected. For flights not in the vicinity of an airport (cross-country flights), you must also have an alternative plan of action in mind if your planned flight cannot be completed, know the fuel requirements for the flight, and get weather reports *and forecasts* for the time of flight.

91.105: Flight crewmembers at stations. During takeoff and landing, each required crewmember must be at his or her station with seatbelt and shoulder harness fastened (if shoulder harnesses are provided). The shoulder harness can be unfastened if you can show that you cannot perform required duties—tune radios or operate controls—with it fastened.

91.107: Use of safety belts. Your passengers must have seatbelts fastened during takeoff and landing, and it is your responsibility to insure that they are fastened and that passengers have been briefed on how to fasten and unfasten their seatbelts.

91.111: Operating near other aircraft. Formation flying looks easy, but it isn't. This regulation prohibits formation flight except by prior arrangement, and forbids formation flight if passengers are carried for hire. Let the pros do air-to-air photography.

91.113: Right-of-way rules. The right-of-way rules are first broken down on the basis of maneuverability, except that an aircraft in distress, regardless of category, has the right of way over all other aircraft (Figure 15-3). Balloons, being least maneuverable, have the right of way over any other category. An

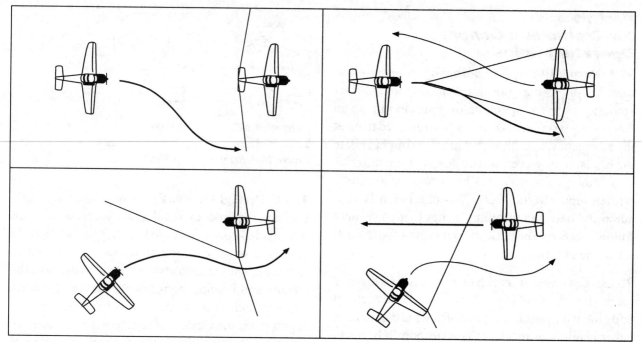

Figure 15-4. Rules of the road

Figure 15-5. Minimum safe altitudes

aircraft towing another aircraft has priority over all other engine-driven aircraft. Gliders have the right of way over airships, airplanes, and rotorcraft. Airships have the right of way over airplanes and rotorcraft. When two aircraft of the same category converge, the one on the right has the right of way. Refer to Figure 15-4 and 91.209 for these situations: the pilot seeing a red light and an anticollision light must pass behind the other airplane (lower left), while the pilot

who sees a green light and an anticollision light maintains course (lower right). In an overtaking situation, the white position light and the anticollision light are visible, and the overtaking airplane must give way to the right while the overtaken airplane maintains course (upper left). When you see both a red and a green light, you are head-on, and both pilots must change course to the right (upper right). A provision of 91.113 that causes problems, usually at non-tower airports, is this: when two aircraft are approaching an airport to land, the lower of the two has the right of way—but it may not take advantage of this rule by cutting in front of the other aircraft.

91.115: Dropping objects. You may not drop or allow to be dropped from your aircraft any object that creates a hazard to persons or property. If reasonable precautions to avoid injury or damage are taken, dropping objects is authorized.

91.117: Aircraft speed. There is no speed limit above 10,000' MSL. That is why the visibility and cloud clearance requirements are more stringent above that altitude. Below 10,000' MSL, the *general speed limit is 250 knots.* When flying on a jet you will experience what seems like a period of "coasting" as you approach the destination airport—your pilot is holding altitude and reducing speed to 250 knots before descending through 10,000'. That 250 knot speed limit extends to the ground in Class B airspace. When you fly beneath the horizontal limits of Class B airspace or in a VFR corridor through Class B airspace your speed is limited to 200 knots—very few student pilots have trouble complying! Within 4 NM of the primary airport of Class C or D airspace, all airplanes are limited to 200 knots.

91.119: Minimum safe altitudes; general. Figure 15-5 illustrates minimum safe altitudes. *Except when necessary for takeoff or landing,* you must always fly high enough to be able to make a safe emergency landing without hazard to persons or property on the ground. Over a congested area, you must fly 1,000' above the highest obstacle within 2,000' horizontally. *Question:* If you are only 1,000' above the highest obstacle over downtown Houston or Chicago, for example, can you make a safe emergency landing? Probably not. Considerably more altitude would be better. Over other than congested areas, you must stay at least 500' above the surface, except that over sparsely settled areas and over water you must stay at least 500' horizontally from any person, vessel, vehicle, or structure on the surface. This means boats, barns, swimmers, etc.

91.121: Altimeter settings. If you can receive an altimeter setting by radio (or by visiting the Flight Service Station) you must adjust your altimeter setting window accordingly. If you are enroute, you must update the altimeter setting by calling a FSS within 100 miles along your route of flight (every time you contact Air Traffic Control or a Flight Service Station you will be given an altimeter setting).

If you are on the ground, and no altimeter setting information is available, you should set your altimeter to read field elevation, and then get a correction as soon as you are able to contact a Flight Service Station by radio. Above 18,000' MSL, all altimeters must be set to 29.92" Hg.

91.123: Compliance with Air Traffic Control clearances and instructions. An air traffic controller can only provide you with vectors and traffic information in controlled airspace—when you enter Class G (uncontrolled) airspace you are on your own. When you receive a clearance from an air traffic controller you must comply *except* when, in your opinion, to do so would be unsafe. Just tell the controller that you can't comply (due to weather, for example). You can always exercise your pilot's emergency authority. *If you are given priority* over other aircraft, even if no emergency is involved, you *may* be requested to make a written report within 48 hours to the Chief of the ATC facility that gave you the priority.

91.125: ATC light signals. Light signals are used by tower controllers when you have no radio or when your radio has failed (Figure 15-6 on Page 15-8). The wisest course, in the event of radio failure, is to land at an uncontrolled airport and make arrangements with the tower controllers by telephone. If this option is not available, you are allowed to join the controlled airport's traffic pattern (after determining the direction of traffic flow) and your actions will be directed with light signals.

91.135: Class A Airspace. As a VFR-rated private pilot you may not climb above 18,000 feet MSL without an instrument rating and an instrument clearance.

91.151: Fuel requirements for flight under VFR. You must carry enough fuel to reach your destination plus 30 minutes reserve for day VFR and 45 minutes for night VFR. It should be apparent that if everyone followed this rule, there would be no fuel exhaustion incidents. Don't be the exception to this rule.

Color and Type of Signal	On the Ground	In Flight
STEADY GREEN	Cleared for takeoff	Cleared to land
FLASHING GREEN	Cleared to taxi	Return for landing (to be followed by steady green at proper time)
STEADY RED	Stop	Give way to other aircraft and continue circling
FLASHING RED	Taxi clear of landing area (runway) in use	Airport unsafe — do not land
FLASHING WHITE	Return to starting point on airport	
ALTERNATING RED & GREEN	General Warning Signal — Exercise Extreme Caution	

Figure 15-6. Light signals

Figure 15-7. Flight plan form

91.153: Flight plan; information required. Figure 15-7 (flight plan form) includes all of the information called for by this section. You should list as your destination airport the last airport at which you intend to land (you can include enroute airports in block 11). Block 12 should reflect total fuel on board. VFR flight plans, although not mandatory, aid in search-and rescue efforts if you do not complete your planned flight.

Airspace	Flight Visibility	Distance from Clouds
Class A	Not Applicable	Not Applicable
Class B	3 statute miles	Clear of clouds
Class C	3 statute miles	500 feet below 1,000 feet above 2,000 feet horizontal
Class D	3 statute miles	500 feet below 1,000 feet above 2,000 feet horizontal
Class E Less than 10,000 feet MSL	3 statute miles	500 feet below 1,000 feet above 2,000 feet horizontal
At or above 10,000 feet MSL	5 statute miles	1,000 feet below 1,000 feet above 1 statute mile horizontal
Class G 1,200 feet or less above the surface (regardless of MSL altitude) Day, except as provided in § 91.155(b)	1 statute mile	Clear of clouds
Night, except as provided in § 91.155(b)	3 statute miles	500 feet below 1,000 feet above 2,000 feet horizontal
More than 1,200 feet above the surface but less than 10,000 feet MSL Day	1 statute mile	500 feet below 1,000 feet above 2,000 feet horizontal
Night	3 statute miles	500 feet below 1,000 feet above 2,000 feet horizontal
More than 1,200 feet above the surface and at or above 10,000 feet MSL	5 statute miles	1,000 feet below 1,000 feet above 1 statute mile horizontal

Table 15-1. Weather minimums

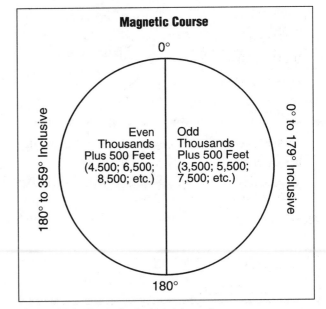

Figure 15-8. Hemispherical cruising rule

Figure 15-9. Certificate of registration and airworthiness certificate

91.155: Basic VFR weather minimums. VFR visibility and cloud clearance requirements have been discussed earlier; this is the table from Part 91 (Table 15-1).

91.159: VFR cruising altitudes or flight levels. This is called the hemispherical rule. It is based on magnetic *course*, not magnetic heading, and applicable only when you are more than 3,000' above the ground (Figure 15-8).

91.203: Certifications required. You must have your aircraft registration certificate and the airplane's *Certificate of Airworthiness* (Figure 15-9) on board at all times; weight and balance data and the FAA Approved Flight Manual must also be carried, although markings and placards can be substituted for the Flight Manual. *Airplane and engine logs are not required to be on board the airplane.* Remember:

A   Certificate of **A**irworthiness.

R   **R**adio station license.

R   **R**egistration.

O   **O**perating limitations (flight manual).

W   **W**eight and balance data.

The Certificate of Airworthiness must be displayed where it can be seen easily by passengers and crew.

91.209: Aircraft lights. During the period from sunset to sunrise (there are special rules for Alaska), you must turn on your position lights: a red light on the left wingtip, green light on the right wingtip, and a white light on the tail. Position lights allow a pilot who sees your lights at night to determine your direction of movement. You must also have a flashing anti-collision light system, either red or white. Many airplanes have both red rotating beacons and white strobe lights—if either system fails, the remaining system meets the requirements of the regulation. The anti-collision system cannot take the place of the position lights, however.

91.211. Supplemental oxygen. If your flight will be above 12,500' MSL for more than 30 minutes, then you, the pilot, must use supplemental oxygen (either a portable tank or a fixed installation) for any time over 30 minutes. If the flight will be above 14,000' MSL, you must use oxygen at all times. At altitudes above 15,000' you must provide oxygen for your passengers. Be sure they know how to use it before you leave the ground and NO SMOKING. Be sure that the oxygen system is serviced with *aviators breathing oxygen!* Medical oxygen contains moisture (which may freeze) and welding oxygen contains impurities which may become health hazards.

91.215: ATC transponder equipment and use. You must have a transponder with altitude encoding (Mode C) capability to enter Class B or C airspace. You also need Mode C to fly above 10,000' MSL, to operate within the horizontal boundaries of Class C airspace and above its ceiling up to 10,000' MSL, and to operate between the surface and 10,000' MSL within 30 miles of the primary airport in Class B airspace (see the blue 30-mile circle on the Seattle chart excerpt).

91.303: Acrobatic flight. Acrobatics are prohibited over a congested area, over an open air assemblage of persons (air shows get waivers of this regulation), within the lateral boundaries of Class B, C, or D airspace or Class E airspace when designated for an airport, below 1,500' AGL, or when flight visibility is less than 3 statute miles.

91.307: Parachutes and parachuting. Parachutes must be worn by all occupants of an aircraft if certain maneuvers are to be performed, unless the maneuvers are being taught in preparation for a certificate or rating. The FAA defines these maneuvers as any bank angle that exceeds 60°, or any nose-up or nose-down attitude that exceeds 30° relative to the horizon. Flight training maneuvers for the private pilot and commercial pilot certificates do not include any of these maneuvers. Any parachute used must have been packed within the preceding 120 days by a rated parachute rigger.

91.313: Restricted Category Civil Aircraft; operating limitations. Restricted category aircraft include cropdusters and banner towing airplanes, and they are not to be operated over congested or densely populated areas.

91.319: Experimental certificates; limitations. You cannot fly an airplane with an *experimental* certificate (such as a homebuilt airplane) over a densely populated area or on a congested airway.

91.403: General. The owner or operator of an aircraft is primarily responsible for maintaining that aircraft in an airworthy condition. If it's your airplane, of course, that's you. If you are a renter, the responsibility lies with the fixed base operator or flight school as "operator." The responsibility for determining that the aircraft is in condition for safe flight is yours as pilot-in-command—that's why you do a preflight check.

91.407: Carrying persons other than crewmembers after repairs or alterations. This section requires a test flight by a *private pilot* or better before passengers can be carried on an airplane that has had maintenance or repair that affected the flight characteristics.

91.409: Inspections. Annual maintenance inspections are required for all airplanes not on an approved progressive maintenance program. An annual inspection expires at the end of the twelfth month following the inspection. 100 hour inspections are required on all airplanes operated for hire, and the FAA interprets 100 hours very strictly. If you want to rent an airplane that received its last inspection when the tachometer read 1259.6 and it now reads 1360.0, don't get in the airplane—it is unairworthy until the inspection has been accomplished.

An annual inspection may substitute for a 100 hour inspection. After a required inspection has been completed, the airplane is "returned to service" by an appropriate logbook entry by the inspector. *The aircraft's Certificate of Airworthiness never expires as long as the required inspections have been made.* An aircraft is "out of license" if an inspection is overdue, and it is the responsibility of the owner or operator to be sure that all required inspections have been performed.

Airworthiness Directives are FAA mandated repairs or inspections, and the aircraft and engine logs should show that all required ADs have been performed. It is the responsibility of the pilot-in-command to insure the airworthiness of the aircraft, and this is usually interpreted to mean that you should make a thorough preflight inspection. As a renter pilot, however, you should also check the aircraft and engine logs.

This section does not contain all of the FARs, only those which in our opinion warranted explanation or illustration. There are many more regulations in Parts 61 and 91 than are covered in this book, and we recommend that you get a copy of the ASA Federal Aviation Regulations or the combined FAR/AIM book published by ASA.

The Aviation Safety Reporting System

The FAA has designated the National Aeronautics and Space Administration (NASA) to administer the Aviation Safety Reporting System. Several times in this text you have been warned that a violation of a Federal Aviation Regulation might result in a penalty and/or loss of your pilot certificate. Under ASRS, if you suspect (or know darn well) that you have inadvertently violated a regulation, you can fill out an ASRS form (ask your instructor, a tower controller, or FSS specialist) with the circumstances of the incident, send it in to NASA at Moffet Field, CA within 10 days (the address is on the form), and the FAA will not be able to take action against you. The error has to be inadvertent, and you can only use this "Get out of jail free" card to avoid certificate action once every five years, but it gets you off the hook. Some pilots say that they file one after every flight, and I'm not sure they're joking.

Accident Reporting

National Transportation Safety Board Regulations, Part 830: These regulations govern accidents and accident reporting. *They are not Federal Aviation Regulations* but will be discussed in this chapter on regulations.

The first thing you should know about Part 830 is the difference between an accident and an incident. An accident is an occurrence during which any person suffers death or serious injury, or one in which the aircraft receives substantial damage. There are fine points on just what constitutes serious injury, of course. An incident is an occurrence, other than an accident, which affects the safety of operations.

The following *incidents* require that the NTSB be notified:

1. Flight control malfunction or failure.
2. Inability of a required flight crewmember to perform flight duties as a result of injury or illness.
3. Failure of structural components of a turbine engine, *excluding* compressor and turbine blades and vanes.
4. In-flight fire.
5. Aircraft collide in flight.

The NTSB must also be notified when an aircraft is overdue and is believed to have been involved in an accident.

The following types of damage are exempt from being defined as "substantial damage":

Engine failure, damage limited to an engine, bent fairings or cowling, dented skin, small puncture holes in the skin or fabric, ground damage to rotor or propeller blades, damage to landing gear, wheels, tires, flaps, engine accessories, brakes, or wingtips.

In practical terms, this means that a gear-up landing in which no one was seriously injured is not a reportable accident. A fire while taxiing is not a reportable accident. Running into a structure or another airplane on the ground is not reportable. Failure of flaps to extend (or failure of one flap to extend) is not reportable, because flaps are not flight controls.

When a reportable accident does occur, the NTSB is to be notified immediately (this is usually, but not always, done by the FAA). If a written report is required, it must be submitted within 10 days. Also, don't let anyone touch or move the airplane until the NTSB arrives at the scene.

Memory Aid: Notify immediately, report within 10 days.

FAR Part 43
Preventive Maintenance

The FAA provides for a limited amount of owner-operator-performed preventive maintenance. FAR Part 43 is the governing regulation, and this is what you can do:

1. Removal, installation, and repair of landing gear tires.
2. Servicing landing gear shock struts by adding oil, air, or both.
3. Servicing landing gear wheel bearings
4. Lubrication not requiring disassembly other than removal of nonstructural items such as coverplates, ings, and fairings.
5. Making simple fabric patches not requiring rib stitching or the removal of structural parts or control surfaces.
6. Replenishing hydraulic fluid in the hydraulic reservoir.
7. Making small, simple repairs to fairings, non-structural cover plates, cowlings, and small patches and reinforcements, but not changing the contour so as to interfere with proper airflow.
8. Replacing safety belts.
9. Replacing seats or belt parts with replacement parts approved for the aircraft, not involving disassembly of any primary structure or operating system.
10. Troubleshooting and repairing broken circuits on landing light wiring circuits.
11. Replacing bulbs, reflectors, and lenses of position and landing lights.
12. Replacing wheels and skis where no weight and balance computation is involved.
13. Replacing or cleaning spark plugs and setting sparkplug gap clearance.
14. Replacing any hose connection except hydraulic connections.
15. Cleaning fuel and oil strainers.
16. Replacing batteries and checking fluid level and specific gravity.

You can perform other preventive maintenance activities under the supervision of a certificated mechanic. FAR 91.173 says that you should keep a record of your preventive maintenance activities (the aircraft and engine logs would seem like a good place).

Chapter 15
Regulations Review Questions

1. What is the general direction of movement of the other aircraft during a night flight if you observe a steady red light and a flashing red light ahead and at the same altitude?

   A—The other aircraft is crossing to the left.
   B—The other aircraft is crossing to the right.
   C—The other aircraft is approaching head-on.

2. If an aircraft is involved in an accident which resulted in substantial damage to the aircraft, the nearest NTSB field office should be notified

   A—immediately.
   B—within 7 days.
   C—within 10 days.

3. Of the following incidents, which would require an immediate notification to the nearest NTSB field office?

   A—An in-flight generator/alternator failure.
   B—An in-flight fire.
   C—Ground damage to the propeller blades.

4. A private pilot acting as pilot-in-command, or in any other capacity as a required pilot flight crewmember, must have in their personal possession while aboard the aircraft

   A—a current logbook endorsement to show that a flight review has been satisfactorily accomplished.
   B—the current and appropriate pilot and medical certificates.
   C—the pilot logbook to show recent experience requirements to serve as pilot-in-command have been met.

5. What is the duration, if any, of a private pilot certificate?

   A—It expires 24 months after issuance.
   B—As long as the flight review and the medical certificate are current.
   C—Indefinite.

6. A third-class medical certificate was issued on May 3, this year. To exercise the privileges of a private pilot certificate, the medical certificate will be valid through

   A—May 31, 1 year later.
   B—May 31, 2 years later.
   C—May 3, 2 years later.

7. To act as pilot-in-command of an airplane that has in more than 200 hp, a person is required to do which of the following?

   A—Make three solo takeoffs and landings in such an airplane.
   B—Receive flight instruction in an airplane that has more than 200-hp.
   C—Hold a 200 hp class rating.

8. To act as pilot-in-command of an airplane with passengers aboard, the pilot must have made at least three takeoffs and landings in an aircraft in the same category and class within the preceding

   A—120 days.
   B—90 days.
   C—12 months.

9. If recency of experience requirements for night flight have not been met and official sunset is 1830, the latest time passengers may be carried is

A—1730.
B—1830.
C—1930.

10. To meet the recent flight experience requirements for acting as pilot-in-command carrying passengers at night, a pilot must have made, within the preceding 90 days and at night, at least

A—three takeoffs and landings to a full stop in the same category and class of aircraft to be used.
B—three takeoffs and landings in the same category and class of aircraft to be used.
C—three takeoffs and landings to a full stop in the same category but not necessarily in the same of aircraft to be used.

11. According to regulations pertaining to general privileges and limitations, a private pilot may

A—not be paid in any manner for the operating expenses of a flight.
B—be paid for the operating expenses of a flight if at least 3 takeoffs and landings were made by the pilot within the preceding 90 days.
C—share the operating expenses of a flight with the passengers.

12. What preflight action is required for every flight?

A—Check weather reports and forecasts.
B—Determine runway length at airports of intended use.
C—Determine alternatives if the flight cannot be completed.

13. In addition to other preflight actions for a VFR flight away from the vicinity of the departure airport, regulations require the pilot-in-command to

A—file a flight plan.
B—check each fuel tank visually to ensure that it is full.
C—determine runway lengths at airports of intended use and the airplane's takeoff and landing distance data.

14. Under what condition may a person act as pilot-in-command of an aircraft after consuming alcohol which may affect that person's faculties?

A—Passengers may not be carried.
B—A waiver must be obtained.
C—Only after the expiration of 8 hours.

15. What is the fuel requirement for flight under VFR at night?

A—Enough to complete the flight at normal cruising flight with adverse wind conditions.
B—Enough to fly to the first point of intended landing and to fly after that for 30 min. at normal cruising speed.
C—Enough to fly to the first point of intended landing and to fly after that for 45 minutes at normal cruising speed.

16. Where, in the 48 contiguous United States and District of Columbia, is a radar beacon transponder equipped with a Mode C required?

A—In Class D Airspace.
B—In Class B airspace and in controlled airspace above 10,000' MSL.
C—In Class B airspace.

17. An aircraft had a 100-hour inspection when the tachometer read 1259.6. When is the next 100-hour inspection due?

A—1269.6 hr.
B—1309.6 hr.
C—1359.6 hr.

18. A 100-hour inspection was due at 3302.5 hr. on the tachometer but was actually done at 3309.5 hr. When is the next 100-hour inspection due?

A—3409.5 hr.
B—3402.5 hr.
C—3809.5 hr.

19. Which operation would be described as preventive maintenance?

A—Removing and installing glider wings.
B—Repair of landing gear brace struts.
C—Refinishing decorative coating of fuselage.

20. Preventive maintenance has been performed on an aircraft. What paperwork is required?

A—A full, detailed description of the work done must be entered in the airframe logbook.
B—The date the work was completed and the name of the person who did the works must be entered in the pilot's logbook.
C—The name of the person performing the work and a description of the work must be entered in the aircraft maintenance records.

21. You plan a night flight in uncontrolled airspace, intending to stay about 1,000 feet above the terrain. What cloud clearance and visibility restrictions must you observe? You do not have an instrument rating.

A—One mile visibility and clear of clouds.
B—Three miles visibility, 500' below, 1,000' above, and 2,000' horizontally from all clouds.
C—One mile visibility, 500' below, 1,000' above, and 2,000' horizontally from all clouds.

22. Would the answer to question 21 be different if you planned to fly more than 1,200 feet above the ground in Class G (uncontrolled) airspace?

Flight Planning

16

Flight Planner

This chapter will give you the opportunity to put together all of the information you have learned from the rest of the book in a practical form. With your knowledge of performance charts, weather, regulations, navigational charts, publications, and the airspace system, you should be able to plan a cross-country flight that is within the capability of your airplane, while complying with the regulations at all times.

Filing a Flight Plan

You will file this VFR flight plan as a round-robin (or round trip), noting in the remarks section that you will be landing at Ellensburg and at Paine Field. The basic purpose for filing a VFR flight plan is to aid Search and Rescue forces if you fail to complete the flight and with that in mind filling out the flight plan form should be easy. *See* Figure 16-1 on Page 16-2, and sectional chart excerpt at the back of the book.

Block 1:
You will be filing a VFR flight plan.

Block 2:
Fill in the complete registration (or "N" number) of your airplane. Be sure that friends or relatives who may be waiting for you know the registration number of your airplane.

Block 3:
Fill in the manufacturer's name and the model of the airplane (Piper PA-28) and the letter designating the equipment on board. The Flight Service Station briefer will help you with this.

Block 4:
Enter your computed true airspeed at your chosen cruising altitude.

Block 5:
Enter the 3-letter identifier for the departure airport or the name of the airport if you don't know the identifier. (It's on the chart.)

Block 6:
Fill in your proposed departure time in the Coordinated Universal Time (ZULU).

Block 7:
Enter your proposed cruising altitude.

Block 8:
Define your route by navigational aids, by airways, or by freeways, but remember that if you do not arrive at your destination, searchers will rely on the information in this block to plan the initial search. If you decide to divert from your planned route *report the change to the FSS* so that searchers will not be misdirected. This information is for your benefit, not the FAA's.

Block 9:
Enter the identifier or name of the destination airport. If it is a round-robin (as is your exercise trip) the departure airport and the destination airport will be the same.

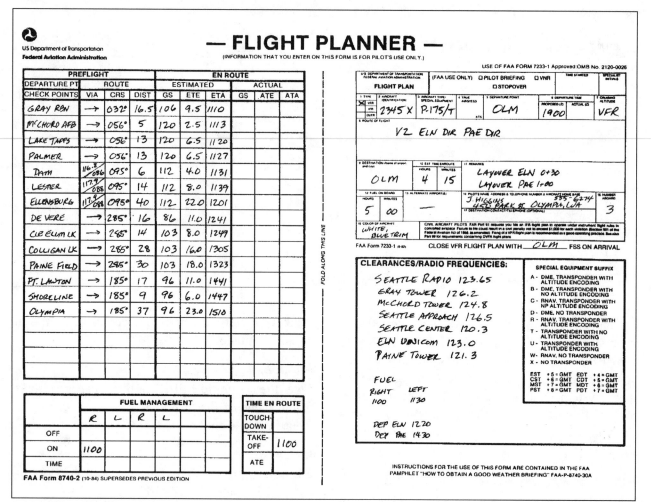

Figure 16-1. *FAA flight planner*

Block 10:

Enter your total planned time enroute including any stops along the way. It is when this total time expires that the FAA becomes concerned for your safety.

Block 11:

This block might include "sightseeing Mt. Rushmore" or "overflying Disney World" to explain planned diversions or, as in the case of your planned trip, to note that you will be on the ground at Ellensburg for 30 minutes and at Paine Field for one hour.

Block 12:

This block should contain the total fuel on board, not how much you expect to use.

Block 13:

As a VFR pilot you are not required to file an alternate airport, but it is an excellent idea if you think that you might not reach the destination airport due to weather, etc. The regulations require that you always have an alternative plan in mind if your original flight cannot be completed.

Block 14:

Fill in your complete name and address, and supply sufficient information to identify the airplane's home base and/or operator. Provide a phone number which will reach someone who is aware of your plans—possibly the airport manager or the owner of the airplane. It is this number that the FAA will call first if you have not closed your flight plan, so don't use your home phone number unless someone there could provide information on your location or plans.

Block 15:

Enter the total number of persons on board.

Block 16:

Enter the predominant colors of the airplane.

Almost all overdue airplane searches end with the first telephone call (the pilot has failed to close the flight plan), or with the second call (the airplane is parked at an enroute airport).

Preparing the Flight Log

Remember that ground speed and wind correction angle calculations require true course, true airspeed, wind direction in relation to true north, and wind velocity. Measure courses as accurately as possible using your flight plotter: this measurement is the only truly accurate element of flight planning. True airspeed figures from the airplane's performance chart were accurate when the airplane was new but its condition may no longer allow it to match the book figures.

Winds aloft as received from the Flight Service Station briefer are only forecasts, and the winds you experience in flight may vary greatly from those forecast. That is why you plan the flight by dead reckoning but fly it by pilotage.

In the calculations below, the forecast wind at cruise altitude is used for figuring ground speed and heading during climb: 90 knots is used as climb true airspeed and time to cruise altitude is based on a climb rate of 500 feet per minute. During the climb, fuel consumption is 9 gallons per hour, while in cruising flight only 7 gallons per hour are consumed.

Route:

Olympia – Ellensburg – Paine Field – Olympia

1st Leg:

Pilotage to V-2, then direct.

2nd Leg:

Direct using VOR navigation.

3rd Leg:

Pilotage.

Airplane:

4 seats, fixed gear.
Gross weight 2,300 lbs., empty weight 1,364 lbs., 150 HP., fixed pitch propeller.
Fuel capacity 38 gallons usable, 100LL.
Oil 8 qts. not included in empty weight.
2 navcomms, 360 channel comm,
200 channel nav. ADF, transponder with Mode C.

Pilot:

190 pounds.

Passengers:

185 and 110 pounds.

Baggage:

25 pounds.

Note: In addition to your Seattle Sectional Chart you should have a Seattle Terminal Area Chart on board.

Weight and Balance Calculation

		Moment
Empty weight (from MFR)	1,364	51.7
Fuel (usable)	228	11.0
Baggage	25	2.0
Oil (2 gals.)	15	-0.2
Pilot and 110 lb. passenger	300	11.2
Rear passenger	185	13.5
Totals	2,117	89.2

See Figure 16-2 (on next page) for the Loading Graph and Center of Gravity Moment Envelope.

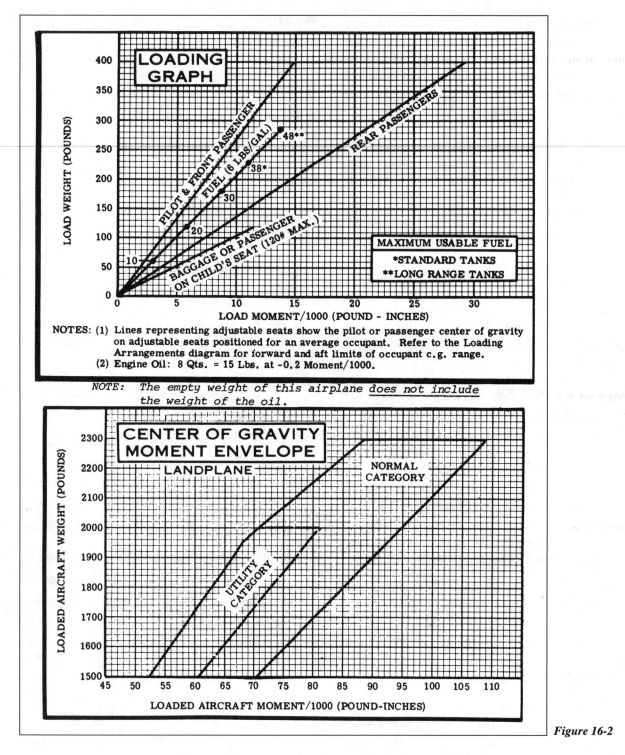

Figure 16-2

Loading is within limits with most adverse weight distribution; moving the 110 pound passenger to the rear seat and the 185 pound passenger to the front seat would move the center of gravity forward. With these passengers and this fuel load you cannot mis-load the airplane.

Weather Briefing

This is a weather briefing from the Seattle Automated Flight Service Station phone (1-800-WX-BRIEF):

"No hazardous weather is forecast for your route and time of flight. The synopsis is for a southwesterly flow aloft over Washington, caused by a stationary low at the surface and aloft 250 miles offshore from Vancouver Island. The airmass is somewhat unstable. At the surface, there is weak high pressure west of the Cascades. Freezing level is 8 thousand along the coast, sloping to 13 thousand at the eastern border.

"The route forecast calls for mountains occasionally obscured in clouds, conditions continuing beyond 0000Z. Olympia is reporting 10,000' scattered and 15 miles at this time. Wenatchee and Yakima report 9,000' broken with 25 mile visibility. We have no weather from Ellensburg. Stampede Pass is reporting a ceiling of 6,000' broken now.

"The route forecast is calling for obscuration of mountain valleys by ground fog which is expected to burn off.

"The Yakima terminal forecast is calling for 10,000 broken until 1800Z then 7,000 scattered, wind 270° at 10 knots. Wenatchee is the same except the wind is forecast to be 320° at 10 knots. Olympia will remain essentially unchanged all day.

"The winds aloft for Seattle at 6,000' are forecast to be 220° at 13 knots, at 9,000' 210° at 12 knots.

"Restricted Area 6714 is active 13,000' and below. The threshold of runway 11 at Paine Field is displaced 1,100' eastward."

If you want to know the status of military Operating Areas or Military Training Routes, you will have to ask the briefer; this information will not be volunteered. Be sure to ask the briefer for NOTAMs (including published NOTAMs) that affect your flight.

Planning the Flight

Your flight planning process will include fuel planning, preparing a flight log, and checking over the proposed route on your chart to be sure you haven't missed anything. In this text all of the details of planning the first leg will be examined, leaving the second and third legs for you to do.

An important part of preflight planning is reviewing your flight on the navigational chart to be sure that you are aware of any airspace restrictions, and that you know who to contact for any required clearances. You should also pick out easily identified ground speed checkpoints, and establish visual "brackets" on either side of your course and at the destination to insure that you do not wander too far off course or overfly the destination.

Planning Considerations, First Leg (Olympia to Ellensburg)

Olympia direct Gray Radio beacon to avoid R-6703A, past the northwest tip of Lake Tapps to intercept V-2 at Palmer, thence via V-2 to Ellensburg.

Overfly Nisqually Wildlife Refuge at least 2,000' AGL.

Use Seattle Approach/Departure Control for advisories (121.1 from Airport/Facility Directory).

Need clearance for Gray AAF and McChord AFB Class D airspace? Not if in contact with Seattle Approach Control or more than 2,800' MSL. (But look out for military aircraft anyway.)

May need clearance to transit Seattle Class B airspace; top of the Class B airspace is 10,000' MSL. You must hear "Cleared to operate in Seattle Class B airspace"; getting a radar vector is not a substitute for a clearance.

Military VFR route crosses V-2 near Lester State. Military flights will be below 1,500' AGL.

Hemispherical rule calls for odd 1,000 plus 500' eastbound when more than 3,000' AGL.

Highest terrain within 5 miles of route is 5,720' MSL.

Ground speed checkpoints: McChord AFB to northwest tip of Lake Tapps 13 NM; 13 NM to Palmer and V-2.

Hanson Reservoir dam to Lester State Airport 14 NM; 40 NM to Ellensburg.

Side brackets: Puget Sound, Cascade Mountains.

End bracket: I-90 freeway.

Frequencies: Gray radiobeacon, Olympia ground control and tower, Seattle Radio (open flight plan) Seattle Approach Control (advisories), Seattle and Ellensburg VORs, Seattle Center (flight following).

Which cruise altitude would you choose for crossing the mountains eastbound?

1. 5,500' MSL.
2. 6,500' MSL.
3. 7,500' MSL.
4. 8,500' MSL.
5. 9,500' MSL.

The hemispherical rule requires that you fly eastbound at an odd-thousand-plus 500 feet, so answer 4 is definitely wrong. The hemispherical rule does not apply within 3,000 feet of the surface, making 6,500' a possible choice, but that altitude is only 1,000' above the ridges, and there is a southwest wind which will create turbulence on the lee slopes. Answer 1 is too close to the terrain. A ceiling of 6,000' at Stampede Pass means a cloud layer at approximately 9,800', ruling out 9,500' as a cruise altitude. Choose 7,500' as your cruise altitude eastbound, and use 8,500' westbound.

In preparing your flight log, you should record the result of your calculations, and not the individual elements. That is, you need to know the magnetic heading, but you do not need to record the true course, the magnetic variation, or the wind for in-flight use. (*See* the FAA Flight Planner, Figure 16-1.) In addition (considering the built-in inaccuracy of the wind forecasts), computing and recording compass deviation and compass heading are unnecessary (although valuable for the written examination). If the heading indicator becomes inoperative, or of questionable accuracy, use your computed magnetic heading and the compass correction card to get compass course to steer. A compass correction card for the airplane you are using in this flight is provided here (Figure 16-3).

Flight Planning, First Leg

Begin by measuring the distance and true course for each leg, using your flight plotter. Here are the figures for the first leg, with variation and deviation applied to derive a compass course (Table 16-1). These are "no wind" courses—when wind is factored in, you have headings to follow.

Eastbound, interpolate the wind at 7,500' from the winds aloft given by the briefer: 220°, 13 knots at 6,000' and 210°, 21 knots at 9,000'. This is how the magnetic heading and ground speed for the first leg is calculated, rounding off fractional results (Table 16-2).

FOR	N	030	060	E	120	150	S	210	240	W	300	330
STEER	0	031	062	094	125	154	181	208	237	266	297	328

Figure 16-3. Compass correction card

	DIST	TC	VAR	MC	DEV	CC
Olympia – Gray Rbn	16.5 NM	049°	-19.5°E	028.5°	+1	029.5°
Gray Rbn – Palmer	31.0 NM	071°	-19.5°E	050.5°	+1.5	052°
Palmer – Ellensburg	58.0 NM	105.5°	-19.5°E	085.0°	+4.0	089°

Table 16-1

	TC	WIND	TAS	WCA	TH	VAR	MH	GS
Olympia – Gray Rbn	049°	215 @ 17	90	2.5°R	052°	20°	032°	106
Gray – V2 airway	071°	215 @ 17	107	5.5°R	076°	20°	056°	120
V2 – Ellensburg	106°	215 @ 17	107	79°R	115°	20°	095°	112

Table 16-2

The wind will have a greater effect during the relatively slow climb than when at cruise. Only the distance, magnetic heading, and ground speed figures from these calculations will appear in your flight log.

Note: Several flight computers, both manual and electronic, were used in making the heading and ground speed calculations. Your own answer may vary slightly.

Fuel Planning the First Leg

The climb from field elevation at Olympia (206' MSL) to the cruising altitude of 7,500' should take 15 minutes and consume 3 gallons of fuel (always round fuel consumption figures off to the next highest figure). Using the most conservative ground speed of 90 knots, you will be 23 miles into the trip with 83 miles to go when you reach cruise altitude. If you plan to descend at cruise speed (TAS 107) maintaining a ground speed of 112 knots, you will reach Ellensburg 44 minutes after leveling off, and will consume 6 gallons during that portion of the trip.

Flying the First Leg

Follow along on the full-color sectional chart excerpt at the back of this book.

Tune the ADF receiver to 216 KHz. After leaving the Olympia Class D airspace, climb as rapidly as possible to pass over wildlife refuge at least 2,000' AGL (Sectional chart legend). Home to Gray radiobeacon. Open VFR flight plan with Seattle Radio on 123.65.

Contact Seattle Approach Control (frequency in A/FD and on back of Sectional) for traffic advisories. No clearance required for Gray AAF or McChord AFB Class D airspace if above 2,800' MSL, but that is too close to the floor of Class B airspace—better talk to the towers. After passing the radiobeacon (start time for ground speed check), steer toward Lake Tapps; call Seattle Approach for clearance into Class B airspace before reaching 3,000'.

Check time at northwest tip of Lake Tapps and compute ground speed. Estimate time of arrival at Palmer. Tune #1 VOR receiver to Seattle frequency and identify. Set omni bearing selector to 085°. Note railroad to right of V-2 passes through Palmer. As VOR course deviation needle centers, turn to predetermined magnetic heading.

Start timing opposite dam at west end of reservoir. Maintain 7,500' MSL to comply with 91.155 (at least 500' below all clouds) and 91.159 (magnetic course 0° through 179° maintain odd thousand + 500') noting that during part of this leg a cruising altitude of 7,500' will be less than 3,000' above the ground and the odd-even rule does not apply. Check time opposite Lester; compute ground speed and estimate time of arrival at Ellensburg. Tune VOR receiver to Ellensburg frequency and identify. Be alert for military traffic beneath you just east of Lester (AIM 3-62). Contact Ellensburg UNICOM or broadcast intentions (AIM 4-9). Note freeway crosses flightpath 10 NM from airport and that airport is north of town. Report on the ground to Seattle Radio on 122.2. *See Table 16-3 and Figure 16-4 on the following page.*

Planning Considerations, Second Leg (Ellensburg to Paine Field)

Ellensburg direct Paine Field via VOR.

Military training route crosses direct course just west of Kachess Lake.

Course crosses Alpine Lakes Wilderness Area (area bounded by blue dots and line).

Flight will enter controlled airspace 700' AGL departing Ellensburg.

Flight will be in Class G airspace briefly while crossing corner of area with 9,500' MSL floor.

Maximum elevation figures show 9,800', 7,900' and 8,400', but highest terrain enroute is 6,680' MSL.

Ground speed checkpoints: DeVere Airport to tip of Cle Elum Lake—14 NM; lake to Paine Field 58 NM.

Side brackets: Mt. Stuart, Mt. Daniel. End bracket: Puget Sound.

Frequencies: Seattle Radio (position report), Seattle Center (flight following), Paine VOR, Paine ATIS, Paine tower and ground control.

Call Seattle Center on 128.5 (from A/FD) for clearance into Class B airspace after crossing foothills if flight is not below 8,000' and 6,000' floors.

First Leg Flight Log

Dep OLM 1100   Cruise 7,500' MSL

CHECKPOINT	ROUTE VIA	CRS*	ESTIMATED DIST	GS	ETE	ETA	ACTUAL GS	ATE	ATA
Gray Rbn	DIR	032°	16.5	106	9.5	1110			
McChord	DIR	056°	5.0	120	2.5	1113			
Lake Tapps	DIR	056°	13.0	120	6.5	1120		8.0	
Palmer	DIR	056°	13.0	120	6.5	1127			
Dam	V-2	095°	6.0	112	4.0	1131			
Lester	V-2	095°	14.0	112	8.0	1139		10.0	
Ellensburg	V-2	095°	40.0	112	22.0	1201			

The actual times en route between ground speed checkpoints have been provided; revise the ETA at Ellensburg based on the measured ground speed.

* When you have completed your wind problems, enter your computed magnetic headings in this column.

Table 16-3

Figure 16-4. *Ellensburg*

Second Leg Flight Log

Dep. ELN 1230 - Cruise altitude 8,500' MSL

CHECKPOINT	VIA	CRS*	DIST	GS	ETE	ETA	GS	ATE	ATA
DeVere Airport	DIR	285°	16.0	86	11.0	1241			
Cle Elum Lake	DIR	285°	14.0	103	8.0	1249		7.0	
Colligan Lake	DIR	285°	28.0	103	16.0	1305			
Paine Field	DIR	285°	30.0	103	18.0	1322			

Are you computing a heading and a ground speed during the climb to cruise altitude at 90 knots and 500' per minute, and also at 107 knots during cruise, this leg is flown using the ELN 285° radial and the PAE 102° radial as backup to ground reference navigation. If the wind forecast is valid, a magnetic heading of 274° should keep the VOR needle centered.

* When you have completed your wind problems, enter your computed magnetic headings in this column.

Table 16-4

Figure 16-5. *Paine Field*

Flight Planning, Second Leg

Since this is a direct flight, the easiest thing to do is to measure the magnetic course from the Ellensburg VORTAC to Paine Field, using the VORTAC's compass rose—285° magnetic. For the wind problem, add 20° for magnetic variation to get the true course. The winds at 8,500 will not be appreciably different than those at 9,000'—use 220° at 21 knots for your heading and ground speed calculations.

Fuel Planning, Second Leg

The climb out of Ellensburg to 8,500' will take approximately 13 minutes and will consume 2 gallons of fuel. You will reach cruising altitude 19 miles from Ellensburg with 69 miles to go at a ground speed of 103 knots (TAS 107), and during the 40 minutes between leveling off and arriving at Paine Field you will consume an additional 5 gallons.

Flying the Second Leg

With VOR receiver tuned to Ellensburg, set OBS on 285°. After takeoff, turn to intercept VOR radial and proceed on course. Contact Seattle Radio on 122.2 and report airborne. Keep freeway and Cle Elum airports on left until high enough to see lakes, and set course across north tips of lakes. Start timing for ground speed check opposite paved DeVere Airport. First half of this leg will be less than 3,000' above terrain and hemispherical rule will not apply. At north tip of Kachess Lake, be alert for military aircraft; tune VOR receiver to Paine Field and identify, make ground speed check and compute ETA at Paine Field. Note that between Snoqualmie Pass and Colligan Lake, controlled airspace floor is 9,500' MSL. Listen to Paine Field ATIS and call tower for clearance into Class D airspace. (The Paine Tower record of your takeoff and landing will serve as a position report if you get lost between Paine and Olympia.) *See* Table 16-4 and Figure 16-5 on Page 16-9.

Planning Considerations, Third Leg (Paine Field to Olympia)

Paine Field direct Olympia via pilotage.

Entire flight is in controlled airspace.

Course line crosses point of land at Fort Lawton.

Lowest floor of Seattle Class B airspace is 3,000' along route.

No conflict with Bremerton National or Tacoma Narrows airports.

Twin obstructions 1,000' MSL left of course line opposite long lake right of course line.

Use Seattle Approach for traffic advisories into Olympia.

Ground speed checkpoints: Fort Lawton to shoreline at Port Orchard—9 miles; shoreline 37 miles to Olympia.

Side brackets: Seattle and Bremerton.

End bracket: Hills south of Olympia.

Frequencies: Paine ground and tower, Paine VOR, Seattle Center, Seattle Approach Control, Olympia VOR, Olympia tower.

Flight Planning, Third Leg

Again, since this is a direct flight, the easiest thing to do is to measure the magnetic course from the Paine VORTAC to Olympia, using the VORTAC's compass rose—185° magnetic. For the wind problem, add 20° for magnetic variation to get the true course. Use the 3,000-foot wind at 210° at 13 knots for your heading and ground speed calculations.

Fuel Planning, Third Leg

Use the winds for 3,000' (210° at 13 knots) and cruise at 2,500 feet MSL. The ground speed works out to 96 knots. Only 3 minutes of climb are involved, so compute the leg at a true airspeed of 107 knots. Fuel consumption for 40 minutes at 7 gallons per hour is 5 gallons.

Flying the Third Leg

Set omni bearing selector to 185° (Paine VORTAC) as backup to pilotage. Set course just west of drive-in theater with point of land off Fort Lawton straight ahead. Start timing for ground speed check off Fort Lawton. Check time over shoreline east of Port Orchard and compute ground speed and ETA at Olympia. Be alert for towers left of course passing long lake. Contact Seattle Approach Control for traffic advisories and vectoring to Olympia traffic pattern. *See* Table 16-5 and Figure 16-6 .

Third Leg Flight Log

Dep Paine 1345 - Cruise 2,500' MSL.

CHECKPOINT	VIA	CRS*	DIST	GS	ETE	ETA	GS	ATE	ATA
Fort Lawton	DIR	185°	17.0		11.0	1356			
Shoreline	DIR	185°	9.0	96	6.0	1402		9.0	
Olympia	DIR	185°	37.0	96	23.0	1426			

This leg is flown using the Paine and Olympia VORs as backups to visual navigation.

Fuel consumption for the trip is planned at 21 gallons. A 30-minute reserve (3.5 gallons) is required for day VFR, so you should have at least that much in the tanks upon landing at Olympia.

Did you close your flight plan with Seattle Radio?

* When you have completed your wind problems, enter your computed magnetic headings in this column.

Table 16-5

Figure 16-6. Olympia

1. Refer to the sectional chart excerpt in the back of the book. Select the true statement regarding Restricted Area R-6703C near Olympia.

   A—The pilot must be instrument rated and file an IFR flight plan before penetrating this area.

   B—Flight within this Restricted Area is prohibited during hours of daylight.

   C—Before penetrating this Restricted Area, authorization must be obtained from the controlling agency.

2. While en route between Olympia and Ellensburg, updated weather information is available by contacting

   A—Ellensburg UNICOM on 123.0 MHz.

   B—Seattle Radio (Flight Service Station) on 122.2 MHz.

   C—Seattle Flight Watch on 122.0 MHz.

3. Assume that you are over the Cle Elum Airport (47°11'00"N 120°53'00"W) flying eastbound at 4,500' MSL. A westbound airplane passes at your altitude. Which statement is correct?

   A—The westbound airplane is legally at 4,500' MSL and you are at the wrong altitude for your direction of flight.

   B—The westbound airplane should be either 1,000' above or below you in controlled airspace.

   C—Both airplanes are being operated legally within 3,000' of the ground, where the hemispherical rule does not apply.

4. Your calls to Ellensburg UNICOM on 123.0 MHz are not answered. What action should you taken?

   A—Cancel your plans to land at Ellensburg because you cannot obtain a landing clearance.

   B—Attempt to obtain landing clearance from Seattle Radio by transmitting on 122.1 MHz and listening on 117.9 MHz.

   C—Enter the Ellensburg traffic pattern and land, announcing your position and intentions on 123.0 MHz.

5. Assume that when you contact the Paine Field tower for landing clearance you are advised that the ceiling is 900' and the visibility is 2 miles. Which statement is correct?

   A—You can proceed into the pattern and land, because all you need only remain clear of all clouds if visibility is at least 1 mile.

   B—You must remain clear of the Paine Field Class D airspace and request a Special VFR clearance from the tower.

   C—You cannot land at Paine Field unless there is at least a 1000' ceiling and 3 miles visibility.

6. On the direct route from Ellensburg to Paine Field you cross the corner of an area marked "9500 MSL". As you fly through this area at 8,500' MSL

A— you must have 3 miles visibility and remain clear of all clouds.
B— you must stay at least 1,000' above, 500' below, and 2,000' horizontally from all clouds and have 3 miles flight visibility.
C— you are in uncontrolled airspace and need only 1 mile visibility and must remain clear of clouds.

7. Refer to the A/FD listings for Ellensburg and Olympia on the back of the sectional chart excerpt. Which one of the following statements is true?

A— The Ellensburg VORTAC is unusable on the 145° radial at 7,500' beyond 25 NM.
B— The Olympia VORTAC is unusable on the 160° radial at 8,500'.
C— The Ellensburg VORTAC is unusable on the 255° radial at 6,700' at a distance of 20 NM.

Figure 17-1. *The CX-1a Pathfinder*

There are different electronic flight computers available on the market. For this chapter, ASA's CX-1a Pathfinder will be used in the step-by-step explanation that follows.

The CX-1a Pathfinder provides an inexpensive, convenient means of solving aviation problems including time-speed-distance, weight and balance, and wind problems. It allows you to make 12 conversions, such as nautical miles to statute miles, and it contains a count-up and count-down timer.

Using the CX-1a (Figure 17-1) is a very much like using a computer. It has a menu section where all of the programs are displayed, cursor movement arrows for selecting the desired program, and an **ENTER** button to store information in the computer's memory. Information stored in the memory can be recalled for use in different programs; for example, you can determine a time en route with the "Leg Time" program and then use that time in the "Fuel Burn" program.

The Keyboard

Before we get into the individual programs, you should become familiar with the keyboard (Figure 17-2). The **ON** switch performs two functions: it turns the calculator on, of course, and it also resets the calculator if you get lost in the middle of a problem and want to start over. The **+ /-** key is used to enter negative numbers, such as temperatures at altitude or weights being removed from the airplane.

The **C** key clears the entry line if you made a wrong keystroke; just press it and re-enter the information. The **T** key is used as a colon when entering time. For example, if you key in 2T40T24T the display will show 02:40:24.

P Alt W DirWT	8 8 8 8 8 8	– Dist LEMAC
TC W Spd I CArm	8 8 8 8 8 8	– GS
CAS Crs Mom Rwy	8 8 8 8 8 8	–Time %MAC
TAS CG	8 8 8 8 8 8	– FPH
MACH # GS RFX-Wind	8 8 8 8 8	– MAC
D AltHdg GWH-Wind	8 8 8 8 8 8	– Fuel

NAUT Plan TAS Hdg/GS Leg Time WT/Arm	CENT Act TAS X/H-Wind Fuel Burn %MAC	FEET Plan M# Wind FPH WT/Mom	CONV Act M# G S Endur Calc	ReqCAS ReqTAS Dst Fln Timer

Figure 17-3. The display screen

The arrows allow you to move around the menu to choose the desired program, and the menu is designed to allow you to move to any program with no more than six keystrokes. When you turn the calculator on, "Leg Time" and "Calc" will be flashing (in this text, of course, it is impossible to show anything flashing, so menu or display screen items which would be flashing on the CX-1a will be enclosed in circles). *See* Figure 17-4.

Figure 17-2. CX-1a keyboard

Plan TAS Hdg/GS (Leg Time) WT/Arm	Act TAS X/H-Wind Fuel Burn %MAC	Plan M# Wind FPH WT/Mom	Act M# G S Endur (Calc)	ReqCAS ReqTAS Dst Fln Timer

Figure 17-4. CX-1a initial display

The **CONV** key is used for all conversions and also starts the countdown timer (in conjunction with the **TIMER** key). The **TIMER** key starts the countup timer; if you want measure elapsed time, turn the CX-1a on and push **TIMER**. It will count up to 99:59:59 (Figure 17-3).

By pushing the left arrow (⬅) you can select any of the programs in the left column: "PlanTAS," "Hdg/GS," "Leg Time," or "WT/Arm."

If you don't want one of those programs, stop at the desired horizontal line and use the ➡ to move to the program you want. If you are in a program on the right side of the display, but not on the same horizontal line as the program you want, the ➡ will cycle through "WT/Mom," "ReqCAS," "ReqTAS," and "Dst Fln."

When you are on the correct horizontal line, use the ← to get to where you want to go. Let's say you want to determine your ground speed after measuring the time to cover a known distance. Turn the CX-1a on, press the ← 3 times to get to "Hdg/GS," then press the → 3 times to get to "GS." With that problem solved and your ground speed in the computer's memory, one push of the ← will put you in the "Wind" program. A few more keystrokes and you will be able to make a pilot report of actual winds aloft. *See* Figure 17-5.

The **ENTER** key is used to enter information into the computer's memory during problem solving. If you don't turn CX-1a off or reset it, any item of information in the memory stays there to be recalled when needed. For example, you might calculate that your time en route will be 3:45:00. That data will be in the "Time" section of the memory when you calculate fuel burn and will not have to be re-entered.

Conversions

Converting one unit of measurement to another is a snap with the CX-1a. Want to convert 125 nautical miles to statute miles? No program selection is required: key in **125 CONV X** (NM to SM) and the answer, 143.847, is displayed instantly. How many gallons does 10 liters equal? **10 CONV 5** (L to G) and the answer is 2.64172.

An outstanding feature of the CX-1a is its ability to make conversions in the middle of a problem. If the problem calls for temperature in Centigrade and all you have is Fahrenheit, key in the F temperature, **CONV**, and = and the Centigrade temperature will appear in the display to be used in the problem.

You will never be unsure of what units to use in a problem, because NAUT, CENT, and FEET (as appropriate) will appear at the top of the menu display when those values are required.

Figure 17-5. *Cursor movement with the* → *and the* ← *keys*

Time

CX-1a's timer counts either up or down. Press **TIMER** to start it counting up and press **TIMER** again to stop. To use it as countdown timer, you must enter the desired time, then press **CONV** followed by **TIMER** to start the countdown (this will be referred to as **CONV>TIMER**). Entering time is easy: Use **T** where you would use a colon in writing down a time in hours, minutes, and seconds. Let's say that you have calculated your fuel endurance as 4:30. Enter **4 T 30 T** and press **CONV>TIMER**. The display will show 04:30:00 and begin counting down. How about a short time—a final approach segment at 2 minutes and 30 seconds. Key in **0 T 2 T 30 T** and press **CONV>TIMER**. (After the entry for seconds you could enter either **T**, **=**, or **+**.)

Time-Speed-Distance Problems

When you turn the CX-1a **ON**, it is ready to solve the most common T-S-D problem: how long it will take to fly a given distance at a known ground speed. Press **ENTER** immediately after pressing **ON** and you are in the "Leg Time" program. Assume that you have measured a leg length of 153 nautical miles and know that your ground speed is 123 knots.

The first prompt is distance: key in **153 ENTER**. The next prompt is GS: key in **123 ENTER**. Time is shown as 01:14:38 (Figure 17-6).

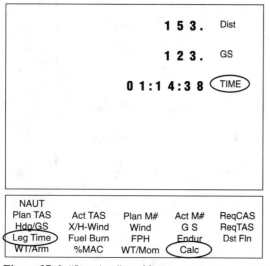

Figure 17-6. *"Leg time" problem*

This time is stored in the computer's memory for you to use in other problems. For example, you now know how long it will take to fly the leg. How much fuel will you burn? Press the ➡ once to get into the "Fuel Burn" program and press **ENTER**.

The display screen now shows the time, flashing. Press **ENTER** to use the time in the "Fuel Burn" program. You are prompted for fuel burn per hour (FPH). Assume a fuel burn rate of 9.5 gallons per hour and key in **9.5 ENTER**. The answer, 11.8 gallons, appears on the display screen (Figure 17-7).

Figure 17-7. *"Fuel burn" problem*

Ground speed (GS) is another useful T-S-D program. Let's assume that in your preflight planning you identified two distinctive landmarks along your courseline and measured the distance between them as 5 nautical miles. As you approach the first checkpoint, turn the CX-1a **ON**, press the ⬅ three times and the ➡ three times to get to the "GS" program. Press **ENTER**.

Distance is flashing. Press **5 ENTER**. Time is flashing. As you pass over the first checkpoint, press **TIMER**, and the built-in stopwatch will begin counting up. When you pass over the second checkpoint, press **TIMER** again to stop the clock. My timer read 00:02:32. Press **ENTER** and read the ground speed from the display screen (Figure 17-8).

Figure 17-8. "GS" problem

Figure 17-9. "Endur" problem

"Distance Flown" (Dst Fln) requires entries of time and ground speed. Enter the program by pressing the right arrow four times and press **ENTER**. You are prompted for time; you could press **TIMER** and time the entire flight, but this would take CX-1a out of action during the flight. Instead, enter the time flown as **HOURS T MINUTES T SECONDS T ENTER**; then key in the ground speed and press **ENTER**. If ground speed exists in the computer's memory as the result of another program, simply press **ENTER**. The display screen will read out distance flown to 3 decimal places.

One time-speed-distance problem with a definite impact on safety is Endurance. Enter the program by pressing the ➡ three times and press **ENTER**. The program will prompt you for fuel quantity. Be conservative and key in the fuel on board minus 45 minutes fuel burn at the cruise power setting. For example, if your airplane holds 45 gallons of usable fuel and burns 9.5 gallons per hour at cruise, key in **38 ENTER** at the fuel prompt and **9.5 ENTER** at the FPH prompt. The display screen will show 04:00:00 endurance (Figure 17-9).

You know that it is the time in the tanks, not the fuel in the tanks, that counts. If you are operating on an IFR flight plan you should be taxiing up to the pumps before 4 hours have gone by.

Rate Problems

A rate problem seeks the answer to "how much/many per hour" questions, and CX-1a offers an easy calculation of fuel burn per hour. The best time to do the Fuel Per Hour ("FPH") program is immediately after having the tanks topped off. You get to the "FPH" program by pressing the ➡ twice after turning the CX-1a **ON** and press **ENTER**. The first prompt is for time, and you should key in the flight time since the tanks were last filled. Let's say 2:35 and key in **2 T 35 T ENTER**. You will be prompted for the amount of fuel burned; key in **34 ENTER** as an example. The answer, 13.2 gallons per hour, appears on the display screen (Figure 17-10).

Figure 17-10. "FPH" problem

Wind Problems

The problem we face most often in flight planning is that of determining heading and ground speed based on a planned true course and true airspeed and the forecast winds. Your CX-1a will provide the answers quickly and easily with no confusion as to which answer is heading and which is ground speed. Get into the "Hdg/GS" program by turning the CX-1a **ON**, pressing the ◀■ three times and press **ENTER**. The first prompt is for wind direction; the wind direction in winds aloft forecasts is always measured in relation to true north, and the wind speed is always in knots. Assume that the forecast for your altitude and route of flight is 3515. Key in **350 ENTER** and **15 ENTER**.

You will have determined the true course from your navigation chart, assuming that the true course is 155°, key in **155 ENTER**. The last entry is true airspeed; get this from the Approved Airplane Flight Manual for your planned cruise altitude (and note the power settings required for that TAS). To finish the problem we'll assume a TAS of 125 knots and key in **125 ENTER**.

The answers, a ground speed of 139.4 knots and a true heading of 153°, appear on the display screen instantly, identified by GS and Hdg. *See* Figure 17-11. Convert true heading to magnetic heading by applying magnetic variation.

As you know, the wind information you get from the Flight Service Station briefer is forecast, not measured wind. You can calculate actual inflight winds and include them in a PIREP for the benefit of other pilots. Of course, it will be necessary for you to make an accurate ground speed check using the "GS" program and to calculate true airspeed using the "Act TAS" program before you enter the "Wind" program.

The first prompt after moving to Wind with three pushes of the ◀■ and two of the ■▶ and pressing **ENTER** is "Hdg". Enter the airplane's magnetic heading and press **ENTER** (we'll use 355° in this example). Now enter your calculated ground speed (128 knots, for example) and press **ENTER**.

The next prompt is TAS, and we will use 145 knots in this example; press **ENTER**. The last prompt is "Crs", and since the problem began with magnetic heading you should enter magnetic course — this will probably be read directly from an omni indicator.

To conclude the example we will key in a magnetic course of 350° and press **ENTER**. The wind is displayed as 028° magnetic at 21 knots. Before you call in your PIREP, however, apply the local magnetic variation to convert the measured wind to true. *See* Figure 17-12.

W Dir	3 5 0.
W Spd	1 5.
Crs	1 5 5.
TAS	1 2 5.
(GS)	1 3 9.4
(Hdg)	1 5 3.

NAUT				
Plan TAS	Act TAS	Plan M#	Act M#	ReqCAS
(Hdg/GS)	X/H-Wind	Wind	G S	ReqTAS
Leg Time	Fuel Burn	FPH	Endur	Dst Fln
WT/Arm	%MAC	WT/Mom	Calc	

Figure 17-11. First "Hdg/GS" problem

(W Dir)	0 2 8.
(W Spd)	2 1.
Crs	3 5 0.
TAS	1 4 5.
GS	1 2 8.
Hdg	3 5 5.

NAUT				
Plan TAS	Act TAS	Plan M#	Act M#	ReqCAS
Hdg/GS	X/H-Wind	(Wind)	G S	ReqTAS
Leg Time	Fuel Burn	FPH	Endur	Dst Fln
WT/Arm	%MAC	WT/Mom	(Calc)	

Figure 17-12. "Wind" problem

The CX-1a has one final wind program that you will find valuable: the "X/H-Wind" program. Its accuracy, of course, is no better than the wind information you receive from the ground. A typical situation calling for the use of this program would find you in cruise flight, listening to the ATIS or other wind and runway information for the destination airport.

For purposes of illustration, assume that the ATIS is reporting the wind as 350° at 10 knots, with runway 3 in use. To enter the program turn the CX-1a **ON** and press the ◄━━ three times and the ━━► once to get to "X/H-Wind;" press **ENTER**. The first prompt is for wind direction: key in **350 ENTER**. The next prompt is for wind speed: key in **10 ENTER**. The final prompt is Rwy: key in **3 ENTER**.

The headwind component is displayed as 8-, indicating an 8 knot headwind. The crosswind component is displayed as -6 knots; the minus sign indicates that it is from the left. A tailwind is displayed as a positive number, and a right crosswind is also displayed as a positive number.

Airspeed Calculations

Most of the problems you must solve as a pilot involve some type of airspeed calculation. During preflight planning you must use *forecast* temperatures and a desired altitude, while inflight problems involve *actual* outside air temperatures and pressure altitude. The CX-1a provides for both situations.

The "Plan TAS" program is used when you have only forecast temperature and a planned cruising altitude available. Move to "Plan TAS" with two pushes of the ◄━━ and press **ENTER**. The first prompt is for pressure altitude; we'll use 8,500 feet. Key in **8500 ENTER**. The next prompt (Figure 17-13) is for temperature; assume that the winds aloft forecast said that the temperature at 8,500 feet will be -5°, slightly colder than standard. Key in **5 +/- ENTER**. *See* Figures 17-13 and 17-14.

The next entry is calibrated airspeed (CAS); you plan to fly at 125 knots CAS, so key in **125 ENTER**. The display screen reads a true airspeed of 141.0 knots and a density altitude of 8,123 feet. *See* Figure 17-15.

Figure 17-13. 8,500 feet P Alt

Figure 17-14. T°C of -5

Figure 17-15. Completed Plan TAS problem

There is no program exclusively for density altitude calculations; it is available as a byproduct of airspeed calculations.

That was a planning function. Now you are cruising at an indicated altitude of 8,500 feet and the OAT gauge reads +3°. It's time for the "Act TAS" program. The CX-1a is programmed to take into account the effects of airspeed on the readings of the outside air temperature gauge in flight.

Assume that the barometer setting window reads 30.15", or .23" higher than the standard pressure of 29.92". Your actual pressure altitude is 8,500 – 230 or 8,270 feet.

Key in **8270 ENTER** when prompted for pressure altitude. The OAT gauge reads +3, so key in **3 ENTER** at the temperature prompt. Assume that the airspeed indicator is showing 160 CAS and key in **160 ENTER**. The display shows the true airspeed to be 180.8 knots and the density altitude to be 8,279 feet. *See* Figure 17-16.

P Alt		8 2 7 0 .
TC		3 .
CAS		1 6 0 .
(TAS)		1 8 0 . 8
(MACH#)		0 . 2 8
(D Alt)		8 2 7 9 .

NAUT	CENT	FEET		
Plan TAS	(Act TAS)	Plan M#	Act M#	ReqCAS
Hdg/GS	X/H-Wind	Wind	GS	ReqTAS
Leg Time	Fuel Burn	FPH	Endur	Dst Fln
WT/Arm	% MAC	WT/MOM	(Calc)	

Figure 17-16. "Act TAS" problem

Required Airspeed

The concept of required airspeed may be foreign to you. It is based on the need for answers to either of these problems: What calibrated airspeed must I maintain to achieve a desired true airspeed? What true airspeed is necessary to make good a desired ground speed?

Let's look at the last situation first. Based on the forecast winds aloft and your fuel calculations, you know that your ground speed must be no less than 150 knots in order for you to land at your destination with 45 minutes fuel on board. Enter the "ReqTAS" program and press **ENTER**. The first prompt is for wind direction. We'll go back to an earlier example and key in **350 ENTER** followed by **15 ENTER** at the windspeed prompt.

The next prompt is "Crs" (true course — remember that the wind direction was true); key in **130 ENTER**. The last thing you are asked for is the required ground speed; key in **150 ENTER**. The required true airspeed is 138.8 knots and the heading will be 126° true. Apply variation as required (Figure 17-17).

W Dir		3 5 0 .
W Spd		1 5 .
Crs		1 3 0 .
(TAS)		1 3 8 . 8
GS		1 5 0 .
(Hdg)		1 2 6 .

NAUT				
Plan TAS	Act TAS	Plan M#	Act M#	ReqCAS
Hdg/GS	X/H-Wind	Wind	GS	(ReqTAS)
Leg Time	Fuel Burn	FPH	Endur	Dst Fln
WT/Arm	% MAC	WT/MOM	(Calc)	

Figure 17-17. "ReqTAS" Problem

Now that you know that the true airspeed must be 139 knots you must calculate the calibrated airspeed necessary to make that true airspeed good. Enter the "ReqCAS" program and press **ENTER**.

The first prompt is for pressure altitude; let's use 9,000 feet again and key in **9000 ENTER**. The next prompt is for temperature.

We are still in the preflight planning stage, and the winds aloft forecast calls for -2°; key in **2 +/- ENTER**. The display reads 138.844 knots TAS. Press **ENTER**. The display reads 121.2 kts CAS, Mach #.22, and 9,098 density altitude (Figure 17-18).

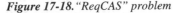

P Alt	9 0 0 0.
TC	2.⁻
(CAS)	1 2 1.2
TAS	1 3 8.844
(MACH#)	0.2 2
D Alt	9 0 9 8.

NAUT	CENT	FEET		
Plan TAS	Act TAS	Plan M#	Act M#	(ReqCAS)
Hdg/GS	X/H-Wind	Wind	GS	ReqTAS
Leg Time	Fuel Burn	FPH	Endur	Dst Fln
WT/Arm	% MAC	WT/MOM	(Calc)	

Figure 17-18. "*ReqCAS*" *problem*

Weight and Balance

The CX-1a contains three weight and balance programs, one for transport category aircraft and two for those who fly little airplanes. We will discuss only the latter two in this book.

WT/Arm

The weight and balance information in your Approved Airplane Flight Manual will always include each loading item's distance (arm) from the datum; if it is called "Station 72," it is 72 inches from the datum. The CX-1a has a "WT/Arm" program for this situation. However, most manufacturers provide the empty aircraft weight and moment but do not provide the empty aircraft center of gravity (arm); you may have to make a one-time calculation by dividing the empty weight into the empty moment. For example, the empty weight and moment/100 for a Beech Sundowner are given as 1,500 pounds and 1,670. Using the calculator function of the CX-1a, divide 165,000 by 1,500 to derive the empty aircraft arm as 110. Record this figure when you have calculated it for your airplane.

Turn the CX-1a **ON** and push the ⬅ once; "WT/Arm" is flashing. Push **ENTER** to get into the program. WT will be flashing at the top of the display: key in the empty weight of the airplane. "Arm" begins flashing: key in the empty airplane arm that you calculated. Now you will encounter something new —reduction factor (RF) is flashing. For "WT/Arm" calculations a reduction factor of 1 is used, because

the distances are in inches (later on you will learn how RF is used in WT/Mom problems.) Simply press **ENTER** to use 1 as a reduction factor. Only one RF entry is required for each problem. Figure 17-19 shows the display screen at the beginning of a problem; the airplane weight is 1,454 pounds and the empty center of gravity position is 39.6 inches aft of datum.

(WT)	1 4 5 4.
Arm	3 9.6
(Mom)	5 7 5 7 8.4
(CG)	3 9.6
RF	1.
(GW)	1 4 5 4.

(WT/Arm)	

Figure 17-19. Initial "WT/Arm" display

	Weight	Arm
Fuel (40 gal.)	240	36.0
Front seat occupants	240	37.0
Rear seat occupants	170	73.0
Baggage	96	95.0

The display shows the weight and arm you have entered, the empty airplane moment (weight x arm), and the center of gravity. WT will be flashing, prompting you to enter the first loading item. Key in the total weight of the pilot and front seat passenger and press **ENTER**. Key in the arm for the front seats found in the flight manual and press **ENTER**. The display now shows the new total weight and the new center of gravity.

Key in the weights and arms for other occupied passenger seats and for cargo compartments and note that you have a running total on weight and on CG position. The manufacturer will provide the arm for fuel tanks and for oil; key in their weights and arms to complete the problem.

The last display screen will show the loaded airplane total weight, total moment, and center of gravity. Check the weight and CG position against the published loading limits to ensure that the airplane is loaded within those limits. Figure 17-20 shows the final display screen after passenger and fuel weights and arms have been entered.

Figure 17-20. Final display of "WT/Arm" problem

If you find the airplane to be overloaded, something has to go. Assume, for example, that the airplane is 50 pounds over gross and the center of gravity exceeds the aft limit. Will offloading 50 pounds of cargo move the CG to a safe location? Press **ON** to reset the computer, and the ⬅ to get back into the WT/Arm program. Key in the total weight and center of gravity from the original problem, remembering to press **ENTER** when prompted for a reduction factor. Now key in **50** followed by the **+/–** key and press **ENTER**. Key in the arm of **95** for the forward compartment and press **ENTER**. Note that the total weight has been reduced by 50 pounds and that the CG has changed to reflect the reduction.

What if the airplane's total weight is within limits but the center of gravity is not? That calls for a weight shift. Let's try moving 230-pound Uncle John from the rear passenger seat (Station 142) to the front passenger seat (Station 104), switching places with 110-pound Aunt Martha. With the CX-1a set up with the results of the original problem, key in **230 +/- ENTER 1 ENTER 142 ENTER** to get Uncle John out of the back seat, and **230 ENTER 104 ENTER**

to get him into the front seat. Key in **110 +/- ENTER 104 ENTER** to get Aunt Martha out of the front seat, and **110 ENTER 142 ENTER** to place her in the back seat. The CX-1a now reads the new center of gravity; if it is within limits, have a good flight!

WT/Mom

If the manufacturer of your airplane has provided weight and moment information, turn the CX-1a **ON**, press the ⬅ once and the ➡ twice to get to the "WT/Mom" program. Press **ENTER** to activate the program. The procedure will be almost identical to the "WT/Arm" program, except that the reduction factor is much more important. If your flight manual lists moments as Mom/1000, enter **1000** when prompted for a reduction factor (RF), or enter **100** when the manual lists Mom/100.

When removing or shifting weights in the "WT/Mom" program, remember that both the weight and the moment are negative numbers and the **+/–** key must be pressed after the weight or moment is keyed in when taking the weight out of a given location.

Let's try a couple of problems to see how it works:

Calculate the center of gravity.

	Weight	Mom/1000
Empty weight	1,350	51.5
Pilot and front passenger	380	14.0
Fuel 48 gal	288	13.8
Oil 8 qts	15	- 0.2

After entering the "WT/Mom" program, your first prompt is for weight: key in **1350 ENTER**. Now enter the moment: key in **51.5 ENTER**. Reduction factor is flashing: key in **1000 ENTER**. You now have the empty center of gravity. Following the same procedure, key in each weight item and its moment. The final screen will show a CG of 38.9" and a weight of 2,033 pounds.

The Approved Airplane Flight Manual should provide the fore and aft center of gravity limits. If the AFM provides only a weight/moment envelope, multiply the weight times the center of gravity (2,033 x 38.9) and divide by the reduction factor. The answer will be a moment of 79.08.

Chaining

The computer contains memory registers for TAS, GS, TIME, FPH, and CG. If any of these values result from a calculation, it is stored in its register, read to be recalled when required by another program. Resetting the computer by pressing **ON** or turning the CX-1a **OFF** causes the loss of this information, so chain calculations should be done without interruption. The menu display of the CX-1a is set up for a logical flow of information from one program to another.

The entire top row of programs in the menu display feed a chain which includes most flight planning problems. This is how it works:

You have checked the en route weather, the winds aloft, and your airplane's performance charts and have chosen 12,000 feet as your cruising altitude. The winds and temperatures aloft forecast for 12,000 feet at your time of flight is 1418+14 and you plan to cruise at 160 knots indicated airspeed on a true course of 280°.

First, call up the "Plan TAS" program and key in **12000**, **14**, and **160** when prompted. The display screen shows the true airspeed as 199.5 knots. Call up the "Hdg/GS" program and key in **140** for wind direction and **18** for wind speed. Key in 280 when prompted for the course. The next prompt is for TAS, and 199.467 shows up from the last problem with no effort on your part. Press **ENTER** to use the true airspeed as a part of the "Hdg/GS" problem. The display screen shows ground speed as 212.9 knots and true heading as 277°.

Note: If you want to use the true airspeed figure from the cruise performance charts, omit the "Plan TAS" program and begin with "Hdg/GS." Move to the "Leg Time" program and press **ENTER**. You have measured the trip length as 465 nautical miles, so key in **465** when prompted for distance. The program supplies the 212.92 knot ground speed; press **ENTER** to use it. The leg time is now displayed as 02:11:02. Move to the "Fuel Burn" program and press **ENTER**.

The first prompt is for time, and 02:11:02 is already displayed; press **ENTER**. The program prompts you for fuel burn per hour, and you key in **9** gallons per hour from the flight manual cruise performance charts. The final answer is a fuel burn of 19.7 gallons.

Your airplane has a usable fuel capacity of 48 gallons but you keep 45 minutes supply at 9 GPH (7 gallons) in reserve. Move to the "Endur" program and press **ENTER**. At the Fuel prompt key in **41** gallons. The fuel burn rate of 9 GPH is supplied by the memory; press **ENTER**. Endurance is 04:33:20.

Now move to the "ReqTAS" program. You will be prompted for the wind direction, wind speed, and course (none of these is retained in memory); GS is supplied from memory, and a TAS of 199.5 knots is displayed. Move to the "ReqCAS" program. You will be prompted for pressure altitude and temperature, but TAS will be supplied from memory. The final display a calibrated airspeed of 160 knots.

You are ready to fill out the flight plan form. You know the true airspeed, the estimated time en route, and the fuel endurance. In flight, you can run a couple of ground speed checks and a "Act TAS" to see how actual conditions might modify these figures.

Miscellaneous Solutions

Several other types of problems can be solved by using the calculator function. For example, assume that you are cruising at 12,000 feet and would like to descend at 120 knots and 500 feet per minute to an airport with a traffic pattern altitude of 1,500 feet MSL. How far from the airport should you begin the descent?

At a speed of two miles per minute your desired descent rate is 250 feet per mile. You have 10,500 feet to lose; divide 10,500 by 250 to get the distance out: 42 nautical miles.

A Standard Instrument Departure requires a climb rate of 350 feet per mile to clear obstacles, and your best climb speed is 115 knots. Will you be able to comply? Divide 115 by 60; your speed is 1.9 miles per minute. Multiply the required climb of 350 feet per mile by 1.9 to derive a climb rate of 665 feet per minute.

The CX-1a Pathfinder takes up little room in your flight case and can be carried in a shirt pocket, ready for use.

This Glossary was compiled to promote a common understanding of the terms used in the Air Traffic Control system. It includes those terms which are intended for pilot/controller communications. Those terms most frequently used in pilot/controller communications are printed in **bold italics**. The definitions are primarily defined in an operational sense applicable to both users and operators of the National Airspace System. Use of the Glossary will preclude any misunderstandings concerning the system's design, function, and purpose.

Because of the international nature of flying, terms used in the *Lexicon*, published by the International Civil Aviation Organization (ICAO), are included when they differ from FAA definitions. These terms are followed by "[ICAO]". For the reader's convenience, there are also cross references to related terms in other parts of the Glossary and to other documents, such as the Federal Aviation Regulations (FAR's) and the Airman's Information Manual (AIM).

This Glossary will be revised, as necessary, to maintain a common understanding of the system.

AAI. (See ARRIVAL AIRCRAFT INTERVAL).

AAR. (See AIRPORT ACCEPTANCE RATE).

ABBREVIATED IFR FLIGHT PLANS. An authorization by ATC requiring pilots to submit only that information needed for the purpose of ATC. It includes only a small portion of the usual IFR flight plan information. In certain instances, this may be only aircraft identification, location, and pilot request. Other information may be requested if needed by ATC for separation control purposes. It is frequently used by aircraft which are airborne and desire an instrument approach or by aircraft which are on the ground and desire a climb to VFR-on-top. *(See VFR-ON-TOP). (Refer to AIM).*

ABEAM. An aircraft is "abeam" a fix, point, or object when that fix, point, or object is approximately 90 degrees to the right or left of the aircraft track. Abeam indicates a general position rather than a precise point.

ABORT. To terminate a preplanned aircraft maneuver; e.g., an aborted takeoff.

ACC [ICAO]. (See AREA CONTROL CENTER).

ACCELERATE-STOP DISTANCE AVAILABLE. The runway plus stopway length declared available and suitable for the acceleration and deceleration of an airplane aborting a takeoff.

ACCELERATE-STOP DISTANCE AVAILABLE [ICAO]. The length of the take-off run available plus the length of the stopway if provided.

ACDO. (See AIR CARRIER DISTRICT OFFICE).

ACKNOWLEDGE [ICAO]. Let me know that you have received my message. *(See ICAO term ACKNOWLEDGE).*

ACKNOWLEDGE [ICAO]. Let me know that you have received and understood this message.

ACLS. (See AUTOMATIC CARRIER LANDING SYSTEM).

ACLT. (See ACTUAL CALCULATED LANDING TIME).

ACROBATIC FLIGHT. An intentional maneuver involving an abrupt change in an aircraft's attitude, an abnormal attitude, or abnormal acceleration not necessary for normal flight. *(Refer to FAR Part 91). (See ICAO term ACROBATIC FLIGHT).*

ACROBATIC FLIGHT [ICAO]. Maneuvers intentionally performed by an aircraft involving an abrupt change in its attitude, an abnormal attitude, or an abnormal variation in speed.

ACTIVE RUNWAY. (See RUNWAY IN USE/ACTIVE RUNWAY/DUTY RUNWAY).

ACTUAL CALCULATED LANDING TIME. ACLT is a flight's frozen calculated landing time. An actual time determined at freeze calculated landing time (FCLT) or meter list display interval (MLDI) for the adapted vertex for each arrival aircraft based upon runway configuration, airport acceptance rate, airport arrival delay period, and other metered arrival aircraft. This time is either the vertex time of arrival (VTA) of the aircraft or the tentative calculated landing time (TCLT)/ACLT of the previous aircraft plus the arrival aircraft interval (AAI), whichever is later. This time will not be updated in response to the aircraft's progress.

ADDITIONAL SERVICES. Advisory information provided by ATC which includes but is not limited to the following:

1. Traffic advisories.
2. Vectors, when requested by the pilot, to assist aircraft receiving traffic advisories to avoid observed traffic.

Continued

3. Altitude deviation information of 300 feet or more from an assigned altitude as observed on a verified (reading correctly) automatic altitude readout (Mode C).

4. Advisories that traffic is no longer a factor.

5. Weather and chaff information.

6. Weather assistance.

7. Bird activity information.

8. Holding pattern surveillance. Additional services are provided to the extent possible contingent only upon the controller's capability to fit them into the performance of higher priority duties and on the basis of limitations of the radar, volume of traffic, frequency congestion, and controller workload. The controller has complete discretion for determining if he is able to provide or continue to provide a service in a particular case. The controller's reason not to provide or continue to provide a service in a particular case is not subject to question by the pilot and need not be made known to him.

(See TRAFFIC ADVISORIES). (Refer to AIM).

ADF. (See AUTOMATIC DIRECTION FINDER).

ADIZ. (See AIR DEFENSE IDENTIFICATION ZONE).

ADLY. (See ARRIVAL DELAY).

ADMINISTRATOR. The Federal Aviation Administrator or any person to whom he has delegated his authority in the matter concerned.

ADVISE INTENTIONS. Tell me what you plan to do.

ADVISORY. Advice and information provided to assist pilots in the safe conduct of flight and aircraft movement. *(See ADVISORY SERVICE).*

ADVISORY FREQUENCY. The appropriate frequency to be used for Airport Advisory Service. (See LOCAL AIRPORT ADVISORY). (See UNICOM). (Refer to ADVISORY CIRCULAR NO. 90-42). (Refer to AIM).

ADVISORY SERVICE. Advice and information provided by a facility to assist pilots in the safe conduct of flight and aircraft movement. *(See LOCAL AIRPORT ADVISORY). (See TRAFFIC ADVISORIES). (See SAFETY ALERT). (See ADDITIONAL SERVICES). (See RADAR ADVISORY). (See EN ROUTE FLIGHT ADVISORY SERVICE). (Refer to AIM).*

AERIAL REFUELING. A procedure used by the military to transfer fuel from one aircraft to another during flight. *(Refer to VFR/IFR Wall Planning Charts).*

AERODROME. A defined area on land or water (including any buildings, installations and equipment) intended to be used either wholly or in part for the arrival, departure, and movement of aircraft.

AERODROME BEACON [ICAO]. Aeronautical beacon used to indicate the location of an aerodrome from the air.

AERODROME CONTROL SERVICE [ICAO]. Air traffic control service for aerodrome traffic.

AERODROME CONTROL TOUR [ICAO]. A unit established to provide air traffic control service to aerodrome traffic.

AERODROME ELEVATION [ICAO]. The elevation of the highest point of the landing area.

AERODROME TRAFFIC CIRCUIT [ICAO]. The specified path to be flown by aircraft operating in the vicinity of an aerodrome.

AERONAUTICAL BEACON. A visual NAVAID displaying flashes of white and/or colored light to indicate the location of an airport, a heliport, a landmark, a certain point of a Federal airway in mountainous terrain, or an obstruction. *(See AIRPORT ROTATING BEACON). (Refer to AIM).*

AERONAUTICAL CHART. A map used in air navigation containing all or part of the following: Topographic features, hazards and obstructions, navigation aids, navigation routes, designated airspace, and airports. Commonly used aeronautical charts are:

1. Sectional Aeronautical Charts (1:500,000). Designed for visual navigation of slow or medium speed aircraft. Topographic information on these charts features the portrayal of relief and a judicious selection of visual check points for VFR flight. Aeronautical information includes visual and radio aids to navigation, airports, controlled airspace, restricted areas, obstructions, and related data.

2. VFR Terminal Area Charts (1:250,000). Depict Class B airspace which provides for the control or segregation of all the aircraft within Class B airspace. The chart depicts topographic information and aeronautical information which includes visual and radio aids to navigation, airports, controlled airspace, restricted areas, obstructions, and related data.

3. World Aeronautical Charts (WAC) (1:1,000,000). Provide a standard series of aeronautical charts covering land areas of the world at a size and scale convenient for navigation by moderate speed aircraft. Topographic information includes cities and towns, principal roads, railroads, distinctive land- marks, drainage, and relief. Aeronautical information includes visual and radio aids to navigation, airports, airways, restricted areas, obstructions, and other pertinent data.

4. En Route Low Altitude Charts. Provide aeronautical information for en route instrument navigation (IFR) in the low altitude stratum. Information includes the portrayal of airways, limits of controlled airspace, position identification and frequencies of radio aids, selected airports, minimum en route and minimum obstruction clearance altitudes, airway distances, reporting points, restricted areas, and related data. Area charts, which are a part of this series, furnish terminal data at a larger scale in congested areas.

5. En Route High Altitude Charts. Provide aeronautical information for en route instrument navigation (IFR) in the high altitude stratum. Information includes the portrayal of jet routes, identification and frequencies of radio aids, selected airports, distances, time zones, special use airspace, and related information.

6. Instrument Approach Procedures (IAP) Charts. Portray the aeronautical data which is required to execute an instrument approach to an airport. These charts depict the procedures, including all related data, and the airport diagram. Each procedure is designated for use with a specific type of electronic navigation system including NDB, TACAN, VOR, ILS/MLS, and RNAV. These charts are identified by the type of navigational aid(s) which provide final approach guidance.

7. Standard Instrument Departure (SID) Charts. Designed to expedite clearance delivery and to facilitate transition between takeoff and en route operations. Each SID procedure is presented as a separate chart and may serve a single airport or more than one airport in a given geographical location.

8. Standard Terminal Arrival (STAR) Charts. Designed to expedite air traffic control arrival procedures and to facilitate transition between en route and instrument approach operations. Each STAR procedure is presented as a separate chart and may serve a single airport or more than one airport in a given geographical location.

9. Airport Taxi Charts. Designed to expedite the efficient and safe flow of ground traffic at an airport. These charts are identified by the official airport name; e.g., Washington National Airport.

(See ICAO term AERONAUTICAL CHART).

AERONAUTICAL CHART [ICAO]. A representation of a portion of the earth, its culture and relief specifically designated to meet the requirements of air navigation.

AERONAUTICAL INFORMATION PUBLICATION [AIP] [ICAO]. A publication issued by or with the authority of a State and containing aeronautical information of a lasting character essential to air navigation.

A/FD. (See AIRPORT/FACILITY DIRECTORY).

AFFIRMATIVE. Yes.

AIM. (See AIRMAN'S INFORMATION MANUAL).

AIP [ICAO]. (See AERONAUTICAL INFORMATION PUBLICATION).

AIRBORNE DELAY. Amount of delay to be encountered in airborne holding.

AIR CARRIER DISTRICT OFFICE. An FAA field office serving an assigned geographical area, staffed with Flight Standards personnel serving the aviation industry and the general public on matters related to the certification and operation of scheduled air carriers and other large aircraft operations.

AIRCRAFT. Device(s) that are used or intended to be used for flight in the air, and when used in air traffic control terminology, may include the flight crew. *(See ICAO term AIRCRAFT).*

AIRCRAFT [ICAO]. Any machine that can derive support in the atmosphere from the reactions of the air other than the reactions of the air against the earth's surface.

AIRCRAFT APPROACH CATEGORY. A grouping of aircraft based on a speed of 1.3 times the stall speed in the landing configuration at maximum gross landing weight. An aircraft shall fit in only one category. If it is necessary to maneuver at speeds in excess of the upper limit of a speed range for a category, the minimums for the next higher category should be used. For example, an aircraft which falls in Category A, but is circling to land at a speed in excess of 91 knots, should use the approach Category B minimums when circling to land. The categories are as follows:

1. Category A. Speed less than 91 knots.
2. Category B. Speed 91 knots or more but less than 121 knots.
3. Category C. Speed 121 knots or more but less than 141 knots.
4. Category D. Speed 141 knots or more but less than 166 knots.
5. Category E. Speed 166 knots or more.

(Refer to FAR FAR Part 1). (Refer to FAR Part 97).

AIRCRAFT CLASSES. For the purposes of Wake Turbulence Separation Minima, ATC classifies aircraft as Heavy, Large, and Small as follows:

1. Heavy. Aircraft capable of takeoff weights of 300,000 pounds or more whether or not they are operating at this weight during a particular phase of flight.
2. Large. Aircraft of more than 12,500 pounds, maximum certificated takeoff weight, up to 300,000 pounds.
3. Small. Aircraft of 12,500 pounds or less maximum certificated takeoff weight.

(Refer to AIM).

AIRCRAFT SITUATION DISPLAY. ASD is a computer system that receives radar track data from all 20 CONUS ARTCCs, organizes this data into a mosaic display, and presents it on a computer screen. The display allows the traffic management coordinator multiple methods of selection and high-lighting of individual aircraft or groups of aircraft. The user has the option of superimposing these aircraft positions over any number of background displays. These background options include ARTCC boundaries, any stratum of en route sector boundaries, fixes, airways, military and other special use airspace, airports, and geopolitical boundaries. By using the ASD, a coordinator can monitor any number of traffic situations or the entire systemwide traffic flows.

AIRCRAFT SURGE LAUNCH AND RECOVERY.
Procedures used at USAF bases to provide increased launch and recovery rates in instrument flight rules conditions. ASLAR is based on:

a. Reduced separation between aircraft which is based on time or distance. Standard arrival separation applies between participants including multiple flights until the DRAG point. The DRAG point is a published location on an ASLAR approach where aircraft landing second in a formation slows to a predetermined airspeed. The DRAG point is the reference point at which MARSA applies as expanding elements effect separation within a flight or between subsequent participating flights.

b. ASLAR procedures shall be covered in a Letter of Agreement between the responsible USAF military ATC facility and the concerned Federal Aviation Administration facility. Initial Approach Fix spacing requirements are normally addressed as a minimum.

AIR DEFENSE EMERGENCY. A military emergency condition declared by a designated authority. This condition exists when an attack upon the continental U.S., Alaska, Canada, or U.S. installations in Greenland by hostile aircraft or missiles is considered probable, is imminent, or is taking place. *(Refer to AIM)*.

AIR DEFENSE IDENTIFICATION ZONE. The area of airspace over land or water, extending upward from the surface, within which the ready identification, the location, and the control of aircraft are required in the interest of national security.

1. Domestic Air Defense Identification Zone. An ADIZ within the United States along an international boundary of the United States.

2. Coastal Air Defense Identification Zone. An ADIZ over the coastal waters of the United States.

3. Distant Early Warning Identification Zone (DEWIZ). An ADIZ over the coastal waters of the State of Alaska.

ADIZ locations and operating and flight plan requirements for civil aircraft operations are specified in Part 99. (Refer to AIM).

AIRMAN'S INFORMATIONAL MANUAL. A primary FAA publication whose purpose is to instruct airmen about operating in the National Airspace System of the U.S. It provides basic flight information, ATC Procedures and general instructional information concerning health, medical facts, factors affecting flight safety, accident and hazard reporting, and types of aeronautical charts and their use.

AIRMAN'S METEOROLOGICAL INFORMATION. (See AIRMET).

AIRMET. In-flight weather advisories issued only to amend the area forecast concerning weather phenomena which are of operational interest to all aircraft and potentially hazardous to aircraft having limited capability because of lack of equipment, instrumentation, or pilot qualifications. AIRMETs concern weather of less severity than that covered by SIGMETs or Convective SIGMETs. AIRMETs cover moderate icing, moderate turbulence, sustained winds of 30 knots or more at the surface, widespread areas of ceilings less than 1,000 feet and/or visibility less than 3 miles, and extensive mountain obscurement. *(See AWW). (See SIGMET). (See CONVECTIVE SIGMET). (See CWA). (Refer to AIM)*.

AIR NAVIGATION FACILITY. Any facility used in, available for use in, or designed for use in, aid of air navigation, including landing areas, lights, any apparatus or equipment for disseminating weather information, for signaling, for radio-directional finding, or for radio or other electrical communication, and any other structure or mechanism having a.similar purpose for guiding or controlling flight in the air or the landing and take-off of aircraft. *(See NAVIGATIONAL AID)*.

AIRPORT. An area on land or water that is used or intended to be used for the landing and takeoff of aircraft and includes its buildings and facilities if any.

AIRPORT ACCEPTANCE RATE. A dynamic input parameter specifying the number of arriving aircraft which an airport or airspace can accept from the ARTCC per hour. The AAR is used to calculate the desired interval between successive arrival aircraft.

AIRPORT ADVISORY AREA. The area within ten miles of an airport without a control tower or where the tower is not in operation, and on which a Flight Service Station is located. *(See LOCAL AIRPORT ADVISORY). (Refer to AIM)*.

AIRPORT ELEVATION. The highest point of an airport's usable runways measured in feet from mean sea level. *(See TOUCHDOWN ZONE ELEVATION). (See ICAO term AERODROME ELEVATION)*.

AIRPORT/FACILITY DIRECTORY. A publication designed primarily as a pilot's operational manual containing all airports, seaplane bases, and heliports open to the public including communications data, navigational facilities, and certain special notices and procedures. This publication is issued in seven volumes according to geographical area.

AIRPORT INFORMATION AID. (See AIRPORT INFORMATION DESK).

AIRPORT INFORMATION DESK. An airport unmanned facility designed for pilot self-service briefing, flight planning, and filing of flight plans. *(Refer to AIM)*.

AIRPORT LIGHTING. Various lighting aids that may be installed on an airport. Types of airport lighting include:

1. Approach Light System (ALS). An airport lighting facility which provides visual guidance to landing aircraft by radiating light beams in a directional pattern by which the pilot aligns the aircraft with the

extended centerline of the runway on his final approach for landing. Condenser-Discharge Sequential Flashing Lights/Sequenced Flashing Lights may be installed in conjunction with the ALS at some airports. Types of Approach Light Systems are:

a. ALSF-1. Approach Light System with Sequenced Flashing Lights in ILS Cat-I configuration.

b. ALSF-2. Approach Light System with Sequenced Flashing Lights in ILS Cat-II configuration. The ALSF-2 may operate as an SSALR when weather conditions permit.

c. SSALF. Simplified Short Approach Light System with Sequenced Flashing Lights.

d. SSALR. Simplified Short Approach Light System with Runway Alignment Indicator Lights.

e. MALSF. Medium Intensity Approach Light System with Sequenced Flashing Lights.

f. MALSR. Medium Intensity Approach Light System with Runway Alignment Indicator Lights.

g. LDIN. Lead-in-light system: Consists of one or more series of flashing lights installed at or near ground level that provides positive visual guidance along an approach path, either curving or straight, where special problems exist with hazardous terrain, obstructions, or noise abatement procedures.

h. RAIL. Runway Alignment Indicator Lights (Sequenced Flashing Lights which are installed only in combination with other light systems).

i. ODALS. Omnidirectional Approach Lighting System consists of seven omnidirectional flashing lights located in the approach area of a nonprecision runway. Five lights are located on the runway centerline extended with the first light located 300 feet from the threshold and extending at equal intervals up to 1,500 feet from the threshold. The other two lights are located, one on each side of the runway threshold, at a lateral distance of 40 feet from the runway edge, or 75 feet from the runway edge when installed on a runway equipped with a VASI. (Refer to Order 6850.2).

2. Runway Lights/Runway Edge Lights. Lights having a prescribed angle of emission used to define the lateral limits of a runway. Runway lights are uniformly spaced at intervals of approximately 200 feet, and the intensity may be controlled or preset.

3. Touchdown Zone Lighting. Two rows of tranverse light bars located symmetrically about the runway centerline normally at 100-foot intervals. The basic system extends 3,000 feet along the runway.

4. Runway Centerline Lighting. Flush centerline lights spaced at 50 foot intervals beginning 75 feet from the landing threshold and extending to within 75 feet of the opposite end of the runway.

5. Threshold Lights. Fixed green lights arranged symmetrically left and right of the runway centerline, identifying the runway threshold.

6. Runway End Identifier Lights (REIL). Two synchronized flashing lights, one on each side of the runway threshold, which provide rapid and positive identification of the approach end of a particular runway.

7. Visual Approach Slope Indicator (VASI). An airport lighting facility providing vertical visual approach slope guidance to aircraft during approach to landing by radiating a directional pattern of high intensity red and white focused light beams which indicate to the pilot that he is "on path" if he sees red/white, "above path" if white/white, and "below path" if red/red. Some airports serving large aircraft have three-bar VASIs which provide two visual glide paths to the same runway.

8. Boundary Lights. Lights defining the perimeter of an airport or landing area.

(Refer to AIM).

AIRPORT MARKING AIDS. Markings used on runway and taxiway surfaces to identify a specific runway, a runway threshold, a centerline, a hold line, etc. A runway should be marked in accordance with its present usage such as:

1. Visual.

2. Nonprecision instrument.

3. Precision instrument.

(Refer to AIM).

AIRPORT RESERVATION OFFICE. Office responsible for monitoring the operation of the high density rule. Receives and processes requests for IFR operations at high density traffic airports.

AIRPORT ROTATING BEACON. A visual NAVAID operated at many airports. At civil airports, alternating white and green flashes indicate the location of the airport. At military airports, the beacons flash alternately white and green, but are differentiated from civil beacons by dual peaked (two quick) white flashes between the green flashes. (See SPECIAL VFR OPERATIONS). (See INSTRUMENT FLIGHT RULES). (Refer to AIM). (See ICAO term AERODROME BEACON).

AIRPORT SURFACE DETECTION EQUIPMENT. Radar equipment specifically designed to detect all principal features on the surface of an airport, including aircraft and vehicular traffic, and to present the entire image on a radar indicator console in the control tower. Used to augment visual observation by tower personnel of aircraft and/or vehicular movements on runways and taxiways.

AIRPORT SURVEILLANCE RADAR. Approach control radar used to detect and display an aircraft's position in the terminal area. ASR provides range and azimuth information but does not provide elevation data. Coverage of the ASR can extend up to 60 miles.

AIRPORT TAXI CHARTS. (See AERONAUTICAL CHART).

AIRPORT TRAFFIC CONTROL SERVICE. A service provided by a control tower for aircraft operating on the movement area and in the vicinity of an airport. *(See MOVEMENT AREA). (See TOWER). (See ICAO term AERODROME CONTROL SERVICE).*

AIRPORT TRAFFIC CONTROL TOWER. (See TOWER).

AIR ROUTE SURVEILLANCE RADAR. Air route traffic control center (ARTCC) radar used primarily to detect and display an aircraft's position while en route between terminal areas. The ARSR enables controllers to provide radar air traffic control service when aircraft are within the ARSR coverage. In some instances, ARSR may enable an ARTCC to provide terminal radar services similar to but usually more limited than those provided by a radar approach control.

AIR ROUTE TRAFFIC CONTROL CENTER. A facility established to provide air traffic control service to aircraft operating on IFR flight plans within controlled airspace and principally during the en route phase of flight. When equipment capabilities and controller workload permit, certain advisory/assistance services may be provided to VFR aircraft. *(See NAS STAGE A). (See EN ROUTE AIR TRAFFIC CONTROL SERVICES). (Refer to AIM).*

AIRSPACE HIERARCHY. Within the airspace classes, there is a hierarchy and, in the event of an overlap of airspace: Class A preempts Class B, Class B preempts Class C, Class C preempts Class D, Class D preempts Class E, and Class E preempts Class G.

AIRSPEED. The speed of an aircraft relative to its surrounding air mass. The unqualified term "airspeed" means one of the following:

1. Indicated Airspeed. The speed shown on the aircraft airspeed indicator. This is the speed used in pilot controller communications under the general term "airspeed." *(Refer to FAR FAR Part 1).*
2. True Airspeed. The airspeed of an aircraft relative to undisturbed air. Used primarily in flight planning and en route portion of flight. When used in pilot/controller communications, it is referred to as "true airspeed" and not shortened to "airspeed."

AIRSTART. The starting of an aircraft engine while the aircraft is airborne, preceded by engine shutdown during training flights or by actual engine failure.

AIR TAXI. Used to describe a helicopter/VTOL aircraft movement conducted above the surface but normally not above 100 feet AGL. The aircraft may proceed either via hover taxi or flight at speeds more than 20 knots. The pilot is solely responsible for selecting a safe airspeed/altitude for the operation being conducted. *(See HOVER TAXI). (Refer to AIM).*

AIR TRAFFIC. Aircraft operating in the air or on an airport surface, exclusive of loading ramps and parking areas. *(See ICAO term AIR TRAFFIC).*

AIR TRAFFIC [ICAO]. All aircraft in flight or operating on the maneuvering area of an aerodrome.

AIR TRAFFIC CLEARANCE. An authorization by air traffic control, for the purpose of preventing collision between known aircraft, for an aircraft to proceed under specified traffic conditions within controlled airspace. The pilot-in-command of an aircraft may not deviate from the provisions of a visual flight rules (VFR) or instrument flight rules (IFR) air traffic clearance unless an amended clearance has been obtained. Additionally, the pilot may request a different clearance from that which has been issued by air traffic control (ATC) if information available to the pilot makes another course of action more practicable or if aircraft equipment limitations or company procedures forbid compliance with the clearance issued. Pilots may also request clarification or amendment, as appropriate, any time a clearance is not fully understood, or considered unacceptable because of safety of flight. Controllers should, in such instances and to the extent of operational practicality and safety, honor the pilot's request. FAR Part 91.3(a) states: "The pilot-in-command of an aircraft is directly responsible for, and is the final authority as to, the operation of that aircraft." THE PILOT IS RESPONSIBLE TO REQUEST AN AMENDED CLEARANCE if ATC issues a clearance that would cause a pilot to deviate from a rule or regulation, or in the pilot's opinion, would place the aircraft in jeopardy. *(See ATC INSTRUCTIONS). (See ICAO term AIR TRAFFIC CONTROL CLEARANCE).*

AIR TRAFFIC CONTROL. A service operated by appropriate authority to promote the safe, orderly and expeditious flow of air traffic. *(See ICAO term AIR TRAFFIC CONTROL SERVICE).*

AIR TRAFFIC CONTROL CLEARANCE [ICAO]. Authorization for an aircraft to proceed under conditions specified by an air traffic control unit.

Note 1: For convenience, the term air traffic control clearance is frequently abbreviated to clearance when used in appropriate contexts.

Note 2: The abbreviated term clearance may be prefixed by the words taxi, takeoff, departure, en route, approach or landing to indicate the particular portion of flight to which the air traffic control clearance relates.

AIR TRAFFIC CONTROL SERVICE. (See AIR TRAFFIC CONTROL).

AIR TRAFFIC CONTROL SERVICE [ICAO]. A service provided for the purpose of:

1. Preventing collisions:
a. Between aircraft; and
b. On the maneuvering area between aircraft and obstructions; and
2. Expediting and maintaining an orderly flow of air traffic.

AIR TRAFFIC CONTROL SPECIALIST. A person authorized to provide air traffic control service. *(See AIR TRAFFIC CONTROL). (See FLIGHT SERVICE STATION). (See ICAO term CONTROLLER).*

AIR TRAFFIC CONTROL SYSTEM COMMAND CENTER. An Air Traffic Operations Service facility consisting of four operational units.

1. Central Flow Control Function (CFCF). Responsible for coordination and approval of all major intercenter flow control restrictions on a system basis in order to obtain maximum utilization of the airspace. *(See QUOTA FLOW CONTROL).*

2. Central Altitude Reservation Function (CARF). Responsible for coordinating, planning, and approving special user requirements under the Altitude Reservation (ALTRV) concept. *(See ALTITUDE RESERVATION).*

3. Airport Reservation Office (ARO). Responsible for approving IFR flights at designated high density traffic airports (John F. Kennedy, La Guardia, O'Hare, and Washington National) during specified hours. *(Refer to FAR Part 93 and AIRPORT/FACILITY DIRECTORY).*

4. ATC Contingency Command Post. A facility which enables the FAA to manage the ATC system when significant portions of the system's capabilities have been lost or are threatened.

AIR TRAFFIC SERVICE. A generic term meaning:

1. Flight Information Service,
2. Alerting Service,
3. Air Traffic Advisory Service,
4. Air Traffic Control Service,
a. Area Control Service,
b. Approach Control Service, or
c. Airport Control Service.

AIRWAY. A Class E airspace area established in the form of a corridor, the centerline of which is defined by radio navigational aids. *(See FEDERAL AIRWAYS). (Refer to Part 71). (Refer to AIM). (See ICAO term AIRWAY).*

AIRWAY [ICAO]. A control area or portion thereof established in the form of corridor equipped with radio navigational aids.

AIRWAY BEACON. Used to mark airway segments in remote mountain areas. The light flashes Morse Code to identify the beacon site. *(Refer to AIM).*

AIT. (See AUTOMATED INFORMATION TRANSFER).

ALERFA (Alert Phase) [ICAO]. A situation wherein apprehension exists as to the safety of an aircraft and its occupants.

ALERT AREA. (See SPECIAL USE AIRSPACE).

ALERT NOTICE. A request originated by a flight service station (FSS) or an air route traffic control center (ARTCC) for an extensive communication search for overdue, unreported, or missing aircraft.

ALERTING SERVICE. A service provided to notify appropriate organizations regarding aircraft in need of search and rescue aid and assist such organizations as required.

ALNOT. (See ALERT NOTICE).

ALPHANUMERIC DISPLAY. Letters and numerals used to show identification, altitude, beacon code, and other information concerning a target on a radar display. *(See AUTOMATED RADAR TERMINAL SYSTEMS). (See NAS STAGE A).*

ALTERNATE AERODROME [ICAO]. An aerodrome to which an aircraft may proceed when it becomes either impossible or inadvisable to proceed to or to land at the aerodrome of intended landing.

Note: The aerodrome from which a flight departs may also be an en route or a destination alternate aerodrome for the flight.

ALTERNATE AIRPORT. An airport at which an aircraft may land if a landing at the intended airport becomes inadvisable. *(See FAA term ICAO term ALTERNATE AERODROME).*

ALTIMETER SETTING. The barometric pressure reading used to adjust a pressure altimeter for variations in existing atmospheric pressure or to the standard altimeter setting (29.92). *(Refer to FAR Part 91). (Refer to AIM).*

ALTITUDE. The height of a level, point, or object measured in feet Above Ground Level (AGL) or from Mean Sea Level (MSL). *(See FLIGHT LEVEL).*

1. MSL Altitude. Altitude expressed in feet measured from mean sea level.

2. AGL Altitude. Altitude expressed in feet measured above ground level.

3. Indicated Altitude. The altitude as shown by an altimeter. On a pressure or barometric altimeter it is altitude as shown uncorrected for instrument error and uncompensated for variation from standard atmospheric conditions. *(See ICAO term ALTITUDE).*

ALTITUDE [ICAO]. The vertical distance of a level, a point or an object considered as a point, measured from mean sea level (MSL).

ALTITUDE READOUT. An aircraft's altitude, transmitted via the Mode C transponder feature, that is visually displayed in 100-foot increments on a radar scope having readout capability. *(See AUTOMATED RADAR TERMINAL SYSTEMS). (See NAS STAGE A). (See ALPHANUMERIC DISPLAY). (Refer to AIM).*

ALTITUDE RESERVATION. Airspace utilization under prescribed conditions normally employed for the mass

Continued

movement of aircraft or other special user requirements which cannot otherwise be accomplished. ALTRVs are approved by the appropriate FAA facility. *(See AIR TRAFFIC CONTROL SYSTEM COMMAND CENTER).*

ALTITUDE RESTRICTION. An altitude or altitudes, stated in the order flown, which are to be maintained until reaching a specific point or time. Altitude restrictions may be issued by ATC due to traffic, terrain, or other airspace considerations.

ALTITUDE RESTRICTIONS ARE CANCELED. Adherence to previously imposed altitude restrictions is no longer required during a climb or descent.

ALTRV. (See ALTITUDE RESERVATION).

AMVER. (See AUTOMATED MUTUAL-ASSISTANCE VESSEL RESCUE SYSTEM).

APPROACH CLEARANCE. Authorization by ATC for a pilot to conduct an instrument approach. The type of instrument approach for which a clearance and other pertinent information is provided in the approach clearance when required. *(See INSTRUMENT APPROACH PROCEDURE). (See CLEARED APPROACH). (Refer to AIM and FAR Part 91).*

APPROACH CONTROL FACILITY. A terminal ATC facility that provides approach control service in a terminal area. *(See APPROACH CONTROL SERVICE). (See RADAR APPROACH CONTROL FACILITY).*

APPROACH CONTROL SERVICE. Air traffic control service provided by an approach control facility for arriving and departing VFR/IFR aircraft and, on occasion, en route aircraft. At some airports not served by an approach control facility, the ARTCC provides limited approach control service. *(Refer to AIM). (See ICAO term APPROACH CONTROL SERVICE).*

APPROACH CONTROL SERVICE [ICAO]. Air traffic control service for arriving or departing controlled flights.

APPROACH GATE. An imaginary point used within ATC as a basis for vectoring aircraft to the final approach course. The gate will be established along the final approach course 1 mile from the outer marker (or the fix used in lieu of the outer marker) on the side away from the airport for precision approaches and 1 mile from the final approach fix on the side away from the airport for nonprecision approaches. In either case when measured along the final approach course, the gate will be no closer than 5 miles from the landing threshold.

APPROACH LIGHT SYSTEM. (See AIRPORT LIGHTING).

APPROACH SEQUENCE. The order in which aircraft are positioned while on approach or awaiting approach clearance. *(See LANDING SEQUENCE). (See ICAO term APPROACH SEQUENCE).*

APPROACH SEQUENCE [ICAO]. The order in which two or more aircraft are cleared to approach to land at the aerodrome.

APPROACH SPEED. The recommended speed contained in aircraft manuals used by pilots when making an approach to landing. This speed will vary for different segments of an approach as well as for aircraft weight and configuration.

APPROPRIATE ATS AUTHORITY [ICAO]. The relevant authority designated by the State responsible for providing air traffic services in the airspace concerned. In the United States, the "appropriate ATS authority" is the Director, Office of Air Traffic System Management, ATM-1.

APPROPRIATE AUTHORITY.

1. Regarding flight over the high seas: the relevant authority is the State of Registry.
2. Regarding flight over other than the high seas: the relevant authority is the State having sovereignty over the territory being overflown.

APPROPRIATE OBSTACLE CLEARANCE MINIMUM ALTITUDE. Any of the following: *(See Minimum IFR Altitude MIA). (See Minimum En Route Altitude MEA). (See Minimum Obstruction Clearance Altitude MOCA). (See Minimum Vectoring Altitude MVA).*

APPROPRIATE TERRAIN CLEARANCE MINIMUM ALTITUDE. Any of the following: *(See Minimum IFR Altitude MIA). (See Minimum En Route Altitude MEA). (See Minimum Obstruction Clearance Altitude MOCA). (See Minimum Vectoring Altitude MVA).*

APRON. A defined area on an airport or heliport intended to accommodate aircraft for purposes of loading or unloading passengers or cargo, refueling, parking, or maintenance. With regard to seaplanes, a ramp is used for access to the apron from the water. *(See ICAO term APRON).*

APRON [ICAO]. A defined area, on a land aerodrome, intended to accommodate aircraft for purposes of loading or unloading passengers, mail or cargo, refueling, parking or maintenance.

ARC. The track over the ground of an aircraft flying at a constant distance from a navigational aid by reference to distance measuring equipment (DME).

AREA CONTROL CENTER [ICAO]. An ICAO term for an air traffic control facility primarily responsible for ATC services being provided IFR aircraft during the en route phase of flight. The U.S. equivalent facility is an air route traffic control center (ARTCC).

AREA NAVIGATION. A method of navigation that permits aircraft operation on any desired course within the coverage of station-referenced navigation signals or within the limits of a self-contained system capability. Random area navigation routes are direct routes, based on area navigation capability, between waypoints defined in terms of latitude/longitude coordinates, degree/distance fixes, or offsets from published or established routes/airways at a specified distance and direction. The major types of equipment are:

1. VORTAC referenced or Course Line Computer (CLC) systems, which account for the greatest number of RNAV units in use. To function, the CLC must be within the service range of a VORTAC.

2. OMEGA/VLF, although two separate systems, can be considered as one operationally. A long-range navigation system based upon Very Low Frequency radio signals transmitted from a total of 17 stations worldwide.

3. Inertial (INS) systems, which are totally self-contained and require no information from external references. They provide aircraft position and navigation information in response to signals resulting from inertial effects on components within the system.

4. MLS Area Navigation (MLS/RNAV), which provides area navigation with reference to an MLS ground facility.

5. LORAN-C is a long-range radio navigation system that uses ground waves transmitted at low frequency to provide user position information at ranges of up to 600 to 1,200 nautical miles at both en route and approach altitudes. The usable signal coverage areas are determined by the signal-to-noise ratio, the envelope-to-cycle difference, and the geometric relationship between the positions of the user and the transmitting stations.

(See ICAO term AREA NAVIGATION).

AREA NAVIGATION [ICAO]. A method of navigation which permits aircraft operation on any desired flight path within the coverage of station-referenced navigation aids or within the limits of the capability of self-contained aids, or a combination of these.

ARINC. An acronym for Aeronautical Radio, Inc., a corporation largely owned by a group of airlines. ARINC is licensed by the FCC as an aeronautical station and contracted by the FAA to provide communications support for air traffic control and meteorological services in portions of international airspace.

ARMY AVIATION FLIGHT INFORMATION BULLETIN. A bulletin that provides air operation data covering Army, National Guard, and Army Reserve aviation activities.

ARO. (See AIRPORT RESERVATION OFFICE).

ARRESTING SYSTEM. A safety device consisting of two major components, namely, engaging or catching devices and energy absorption devices for the purpose of arresting both tailhook and/or nontailhook-equipped aircraft. It is used to prevent aircraft from overrunning runways when the aircraft cannot be stopped after landing or during aborted takeoff. Arresting systems have various names; e.g., arresting gear, hook device, wire barrier cable. *(See ABORT). (Refer to AIM).*

ARRIVAL AIRCRAFT INTERVAL. An internally generated program in hundredths of minutes based upon the AAR. AAI is the desired optimum interval between successive arrival aircraft over the vertex.

ARRIVAL CENTER. The ARTCC having jurisdiction for the impacted airport.

ARRIVAL DELAY. A parameter which specifies a period of time in which no aircraft will be metered for arrival at the specified airport.

ARRIVAL SECTOR. An operational control sector containing one or more meter fixes.

ARRIVAL SECTOR ADVISORY LIST. An ordered list of data on arrivals displayed at the PVD of the sector which controls the meter fix.

ARRIVAL SEQUENCING PROGRAM. The automated program designed to assist in sequencing aircraft destined for the same airport.

ARRIVAL TIME. The time an aircraft touches down on arrival.

ARSR. (See AIR ROUTE SURVEILLANCE RADAR).

ARTCC. (See AIR ROUTE TRAFFIC CONTROL CENTER).

ARTS. (See AUTOMATED RADAR TERMINAL SYSTEMS).

ASD. (See AIRCRAFT SITUATION DISPLAY).

ASDAR. (See ACCELERATE-STOP DISTANCE AVAILABLE).

ASDA [ICAO]. (See ICAO Term ACCELERATE-STOP DISTANCE AVAILABLE).

ASDE. (See AIRPORT SURFACE DETECTION EQUIPMENT).

ASLAR. (See AIRCRAFT SURGE LAUNCH AND RECOVERY).

ASP. (See ARRIVAL SEQUENCING PROGRAM).

ASR. (See AIRPORT SURVEILLANCE RADAR).

ASR APPROACH. (See SURVEILLANCE APPROACH).

ATC. (See AIR TRAFFIC CONTROL).

ATCAA. (See ATC ASSIGNED AIRSPACE).

ATC ADVISES. Used to prefix a message of noncontrol information when it is relayed to an aircraft by other than an air traffic controller. *(See ADVISORY).*

ATC ASSIGNED AIRSPACE. Airspace of defined vertical/lateral limits, assigned by ATC, for the purpose of providing air traffic segregation between the specified activities being conducted within the assigned airspace and other IFR air traffic. *(See SPECIAL USE AIRSPACE).*

ATC CLEARANCE. (See AIR TRAFFIC CLEARANCE).

ATC CLEARS. Used to prefix an ATC clearance when it is relayed to an aircraft by other than an air traffic controller.

ATC INSTRUCTIONS. Directives issued by air traffic control for the purpose of requiring a pilot to take specific actions; e.g., "Turn left heading two five zero," "Go around," "Clear the runway." *(Refer to FAR Part 91).*

ATCRBS. (See RADAR).

ATC REQUESTS. Used to prefix an ATC request when it is relayed to an aircraft by other than an air traffic controller.

ATCSCC. (See AIR TRAFFIC CONTROL SYSTEM COMMAND CENTER).

ATCSCC DELAY FACTOR. The amount of delay calculated to be assigned prior to departure.

ATCT. (See TOWER).

ATIS. (See AUTOMATIC TERMINAL INFORMATION SERVICE).

ATIS [ICAO]. (See ICAO Term AUTOMATIC TERMINAL INFORMATION SERVICE).

ATS Route [ICAO]. A specified route designed for channeling the flow of traffic as necessary for the provision of air traffic services.

Note: The term "ATS route" is used to mean variously, airway, advisory route, controlled or uncontrolled route, arrival or departure, etc.

AUTOLAND APPROACH. An autoland approach is a precision instrument approach to touchdown and, in some cases, through the landing rollout. An autoland approach is performed by the aircraft autopilot which is receiving position information and/or steering commands from onboard navigation equipment. (See COUPLED APPROACH).

Note: Autoland and coupled approaches are flown in VFR and IFR. It is common for carriers to require their crews to fly coupled approaches and autoland approaches (if certified) when the weather conditions are less than approximately 4,000 RVR.

AUTOMATED INFORMATION TRANSFER. A precoordinated process, specifically defined in facility directives, during which a transfer of altitude control and/or radar identification is accomplished without verbal coordination between controllers using information communicated in a full data block.

AUTOMATED MUTUAL-ASSISTANCE VESSEL RESCUE SYSTEM. A facility which can deliver, in a matter of minutes, a surface picture (SURPIC) of vessels in the area of a potential or actual search and rescue incident, including their predicted positions and their characteristics. *(See Order 7110.65, paragraph 10-73, In-Flight Contingencies).*

AUTOMATED RADAR TERMINAL SYSTEMS. The generic term for the ultimate in functional capability afforded by several automation systems. Each differs in functional capabilities and equipment. ARTS plus a suffix roman numeral denotes a specific system. A following letter indicates a major modification to that system. In general, an ARTS displays for the terminal controller aircraft identification, flight plan data, other flight associated information; e.g., altitude, speed, and aircraft position symbols in conjunction with his radar presentation. Normal radar co-exists with the alphanumeric display. In addition to enhancing visualization of the air traffic situation, ARTS facilitate intra/inter-facility transfer and coordination of flight information. These capabilities are enabled by specially designed computers and subsystems tailored to the radar and communications equipments and operational requirements of each automated facility. Modular design permits adoption of improvements in computer software and electronic technologies as they become available while retaining the characteristics unique to each system.

1. ARTS II. A programmable nontracking, computer-aided display subsystem capable of modular expansion. ARTS II systems provide a level of automated air traffic control capability at terminals having low to medium activity. Flight identification and altitude may be associated with the display of secondary radar targets. The system has the capability of communicating with ARTCC's and other ATRS II, IIA, III, and IIIA facilities.

2. ARTS IIA. A programmable radar-tracking computer subsystem capable of modular expansion. The ARTS IIA detects, tracks, and predicts secondary radar targets. The targets are displayed by means of computer-generated symbols, ground speed, and flight plan data. Although it does not track primary radar targets, they are displayed coincident with the secondary radar as well as the symbols and alphanumerics. The system has the capability of communicating with ARTCCs and other ARTS II, IIA, III, and IIIA facilities.

3. ARTS III. The Beacon Tracking Level of the modular programmable automated radar terminal system in use at medium to high activity terminals. ARTS III detects, tracks, and predicts secondary radar-derived aircraft targets. These are displayed by means of computer-generated symbols and alpha-numeric characters depicting flight identification, aircraft altitude, ground speed, and flight plan data. Although it does not track primary targets, they are displayed coincident with the secondary radar as well as the symbols and alphanumerics. The system has the capability of communicating with ARTCC's and other ARTS III facilities.

4. ARTS IIIA. The Radar Tracking and Beacon Tracking Level (RT&BTL) of the modular, programmable automated radar terminal system. ARTS IIIA detects, tracks, and predicts primary as well as secondary radar-derived aircraft targets. This more sophisticated computer-driven system upgrades the existing ARTS III system by providing improved tracking, continuous data recording, and fail-soft capabilities.

AUTOMATIC ALTITUDE REPORT. (See ALTITUDE READOUT).

AUTOMATIC ALTITUDE REPORTING. That function of a transponder which responds to Mode C interrogations by transmitting the aircraft's altitude in 100-foot increments.

AUTOMATIC CARRIER LANDING SYSTEM. U.S. Navy final approach equipment consisting of precision tracking radar coupled to a computer data link to provide continuous information to the aircraft, monitoring capability to the pilot, and a backup approach system.

AUTOMATIC DIRECTION FINDER. An aircraft radio navigation system which senses and indicates the direction to a L/MF nondirectional radio beacon (NDB) ground transmitter. Direction is indicated to the pilot as a magnetic bearing or as a relative bearing to the longitudinal axis of the aircraft depending on the type of indicator installed in the aircraft. In certain applications, such as military, ALF operations may be based on airborne and ground transmitters in the VHF/UHF frequency spectrum. *(See BEARING). (See NONDIRECTIONAL BEACON).*

AUTOMATIC TERMINAL INFORMATION SERVICE. The continuous broadcast of recorded noncontrol information in selected terminal areas. Its purpose is to improve controller effectiveness and to relieve frequency congestion by automating the repetitive transmission of essential but routine information; e.g., "Los Angeles information Alfa. One three zero zero Coordinated Universal Time. Weather, measured ceiling two thousand overcast, visibility three, haze, smoke, temperature seven one, dew point five seven, wind two five zero at five, altimeter two niner niner six. I-L-S Runway Two Five Left approach in use, Runway Two Five Right closed, advise you have Alfa." *(Refer to AIM). (See ICAO term AUTOMATIC TERMINAL INFORMATION SERVICE).*

AUTOMATIC TERMINAL INFORMATION SERVICE [ICAO]. The provision of current, routine information to arriving and departing aircraft by means of continuous and repetitive broadcasts throughout the day or a specified portion of the day.

AUTOROTATION. A rotorcraft flight condition in which the lifting rotor is driven entirely by action of the air when the rotorcraft is in motion.

1. Autorotative Landing/Touchdown Autorotation. Used by a pilot to indicate that he will be landing without applying power to the rotor.

2. Low Level Autorotation. Commences at an altitude well below the traffic pattern, usually below 100 feet AGL and is used primarily for tactical military training.

3. 180 degrees Autorotation. Initiated from a down wind heading and is commenced well inside the normal traffic pattern. "Go around" may not be possible during the latter part of this maneuver.

AVIATION WEATHER SERVICE. A service provided by the National Weather Service (NWS) and FAA which collects and disseminates pertinent weather information for pilots, aircraft operators, and ATC. Available aviation weather reports and forecasts are displayed at each NWS office and FAA FSS. *(See EN ROUTE FLIGHT ADVISORY SERVICE). (See TRANSCRIBED WEATHER BROADCAST). (See ETHER ADVISORY). (See PILOTS AUTOMATIC TELEPHONE WEATHER ANSWERING SERVICE). (Refer to AIM).*

AWW. (See SEVERE WEATHER FORECAST ALERTS).

AZIMUTH (MLS). A magnetic bearing extending from an MLS navigation facility.

Note: Azimuth bearings are described as magnetic and are referred to as "azimuth" in radio telephone communications.

BASE LEG. (See TRAFFIC PATTERN).

BEACON. (See RADAR). *(See NONDIRECTIONAL BEACON). (See MARKER BEACON). (See AIRPORT ROTATING BEACON). (See AERONAUTICAL BEACON). (See AIRWAY BEACON).*

BEARING. The horizontal direction to or from any point, usually measured clockwise from true north, magnetic north, or some other reference point through 360 degrees. *(See NONDIRECTIONAL BEACON).*

BELOW MINIMUM. Weather conditions below the minimums prescribed by regulation for the particular action involved; e.g., landing minimums, takeoff minimums.

BLAST FENCE. A barrier that is used to divert or dissipate jet or propeller blast.

BLIND SPEED. The rate of departure or closing of a target relative to the radar antenna at which cancellation of the primary radar target by moving target indicator (MTI) circuits in the radar equipment causes a reduction or complete loss of signal. *(See ICAO term BLIND VELOCITY).*

BLIND SPOT. An area from which radio transmissions and/or radar echoes cannot be received. The term is also used to describe portions of the airport not visible from the control tower.

BLIND TRANSMISSION. (See TRANSMITTING IN THE BLIND).

BLIND VELOCITY [ICAO]. The radial velocity of a moving target such that the target is not seen on primary radars fitted with certain forms of fixed echo suppression.

BLIND ZONE. (See BLIND SPOT).

BLOCKED. Phraseology used to indicate that a radio transmission has been distorted or interrupted due to multiple simultaneous radio transmissions.

BOUNDARY LIGHTS. (See AIRPORT LIGHTING).

BRAKING ACTION (GOOD, FAIR, POOR, OR NIL). A report of conditions on the airport movement area providing a pilot with a degree/quality of braking that he might expect. Braking action is reported in terms of good, fair, poor, or nil. *(See RUNWAY CONDITION READING).*

BRAKING ACTION ADVISORIES. When tower controllers have received runway braking action reports which include the terms "poor" or "nil," or whenever weather conditions are conducive to deteriorating or rapidly changing runway braking conditions, the tower will include on the ATIS broadcast the statement, "BRAKING ACTION ADVISORIES ARE IN EFFECT." During the time Braking Action Advisories are in effect, ATC will issue the latest braking action report for the runway in use to each arriving and departing aircraft. Pilots should be prepared for deteriorating braking conditions and should request current runway condition information if not volunteered by controllers. Pilots should also be prepared to provide a descriptive runway condition report to controllers after landing.

BROADCAST. Transmission of information for which an acknowledgment is not expected. *(See ICAO tea BROADCAST).*

BROADCAST [ICAO]. A transmission of information relating to air navigation that is not addressed to a specific station or stations.

CALCULATED LANDING TIME. A term that may be used in place of tentative or actual calculated landing time, whichever applies.

CALL UP. Initial voice contact between a facility and an aircraft, using the identification of the unit being called and the unit initiating the call. *(Refer to AIM).*

CALL FOR RELEASE. Wherein the overlying ARTCC requires a terminal facility to initiate verbal coordination to secure ARTCC approval for release of a departure into the en route environment.

CANADIAN MINIMUM NAVIGATION PERFORMANCE SPECIFICATION AIRSPACE. That portion of Canadian domestic airspace within which MNPS separation may be applied.

CARDINAL ALTITUDES. "Odd" or "Even" thousand-foot altitudes or flight levels; e.g. 5,000, 6,000, 7,000, FL 250, FL 260, FL 270. *(See ALTITUDE). (See FLIGHT LEVEL).*

CARDINAL FLIGHT LEVELS. (See CARDINAL ALTITUDES).

CAT. (See CLEAR-AIR TURBULENCE).

CDT PROGRAMS. (See CONTROLLED DEPARTURE TIME PROGRAMS).

CEILING. The heights above the earth's surface of the lowest layer of clouds or obscuring phenomena that is reported as "broken," "overcast," or "obscuration," and not classified as "thin" or "partial". *(See ICAO term CEILING).*

CEILING [ICAO]. The height above the ground or water of the base of the lowest layer of cloud below 6,000 metres (20,000 feet) covering more than half the sky.

CENRAP. (See CENTER RADAR ARTS PRESENTATION/PROCESSING).

CENRAP-PLUS. (See CENTER RADAR ARTS PRESENTATION/PROCESSING-PLUS).

CENTER. (See AIR ROUTE TRAFFIC CONTROL CENTER).

CENTER'S AREA. The specified airspace within which an air route traffic control center (ARTCC) provides air traffic control and advisory service. *(See AIR ROUTE TRAFFIC CONTROL CENTER). (Refer to AIM).*

CENTER RADAR ARTS PRESENTATION/PROCESSING. A computer program developed to provide a back-up system for airport surveillance radar in the event of a failure or malfunction. The program uses air route traffic control center radar for the processing and presentation of data on the ARTS IIA or IIIA displays.

CENTER RADAR ARTS PRESENTATION/PROCESSING-PLUS. A computer program developed to provide a back-up system for airport surveillance radar in the event of a terminal secondary radar system failure. The program uses a combination of Air Route Traffic Control Center Radar and terminal airport surveillance radar primary targets displayed simultaneously for the processing and presentation of data on the ARTS IIA or IIIA displays.

CENTER WEATHER ADVISORY. An unscheduled weather advisory issued by Center Weather Service Unit meteorologists for ATC use to alert pilots of existing or anticipated adverse weather conditions within the next 2 hours. A CWA may modify or redefine a SIGMET. *(See AWW). (See SIGMET). (See CONVECTIVE SIGMET). (See AIRMET). (Refer to AIM).*

CENTRAL EAST PACIFIC. An organized route system between the U.S. West Coast and Hawaii.

CEP. (See CENTRAL EAST PACIFIC).

CERAP. (See COMBINED CENTER-RAPCON).

CFR. (See CALL FOR RELEASE).

CHAFF. Thin, narrow metallic reflectors of various lengths and frequency responses, used to reflect radar energy. These reflectors when dropped from aircraft and allowed to drift downward result in large targets on the radar display.

CHARTED VFR FLYWAYS. Charted VFR Flyways are flight paths recommended for use to bypass areas heavily traversed by large turbine-powered aircraft. Pilot compliance with recommended flyways and associated altitudes is strictly voluntary. VFR Flyway Planning charts are published on the back of existing VFR Terminal Area charts.

CHARTED VISUAL FLIGHT PROCEDURE APPROACH. An approach wherein a radar-controlled aircraft on an IFR flight plan, operating in VFR conditions and having an ATC authorization, may proceed to the airport of intended landing via visual landmarks and altitudes depicted on a charted visual flight procedure.

CHASE. An aircraft flown in proximity to another aircraft normally to observe its performance during training or testing.

CHASE AIRCRAFT. (See CHASE).

CIRCLE-TO-LAND MANEUVER. A maneuver initiated by the pilot to align the aircraft with a runway for landing when a straight-in landing from an instrument approach is not possible or is not desirable. This maneuver is made only after ATC authorization has been obtained and the pilot has established required visual reference to the airport *(See CIRCLE TO RUNWAY). (See LANDING MINIMUM). (Refer to AIM).*

CIRCLE TO RUNWAY (RUNWAY NUMBER). Used by ATC to inform the pilot that he must circle to land because the runway in use is other than the runway aligned with the instrument approach procedure. When the direction of the circling maneuver in relation to the airport/ runway is required, the controller will state the direction (eight cardinal compass points) and specify a left or right downwind or base leg as appropriate; e.g., "Cleared VOR Runway Three Six Approach circle to Runway Two Two," or "Circle northwest of the airport for a right downwind to Runway Two Two." *(See CIRCLE-TO-LAND MANEUVER). (See LANDING MINIMUMS). (Refer to AIM).*

CIRCLING APPROACH. (See CIRCLE-TO-LAND MANEUVER).

CIRCLING MANEUVER. (See CIRCLE-TO-LAND MANEUVER).

CIRCLING MINIMA. (See LANDING MINIMUMS).

CLASS A AIRSPACE. (See Controlled Airspace).

CLASS B AIRSPACE. (See Controlled Airspace).

CLASS C AIRSPACE. (See Controlled Airspace).

CLASS D AIRSPACE. (See Controlled Airspace).

CLASS E AIRSPACE. (See Controlled Airspace).

CLASS G AIRSPACE. That airspace not designated as Class A, B, C, D or E.

CLEAR-AIR TURBULENCE. Turbulence encountered in air where no clouds are present. This term is commonly applied to high-level turbulence associated with wind shear. CAT is often encountered in the vicinity of the jet stream. *(See WIND SHEAR). (See JET STREAM).*

CLEAR OF THE RUNWAY.

1. A taxiing aircraft, which is approaching a runway, is clear of the runway when all parts of the aircraft are held short of the applicable holding position marking.

2. A pilot or controller may consider an aircraft, which is exiting or crossing a runway, to be clear of the runway when all parts of the aircraft are beyond the runway edge and there is no ATC restriction to its continued movement beyond the applicable holding position marking.

3. Pilots and controllers shall exercise good judgment to ensure that adequate separation exists between all aircraft on runways and taxiways at airports with inadequate runway edge lines or holding position markings.

CLEARANCE. (See AIR TRAFFIC CLEARANCE).

CLEARANCE LIMIT. The fix, point, or location to which an aircraft is cleared when issued an air traffic clearance.

(See ICAO term CLEARANCE LIMIT).

CLEARANCE LIMIT [ICAO]. The point of which an aircraft is granted an air traffic control clearance.

CLEARANCE VOID IF NOT OFF BY (TIME). Used by ATC to advise an aircraft that the departure clearance is automatically canceled if takeoff is not made prior to a specified time. The pilot must obtain a new clearance or cancel his IFR flight plan if not off by the specified time. *(See ICAO term CLEARANCE VOID TIME).*

CLEARANCE VOID TIME [ICAO]. A time specified by an air traffic control unit at which a clearance ceases to be valid unless the aircraft concerned has already taken action to comply therewith.

CLEARED AS FILED. Means the aircraft is cleared to proceed in accordance with the route of flight filed in the flight plan. This clearance does not include the altitude, SID, or SID Transition. *(See REQUEST FULL ROUTE CLEARANCE). (Refer to AIM).*

CLEARED (Type of) APPROACH. ATC authorization for an aircraft to execute a specific instrument approach procedure to an airport; e.g., "Cleared ILS Runway Three Six Approach." *(See INSTRUMENT APPROACH PROCEDURE). (See APPROACH CLEARANCE). (Refer to AIM). (Refer to FAR Part 91).*

CLEARED APPROACH. ATC authorization for an aircraft to execute any standard or special instrument approach procedure for that airport. Normally, an aircraft will be cleared for a specific instrument approach procedure. *(See INSTRUMENT APPROACH PROCEDURE). (See CLEARED (TYPE OF) APPROACH). (Refer to AIM). (Refer to FAR Part 91).*

CLEARED FOR TAKEOFF. ATC authorization for an aircraft to depart. It is predicated on known traffic and known physical airport conditions.

CLEARED FOR THE OPTION. ATC authorization for an aircraft to make a touch-and-go, low approach, missed approach, stop and go, or full stop landing at the discretion of the pilot. It is normally used in training so that an instructor can evaluate a student's performance under changing situations. *(See OPTION APPROACH). (Refer to AIM).*

CLEARED THROUGH. ATC authorization for an aircraft to make intermediate stops at specified airports without refiling a flight plan while en route to the clearance limit.

CLEARED TO LAND. ATC authorization for an aircraft to land. It is predicated on known traffic and known physical airport conditions.

CLEARWAY. An area beyond the takeoff runway under the control of airport authorities within which terrain or fixed obstacles may not extend above specified limits. These areas may be required for certain turbine-powered operations and the size and upward slope of the clearway will differ depending on when the aircraft was certificated. *(Refer to FAR Part 1)*.

CLIMBOUT. That portion of flight operation between takeoff and the initial cruising altitude.

CLIMB TO VFR. ATC authorization for an aircraft to climb to VFR conditions within Class B, C, D, and E surface areas when the only weather limitation is restricted visibility. The aircraft must remain clear of clouds while climbing to VFR. *(See Special VFR)*. *(Refer to AIM)*.

CLOSED RUNWAY. A runway that is unusable for aircraft operations. Only the airport management/military operations office can close a runway.

CLOSED TRAFFIC. Successive operations involving takeoffs and landings or low approaches where the aircraft does not exit the traffic pattern.

CLT. (See CALCULATED LANDING TIME).

CLUTTER. In radar operations, clutter refers to the reception and visual display of radar returns caused by precipitation, chart terrain, numerous aircraft targets, or other phenomena. Such returns may limit or preclude ATC from providing services based on radar. *(See GROUND CLUTTER)*. *(See CHAFF)*. *(See PRECIPITATION)*. *(See TARGET)*. *(See ICAO term Radar Clutter)*.

CMNPS. (See CANADIAN MINIMUM NAVIGATION PERFORMANCE SPECIFICATION AIRSPACE).

COASTAL FIX. A navigation aid or intersection where an aircraft transitions between the domestic route structure and the oceanic route structure.

CODES. The number assigned to a particular multiple pulse reply signal transmitted by a transponder. *(See DISCRETE CODE)*.

COMBINED CENTER-RAPCON. An air traffic facility which combines the functions of an ARTCC and a radar approach control facility. *(See AIR ROUTE TRAFFIC CONTROL CENTER)*. *(See RADAR APPROACH CONTROL FACILITY)*.

COMMON POINT. A *significant point* over which two or more aircraft will report passing or have reported passing before proceeding on the same or diverging tracks. To establish/maintain longitudinal separation, a controller may determine a common point not originally in the aircraft's flight plan and then clear the aircraft to fly over the point. *(See Significant Point)*.

COMMON PORTION. (See COMMON ROUTE).

COMMON ROUTE. That segment of a North American Route between the inland navigation facility and the coastal fix.

COMMON TRAFFIC ADVISORY FREQUENCY (CTAF). A frequency designed for the purpose of carrying out airport advisory practices while operating to or from an airport without an operating control tower. The CTAF may be a UNICOM, Multicom, FSS, or tower frequency and is identified in appropriate aeronautical publications. *(Refer to AC 90-42)*.

COMPASS LOCATOR. A low power, low or medium frequency (L/MF) radio beacon installed at the site of the outer or middle marker of an instrument landing system (ILS). It can be used for navigation at distances of approximately 15 miles or as authorized in the approach procedure.

1. Outer Compass Locator (LOM). A compass locator installed at the site of the outer marker of an instrument landing system. *(See OUTER MARKER)*.

2. Middle Compass Locator (LMM). A compass locator installed at the site of the middle marker of an instrument landing system. *(See MIDDLE MARKER)*. *(See ICAO term LOCATOR)*.

COMPASS ROSE. A circle, graduated in degrees, printed on some charts or marked on the ground at an airport. It is used as a reference to either true or magnetic direction.

COMPOSITE FLIGHT PLAN. A flight plan which specifies VFR operation for one portion of flight and IFR for another portion. It is used primarily in military operations. *(Refer to AIM)*.

COMPOSITE ROUTE SYSTEM. An organized oceanic route structure, incorporating reduced lateral spacing between routes, in which composite separation is authorized.

COMPOSITE SEPARATION. A method of separating aircraft in a composite route system where, by management of route and altitude assignments, a combination of half the lateral minimum specified for the area concerned and half the vertical minimum is applied.

COMPULSORY REPORTING POINTS. Reporting points which must be reported to ATC. They are designated on aeronautical charts by solid triangles or filed in a flight plan as fixes selected to define direct routes. These points are geographical locations which are defined by navigation aids/fixes. Pilots should discontinue position reporting over compulsory reporting points when informed by ATC that their aircraft is in "radar contact."

CONFLICT ALERT. A function of certain air traffic control automated systems designed to alert radar controllers to existing or pending situations between tracked targets (known IFR or VFR aircraft) that require his immediate attention/action. *(See MODE C INTRUDER ALERT).*

CONFLICT RESOLUTION. The resolution of potential conflictions between aircraft that are radar identified and in communication with ATC by ensuring that radar targets do not touch. Pertinent traffic advisories shall be issued when this procedure is applied.

Note: This procedure shall not be provided utilizing mosaic radar systems.

CONSOLAN. A low frequency, long-distance NAVAID used principally for transoceanic navigations.

CONTACT.

1. Establish communication with (followed by the name of the facility and, if appropriate, the frequency to be used).

2. A flight condition wherein the pilot ascertains the attitude of his aircraft and navigates by visual reference to the surface.

(See CONTACT APPROACH). (See RADAR CONTACT).

CONTACT APPROACH. An approach wherein an aircraft on an IFR flight plan, having an air traffic control authorization, operating clear of clouds with at least 1 mile flight visibility and a reasonable expectation of continuing to the destination airport in those conditions, may deviate from the instrument approach procedure and proceed to the destination airport by visual reference to the surface. This approach will only be authorized when requested by the pilot and the reported ground visibility at the destination airport is at least 1 statute mile. *(Refer to AIM).*

CONTERMINOUS U.S.. The 48 adjoining States and the District of Columbia.

CONTINENTAL UNITED STATES. The 49 States located on the continent of North America and the District of Columbia.

CONTROL AREA [ICAO]. A controlled airspace extending upwards from a specified limit above the earth.

CONTROLLED AIRSPACE. An airspace of defined dimensions within which air traffic control service is provided to IFR flights and to VFR flights in accordance with the airspace classification.

Note 1: Controlled airspace is a generic term that covers Class A, Class B, Class C, Class D, and Class E airspace.

Note 2: Controlled airspace is also that airspace within which all aircraft operators are subject to certain pilot qualifications, operating rules, and equipment requirements in FAR Part 91 (for specific operating requirements, please refer to FAR Part 91). For IFR operations in any class of controlled airspace, a pilot must file an IFR flight plan and receive an appropriate ATC clearance. Each Class B, Class C, and Class D airspace area designated for an airport contains at least one primary airport around which the airspace is designated (for specific designations and descriptions of the airspace classes, please refer to Part 71).

Controlled airspace in the United States is designated as follows:

1. CLASS A: Generally, that airspace from 18,000 feet MSL up to and including FL600, including the airspace overlying the waters within 12 nautical miles of the coast of the 48 contiguous States and Alaska. Unless otherwise authorized, all persons must operate their aircraft under IFR.

2. CLASS B: Generally, that airspace from the surface to 10,000 feet MSL surrounding the nation's busiest airports in terms of airport operations or passenger enplanements. The configuration of each Class B airspace area is individually tailored and consists of a surface area and two or more layers (some Class B airspaces areas resemble upside-down wedding cakes), and is designed to contain all published instrument procedures once an aircraft enters the airspace. An ATC clearance is required for all aircraft to operate in the area, and all aircraft that are so cleared receive separation services within the airspace. The cloud clearance requirement for VFR operations is "clear of clouds."

3. CLASS C: Generally, that airspace from the surface to 4,000 feet above the airport elevation (charted in MSL) surrounding those airports that have an operational control tower, are serviced by a radar approach control, and that have a certain number of IFR operations or passenger enplanements. Although the configuration of each Class C airspace area is individually tailored, the airspace usually consists of a surface area with a 5 nm radius, and an outer area with a 10 nm radius that extends from 1,200 feet to 4,000 feet above the airport elevation. Each person must establish two-way radio communications with the ATC facility providing air traffic services prior to entering the airspace and thereafter maintain those communications while within the airspace. VFR aircraft are only separated from IFR aircraft within the airspace.

4. CLASS D: Generally, that airspace from the surface to 2,500 feet above the airport elevation (charted in MSL) surrounding those airports that have an operational control tower. The configuration of each Class D airspace area is individually tailored and when instrument procedures are published, the airspace will normally be designed to contain the procedures. Arrival extensions for instrument approach procedures may be Class D or Class E airspace. Unless otherwise authorized, each person must establish two-way radio communications with the ATC facility providing air traffic services prior entering the airspace and thereafter maintain those communications while in the airspace. No separation services are provided to VFR aircraft.

Continued

5. CLASS E: Generally, if the airspace is not Class A, Class B, Class C, or Class D, and it is controlled airspace, it is Class E airspace. Class E airspace extends upward from either the surface or a designated altitude to the overlying or adjacent controlled airspace. When designated as a surface area, the airspace will be configured to contain all instrument procedures. Also in this class are Federal airways, airspace beginning at either 700 or 1,200 feet AGL used to transition to/from the terminal or enroute environment, enroute domestic, and offshore airspace areas designated below 18,000 feet MSL. Unless designated at a lower altitude, Class E airspace begins at 14,500 MSL over the United States, including that airspace overlying the waters within 12 nautical miles of the coast of the 48 contiguous States and Alaska, up to, but not including 18,000 feet MSL, and the airspace above FL 600.

CONTROLLED AIRSPACE [ICAO]. An airspace of defined dimensions within which air traffic control service is provided to IFR flights and to VFR flights in accordance with the airspace classification.

Note: Controlled airspace is a generic term which covers ATS airspace Classes A, B, C, D, and E.

CONTROLLED DEPARTURE TIME PROGRAMS. These programs are the flow control process whereby aircraft are held on the ground at the departure airport when delays are projected to occur in either the en route system or the terminal of intended landing. The purpose of these programs is to reduce congestion in the air traffic system or to limit the duration of airborne holding in the arrival center or terminal area. A CDT is a specific departure slot shown on the flight plan as an expected departure clearance time (EDCT).

CONTROLLED TIME OF ARRIVAL. The original estimated time of arrival adjusted by the ATCSCC ground delay factor.

CONTROLLER. (See AIR TRAFFIC CONTROL SPECIALIST).

CONTROLLER [ICAO]. A person authorized to provide air traffic control services.

CONTROL SECTOR. An airspace area of defined horizontal and vertical dimensions for which a controller or group of controllers has air traffic control responsibility, normally within an air route traffic control center or an approach control facility. Sectors are established based on predominant traffic flows, altitude strata, and controller workload. Pilot-communications during operations within a sector are normally maintained on discrete frequencies assigned to the sector. *(See DISCRETE FREQUENCY).*

CONTROL SLASH. A radar beacon slash representing the actual position of the associated aircraft. Normally, the control slash is the one closest to the interrogating radar beacon site. When ARTCC radar is operating in narrow band (digitized) mode, the control slash is converted to a target symbol.

CONVECTIVE SIGMET. A weather advisory concerning convective weather significant to the safety of all aircraft. Convective SIGMET's are issued for tornadoes, lines of thunderstorms, embedded thunderstorms of any intensity level, areas of thunderstorms greater than or equal to VIP level 4 with an area coverage of 4/10 (40%) or more, and hail 3/4 inch or greater. *(See AWW). (See SIGMET). (See CWA). (See AIRMET). (Refer to AIM).*

CONVECTIVE SIGNIFICANT METEOROLOGICAL INFORMATION. (See CONVECTIVE SIGMET).

COORDINATES. The intersection of lines of reference, usually expressed in degrees/minutes/seconds of latitude and longitude, used to determine position or location.

COORDINATION FIX. The fix in relation to which facilities will handoff, transfer control of an aircraft, or coordinate flight progress data. For terminal facilities, it may also serve as a clearance for arriving aircraft.

COPTER. (See HELICOPTER).

CORRECTION. An error has been made in the transmission and the correct version follows.

COUPLED APPROACH. A coupled approach is an instrument approach performed by the aircraft autopilot which is receiving position information and/or steering commands from onboard navigation equipment. In general, coupled nonprecision approaches must be discontinued and flown manually at altitudes lower than 50 feet below the minimum descent altitude, and coupled precision approaches must be flown manually below 50 feet ALG *(See AUTOLAND APPROACH).*

Note: Coupled and autoland approaches are flown in VFR and IFR. It is common for carriers to require their crews to fly coupled approaches and autoland approaches (if certified) when the weather conditions are less than approximately 4,000 RVR.

COURSE.

1. The intended direction of flight in the horizontal plane measured in degrees from north.
2. The ILS localizer signal pattern usually specified as the front course or the back course.
3. The intended track along a straight, curved, or segmented MLS path.

(See BEARING). (See RADIAL). (See INSTRUMENT LANDING SYSTEM). (See MICROWAVE LANDING SYSTEM).

CPL [ICAO]. (See CURRENT FLIGHT PLAN).

CRITICAL ENGINE. The engine which, upon failure, would most adversely affect the performance or handling qualities of an aircraft.

CROSS (FIX) AT (ALTITUDE). Used by ATC when a specific altitude restriction at a specified fix is required.

CROSS (FIX) AT OR ABOVE (ALTITUDE). Used by ATC when an altitude restriction at a specified fix is required. It does not prohibit the aircraft from crossing the fix at a higher altitude than specified; however, the higher altitude may not be one that will violate a succeeding altitude restriction or altitude assignment. *(See ALTITUDE RESTRICTION). (Refer to AIM).*

CROSS (FIX) AT OR BELOW (ALTITUDE). Used by ATC when a maximum crossing altitude at a specific fix is required. It does not prohibit the aircraft from crossing the fix at a lower altitude; however, it must be at or above the minimum IFR altitude. *(See MINIMUM IFR ALTITUDES). (See ALTITUDE RESTRICTION). (Refer to FAR Part 91).*

CROSSWIND.

1. When used concerning the traffic pattern, the word means "crosswind leg." *(See TRAFFIC PATTERN).*

2. When used concerning wind conditions, the word means a wind not parallel to the runway or the path of an aircraft.

(See CROSSWIND COMPONENT).

CROSSWIND COMPONENT. The wind component measured in knots at 90 degrees to the longitudinal axis of the runway.

CRUISE. Used in an ATC clearance to authorize a pilot to conduct flight at any altitude from the minimum IFR altitude up to and including the altitude specified in the clearance. The pilot may level off at any intermediate altitude within this block of airspace. Climb/descent within the block is to be made at the discretion of the pilot. However, once the pilot starts descent and verbally reports leaving an altitude in the block, he may not return to that altitude without additional ATC clearance. Further, it is approval for the pilot to proceed to and make an approach at destination airport and can be used in conjunction with:

1. An airport clearance limit at locations with a standard/special instrument approach procedure. The FAR's require that if an instrument letdown to an airport is necessary, the pilot shall make the letdown in accordance with a standard/special instrument approach procedure for that airport, or

2. An airport clearance limit at locations that are within/below/outside controlled airspace and without a standard/special instrument approach procedure. Such a clearance is NOT AUTHORIZATION for the pilot to descend under IFR conditions below the applicable minimum IFR altitude nor does it imply that ATC is exercising control over aircraft in Class G airspace; however, it provides a means for the aircraft to proceed to destination airport, descend, and land in accordance with applicable FAR's governing VFR flight operations. Also, this provides search and rescue protection until such time as the IFR flight plan is closed.

(See INSTRUMENT APPROACH PROCEDURE).

CRUISING ALTITUDE. An altitude or flight level maintained during en route level flight. This is a constant altitude and should not be confused with a cruise clearance. *(See ALTITUDE). (See ICAO term CRUISING LEVEL).*

CRUISING LEVEL [ICAO]. A level maintained during a significant portion of a flight.

CRUISE CLIMB. A climb technique employed by aircraft, usually at a constant power setting, resulting in an increase of altitude as the aircraft weight decreases.

CRUISING LEVEL. *(See CRUISING ALTITUDE).*

CT MESSAGE. An EDCT time generated by the ATCSCC to regulate traffic at arrival airports. Normally, a CT message is automatically transferred from the Traffic Management System computer to the NAS en route computer and appears as an EDCT. In the event of a communication failure between the TMS and the NAS, the CT message can be manually entered by the TMC at the en route facility.

CTA. *(See CONTROLLED TIME OF ARRIVAL).*

CTA. *(See CONTROL AREA [ICAO]).*

CTAF. *(See COMMON TRAFFIC ADVISORY FREQUENCY).*

CURRENT FLIGHT PLAN [ICAO]. The flight plan, including changes, if any, brought about by subsequent clearances.

CVFP APPROACH. *(See CHARTED VISUAL FLIGHT PROCEDURE APPROACH).*

CWA. *(See CENTER WEATHER ADVISORY). (See WEATHER ADVISORY).*

DA [ICAO]. *(See ICAO Term DECISION ALTITUDE/DECISION HEIGHT).*

DAIR. *(See DIRECT ALTITUDE AND IDENTITY READOUT).*

DANGER AREA [ICAO]. An airspace of defined dimensions within which activities dangerous to the flight of aircraft may exist at specified times.

Note: The term "Danger Area" is not used in reference to areas within the United States or any of its possessions or territories.

DATA BLOCK. *(See ALPHANUMERIC DISPLAY).*

DEAD RECKONING. Dead reckoning, as applied to flying, is the navigation of an airplane solely by means of computations based on airspeed, course, heading, wind direction, and speed, groundspeed, and elapsed time.

DECISION ALTITUDE/DECISION HEIGHT [ICAO]. A specified altitude or height (A/H) in the precision approach at which a missed approach must be initiated if the required visual reference to continue the approach has not been established.

Note 1: Decision altitude [DA] is referenced to mean sea level [MSL] and decision height [DH] is referenced to the threshold elevation.

Note 2: The required visual reference means that section of the visual aids or of the approach area which should have been in view for sufficient time for the pilot to have made an assessment of the aircraft position and rate of change of position, in relation to the desired flight path.

DECISION HEIGHT. With respect to the operation of aircraft, means the height at which a decision must be made during an ILS, MLS, or PAR instrument approach to either continue the approach or to execute a missed approach. *(See ICAO term DECISION ALTITUDE/ DECISION HEIGHT).*

DECODER. The device used to decipher signals received from ATCRBS transponders to effect their display as select codes. *(See CODES). (See RADAR).*

DEFENSE VISUAL FLIGHT RULES. Rules applicable to flights within an ADIZ conducted under the visual flight rules in FAR Part 91. *(See AIR DEFENSE IDENTIFICATION ZONE). (Refer to FAR Part 91). (Refer to Part 99).*

DELAY INDEFINITE (REASON IF KNOWN) EXPECT FURTHER CLEARANCE (TIME). Used by ATC to inform a pilot when an accurate estimate of the delay time and the reason for the delay cannot immediately be determined; e.g., a disabled aircraft on the runway, terminal or center area saturation, weather below landing minimums, etc. *(See EXPECT FURTHER CLEARANCE (TIME)).*

DELAY TIME. The amount of time that the arrival must lose to cross the meter fix at the assigned meter fix time. This is the difference between ACLT and VTA.

DEPARTURE CENTER. The ARTCC having jurisdiction for the airspace that generates a flight to the impacted airport.

DEPARTURE CONTROL. A function of an approach control facility providing air traffic control service for departing IFR and, under certain conditions, VFR aircraft. *(See APPROACH CONTROL FACILITY). (Refer to AIM).*

DEPARTURE SEQUENCING PROGRAM. A program designed to assist in achieving a specified interval over a common point for departures.

DEPARTURE TIME. The time an aircraft becomes airborne.

DESCENT SPEED ADJUSTMENTS. Speed deceleration calculations made to determine an accurate VTA. These calculations start at the transition point and use arrival speed segments to the vertex.

DETRESFA (DISTRESS PHASE) [ICAO]. The code word used to designate an emergency phase wherein there is reasonable certainty that an aircraft and its occupants are threatened by grave and imminent danger or require immediate assistance.

DEVIATIONS.

1. A departure from a current clearance, such as an off course maneuver to avoid weather or turbulence.

2. Where specifically authorized in the FAR's and requested by the pilot, ATC may permit pilots to deviate from certain regulations.

(Refer to AIM).

DF. (See DIRECTION FINDER).

DF APPROACH PROCEDURE. Used under emergency conditions where another instrument approach procedure cannot be executed. DF guidance for an instrument approach is given by ATC facilities with DF capability. *(See DF GUIDANCE). (See DIRECTION FINDER). (Refer to AIM).*

DF FIX. The geographical location of an aircraft obtained by one or more direction finders. *(See DIRECTION FINDER).*

DF GUIDANCE. Headings provided to aircraft by facilities equipped with direction finding equipment. These headings, if followed, will lead the aircraft to a predetermined point such as the DF station or an airport. DF guidance is given to aircraft in distress or to other aircraft which request the service. Practice DF guidance is provided when workload permits. *(See DIRECTION FINDER). (See DF FIX). (Refer to AIM).*

DF STEER. (See DF GUIDANCE).

DH. (See DECISION HEIGHT).

DH [ICAO]. (See ICAO Term DECISION ALTITUDE/ DECISION HEIGHT).

DIRECT. Straight line flight between two navigational aids, fixes, points, or any combination thereof. When used by pilots in describing off airway routes, points defining direct route segments become compulsory reporting points unless the aircraft is under radar contact.

DIRECT ALTITUDE AND IDENTITY READOUT. The DAIR System is a modification to the AN/TPX-42 Interrogator System. The Navy has two adaptations of the DAIR System-Carrier Air Traffic Control Direct Altitude and Identification Readout System for Aircraft Carriers and Radar Air Traffic Control Facility Direct Altitude and Identity Readout System for land-based terminal operations. The DAIR detects, tracks, and predicts secondary radar aircraft targets. Targets are displayed by means of computer-generated symbols and alphanumeric characters depicting flight identification, altitude, ground speed, and flight plan data. The DAIR System is capable of interfacing with ARTCCs.

DIRECTION FINDER. A radio receiver equipped with a directional sensing antenna used to take bearings on a radio transmitter. Specialized radio direction finders are used in aircraft as air navigation aids. Others are ground-based, primarily to obtain a "fix" on a pilot requesting orientation assistance or to locate downed aircraft. A location "fix" is established by the intersection of two or more bearing lines plotted on a navigational chart using either two separately located Direction Finders to obtain a fix on an aircraft or by a pilot plotting the bearing indications of his DF on two separately located ground-based transmitters, both of which can be identified on his chart. UDF's receive signals in the ultra high frequency radio broadcast band; VDF's in the very high frequency band; and UVDF's in both bands. ATC provides DF service at those air traffic control towers and flight service stations listed in the Airport/Facility Directory and the DOD FLIP IFR En Route Supplement. *(See DF GUIDANCE). (See DF FIX).*

DISCRETE BEACON CODE. (See DISCRETE CODE).

DISCRETE CODE. As used in the Air Traffic Control Radar Beacon System (ATCRBS), any one of the 4096 selectable Mode 3/A aircraft transponder codes except those ending in zero zero; e.g., discrete codes: 0010, 1201, 2317, 7777; nondiscrete codes: 0100, 1200, 7700. Nondiscrete codes are normally reserved for radar facilities that are not equipped with discrete decoding capability and for other purposes such as emergencies (7700), VFR aircraft (1200), etc. *(See RADAR). (Refer to AIM).*

DISCRETE FREQUENCY. A separate radio frequency for use in direct pilot-controller communications in air traffic control which reduces frequency congestion by controlling the number of aircraft operating on a particular frequency at one time. Discrete frequencies are normally designated for each control sector in en route/terminal ATC facilities. Discrete frequencies are listed in the Airport/Facility Directory and the DOD FLIP IFR En Route Supplement. *(See CONTROL SECTOR).*

DISPLACED THRESHOLD. A threshold that is located at a point on the runway other than the designated beginning of the runway. *(See THRESHOLD). (Refer to AIM).*

DISTANCE MEASURING EQUIPMENT. Equipment (airborne and ground) used to measure, in nautical miles, the slant range distance of an aircraft from the DME navigational aid. *(See TACAN). (See VORTAC). (See MICROWAVE LANDING SYSTEM).*

DISTRESS. A condition of being threatened by serious and/or imminent danger and of requiring immediate assistance.

DIVE BRAKES. (See SPEED BRAKES).

DIVERSE VECTOR AREA. In a radar environment, that area in which a prescribed departure route is not required as the only suitable route to avoid obstacles. The area in which random radar vectors below the MVA/MIA, established in accordance with the TERPS criteria for diverse departures obstacles and terrain avoidance, may be issued to departing aircraft.

DME. (See DISTANCE MEASURING EQUIPMENT).

DME FIX. A geographical position determined by reference to a navigational aid which provides distance and azimuth information. It is defined by a specific distance in nautical miles and a radial, azimuth, or course (i.e., localizer) in degrees magnetic from that aid. *(See DISTANCE MEASURING EQUIPMENT). (See FIX). (See MICROWAVE LANDING SYSTEM).*

DME SEPARATION. Spacing of aircraft in terms of distances (nautical miles) determined by reference to distance measuring equipment (DME). *(See DISTANCE MEASURING EQUIPMENT).*

DOD FLIP. Department of Defense Flight Information Publications used for flight planning, en route, and terminal operations. FLIP is produced by the Defense Mapping Agency for world-wide use. United States Government Flight Information Publications (en route charts and instrument approach procedure charts) are incorporated in DOD FLIP for use in the National Airspace System (NAS).

DOMESTIC AIRSPACE. Airspace which overlies the continental land mass of the United States plus Hawaii and U.S. possessions. Domestic airspace extends to 12 miles offshore.

DOWNBURST. A strong downdraft which induces an outburst of damaging winds on or near the ground. Damaging winds, either straight or curved, are highly divergent. The sizes of downbursts vary from 1/2 mile or less to more than 10 miles. An intense down burst often causes widespread damage. Damaging winds, lasting 5 to 30 minutes, could reach speeds as high as 120 knots.

DOWNWIND LEG. (See TRAFFIC PATTERN).

DRAG CHUTE. A parachute device installed on certain aircraft which is deployed on landing roll to assist in deceleration of the aircraft.

DSP. (See DEPARTURE SEQUENCING PROGRAM).

DT. (See DELAY TIME).

DUE REGARD. A phase of flight wherein an aircraft commander of a State-operated aircraft assumes responsibility to separate his aircraft from all other aircraft. *(See also AIM Chapter 1, Word Meanings).*

DUTY RUNWAY. (See RUNWAY IN USE/ACTIVE RUNWAY/DUTY RUNWAY).

DVA. (See DIVERSE VECTOR AREA).

DVFR. (See DEFENSE VISUAL FLIGHT RULES).

DVFR FLIGHT PLAN. A flight plan filed for a VFR aircraft which intends to operate in airspace within which the ready identification, location, and control of aircraft are required in the interest of national security.

DYNAMIC. Continuous review, evaluation, and change to meet demands.

DYNAMIC RESTRICTIONS. Those restrictions imposed by the local facility on an "as needed" basis to manage unpredictable fluctuations in traffic demands.

EARTS. (See EN ROUTE AUTOMATED RADAR TRACING SYSTEM).

EDCT. (See EXPECTED DEPARTURE CLEARANCE TIME).

EFC. (See EXPECT FURTHER CLEARANCE (TIME)).

ELT. (See EMERGENCY LOCATOR TRANSMITTER).

EMERGENCY. A *distress* or an *urgency* condition.

EMERGENCY LOCATOR TRANSMITTER. A radio transmitter attached to the aircraft structure which operates from its own power source on 121.5 mHz and 243.0 mHz. It aids in locating downed aircraft by radiating a downward sweeping audio tone, 2-4 times per second. It is designed to function without human action after an accident. *(Refer to FAR Part 91.9). (Refer to AIM)*.

EMERGENCY SAFE ALTITUDE. (See MINIMUM SAFE ALTITUDE).

E-MSAW. (See EN ROUTE MINIMUM SAFE ALTITUDE WARNING).

ENTRY POINT. The point at which an aircraft transitions from an offshore control area to oceanic airspace.

ENGINEERED PERFORMANCE STANDARDS. A mathematically derived runway capacity standard. EPS's are calculated for each airport on an individual basis and reflect that airport's aircraft mix, operating procedures, runway layout, and specific weather conditions. EPS's do not give consideration to starting, experience levels, equipment outages, and in-trail restrictions as does the AAR.

EN ROUTE AIR TRAFFIC CONTROL SERVICES. Air traffic control service provided aircraft on IFR flight plans, generally by centers, when these aircraft are operating between departure and destination terminal areas. When equipment, capabilities, and controller workload permit, certain advisory/assistance services may be provided to VFR aircraft. *(See NAS STAGE A). (See AIR ROUTE TRAFFIC CONTROL CENTER). (Refer to AIM)*.

EN ROUTE AUTOMATED RADAR TRACKING SYSTEM. An automated radar and radar beacon tracking system. Its functional capabilities and design are essentially the same as the terminal ARTS IIIA system except for the EARTS capability of employing both short-range (ASR) and long-range (ARSR) radars, use of full digital radar displays, and fail-safe design. *(See AUTOMATED RADAR TERMINAL SYSTEMS)*.

EN ROUTE CHARTS. (See AERONAUTICAL CHART).

EN ROUTE DESCENT. Descent from the en route cruising altitude which takes place along the route of flight.

EN ROUTE FLIGHT ADVISORY SERVICE. A service specifically designed to provide, upon pilot request, timely weather information pertinent to his type of flight, intended route of flight, and altitude. The FSS's providing this service are listed in the Airport/Facility Directory.

(See FLIGHT WATCH). (Refer to AIM).

EN ROUTE HIGH ALTITUDE CHARTS. (See AERONAUTICAL CHART).

EN ROUTE LOW ALTITUDE CHART. (See AERONAUTICAL CHART).

EN ROUTE MINIMUM SAFE ALTITUDE WARNING. A function of the NAS Stage A en route computer that aids the controller by alerting him when a tracked aircraft is below or predicted by the computer to go below a predetermined minimum IFR altitude (MIA).

EN ROUTE SPACING PROGRAM. A program designed to assist the exit sector in achieving the required in-trail spacing.

EPS. (See ENGINEERED PERFORMANCE STANDARDS).

ESP. (See EN ROUTE SPACING PROGRAM).

ESTIMATED ELAPSED TIME [ICAO]. The estimated time required to proceed from one significant point to another. *(See ICAO Term TOTAL ESTIMATED ELAPSED TIME)*.

ESTIMATED OFF-BLOCK TIME [ICAO]. The estimated time at which the aircraft will commence movement associated with departure.

ESTIMATED TIME OF ARRIVAL. The time the flight is estimated to arrive at the gate (scheduled operators) or the actual runway on times for nonscheduled operators.

ESTIMATED TIME EN ROUTE. The estimated flying time from departure point to destination (lift-off to touchdown).

ETA. (See ESTIMATED TIME OF ARRIVAL).

ETE. (See ESTIMATED TIME EN ROUTE).

EXECUTE MISSED APPROACH. Instructions issued to a pilot making an instrument approach which means continue inbound to the missed approach point and execute the missed approach procedure as described on the Instrument Approach Procedure Chart or as previously assigned by ATC. The pilot may climb immediately to the altitude specified in the missed approach procedure upon making a missed approach. No turns should be initiated prior to reaching the missed approach point. When conducting an ASR or PAR approach, execute the assigned missed approach procedure immediately upon receiving instructions to "execute missed approach." *(Refer to AIM)*.

EXPECT (ALTITUDE) AT (TIME) or (FIX). Used under certain conditions to provide a pilot with an altitude to be used in the event of two-way communications failure. It also provides altitude information to assist the pilot in planning. *(Refer to AIM)*.

EXPECTED DEPARTURE CLEARANCE TIME. The runway release time assigned to an aircraft in a controlled departure time program and shown on the flight progress strip as an EDCT.

EXPECT FURTHER CLEARANCE (TIME). The time a pilot can expect to receive clearance beyond a clearance limit.

EXPECT FURTHER CLEARANCE VIA (AIRWAYS, ROUTES OR FIXES). Used to inform a pilot of the routing he can expect if any part of the route beyond a short range clearance limit differs from that filed.

EXPEDITE. Used by ATC when prompt compliance is required to avoid the development of an imminent situation.

FAF. (See FINAL APPROACH FIX).

FA MESSAGE. The data entered into the ARTCC computers that activates delay processing for an impacted airport. The FA data includes the delay factor for flight plans that have not been assigned delays under CT message processing. The delay factor appears on flight progress strips in the form of an EDCT (e.g., EDCT 1820). FA processing assigns delays in 1-minute time blocks. FA's control numbers of aircraft within a specified time block but do not spread aircraft out evenly throughout the time block.

FAP. (See FINAL APPROACH POINT).

FAST FILE. A system whereby a pilot files a flight plan via telephone that is tape recorded and then transcribed for transmission to the appropriate air traffic facility. Locations having a fast file capability are contained in the Airport/Facility Directory. *(Refer to AIM)*.

FCLT. (See FREEZE CALCULATED LANDING TIME).

FEATHERED PROPELLER. A propeller whose blades have been rotated so that the leading and trailing edges are nearly parallel with the aircraft flight path to stop or minimize drag and engine rotation. Normally used to indicate shutdown of a reciprocating or turboprop engine due to malfunction.

FEDERAL AIRWAYS. (See LOW ALTITUDE AIRWAY STRUCTURE).

FEEDER FIX. The fix depicted on Instrument Approach Procedure Charts which establishes the starting point of the feeder route.

FEEDER ROUTE. A route depicted on instrument approach procedure charts to designate routes for aircraft to proceed from the en route structure to the initial approach fix (IAF). *(See INSTRUMENT APPROACH PROCEDURE)*.

FERRY FLIGHT. A flight for the purpose of:

1. Returning an aircraft to base.
2. Delivering an aircraft from one location to another.
3. Moving an aircraft to and from a maintenance base.

Ferry flights, under certain conditions, may be conducted under terms of a special flight permit.

FIELD ELEVATION. (See AIRPORT ELEVATION).

FILED. Normally used in conjunction with flight plans, meaning a flight plan has been submitted to ATC.

FILED EN ROUTE DELAY. Any of the following preplanned delays at points/areas along the route of flight which require special flight plan filing and handling techniques.

1. Terminal Area Delay. A delay within a terminal area for touch-and-go, low approach, or other terminal area activity.

2. Special Use Airspace Delay. A delay within a Military Operating Area, Restricted Area, Warning Area, or ATC Assigned Airspace.

3. Aerial Refueling Delay. A delay within an Aerial Refueling Track or Anchor.

FILED FLIGHT PLAN. The flight plan as filed with an ATS unit by the pilot or his designated representative without any subsequent changes or clearances.

FINAL. Commonly used to mean that an aircraft is on the final approach course or is aligned with a landing area. *(See FINAL APPROACH COURSE)*. *(See FINAL APPROACH–IFR)*. *(See TRAFFIC PATTERN)*. *(See SEGMENTS OF AN INSTRUMENT APPROACH PROCEDURE)*.

FINAL APPROACH [ICAO]. That part of an instrument approach procedure which commences at the specified final approach fix or point, or where such a fix or point is not specified,

a) At the end of the last procedure turn, base turn or inbound turn of a racetrack procedure, if specified; or

b) At the point of interception of the last track specified in the approach procedure; and ends at a point in the vicinity of an aerodrome from which:

1) A landing can be made; or

2) A missed approach procedure is initiated.

FINAL APPROACH COURSE. A published MLS course, a straight line extension of a localizer, a final approach radial/bearing, or a runway centerline all without regard to distance. *(See FINAL APPROACH–IFR)*. *(See TRAFFIC PATTERN)*.

FINAL APPROACH FIX. The fix from which the final approach (IFR) to an airport is executed and which identifies the beginning of the final approach segment. It is designated on Government charts by the Maltese Cross symbol for nonprecision approaches and the lightning bolt symbol for precision approaches; or when ATC directs a lower-than-published Glideslope/path Intercept Altitude, it is the resultant actual point of the glideslope/path intercept.

(See FINAL APPROACH POINT). *(See GLIDESLOPE INTERCEPT ALTITUDE)*. *(See SEGMENTS OF AN INSTRUMENT APPROACH PROCEDURE)*.

FINAL APPROACH-IFR. The flight path of an aircraft which is inbound to an airport on a final instrument approach course, beginning at the final approach fix or point and extending to the airport or the point where a circle-to-land maneuver or a missed approach is executed. *(See SEGMENTS OF AN INSTRUMENT APPROACH PROCEDURE). (See FINAL APPROACH FIX). (See FINAL APPROACH COURSE). (See FINAL APPROACH POINT). (See ICAO term FINAL APPROACH).*

FINAL APPROACH POINT. The point, applicable only to a nonprecision approach with no depicted FAF (such as an on-airport VOR), where the aircraft is established inbound on the final approach course from the procedure turn and where the final approach descent may be commenced. The FAP serves as the FAF and identifies the beginning of the final approach segment. *(See FINAL APPROACH FIX). (See SEGMENTS OF AN INSTRUMENT APPROACH PROCEDURE).*

FINAL APPROACH SEGMENT. (See SEGMENTS OF AN INSTRUMENT APPROACH PROCEDURE).

FINAL APPROACH SEGMENT [ICAO]. That segment of an instrument approach procedure in which alignment and descent for landing are accomplished.

FINAL APPROACH-VFR. (See TRAFFIC PATTERN).

FINAL CONTROLLER. The controller providing information and final approach guidance during PAR and ASR approaches utilizing radar equipment. *(See RADAR APPROACH).*

FINAL MONITOR AID. A high resolution color display that is equipped with the controller alert system hardware/software which is used in the precision runway monitor (PRM) system. The display includes alert algorithms providing the target predictors, a color change alert when a target penetrates or is predicted to penetrate the no transgression zone (NTZ), a color change alert if the aircraft transponder becomes inoperative, synthesized voice alerts, digital mapping, and like features contained in the PRM system. *(See RADAR APPROACH).*

FIR. (See FLIGHT INFORMATION REGION).

FIRST TIER CENTER. The ARTCC immediately adjacent to the impacted center.

FIX. A geographical position determined by visual reference to the surface, by reference to one or more radio NAVAIDs, by celestial plotting, or by another navigational device.

FIX BALANCING. A process whereby aircraft are evenly distributed over several available arrival fees reducing delays and controller workload.

FLA. A warning device incorporated in certain airborne navigation and flight instruments indicating that:

1. Instruments are inoperative or otherwise not operating satisfactorily, or

2. Signal strength or quality of the received signal falls below acceptable values.

FLAG ALARM. (See FLAG).

FLAMEOUT. Unintended loss of combustion in turbine engines resulting in the loss of engine power.

FLIGHT CHECK. A call-sign prefix used by FAA aircraft engaged in flight inspection/certification of navigational aids and flight procedures. The word "recorded" may be added as a suffix; e.g., "Flight Check 320 recorded" to indicate that an automated flight inspection is in progress in terminal areas. *(See FLIGHT INSPECTION). (Refer to AIM).*

FLIGHT FOLLOWING. (See TRAFFIC ADVISORIES).

FLIGHT INFORMATION REGION. An airspace of defined dimensions within which Flight Information Service and Alerting Service are provided.

1. Flight Information Service. A service provided for the purpose of giving advice and information useful for the safe and efficient conduct of flights.

2. Alerting Service. A service provided to notify appropriate organizations regarding aircraft in need of search and rescue aid and to assist such organizations as required.

FLIGHT INFORMATION SERVICE. A service provided for the purpose of giving advice and information useful for the safe and efficient conduct of flights.

FLIGHT INSPECTION. Inflight investigation and evaluation of a navigational aid to determine whether it meets established tolerances. *(See NAVIGATIONAL AID). (See FLIGHT CHECK).*

FLIGHT LEVEL. A level of constant atmospheric pressure related to a reference datum of 29.92 inches of mercury. Each is stated in three digits that represent hundreds of feet. For example, flight level 250 represents a barometric altimeter indication of 25,000 feet; flight level 255, an indication of 25,500 feet. *(See ICAO term FLIGHT LEVEL).*

FLIGHT LEVEL [ICAO]. A surface of constant atmospheric pressure which is related to a specific pressure datum, 1013.2 hPa (1013.2 mb), and is separated from other such surfaces by specific pressure intervals.

Note 1: A pressure tee altimeter calibrated in accordance with the standard atmosphere:

a) When set to a QNH altimeter setting, will indicate altitude;

b) When set to a QFE altimeter setting, will indicate height above the QFE reference datum; and

c) When set to a pressure of 1013.2 hPa (1013.2 mb), may be used to indicate flight levels.

Note 2: The terms "height" and "altitude", used in Note 1 above, indicate altimetric rather than geometric heights and altitudes.

FLIGHT LINE. A term used to describe the precise movement of a civil photogrammetric aircraft along a predetermined course(s) at a predetermined altitude during the actual photographic run.

FLIGHT MANAGEMENT SYSTEMS. A computer system that uses a large data base to allow routes to be preprogrammed and fed into the system by means of a data loader. The system is constantly updated with respect to position accuracy by reference to conventional navigation aids. The sophisticated program and its associated data base insures that the most appropriate aids are automatically selected during the information update cycle.

FLIGHT MANAGEMENT SYSTEM PROCEDURE. An arrival, departure, or approach procedure developed for use by aircraft with a slant (/) G equipment suffix.

FLIGHT PATH. A line, course, or track along which an aircraft is flying or intended to be flown. *(See TRACK). (See COURSE).*

FLIGHT PLAN. Specified information relating to the intended flight of an aircraft that is filed orally or in writing with an FSS or an ATC facility. *(See FAST FILE). (See FILED). (Refer to AIM).*

FLIGHT PLAN AREA. The geographical area assigned by regional air traffic divisions to a flight service station for the purpose of search and rescue for VFR aircraft, issuance of notams, pilot briefing, in-flight services, broadcast, emergency services, flight data processing, international operations, and aviation weather services. Three letter identifiers are assigned to every flight service station and are annotated in AFDs and Order 7350.6 as tie-in-facilities. *(See FAST FILE). (See FILED). (Refer to AIM).*

FLIGHT RECORDER. A general term applied to any instrument or device that records information about the performance of an aircraft in flight or about conditions encountered in flight. Flight recorders may make records of airspeed, outside air temperature, vertical acceleration, engine RPM, manifold pressure, and other pertinent variables for a given flight. *(See ICAO term FLIGHT RECORDER).*

FLIGHT RECORDER [ICAO]. Any type of recorder installed in the aircraft for the purpose of complementing accident/incident investigation.

Note: See Annex 6 Part I, for specifications relating to flight recorders.

FLIGHT SERVICE STATION. Air traffic facilities which provide pilot briefing, en route communications and VFR search and rescue services, assist lost aircraft and aircraft in emergency situations, relay ATC clearances, originate Notices to Airmen, broadcast aviation weather and HAS information, receive and process IFR flight plans, and monitor NAVAID's. In addition, at selected locations, FSS's provide Enroute Flight Advisory Service (Flight Watch), take weather observations, issue airport advisories, and advise Customs and Immigration of transborder flights. *(Refer to AIM).*

FLIGHT STANDARDS DISTRICT OFFICE. An FAA field office serving an assigned geographical area and staffed with Flight Standards personnel who serve the aviation industry and the general public on matters relating to the certification and operation of air carrier and general aviation aircraft. Activities include general surveillance of operational safety, certification of airmen and aircraft, accident prevention, investigation, enforcement, etc.

FLIGHT TEST. A flight for the purpose of:

1. Investigating the operation/flight characteristics of an aircraft or aircraft component.

2. Evaluating an applicant for a pilot certificate or rating.

FLIGHT VISIBILITY. (See VISIBILITY).

FLIGHT WATCH. A shortened term for use in air-ground contacts to identify the flight service station providing En Route Flight Advisory Service; e.g., "Oakland Flight Watch." *(See EN ROUTE FLIGHT ADVISORY SERVICE).*

FLIP. (See DOD FLIP).

FLOW CONTROL. Measures designed to adjust the flow of traffic into a given airspace, along a given route, or bound for a given aerodrome (airport) so as to ensure the most effective utilization of the airspace. *(See QUOTA FLOW CONTROL). (Refer to AIRPORT/FACILITY DIRECTORY).*

FLY HEADING (DEGREES). Informs the pilot of the heading he should fly. The pilot may have to turn to, or continue on, a specific compass direction in order to comply with the instructions. The pilot is expected to turn in the shorter direction to the heading unless otherwise instructed by ATC.

FMA. (See FIND MONITOR AID).

FMS. (See FLIGHT MANAGEMENT SYSTEM).

FMSP. (See FLIGHT MANAGEMENT SYSTEM PROCEDURE).

FORMATION FLIGHT. More than one aircraft which, by prior arrangement between the pilots, operate as a single aircraft with regard to navigation and position reporting. Separation between aircraft within the formation is the responsibility of the flight leader and the pilots of the other aircraft in the flight. This includes transition periods when aircraft within the formation are maneuvering to attain separation from each other to effect individual control and during join-up and breakaway.

1. A standard formation is one in which a proximity of no more than 1 mile laterally or longitudinally and within 100 feet vertically from the flight leader is maintained by each wingman.

2. Nonstandard formations are those operating under any of the following conditions:

Continued

a. When the flight leader has requested and ATC has approved other than standard formation dimensions.

b. When operating within an authorized altitude reservation (ALTRV) or under the provisions of a letter of agreement.

c. When the operations are conducted in airspace specifically designed for a special activity.

(See ALTITUDE RESERVATION). (Refer to FAR Part 91).

FRC. (See REQUEST FULL ROUTE CLEARANCE).

FREEZE/FROZEN. Terms used in referring to arrivals which have been assigned ACLT's and to the lists in which they are displayed.

FREEZE CALCULATED LANDING TIME. A dynamic parameter number of minutes prior to the meter fix calculated time of arrival for each aircraft when the TCLT is frozen and becomes an ACLT (i.e., the VTA is updated and consequently the TCLT is modified as appropriate until FCLT minutes prior to meter fix calculated time of arrival, at which time updating is suspended and an ACLT and a frozen meter fix crossing time (MFT) is assigned).

FREEZE SPEED PARAMETER. A speed adapted for each aircraft to determine fast and slow aircraft. Fast aircraft freeze on parameter FCLT and slow aircraft freeze on parameter MLDI.

FSDO. (See FLIGHT STANDARDS DISTRICT OFFICE).

FSPD. (See FREEZE SPEED PARAMETER).

FSS. (See FLIGHT SERVICE STATION).

FUEL DUMPING. Airborne release of usable fuel. This does not include the dropping of fuel tanks. *(See JETTISONING OF EXTERNAL STORES).*

FUEL REMAINING. A phrase used by either pilots or controllers when relating to the fuel remaining on board until actual fuel exhaustion. When transmitting such information in response to either a controller question or pilot initiated cautionary advisory to air traffic control, pilots will state the APPROXIMATE NUMBER OF MINUTES the flight can continue with the fuel remaining. All reserve fuel SHOULD BE INCLUDED in the time stated, as should an allowance for established fuel gauge system error.

FUEL SIPHONING. Unintentional release of fuel caused by overflow, puncture, loose cap, etc.

FUEL VENTING. (See FUEL SIPHONING).

GADO. (See GENERAL AVIATION DISTRICT OFFICE).

GATE HOLD PROCEDURES. Procedures at selected airports to hold aircraft at the gate or other ground location whenever departure delays exceed or are anticipated to exceed 15 minutes. The sequence for departure will be maintained in accordance with initial call-up unless modified by flow control restrictions. Pilots should monitor the ground control/clearance delivery frequency for engine start/taxi advisories or new proposed start/taxi time if the delay changes. *(See FLOW CONTROL).*

GCA. (See GROUND CONTROLLED APPROACH).

GENERAL AVIATION. That portion of civil aviation which encompasses all facets of aviation except air carriers holding a certificate of public convenience and necessity from the Civil Aeronautics Board and large aircraft commercial operators. *(See ICAO term GENERAL AVIATION).*

GENERAL AVIATION [ICAO]. All civil aviation operations other than scheduled air services and nonscheduled air transport operations for remuneration or hire.

GENERAL AVIATION DISTRICT OFFICE. An FAA field office serving a designated geographical area and staffed with Flight Standards personnel who have the responsibility for serving the aviation industry and the general public on all matters relating to the certification and operation of general aviation aircraft.

GEO MAP. The digitized map markings associated with the ASR-9 Radar System.

GLIDEPATH. (See GLIDESLOPE).

GLIDEPATH INTERCEPT ALTITUDE. (See GLIDESLOPE INTERCEPT ALTITUDE).

GLIDESLOPE. Provides vertical guidance for aircraft during approach and landing. The glideslope/glidepath is based on the following:

1. Electronic components emitting signals which provide vertical guidance by reference to airborne instruments during instrument approaches such as ILS/MLS, or

2. Visual ground aids, such as VASI, which provide vertical guidance for a VFR approach or for the visual portion of an instrument approach and landing.

3. PAR. Used by ATC to inform an aircraft making a PAR approach of its vertical position (elevation) relative to the descent profile.

(See ICAO term GLIDEPATH).

GLIDEPATH [ICAO]. A descent profile determined for vertical guidance during a final approach.

GLIDESLOPE INTERCEPT ALTITUDE. The minimum altitude to intercept the glideslope/path on a precision approach. The intersection of the published intercept altitude with the glideslope/path, designated on Government charts by the lightning bolt symbol, is the precision FAF; however, when ATC directs a lower altitude the resultant lower intercept position is then the FAF. *(See FINAL APPROACH FIX). (See SEGMENTS OF AN INSTRUMENT APPROACH PROCEDURE).*

GLOBAL POSITIONING SYSTEM. A space-base radio positioning, navigation, and time-transfer system being developed by Department of Defense. When fully deployed, the system is intended to provide highly accurate position and velocity information, and precise time, on a continuous global basis, to an unlimited number of properly equipped users. The system will be unaffected by weather, and will provide a worldwide common grid reference system. The GPS concept is predicated upon accurate and continuous knowledge of the spatial position of each satellite in the system with respect to time and distance from a transmitting satellite to the user. The GPS receiver automatically selects appropriate signals from the satellites in view and translates these into a three-dimensional position, velocity, and time. Predictable system accuracy for civil users is projected to be 100 meters horizontally. Performance standards and certification criteria have not yet been established.

GO AHEAD. Proceed with your message. Not to be used for any other purpose.

GO AROUND. Instructions for a pilot to abandon his approach to landing. Additional instructions may follow. Unless otherwise advised by ATC, a VFR aircraft or an aircraft conducting visual approach should overfly the runway while climbing to traffic pattern altitude and enter the traffic pattern via the crosswind leg. A pilot on an IFR flight plan making an instrument approach should execute the published missed approach procedure or proceed as instructed by ATC; e.g., "Go around" (additional instructions if required). *(See LOW APPROACH). (See MISSED APPROACH)*.

GPS. (See Global Positioning System)

GROUND CLUTTER. A pattern produced on the radar scope by ground returns which may degrade other radar returns in the affected area. The effect of ground clutter is minimized by the use of moving target indicator (MTI) circuits in the radar equipment resulting in a radar presentation which displays only targets which are in motion. *(See CLUTTER)*.

GROUND CONTROLLED APPROACH. A radar approach system operated from the ground by air traffic control personnel transmitting instructions to the pilot by radio. The approach may be conducted with surveillance radar (ASR) only or with both surveillance and precision approach radar (PAR). Usage of the term "GCA" by pilots is discouraged except when referring to a GCA facility. Pilots should specifically request a "PAR" approach when a precision radar approach is desired or request an "ASR" or "surveillance" approach when a nonprecision radar approach is desired. *(See RADAR APPROACH)*.

GROUND DELAY. The amount of delay attributed to ATC, encountered prior to departure, usually associated with a CDT program.

GROUND SPEED. The speed of an aircraft relative to the surface of the earth.

GROUND STOP. Normally, the last initiative to be utilized; this method mandates that the terminal facility will not allow any departures to enter the ARTCC airspace until further notified.

GROUND VISIBILITY. (See VISIBILITY).

HAA. (See HEIGHT ABOVE AIRPORT).

HAL. See HEIGHT ABOVE LANDING).

HANDOFF. An action taken to transfer the radar identification of an aircraft from one controller to another if the aircraft will enter the receiving controller's airspace and radio communications with the aircraft will be transferred.

HAT. (See HEIGHT ABOVE TOUCHDOWN).

HAVE NUMBERS. Used by pilots to inform ATC that they have received runway, wind, and altimeter information only.

HAZARDOUS INFLIGHT WEATHER ADVISORY SERVICE. Continuous recorded hazardous inflight weather forecasts broadcasted to airborne pilots over selected VOR outlets defined as an HIWAS BROADCAST AREA.

HAZARDOUS WEATHER INFORMATION. Summary of significant meteorological information (SIGMET, WS), convective significant meteorological information (convective SIGMET/WST), urgent pilot weather reports (urgent PIREP/UUA), center weather advisories (CWA), airmen's meteorological information (AIRMET/WA) and any other weather such as isolated thunderstorms that are rapidly developing and increasing in intensity, or low ceilings and visibilities that are becoming widespread which is considered significant and are not included in a current hazardous weather advisory.

HEAVY (AIRCRAFT). (See AIRCRAFT CLASSES).

HEIGHT ABOVE AIRPORT. The height of the Minimum Descent Altitude above the published airport elevation. This is published in conjunction with circling minimums. *(See MINIMUM DESCENT ALTITUDE)*.

HEIGHT ABOVE LANDING. The height above a designated helicopter landing area used for helicopter instrument approach procedures. *(Refer to FAR Part 97)*.

HEIGHT ABOVE TOUCHDOWN. The height of the Decision Height or Minimum Descent Altitude above the highest runway elevation in the touchdown zone (first 3,000 feet of the runway). HAT is published on instrument approach charts in conjunction with all straight-in minimums. *(See DECISION HEIGHT). (See MINIMUM DESCENT ALTITUDE)*.

HELICOPTER. Rotorcraft that, for its horizontal motion, depends principally on its engine-driven rotors. *(See ICAO term HELICOPTER)*.

HELICOPTER [ICAO]. A heavier-than-air aircraft supported in flight chiefly by the reactions of the air on one or more power-driven rotors on substantially vertical axes.

HELIPAD. A small, designated area, usually with a prepared surface, on a heliport, airport, landing/takeoff area, apron/ramp, or movement area used for takeoff landing, or parking of helicopters.

HELIPORT. An area of land, water, or structure used or intended to be used for the landing and takeoff of helicopters and includes its buildings and facilities if any.

HERTZ. The standard radio equivalent of frequency in cycles per second of an electromagnetic wave. Kilohertz (kHz) is a frequency of one thousand cycles per second. Megahertz (mHz) is a frequency of one million cycles per second.

HF. (See HIGH FREQUENCY).

HF COMMUNICATIONS. (See HIGH FREQUENCY COMMUNICATIONS).

HIGH FREQUENCY. The frequency band between 3 and 30 mHz. *(See HIGH FREQUENCY COMMUNICATIONS)*.

HIGH FREQUENCY COMMUNICATIONS. High radio frequencies (HF) between 3 and 30 mHz used for air-to-ground voice communication in overseas operations.

HIGH SPEED EXIT. (See HIGH SPEED TAXIWAY).

HIGH SPEED TAXIWAY. A long radius taxiway designed and provided with lighting or marking to define the path of aircraft, traveling at high speed (up to 60 knots), from the runway center to a point on the center of a taxiway. Also referred to as long radius exit or turn-off taxiway. The high speed taxiway is designed to expedite aircraft turning off the runway after landing, thus reducing runway occupancy time.

HIGH SPEED TURNOFF. (See HIGH SPEED TAXIWAY).

HIWAS. (See HAZARDOUS INFLIGHT WEATHER ADVISORY SERVICE).

HIWAS AREA. (See HAZARDOUS INFLIGHT WEATHER ADVISORY SERVICE).

HIWAS BROADCAST AREA. A geographical area of responsibility including one or more HIWAS outlet areas assigned to an AFSS/FSS for hazardous weather advisory broadcasting.

HIWAS OUTLET AREA. An area defined as a 160 NM radius of a HIWAS outlet, expanded as necessary to provide coverage.

HOLDING PROCEDURE. (See HOLD PROCEDURE).

HOLD PROCEDURE. A predetermined maneuver which keeps aircraft within a specified airspace while awaiting further clearance from air traffic control. Also used during ground operations to keep aircraft within a specified area

or at a specified point while awaiting further clearance from air traffic control. *(See HOLDING FIX)*. *(Refer to AIM)*.

HOLDING FIX. A specified fix identifiable to a pilot by NAVAIDs or visual reference to the ground used as a reference point in establishing and maintaining the position of an aircraft while holding. *(See FIX)*. *(See VISUAL HOLDING)*. *(Refer to AIM)*.

HOLDING POINT [ICAO]. A specified location, identified by visual or other means, in the vicinity of which the position of an aircraft in flight is maintained in accordance with air traffic control clearances.

HOLD FOR RELEASE. Used by ATC to delay an aircraft for traffic management reasons; i.e., weather, traffic volume, etc. Hold for release instructions (including departure delay information) are used to inform a pilot or a controller (either directly or through an authorized relay) that an IFR departure clearance is not valid until a release time or additional instructions have been received. *(See ICAO term HOLDING POINT)*.

HOMING. Flight toward a NAVAID, without correcting for wind, by adjusting the aircraft heading to maintain a relative bearing of zero degrees. *(See BEARING)*. *(See ICAO term HOMING)*.

HOMING [ICAO]. The procedure of using the direction-finding equipment of one radio station with the emission of another radio station, where at least one of the stations is mobile, and whereby the mobile station proceeds continuously towards the other station.

HOVER CHECK. Used to describe when a helicopter/VTOL aircraft requires a stabilized hover to conduct a performance/power check prior to hover taxi, air taxi, or takeoff. Altitude of the hover will vary based on the purpose of the check.

HOVER TAXI. Used to describe a helicopter/VTOL aircraft movement conducted above the surface and in ground effect at airspeeds less than approximately 20 knots. The actual height may vary, and some helicopters may require hover taxi above 25 feet AGL to reduce ground effect turbulence or provide clearance for cargo slingloads. *(See AIR TAXI)*. *(See HOVER CHECK)*. *(Refer to AIM)*.

HOW DO YOU HEAR ME?. A question relating to the quality of the transmission or to determine how well the transmission is being received.

HZ. (See HERTZ).

IAF. (See INITIAL APPROACH FIX).

IAP. (See INSTRUMENT APPROACH PROCEDURE).

ICAO. (See INTERNATIONAL CIVIL AVIATION ORGANIZATION).

ICAO [ICAO]. (See ICAO Term INTERNATIONAL CIVIL AVIATION ORGANIZATION).

IDENT. A request for a pilot to activate the aircraft transponder identification feature. This will help the controller to confirm an aircraft identity or to identify an aircraft. *(Refer to AIM)*

IDENT FEATURE. The special feature in the Air Traffic Control Radar Beacon System (ATCRBS) equipment. It is used to immediately distinguish one displayed beacon target from other beacon targets. *(See IDENT)*.

IF. (See INTERMEDIATE FIX).

IFIM. (See INTERNATIONAL FLIGHT INFORMATION MANUAL).

IF NO TRANSMISSION RECEIVED FOR (TIME). Used by ATC in radar approaches to prefix procedures which should be followed by the pilot in event of lost communications. *(See LOST COMMUNICATIONS)*.

IFR. (See INSTRUMENT FLIGHT RULES).

IFR AIRCRAFT. An aircraft conducting flight in accordance with instrument flight rules.

IFR CONDITIONS. Weather conditions below the minimum for flight under visual flight rules. *(See INSTRUMENT METEOROLOGICAL CONDITIONS)*.

IFR DEPARTURE PROCEDURE. (See IFR TAKEOFF MINIMUMS AND DEPARTURE PROCEDURES). *(Refer to AIM)*.

IFR FLIGHT. (See IFR AIRCRAFT).

IFR LANDING MINIMUMS. (See LANDING MINIMUMS).

IFR MILITARY TRAINING ROUTES (IR). Routes used by the Department of Defense and associated Reserve and Air Guard units for the purpose of conducting low-altitude navigation and tactical training in both IFR and VFR weather conditions below 10,000 feet MSL at airspeeds in excess of 250 knots LAS.

IFR TAKEOFF MINIMUMS AND DEPARTURE PROCEDURES. Federal Aviation Regulations, FAR Part 91, prescribes standard takeoff rules for certain civil users. At some airports, obstructions or other factors require the establishment of nonstandard takeoff minimums, departure procedures, or both to assist pilots in avoiding obstacles during climb to the minimum en route altitude. Those airports are listed in NOS/DOD Instrument Approach Charts (IAP's) under a section entitled "IFR Takeoff Minimums and Departure Procedures." The NOS/DOD IAP chart legend illustrates the symbol used to alert the pilot to nonstandard takeoff minimums and departure procedures. When departing IFR from such airports or from any airports where there are no departure procedures, SID's, or ATC facilities available, pilots should advise ATC of any departure limitations. Controllers may query a pilot to determine acceptable departure directions, turns, or headings after takeoff. Pilots should be familiar with the departure procedures and must assure that their aircraft can meet or exceed any specified climb gradients.

ILS. (See INSTRUMENT LANDING SYSTEM).

ILS CATEGORIES.

1. ILS Category I. An ILS approach procedure which provides for approach to a height above touchdown of not less than 200 feet and with runway visual range of not less than 1,800 feet.

2. ILS Category II. An ILS approach procedure which provides for approach to a height above touchdown of not less than 100 feet and with runway visual range of not less than 1,200 feet.

3. ILS Category III:

a. IIIA: An ILS approach procedure which provides for approach without a decision height minimum and with runway visual range of not less than 700 feet.

b. IIIB: An ILS approach procedure which provides for approach without a decision height minimum and with runway visual range of not less than 150 feet.

c. IIIC: An ILS approach procedure which provides for approach without a decision height minimum and without runway visual range minimum.

IM. (See INNER MARKER).

IMC. (See INSTRUMENT METEOROLOGICAL CONDITIONS).

IMMEDIATELY. Used by ATC when such action compliance is required to avoid an imminent situation.

INCERFA (Uncertainty Phase) [ICAO]. A situation wherein uncertainty exists as to the safety of an aircraft and its occupants.

INCREASE SPEED TO (SPEED). (See SPEED ADJUSTMENT).

INERTIAL NAVIGATION SYSTEM. An RNAV system which is a form of self-contained navigation. *(See Area Navigationl RNAV.)*.

INFLIGHT REFUELING. (See AERIAL REFUELING).

INFLIGHT WEATHER ADVISORY. (See WEATHER ADVISORY).

INFORMATION REQUEST. A request originated by an FSS for information concerning an overdue VFR aircraft.

INITIAL APPROACH FIX. The fixes depicted on instrument approach procedure charts that identify the beginning of the initial approach segment(s). *(See FIX)*. *(See SEGMENTS OF AN INSTRUMENT APPROACH PROCEDURE)*.

INITIAL APPROACH SEGMENT. (See SEGMENTS OF AN INSTRUMENT APPROACH PROCEDURE).

INITIAL APPROACH SEGMENT [ICAO]. That segment of an instrument approach procedure between the initial approach fix and the intermediate approach fix or, where applicable, the final approach fix or point.

INLAND NAVIGATION FACILITY. A navigation aid on a North American Route at which the common route and/or the noncommon route begins or ends.

INNER MARKER. A marker beacon used with an ILS (CAT II) precision approach located between the middle marker and the end of the ILS runway, transmitting a radiation pattern keyed at six dots per second and indicating to the pilot, both aurally and visually, that he is at the designated decision height (DH), normally 100 feet above the touchdown zone elevation, on the ILS CAT II approach. It also marks progress during a CAT III approach. *(See INSTRUMENT LANDING SYSTEM). (Refer to AIM).*

INNER MARKER BEACON. (See INNER MARKER).

INREQ. (See INFORMATION REQUEST).

INS. (See INERTIAL NAVIGATION SYSTEM).

INSTRUMENT APPROACH. (See INSTRUMENT APPROACH PROCEDURE).

INSTRUMENT APPROACH PROCEDURE. A series of predetermined maneuvers for the orderly transfer of an aircraft under instrument flight conditions from the beginning of the initial approach to a landing or to a point from which a landing may be made visually. It is prescribed and approved for a specific airport by competent authority. *(See SEGMENTS OF AN INSTRUMENT APPROACH PROCEDURE). (Refer to FAR Part 91). (See AIM).*

1. U.S. civil standard instrument approach procedures are approved by the FAA as prescribed under Part 97 and are available for public use.

2. U.S. military standard instrument approach procedures are approved and published by the Department of Defense.

3. Special instrument approach procedures are approved by the FAA for individual operators but are not published in Part 97 for public use. *(See ICAO term INSTRUMENT APPROACH PROCEDURE).*

INSTRUMENT APPROACH PROCEDURE [ICAO]. A series of predetermined manoeuvres by reference to flight instruments with specified protection from obstacles from the initial approach fix, or where applicable, from the beginning of a defined arrival route to a point from which a landing can be completed and thereafter, if a landing is not completed, to a position at which holding or en route obstacle clearance criteria apply.

INSTRUMENT APPROACH PROCEDURES CHARTS. (See AERONAUTICAL CHART).

INSTRUMENT FLIGHT RULES. Rules governing the procedures for conducting instrument flight. Also a term used by pilots and controllers to indicate type of flight plan. *(See VISUAL FLIGHT RULES). (See INSTRUMENT METEOROLOGICAL CONDITIONS). (See VISUAL METEOROLOGICAL CONDITIONS). (Refer to AIM). (See ICAO term INSTRUMENT FLIGHT RULES).*

INSTRUMENT FLIGHT RULES [ICAO]. A set of rules governing the conduct of flight under instrument meteorological conditions.

INSTRUMENT LANDING SYSTEM. A precision instrument approach system which normally consists of the following electronic components and visual aids:

1. Localizer. (See LOCALIZER).
2. Glideslope. (See GLIDESLOPE).
3. Outer Marker. (See OUTER MARKER).
4. Middle Marker. (See MIDDLE MARKER).
5. Approach Lights. (See AIRPORT LIGHTING).

(Refer to FAR Part 91). (See AIM).

INSTRUMENT METEOROLOGICAL CONDITIONS. Meteorological conditions expressed in terms of visibility, distance from cloud, and ceiling less than the minima specified for visual meteorological conditions. *(See VISUAL METEOROLOGICAL CONDITIONS). (See INSTRUMENT FLIGHT RULES). (See VISUAL FLIGHT RULES).*

INSTRUMENT RUNWAY. A runway equipped with electronic and visual navigation aids for which a precision or nonprecision approach procedure having straight-in landing minimums has been approved. *(See ICAO term INSTRUMENT RUNWAY).*

INSTRUMENT RUNWAY [ICAO]. One of the following types of runways intended for the operation of aircraft using instrument approach procedures:

a) *Nonprecision Approach Runway.* An instrument runway served by visual aids and a nonvisual aid providing at least directional guidance adequate for a straight-in approach.

b) *Precision Approach Runway, Category I.* An instrument runway served by ILS and visual aids intended for operations down to 60 m (200 feet) decision height and down to an RVR of the order of 800 m.

c) *Precision Approach Runway, Category II.* An instrument runway served by ILS and visual aids intended for operations down to 30 m (100 feet) decision height and down to an RVR of the order of 400 m.

d) *Precision Approach Runway, Category III.* An instrument runway served by ILS to and along the surface of the runway and:

A. Intended for operations down to an RVR of the order of 200 m (no decision height being applicable) using visual aids during the final phase of landing;

B. Intended for operations down to an RVR of the order of 50 m (no decision height being applicable) using visual aids for taxiing;

C. Intended for operations without reliance on visual reference for landing or taxiing.

Note 1: See Annex 10 Volume I, Part I Chapter 3, for related ILS specifications.

Note 2: Visual aids need not necessarily be matched to the scale of nonvisual aids provided. The criterion for the selection of visual aids is the conditions in which operations are intended to be conducted.

INTERMEDIATE APPROACH SEGMENT. (See SEGMENTS OF AN INSTRUMENT APPROACH PROCEDURE).

INTERMEDIATE APPROACH SEGMENT [ICAO]. That segment of an instrument approach procedure between either the intermediate approach fix and the final approach fix or point, or between the end of a reversal, race track or dead reckoning track procedure and the final approach fix or point, as appropriate.

INTERMEDIATE FIX. The fix that identifies the beginning of the intermediate approach segment of an instrument approach procedure. The fix is not normally identified on the instrument approach chart as an intermediate fix (IF). *(See SEGMENTS OF AN INSTRUMENT APPROACH PROCEDURE).*

INTERMEDIATE LANDING. On the rare occasion that this option is requested, it should be approved. The departure center, however, must advise the ATCSCC so that the appropriate delay is carried over and assigned at the intermediate airport. An intermediate landing airport within the arrival center will not be accepted without coordination with and the approval of the ATCSCC.

INTERNATIONAL AIRPORT. Relating to international flight, it means:

1. An airport of entry which has been designated by the Secretary of Treasury or Commissioner of Customs as an international airport for customs service.

2. A landing rights airport at which specific permission to land must be obtained from customs authorities in advance of contemplated use.

3. Airports designated under the Convention on International Civil Aviation as an airport for use by international commercial air transport and/or international general aviation.

(Refer to AIRPORT/FACILITY DIRECTORY). (Refer to IFIM). (See ICAO term INTERNATIONAL AIRPORT).

INTERNATIONAL AIRPORT [ICAO]. Any airport designated by the Contracting State in whose territory it is situated as an airport of entry and departure for international air traffic, where the formalities incident to customs, immigration, public health, animal and plant quarantine and similar procedures are carried out.

INTERNATIONAL CIVIL AVIATION ORGANIZATION [ICAO]. A specialized agency of the United Nations whose objective is to develop the principles and techniques of international air navigation and to foster planning and development of international civil air transport.

ICAO Regions include:

AFI. African-Indian Ocean Region

CAR. Caribbean Region
EUR. European Region
MID/ASIA. Middle East/Asia Region
NAM. North American Region
NAT. North Atlantic Region
PAC. Pacific Region
SAM. South American Region

INTERNATIONAL FLIGHT INFORMATION MANUAL. A publication designed primarily as a pilot's preflight planning guide for flights into foreign airspace and for flights returning to the U.S. from foreign locations.

INTERROGATOR. The ground-based surveillance radar beacon transmitter-receiver, which normally scans in synchronism with a primary radar, transmitting discrete radio signals which repetitively request all transponders on the mode being used to reply. The replies received are mixed with the primary radar returns and displayed on the same plan position indicator (radar scope). Also, applied to the airborne element of the TACAN/DME system. *(See TRANSPONDER). (Refer to AIM).*

INTERSECTING RUNWAYS. Two or more runways which cross or meet within their lengths. *(See INTERSECTION).*

INTERSECTION.

1. A point defined by any combination of courses, radials, or bearings of two or more navigational aids.

2. Used to describe the point where two runways, a runway and a taxiway, or two taxiways cross or meet.

INTERSECTION DEPARTURE. A departure from any runway intersection except the end of the runway. *(See INTERSECTION).*

INTERSECTION TAKEOFF. (See INTERSECTION DEPARTURE).

IR. (See IFR MILITARY TRAINING ROUTES).

I SAY AGAIN. The message will be repeated.

JAMMING. Electronic or mechanical interference which may disrupt the display of aircraft on radar or the transmission/reception of radio communications/navigation.

JET BLAST. Jet engine exhaust (thrust stream turbulence). *(See WAKE TURBULENCE).*

JET ROUTE. A route designed to serve aircraft operations from 18,000 feet MSL up to and including flight level 450. The routes are referred to as "J" routes with numbering to identify the designated route; e.g., J105. *(See Class A airspace). (Refer to Part 71).*

JET STREAM. A migrating stream of high-speed winds present at high altitudes.

JETTISONING OF EXTERNAL STORES. Airborne release of external stores; e.g., tiptanks, ordnance. *(See FUEL DUMPING). (Refer to FAR Part 91).*

JOINT USE RESTRICTED AREA. (See RESTRICTED AREA).

KNOWN TRAFFIC. With respect to ATC clearances, means aircraft whose altitude, position, and intentions are known to ATC.

LAA. (See LOCAL AIRPORT ADVISORY).

LAAS. (See LOW ALTITUDE ALERT SYSTEM).

LANDING AREA. Any locality either on land, water, or structures, including airports/heliports and intermediate landing fields, which is used, or intended to be used, for the landing and takeoff of aircraft whether or not facilities are provided for the shelter, servicing, or for receiving or discharging passengers or cargo. *(See ICAO term LANDING AREA).*

LANDING AREA [ICAO]. That part of a movement area intended for the landing or takeoff of aircraft.

LANDING DIRECTION INDICATOR. A device which visually indicates the direction in which landings and takeoffs should be made. *(See TETRAHEDRON). (Refer to AIM).*

LANDING DISTANCE AVAILABLE [ICAO]. The length of runway which is declared available and suitable for the ground run of an aeroplane landing.

LANDING MINIMUMS. The minimum visibility prescribed for landing a civil aircraft while using an instrument approach procedure. The minimum applies with other limitations set forth in FAR Part 91 with respect to the Minimum Descent Altitude (MDA) or Decision Height (DH) prescribed in the instrument approach procedures as follows:

1. Straight-in landing minimums. A statement of MDA and visibility, or DH and visibility, required for a straight-in landing on a specified runway, or
2. Circling minimums. A statement of MDA and visibility required for the circle-to-land maneuver.

Decent below the established MDA or DH is not authorized during an approach unless the aircraft is in a position from which a normal approach to the runway of intended landing can be made and adequate visual reference to required visual cues is maintained.

(See STRAIGHT-IN LANDING). (See CIRCLE-TO-LAND MANEUVER). (See DECISION HEIGHT). (See MINIMUM DESCENT ALTITUDE). (See VISIBILITY). (See INSTRUMENT APPROACH PROCEDURE). (Refer to FAR Part 91).

LANDING ROLL. The distance from the point of touchdown to the point where the aircraft can be brought to a stop or exit the runway.

LANDING SEQUENCE. The order in which aircraft are positioned for landing. *(See APPROACH SEQUENCE).*

LAST ASSIGNED ALTITUDE. The last altitude/flight level assigned by ATC and acknowledged by the pilot. *(See MAINTAIN). (Refer to FAR Part 91).*

LATERAL SEPARATION. The lateral spacing of aircraft at the same altitude by requiring operation on different routes or in different geographical locations. *(See SEPARATION).*

LDA. (See LOCALIZER TYPE DIRECTIONAL AID).

LDA [ICAO]. (See ICAO Term LANDING DISTANCE AVAILABLE).

LF. (See LOW FREQUENCY).

LIGHTED AIRPORT. An airport where runway and obstruction lighting is available. *(See AIRPORT LIGHTING). (Refer to AIM).*

LIGHT GUN. A handheld directional light signaling device which emits a brilliant narrow beam of white, green, or red light as selected by the tower controller. The color and type of light transmitted can be used to approve or disapprove anticipated pilot actions where radio communication is not available. The light gun is used for controlling traffic operating in the vicinity of the airport and on the airport movement area. (Refer to AIM).

LOCALIZER. The component of an ILS which provides course guidance to the runway. *(See INSTRUMENT LANDING SYSTEM). (Refer to AIM). (See ICAO term LOCALIZER COURSE).*

LOCALIZER COURSE [ICAO]. The locus of points, in any given horizontal plane, at which the DDM (difference in depth of modulation) is zero.

LOCALIZER TYPE DIRECTIONAL AID–A NAVAID used for nonprecision instrument approaches with utility and accuracy comparable to a localizer but which is not a part of a complete ILS and is not aligned with the runway. *(Refer to AIM).*

LOCALIZER USABLE DISTANCE. The maximum distance from the localizer transmitter at a specified altitude, as verified by flight inspection, at which reliable course information is continuously received. *(Refer to AIM).*

LOCAL AIRPORT ADVISORY [LAA]. A service provided by flight service stations or the military at airports not serviced by an operating control tower. This service consists of providing information to arriving and departing aircraft concerning wind direction and speed, favored runway, altimeter setting, pertinent known traffic, pertinent known field conditions, airport taxi routes and traffic patterns, and authorized instrument approach procedures. This information is advisory in nature and does not constitute an ATC clearance. *(See AIRPORT ADVISORY AREA).*

LOCAL TRAFFIC. Aircraft operating in the traffic pattern or within sight of the tower, or aircraft known to be departing or arriving from flight in local practice areas, or aircraft executing practice instrument approaches at the airport. *(See TRAFFIC PATTERN).*

LOCATOR [ICAO]. An LM/MF NDB used as an aid to final approach.

Note: A locator usually has an average radius of rated coverage of between 18.6 and 48.3 km (10 and 25 NM).

LONGITUDINAL SEPARATION. The longitudinal spacing of aircraft at the same altitude by a minimum distance expressed in units of time or miles. *(See SEPARATION). (Refer to AIM).*

LONG RANGE NAVIGATION. (See LORAN).

LORAN. An electronic navigational system by which hyperbolic lines of position are determined by measuring the difference in the time of reception of synchronized pulse signals from two fixed transmitters. Loran A operates in the 1750-1950 kHz frequency band. Loran C and D operate in the 10-110 kHz frequency band. *(Refer to AIM).*

LOST COMMUNICATIONS. Loss of the ability to communicate by radio. Aircraft are sometimes referred to as NORDO (No Radio). Standard pilot procedures are specified in FAR Part 91. Radar controllers issue procedures for pilots to follow in the event of lost communications during a radar approach when weather reports indicate that an aircraft will likely encounter IFR weather conditions during the approach. *(Refer to FAR Part 91). (See AIM).*

LOW ALTITUDE AIRWAY STRUCTURE. The network of airways serving aircraft operations up to but not including 18,000 feet MSL. *(See AIRWAY). (Refer to AIM).*

LOW ALTITUDE ALERT, CHECK YOUR ALTITUDE IMMEDIATELY. (See SAFETY ALERT).

LOW ALTITUDE ALERT SYSTEM. An automated function of the TPX-42 that alerts the controller when a Mode C transponder-equipped aircraft on an IFR flight plan is below a predetermined minimum safe altitude. If requested by the pilot, LAAS monitoring is also available to VFR Mode C transponder-equipped aircraft.

LOW APPROACH. An approach over an airport or runway following an instrument approach or a VFR approach including the go-around maneuver where the pilot intentionally does not make contact with the runway. *(Refer to AIM).*

LOW FREQUENCY. The frequency band between 30 and 300 kHz. *(Refer to AIM).*

MAA. (See MAXIMUM AUTHORIZED ALTITUDE).

MACH NUMBER. The ratio of true airspeed to the speed of sound; e.g., MACH 82, MACH 1.6. *(See AIRSPEED).*

MACH TECHNIQUE [ICAO]. Describes a control technique used by air traffic control whereby turbojet aircraft operating successively along suitable routes are cleared to maintain appropriate MACH numbers for a relevant portion of the en route phase of flight. The principle objective is to achieve improved utilization of the airspace and to ensure that separation between successive aircraft does not decrease below the established minima.

MAINTAIN.

1. Concerning altitude/flight level, the term means to remain at the altitude/flight level specified. The phrase "climb and" or "descend and" normally precedes "maintain" and the altitude assignment; e.g., "descend and maintain 5,000."

2. Concerning other ATC instructions, the term is used in its literal sense; e.g., maintain VFR.

MAKE SHORT APPROACH. Used by ATC to inform a pilot to alter his traffic pattern so as to make a short final approach. *(See TRAFFIC PATTERN).*

MANDATORY ALTITUDE. An altitude depicted on an instrument Approach Procedure Chart requiring the aircraft to maintain altitude at the depicted value.

MAP. (See MISSED APPROACH POINT).

MARKER BEACON. An electronic navigation facility transmitting a 75 mHz vertical fan or boneshaped radiation pattern. Marker beacons are identified by their modulation frequency and keying code, and when received by compatible airborne equipment, indicate to the pilot, both aurally and visually, that he is passing over the facility.

(See OUTER MARKER). (See MIDDLE MARKER). (See INNER MARKER). (Refer to AIM).

MARSA. (See MILITARY AUTHORITY ASSUMES RESPONSIBILITY FOR SEPARATION OF AIRCRAFT).

MAXIMUM AUTHORIZED ALTITUDE. A published altitude representing the maximum usable altitude or flight level for an airspace structure or route segment. It is the highest altitude on a Federal airway, jet route, area navigation low or high route, or other direct route for which an MEA is designated in FAR Part 95 at which adequate reception of navigation aid signals is assured.

MAYDAY. The international radiotelephony distress signal. When repeated three times, it indicates imminent and grave danger and that immediate assistance is requested. *(See PAN-PAN). (Refer to AIM).*

MCA. (See MINIMUM CROSSING ALTITUDE).

MDA. (See MINIMUM DESCENT ALTITUDE).

MEA. (See MINIMUM EN ROUTE IFR ALTITUDE).

METEOROLOGICAL IMPACT STATEMENT. An unscheduled planning forecast describing conditions expected to begin within 4 to 12 hours which may impact the flow of air traffic in a specific center's (ARTCC) area.

METER FIX TIME/SLOT TIME. A calculated time to depart the meter fix in order to cross the vertex at the ACLT. This time reflects descent speed adjustment and any applicable time that must be absorbed prior to crossing the meter fix.

METER LIST DISPLAY INTERVAL. A dynamic parameter which controls the number of minutes prior to the flight plan calculated time of arrival at the meter fix for each aircraft, at which time the TCLT is frozen and becomes an ACLT; i.e., the VTA is updated and consequently the TCLT modified as appropriate until frozen at which time updating is suspended and an ACLT is assigned. When frozen, the flight entry is inserted into the arrival sector's meter list for display on the sector PVD. MLDI is used if filed true airspeed is less than or equal to freeze speed parameters (FSPD).

METERING. A method of time-regulating arrival traffic flow into a terminal area so as not to exceed a predetermined terminal acceptance rate.

METERING AIRPORTS. Airports adapted for metering and for which optimum flight paths are defined. A maximum of 15 airports may be adapted.

METERING FIX. A fix along an established route from over which aircraft will be metered prior to entering terminal airspace. Normally, this fix should be established at a distance from the airport which will facilitate a profile descent 10,000 feet above airport elevation [AAE] or above.

METERING POSITION(S). Adapted PVD's and associated "D" positions eligible for display of a metering position list. A maximum of four PVD's may be adapted.

METERING POSITION LIST. An ordered list of data on arrivals for a selected metering airport displayed on a metering position PVD.

MFT. (See METER FIX TIME/SLOT TIME).

MHA. (See MINIMUM HOLDING ALTITUDE).

MIA. (See MINIMUM IFR ALTITUDES).

MICROBURST. A small downburst with outbursts of damaging winds extending 2.5 miles or less. In spite of its small horizontal scale, an intense microburst could induce wind speeds as high as 150 knots. (Refer to AIM).

MICROWAVE LANDING SYSTEM. A precision instrument approach system operating in the microwave spectrum which normally consists of the following components:

1. Azimuth Station.
2. Elevation Station.
3. Precision Distance Measuring Equipment.
(See MLS CATEGORIES).

MIDDLE COMPASS LOCATOR. (See COMPASS LOCATOR).

MIDDLE MARKER. A marker beacon that defines a point along the glideslope of an ILS normally located at or near the point of decision height (ILS Category I). It is keyed to transmit alternate dots and dashes, with the alternate dots and dashes keyed at the rate of 95 dot/dash

combinations per minute on a 1300 Hz tone, which is received aurally and visually by compatible airborne equipment. (See MARKER BEACON). (See INSTRUMENT LANDING SYSTEM). (Refer to AIM).

MID RVR. (See VISIBILITY).

MILES-IN-TRAIL. A specified distance between aircraft, normally, in the same stratum associated with the same destination or route of flight.

MILITARY AUTHORITY ASSUMES RESPONSIBILITY FOR SEPARATION OF AIRCRAFT. A condition whereby the military services involved assume responsibility for separation between participating military aircraft in the ATC system. It is used only for required IFR operations which are specified in letters of agreement or other appropriate FAA or military documents.

MILITARY OPERATIONS AREA. (See SPECIAL USE AIRSPACE).

MILITARY TRAINING ROUTES. Airspace of defined vertical and lateral dimensions established for the conduct of military flight training at airspeeds in excess of 250 knots IAS. (See IFR MILITARY TRAINING ROUTES). (See VFR MILITARY TRAINING ROUTES).

MINIMA. (See MINIMUMS).

MINIMUM CROSSING ALTITUDE. The lowest altitude at certain fixes at which an aircraft must cross when proceeding in the direction of a higher minimum en route IFR altitude (MEA). (See MINIMUM EN ROUTE IFR ALTITUDE).

MINIMUM DESCENT ALTITUDE. The lowest altitude, expressed in feet above mean sea level, to which descent is authorized on final approach or during circle-to-land maneuvering in execution of a standard instrument approach procedure where no electronic glideslope is provided. (See NONPRECISION APPROACH PROCEDURE).

MINIMUM EN ROUTE IFR ALTITUDE. The lowest published altitude between radio fixes which assures acceptable navigational signal coverage and meets obstacle clearance requirements between those fixes. The MEA prescribed for a Federal airway or segment thereof, area navigation low or high route, or other direct route applies to the entire width of the airway, segment, or route between the radio fixes defining the airway, segment, or route. (Refer to FAR Part 91). (Refer to FAR Part 95). (Refer to AIM).

MINIMUM FUEL. Indicates that an aircraft's fuel supply has reached a state where, upon reaching the destination, it can accept little or no delay. This is not an emergency situation but merely indicates an emergency situation is possible should any undue delay occur. (Refer to AIM).

MINIMUM HOLDING ALTITUDE. The lowest altitude prescribed for a holding pattern which assures navigational signal coverage, communications, and meets obstacle clearance requirements.

MINIMUM IFR ALTITUDES. Minimum altitudes for IFR operations as prescribed in FAR Part 91. These altitudes are published on aeronautical charts and prescribed in FAR Part 95 for airways and routes, and in Part 97 for standard instrument approach procedures. If no applicable minimum altitude is prescribed in FAR 95 or FAR 97, the following minimum IFR altitude applies:

1. In designated mountainous areas, 2,000 feet above the highest obstacle within a horizontal distance of 4 nautical miles from the course to be flown; or

2. Other than mountainous areas, 1,000 feet above the highest obstacle within a horizontal distance of 4 nautical miles from the course to be flown; or

3. As otherwise authorized by the Administrator or assigned by ATC.

(See MINIMUM ENROUTE IFR ALTITUDE). (See MINIMUM OBSTRUCTION CLEARANCE ALTITUDE). (See MINIMUM CROSSING ALTITUDE). (See MINIMUM SAFE ALTITUDE). (See MINIMUM VECTORING ALTITUDE). (Refer to FAR Part 91).

MINIMUM NAVIGATION PERFORMANCE SPECIFICATION. A set of standards which require aircraft to have a minimum navigation performance capability in order to operate in MNPS designated airspace. In addition, aircraft must be certified by their State of Registry for MNPS operation.

MINIMUM NAVIGATION PERFORMANCE SPECIFICATIONS AIRSPACE. Designated airspace in which MNPS procedures are applied between MNPS certified and equipped aircraft. Under certain conditions, non-MNPS aircraft can operate in MNPSA. However, standard oceanic separation minima is provided between the non-MNPS aircraft and other traffic. Currently, the only designated MNPSA is described as follows:

1. Between FL 275 and FL 400;

2. Between latitudes 27- N and the North Pole;

3. In the east, the eastern boundaries of the CTAs Santa Maria Oceanic, Shanwick Oceanic, and Reykjavik;

4. In the west, the western boundaries of CTAs Reykjavik and Gander Oceanic and New York Oceanic excluding the area west of 60- W and south of 3-30'N.

MINIMUM OBSTRUCTION CLEARANCE ALTITUDE. The lowest published altitude in effect between radio fixes on VOR airways, off airway routes, or route segments which meets obstacle clearance requirements for the entire route segment and which assures acceptable navigational signal coverage only within 25 statute (22 nautical) miles of a VOR. *(Refer to FAR Part 91). (Refer to FAR FAR Part 95).*

MINIMUM RECEPTION ALTITUDE. The lowest altitude at which an intersection can be determined. *(Refer to FAR FAR Part 95).*

MINIMUM SAFE ALTITUDE.

1. The minimum altitude specified in FAR Part 91 for various aircraft operations.

2. Altitudes depicted on approach charts which provide at least 1,000 feet of obstacle clearance for emergency use within a specified distance from the navigation facility upon which a procedure is predicated. These altitudes will be identified as Minimum Sector Altitudes or Emergency Safe Altitudes and are established as follows:

a. Minimum Sector Altitudes. Altitudes depicted on approach charts which provide at least 1,000 feet of obstacle clearance within a 25-mile radius of the navigation facility upon which the procedure is predicated. Sectors depicted on approach charts must be at least 90 degrees in scope. These altitudes are for emergency use only and do not necessarily assure acceptable navigational signal coverage. *(See ICAO term Minimum Sector Altitude).*

b. Emergency Safe Altitudes. Altitudes depicted on approach charts which provide at least 1,000 feet of obstacle clearance in nonmountainous areas and 2,000 feet of obstacle clearance in designated mountainous areas within a 10~mile radius of the navigation facility upon which the procedure is predicated and normally used only in military procedures. These altitudes are identified on published procedures as "Emergency Safe Altitudes."

MINIMUM SAFE ALTITUDE WARNING. A function of the ARTS III computer that aids the controller by alerting him when a tracked Mode–C equipped aircraft is below or is predicted by the computer to go below a predetermined minimum safe altitude. *(Refer to AIM).*

MINIMUM SECTOR ALTITUDE [ICAO]. The lowest altitude which may be used under emergency conditions which will provide a minimum clearance of 300 m (1,000 feet) above all obstacles located in an area contained within a sector of a circle of 46 km (25 NM) radius centered on a radio aid to navigation.

MINIMUMS. Weather condition requirements established for a particular operation or type of operation; e.g., IFR takeoff or landing, alternate airport for IFR flight plans, VFR flight, etc. *(See LANDING MINIMUMS). (See IFR TAKEOFF MINIMUMS AND DEPARTURE PROCEDURES). (See VFR CONDITIONS). (See IFR CONDITIONS). (Refer to FAR Part 91). (Refer to AIM).*

MINIMUM VECTORING ALTITUDE. The lowest MSL altitude at which an IFR aircraft will be vectored by a radar controller, except as otherwise authorized for radar approaches, departures, and missed approaches. The altitude meets IFR obstacle clearance criteria. It may be lower than the published MEA along an airway or J-route segment. It may be utilized for radar vectoring only upon the controller's determination that an adequate radar return is being received from the aircraft being controlled. Charts depicting minimum vectoring altitudes are normally available only to the controllers and not to pilots. *(Refer to AIM).*

MINUTES-IN-TRAIL. A specified interval between aircraft expressed in time. This method would more likely be utilized regardless of altitude.

MIS. (See METEOROLOGICAL IMPACT STATEMENT).

MISSED APPROACH.

1. A maneuver conducted by a pilot when an instrument approach cannot be completed to a landing. The route of flight and altitude are shown on instrument approach procedure charts. A pilot executing a missed approach prior to the Missed Approach Point (MAP) must continue along the final approach to the MAP. The pilot may climb immediately to the altitude specified in the missed approach procedure.

2. A term used by the pilot to inform ATC that he is executing the missed approach.

3. At locations where ATC radar service is provided, the pilot should conform to radar vectors when provided by ATC in lieu of the published missed approach procedure.

(See Missed Approach Point) (Refer to AIM).

MISSED APPROACH POINT. A point prescribed in each instrument approach procedure at which a missed approach procedure shall be executed if the required visual reference does not exist. *(See MISSED APPROACH). (See SEGMENTS OF AN INSTRUMENT APPROACH PROCEDURE).*

MISSED APPROACH PROCEDURE [ICAO]. The procedure to be followed if the approach cannot be continued.

MISSED APPROACH SEGMENT. (See SEGMENTS OF AN INSTRUMENT APPROACH PROCEDURE).

MLDI. (See METER LIST DISPLAY INTERVAL).

MLS. (See MICROWAVE LANDING SYSTEM).

MLS CATEGORIES.

1. MLS Category I. An MLS approach procedure which provides for an approach to a height above touchdown of not less than 200 feet and a runway visual range of not less than 1,800 feet.

2. MLS Category II. Undefined until data gathering/analysis completion.

3. MLS Category III. Undefined until data gathering/analysis completion.

MM. (See MIDDLE MARKER).

MNPS. (See MINIMUM PERFORMANCE SPECIFICATION).

MNPSA. (See MINIMUM PERFORMANCE SPECIFICATIONS AIRSPACE).

MOA. (See MILITARY OPERATIONS AREA).

MOCA. (See MINIMUM OBSTRUCTION CLEARANCE ALTITUDE).

MODE. The letter or number assigned to a specific pulse spacing of radio signals transmitted or received by ground interrogator or airborne transponder components of the Air Traffic Control Radar Beacon System (ATCRBS). Mode A (military Mode 3) and Mode C (altitude reporting) are used in air traffic control. *(See TRANSPONDER). (See INTERROGATOR). (See RADAR). (Refer to AIM). (See ICAO term MODE).*

MODE (SSR MODE) [ICAO]. The letter or number assigned to a specific pulse spacing of the interrogation signals transmitted by an interrogator. There are 4 modes, A, B, C and D specified in Annex 10, corresponding to four different interrogation pulse spacings.

MODE C INTRUDER ALERT. A function of certain air traffic control automated systems designed to alert radar controllers to existing or pending situations between a tracked target (known IFR or VFR aircraft) and an untracked target (unknown IFR or VFR aircraft) that requires immediate attention/action. *(See CONFLICT ALERT).*

MONITOR. (When used with communication transfer) listen on a specific frequency and stand by for instructions. Under normal circumstances do not establish communications.

MOVEMENT AREA. The runways, taxiways, and other areas of an airport/heliport which are utilized for taxiing/hover taxiing, air taxiing, takeoff, and landing of aircraft, exclusive of loading ramps and parking areas. At those airports/heliports with a tower, specific approval for entry onto the movement area must be obtained from ATC. *(See ICAO term MOMENT AREA).*

MOVEMENT AREA [ICAO]. That part of an aerodrome to be used for the takeoff landing and taxiing of aircraft, consisting of the manoeuvreing area and the apron(s).

MOVING TARGET INDICATOR. An electronic device which will permit radar scope presentation only from targets which are in motion. A partial remedy for ground clutter.

MRA. (See MINIMUM RECEPTION ALTITUDE).

MSA. (See MINIMUM SAFE ALTITUDE).

MSAW. (See MINIMUM SAFE ALTITUDE WARNING).

MTI. (See MOVING TARGET INDICATOR).

MTR. (See MILITARY TRAINING ROUTES).

MULTICOM. A mobile service not open to public correspondence used to provide communications essential to conduct the activities being performed by or directed from private aircraft.

MULTIPLE RUNWAYS. The utilization of a dedicated arrival runway(s) for departures and a dedicated departure runway(s) for arrivals when feasible to reduce delays and enhance capacity.

MVA. (See MINIMUM VECTORING ALTITUDE).

NAS. (See NATIONAL AIRSPACE SYSTEM).

NAS STAGE A. The en route ATC system's radar, computers and computer programs, controller plan view displays (PVDs/Radar Scopes), input/output devices, and the related communications equipment which are integrated to form the heart of the automated IFR air traffic control system. This equipment performs Flight Data Processing (FDP) and Radar Data Processing (RDP). It interfaces with automated terminal systems and is used in the control of en route IFR aircraft. *(Refer to AIM)*.

NATIONAL AIRSPACE SYSTEM. The common network of U.S. airspace; air navigation facilities, equipment and services, airports or landing areas; aeronautical charts, information and services; rules, regulations and procedures, technical information, and manpower and material. Included are system components shared jointly with the military.

NATIONAL BEACON CODE ALLOCATION PLAN AIRSPACE. Airspace over United States territory located within the North American continent between Canada and Mexico, including adjacent territorial waters outward to about boundaries of oceanic control areas (CTA)/ Flight Information Regions (FIR). *(See FLIGHT INFORMATION REGION)*.

NATIONAL FLIGHT DATA CENTER. A facility in Washington D.C., established by FAA to operate a central aeronautical information service for the collection, validation, and dissemination of aeronautical data in support of the activities of government, industry, and the aviation community. The information is published in the National Flight Data Digest. *(See NATIONAL FLIGHT DATA DIGEST)*.

NATIONAL FLIGHT DATA DIGEST. A daily (except weekends and Federal holidays) publication of flight information appropriate to aeronautical charts, aeronautical publications, Notices to Airmen, or other media serving the purpose of providing operational flight data essential to safe and efficient aircraft operations.

NATIONAL SEARCH AND RESCUE PLAN. An interagency agreement which provides for the effective utilization of all available facilities in all types of search and rescue missions.

NAVAID. (See NAVIGATIONAL AID).

NAVAID CLASSES. VOR, VORTAC, and TACAN aids are classed according to their operational use. The three classes of NAVAID's are:

    T- Terminal.

    L- Low altitude.

    H- High altitude.

The normal service range for T, L, and H class aids is found in the FAAAIMTOC. Certain operational requirements make it necessary to use some of these aids at greater service ranges than specified. Extended range is made possible through flight inspection determinations. Some aids also have lesser service range due to location, terrain, frequency protection, etc. Restrictions to service range are listed in Airport/Facility Directory.

NAVIGABLE AIRSPACE. Airspace at and above the minimum flight altitudes prescribed in the FARs including airspace needed for safe takeoff and landing. *(Refer to FAR Part 91)*.

NAVIGATIONAL AID. Any visual or electronic device airborne or on the surface which provides point-to-point guidance information or position data to aircraft in flight. *(See AIR NAVIGATION FACILITY)*.

NBCAP AIRSPACE. (See NATIONAL BEACON CODE ALLOCATION PLAN AIRSPACE).

NDB. (See NONDIRECTIONAL BEACON).

NEGATIVE. "No," or "permission not granted," or "that is not correct."

NEGATIVE CONTACT. Used by pilots to inform ATC that:

1. Previously issued traffic is not in sight. It may be followed by the pilot's request for the controller to provide assistance in avoiding the traffic.

2. They were unable to contact ATC on a particular frequency.

NFDC. (See NATIONAL FLIGHT DATA CENTER).

NFDD. (See NATIONAL FLIGHT DATA DIGEST).

NIGHT. The time between the end of evening civil twilight and the beginning of morning civil twilight, as published in the American Air Almanac, converted to local time. *(See ICAO term NIGHT)*.

NIGHT [ICAO]. The hours between the end of evening civil twilight and the beginning of morning civil twilight or such other period between sunset and sunrise as may be specified by the appropriate authority.

Note: Civil twilight ends in the evening when the center of the sun's disk is 6 degrees below the horizon and begins in the morning when the centre of the sun's disk is 6 degrees below the horizon.

NO GYRO APPROACH. A radar approach/vector provided in case of a malfunctioning gyro-compass or directional gyro. Instead of providing the pilot with headings to be flown, the controller observes the radar track and issues control instructions "turn right/left" or "stop turn" as appropriate. *(Refer to AIM)*.

NO GYRO VECTOR. (See NO GYRO APPROACH).

NONAPPROACH CONTROL TOWER. Authorizes aircraft to land or takeoff at the airport controlled by the tower or to transit the Class D airspace. The primary function of a nonapproach control tower is the sequencing

Continued

of aircraft in the traffic pattern and on the landing area. Nonapproach control towers also separate aircraft operating under instrument flight rules clearances from approach controls and centers. They provide ground control services to aircraft, vehicles, personnel, and equipment on the airport movement area.

NONCOMMON ROUTE/PORTION. That segment of a North American Route between the inland navigation facility and a designated North American terminal.

NONCOMPOSITE SEPARATION. Separation in accordance with minima other than the composite separation minimum specified for the area concerned.

NONDIRECTIONAL BEACON. An L/MF or UHF radio beacon transmitting nondirectional signals whereby the pilot of an aircraft equipped with direction finding equipment can determine his bearing to or from the radio beacon and "home" on or track to or from the station. When the radio beacon is installed in conjunction with the Instrument Landing System marker, it is normally called a Compass Locator. *(See COMPASS LOCATOR). (See AUTOMATIC DIRECTION FINDER).*

NONMOVEMENT AREAS. Taxiways and apron (ramp) areas not under the control of air traffic.

NONPRECISION APPROACH. (See NONPRECISION APPROACH PROCEDURE).

NONPRECISION APPROACH PROCEDURE. A standard instrument approach procedure in which no electronic glideslope is provided; e.g., VOR, TACAN, NDB, LOC, ASR, LDA, or SDF approaches.

NONRADAR. Precedes other terms and generally means without the use of radar, such as:

1. Nonradar Approach. Used to describe instrument approaches for which course guidance on final approach is not provided by ground-based precision or surveillance radar. Radar vectors to the final approach course may or may not be provided b) ATC. Examples of nonradar approaches are VOR NDB, TACAN, and ILS/MLS approaches. *(See FINAL APPROACH-IFR). (See FINAL APPROACH COURSE). (See RADAR APPROACH). (See INSTRUMENT APPROACH PROCEDURE).*

2. Nonradar Approach Control. An ATC facility providing approach control service without the use of radar. *(See APPROACH CONTROL FACILITY). (See APPROACH CONTROL SERVICE).*

3. Nonradar Arrival. An aircraft arriving at an airport without radar service or at an airport served by a radar facility and radar contact has not been established or has been terminated due to a lack of radar service to the airport. *(See RADAR ARRIVAL).(See RADAR SERVICE).*

4. Nonradar Route. A flight path or route over which the pilot is performing his own navigation. The pilot may be receiving radar separation, radar monitoring, or other ATC services while on a nonradar route. *(See RADAR ROUTE).*

5. Nonradar Separation. The spacing of aircraft in accordance with established minima without the use of radar; e.g., vertical, lateral, or longitudinal separation. *See RADAR SEPARATION). (See ICAO term NONRADAR SEPARATION).*

NONRADAR SEPARATION [ICAO]. The separation used when aircraft position information is derived from sources other than radar.

NOPAC. (See NORTH PACIFIC).

NORDO. (See LOST COMMUNICATIONS).

NORTH AMERICAN ROUTE. A numerically coded route preplanned over existing airway and route systems to and from specific coastal fixes serving the North Atlantic. North American Routes consist of the following:

1. Common Route/Portion. That segment of a North American Route between the inland navigation facility and the coastal fix.

2. NonCommon Route/Portion. That segment of a North American Route between the inland navigation facility and a designated North American terminal.

3. Inland Navigation Facility. A navigation aid on a North American Route at which the common route and/or the noncommon route begins or ends.

4. Coastal Fix. A navigation aid or intersection where an aircraft transitions between the domestic route structure and the oceanic route structure.

NORTH MARK. A beacon data block sent by the host computer to be displayed by the ARTS on a 360 degree bearing at a locally selected radar azimuth and distance. The North Mark is used to ensure correct range/azimuth orientation during periods of CENRAP.

NORTH PACIFIC. An organized route system between the Alaskan west coast and Japan.

NOTAM. (See NOTICE TO AIRMEN).

NOTICE TO AIRMEN. A notice containing information (not known sufficiently in advance to publicize by other means) concerning the establishment, condition, or change in any component (facility, service, or procedure of, or hazard in the National Airspace System) the timely knowledge of which is essential to personnel concerned with flight operations.

1. NOTAM(D). A NOTAM given (in addition to local dissemination) distant dissemination beyond the area of responsibility of the Flight Service Station. These NOTAMs will be stored and available until canceled.

2. NOTAM(L). A NOTAM given local dissemination by voice and other means, such as telautograph and telephone, to satisfy local user requirements.

3. FDC NOTAM. A NOTAM regulatory in nature, transmitted by USNOF and given system wide dissemination.

(See ICAO Term NOTAM).

NOTAM [ICAO]. A notice containing information concerning the establishment, condition or change in any aeronautical facility, service, procedure or hazard, the timely knowledge of which is essential to personnel concerned with flight operations.

Class I Distribution. Distribution by means of telecommunication.

Class II Distribution. Distribution by means other than telecommunications.

NOTICES TO AIRMEN PUBLICATION. A publication issued every 14 days, designed primarily for the pilot, which contains current NOTAM information considered essential to the safety of flight as well as supplemental data to other aeronautical publications. The contraction NTAP is used in NOTAM text. *(See NOTICE TO AIRMEN).*

NTAP. (See NOTICES TO AIRMEN PUBLICATION).

NUMEROUS TARGETS VICINITY (LOCATION). A traffic advisory issued by ATC to advise pilots that targets on the radar scope are too numerous to issue individually. *(See TRAFFIC ADVISORIES).*

OALT. (See OPERATIONS ACCEPTABLE LEVEL OF TRAFFIC).

OBSTACLE. An existing object, object of natural growth, or terrain at a fixed geographical location or which may be expected at a fixed location within a prescribed area with reference to which vertical clearance is or must be provided during flight operation.

OBSTACLE FREE ZONE. The OFZ is a three dimensional volume of airspace which protects for the transition of aircraft to and from the runway. The OFZ clearing standard precludes taxiing and parked airplanes and object penetrations, except for frangible NAVAID locations that are fixed by function. Additionally, vehicles, equipment, and personnel may be authorized by air traffic control to enter the area using the provisions of Order 7110.65, Air Traffic Control, paragraph 3-5. The runway OFZ and when applicable, the inner-approach OFZ, and the inner-transitional OFZ, comprise the OFZ.

1. Runway OFZ. The runway OFZ is a defined volume of airspace centered above the runway. The runway OFZ is the airspace above a surface whose elevation at any point is the same as the elevation of the nearest point on the runway centerline. The runway OFZ extends 200 feet beyond each end of the runway. The width is as follows:

(a) For runways serving large airplanes, the greater of:

(1) 400 feet, or

(2) 180 feet, plus the wingspan of the most demanding airplane, plus 20 feet per 1,000 feet of airport elevation.

(b) For runways serving only small airplanes:

(1) 300 feet for precision instrument runways.

(2) 250 feet for other runways serving small airplanes with approach speeds of 50 knots, or more.

(3) 120 feet for other runways serving small airplanes with approach speeds of less than 50 knots.

2. Inner-approach OFZ. The inner-approach OFZ is a defined volume of airspace centered on the approach area. The inner-approach OFZ applies only to runways with an approach lighting system. The inner-approach OFZ begins 200 feet from the runway threshold at the same elevation as the runway threshold and extends 200 feet beyond the last light unit in the approach lighting system. The width of the inner-approach OFZ is the same as the runway OFZ and rises at a slope of 50 (horizontal) to 1 (vertical) from the beginning.

3. Inner-transitional OFZ. The inner transitional surface OFZ is a defined volume of airspace along the sides of the runway and inner-approach OFZ and applies only to precision instrument runways. The inner-transitional surface OFZ slopes 3 (horizontal) to 1 (vertical) out from the edges of the runway OFZ and inner-approach OFZ to a height of 150 feet above the established airport elevation.

(Refer to AC 150/5300-13, Chapter 3 and FAA Order 7110.65 paragraph -5).

OBSTRUCTION. Any object/obstacle exceeding the obstruction standards specified by Part 77, Subpart C.

OBSTRUCTION LIGHT. A light or one of a group of lights, usually red or white, frequently mounted on a surface structure or natural terrain to warn pilots of the presence of an obstruction.

OCEANIC AIRSPACE. Airspace over the oceans of the world, considered international airspace, where oceanic separation and procedures per the International Civil Aviation Organization are applied. Responsibility for the provisions of air traffic control service in this airspace is delegated to various countries, based generally upon geographic proximity and the availability of the required resources.

OCEANIC DISPLAY AND PLANNING SYSTEM. An automated digital display system which provides flight data processing, conflict probe, and situation display for oceanic air traffic control.

OCEANIC NAVIGATIONAL ERROR REPORT. A report filed when an aircraft exiting oceanic airspace has been observed by radar to be off course. ONER reporting parameters and procedures are contained in Order 7110.82, Monitoring of Navigational Performance In Oceanic Areas.

OCEANIC PUBLISHED ROUTE. A route established in international airspace and charted or described in flight information publications, such as Route Charts, DOD Enroute Charts, Chart Supplements, NOTAMs, and Track Messages.

OCEANIC TRANSITION ROUTE. An ATS route established for the purpose of transitioning aircraft to/from an organized track system.

ODAPS. (See OCEANIC DISPLAY AND PLANNING SYSTEM).

OFF COURSE. A term used to describe a situation where an aircraft has reported a position fix or is observed on radar at a point not on the ATC-approved route of flight.

OFFSHORE CONTROL AREA. That portion of airspace between the U.S 12-mile limit and the oceanic CTA/FIR boundary within which air traffic control is exercised. These areas are established to permit the application of domestic procedures in the provision of air traffic control services. Offshore control area is generally synonymous with Federal Aviation Regulations, Part 71, Subpart E, "Control Areas and Control Area Extensions."

OFF-ROUTE VECTOR. A vector by ATC which takes an aircraft off a previously assigned route. Altitudes assigned by ATC during such vectors provide required obstacle clearance.

OFFSET PARALLEL RUNWAYS. Staggered runways having centerlines which are parallel.

OFT. (See OUTER FIX TIME).

OM. (See OUTER MARKER).

OMEGA. An RNAV system designed for long-range navigation based upon ground-based electronic navigational aid signals.

ONER. (See OCEANIC NAVIGATIONAL ERROR REPORT).

OPERATIONAL. (See DUE REGARD).

ON COURSE.

1. Used to indicate that an aircraft is established on the route centerline.
2. Used by ATC to advise a pilot making a radar approach that his aircraft is lined up on the final approach course.

(See ON-COURSE INDICATION).

ON-COURSE INDICATION. An indication on an instrument, which provides the pilot a visual means of determining that the aircraft is located on the centerline of a given navigational track, or an indication on a radar scope that an aircraft is on a given track.

OPERATIONAL ACCEPTABLE LEVEL OF TRAFFIC. An air traffic activity level associated with the designed capacity for a sector or airport. The OALT considers dynamic changes in staffing, personnel experience levels, equipment outages, operational configurations, weather, traffic complexity, aircraft performance mixtures, transitioning flights, adjacent airspace, handoff/point-out responsibilities, and other factors that may affect an air traffic operational position or system element.

The OALT is normally considered to be the total number of aircraft that any air traffic functional position can accommodate for a defined period of time under a given set of circumstances.

OPPOSITE DIRECTION AIRCRAFT. Aircraft are operating in opposite directions when:

1. They are following the same track in reciprocal directions; or
2. Their tracks are parallel and the aircraft are flying in reciprocal directions; or
3. Their tracks intersect at an angle of more than 135°.

OPTION APPROACH. An approach requested and conducted by a pilot which will result in either a touch-and-go, missed approach, low approach, stop-and-go, or full stop landing. *(See CLEARED FOR THE OPTION). (Refer to AIM).*

ORGANIZED TRACK SYSTEM. A movable system of oceanic tracks that traverses the North Atlantic between Europe and North America the physical position of which is determined twice daily taking the best advantage of the winds aloft.

ORGANIZED TRACK SYSTEM. A series of ATS routes which are fixed and charted; i.e., CEP, NOPAC, or flexible and described by NOTAM; i.e., NAT TRACK MESSAGE.

OTR. (See OCEANIC TRANSITION ROUTE).

OTS. (See ORGANIZED TRACK SYSTEM).

OUT. The conversation is ended and no response is expected.

OUTER AREA (associated with Class C airspace). Nonregulatory airspace surrounding designated Class C airspace airports wherein ATC provides radar vectoring and sequencing on a full-time basis for all IFR and participating VFR aircraft. The service provided in the outer area is called Class C service which includes: IFR/IFR-standard IFR separation; IFR/VFR-traffic advisories and conflict resolution; and VFR/VFR-traffic advisories and, as appropriate, safety alerts. The normal radius will be 20 nautical miles with some variations based on site-specific requirements. The outer area extends outward from the primary Class C airspace airport and extends from the lower limits of radar/ radio coverage up to the ceiling of the approach control's delegated airspace excluding the Class C charted area and other airspace as appropriate. *(See CONTROLLED AIRSPACE). (See CONFLICT RESOLUTION).*

OUTER COMPASS LOCATOR. (See COMPASS LOCATOR).

OUTER FIX. A general term used within ATC to describe fixes in the terminal area, other than the final approach fix. Aircraft are normally cleared to these fixes by an Air Route Traffic Control Center or an Approach Control Facility. Aircraft are normally cleared from these fixes to the final approach fix or final approach course.

OUTER FIX. An adapted fix along the converted route of flight, prior to the meter fix, for which crossing times are calculated and displayed in the metering position list.

OUTER FIX TIME. A calculated time to depart the outer fix in order to cross the vertex at the ACLT. The time reflects descent speed adjustments and any applicable delay time that must be absorbed prior to crossing the meter fix.

OUTER MARKER. A marker beacon at or near the glideslope intercept altitude of an ILS approach. It is keyed to transmit two dashes per second on a 400 Hz tone, which is received aurally and visually by compatible airborne equipment. The OM is normally located four to seven miles from the runway threshold on the extended centerline of the runway. *(See MARKER BEACON). (See INSTRUMENT LANDING SYSTEM). (Refer to AIM).*

OVER. My transmission is ended; I expect a response.

OVERHEAD MANEUVER. A series of predetermined maneuvers prescribed for aircraft (often in formation) for entry into the visual flight rules (VFR) traffic pattern and to proceed to a landing. An overhead maneuver is not an instrument flight rules (IFR) approach procedure. An aircraft executing an overhead maneuver is considered VFR and the IFR flight plan is canceled when the aircraft reaches the "initial point" on the initial approach portion of the maneuver. The pattern usually specifies the following:

1. The radio contact required of the pilot.
2. The speed to be maintained.
3. An initial approach 3 to 5 miles in length.
4. An elliptical pattern consisting of two 180 degree turns.
5. A break point at which the first 180 degree turn is started.
6. The direction of turns.
7. Altitude (at least 500 feet above the conventional pattern).
8. A "Roll-out" on final approach not less than 1/4 mile from the landing threshold and not less than 300 feet above the ground.

OVERLYING CENTER. The ARTCC facility that is responsible for arrival/departure operations at a specific terminal.

P TIME. (See PROPOSED DEPARTURE TIME).

PAN-PAN. The international radio-telephony urgency signal. When repeated three times, indicates uncertainty or alert followed by the nature of the urgency. *(See MAYDAY). (Refer to AIM).*

PAR. (See PRECISION APPROACH RADAR).

PAR [ICAO]. (See ICAO Term PRECISION APPROACH RADAR).

PARALLEL ILS APPROACHES. Approaches to parallel runways by IFR aircraft which, when established inbound toward the airport on the adjacent final approach courses, are radar-separated by at least 2 miles. *(See FINAL APPROACH COURSE). (See SIMULTANEOUS ILS APPROACHES).*

PARALLEL MLS APPROACHES. (See PARALLEL ILS APPROACHES).

PARALLEL OFFSET ROUTE. A parallel track to the left or right of the designated or established airway/route. Normally associated with Area Navigation (RNAV) operations. *(See AREA NAVIGATION).*

PARALLEL RUNWAYS. Two or more runways at the same airport whose centerlines are parallel. In addition to runway number, parallel runways are designated as L (left) and R (right) or, if three parallel runways exist, L (left), C (center), and R (right).

PATWAS. (See PILOTS AUTOMATIC TELEPHONE WEATHER ANSWERING SERVICE).

PBCT. (See PROPOSED BOUNDARY CROSSING TIME).

PERMANENT ECHO. Radar signals reflected from fixed objects on the earth's surface; e.g., buildings, towers, terrain. Permanent echoes are distinguished from "ground clutter" by being definable locations rather than large areas. Under certain conditions they may be used to check radar alignment.

PHOTO RECONNAISSANCE. Military activity that requires locating individual photo targets and navigating to the targets at a preplanned angle and altitude. The activity normally requires a lateral route width of 16 NM and altitude range of 1,500 feet to 10,000 feet AGL.

PIDP. (See PROGRAMMABLE INDICATOR DATA PROCESSOR).

PILOT BRIEFING. A service provided by the FSS to assist pilots in flight planning. Briefing items may include weather information, NOTAMS, military activities, flow control information, and other items as requested. *(Refer to AIM).*

PILOT-IN-COMMAND. The pilot responsible for the operation and safety of an aircraft during flight time. *(Refer to FAR Part 91).*

PILOTS AUTOMATIC TELEPHONE WEATHER ANSWERING SERVICE. A continuous telephone recording containing current and forecast weather information for pilots. *(See FLIGHT SERVICE STATION). (Refer to AIM).*

PILOT'S DISCRETION. When used in conjunction with altitude assignments, means that ATC has offered the pilot the option of starting climb or descent whenever he wishes and conducting the climb or descent at any rate he wishes. He may temporarily level off at any intermediate altitude. However, once he has vacated an altitude, he may not return to that altitude.

PILOT WEATHER REPORT. A report of meteorological phenomena encountered by aircraft in flight. *(Refer to AIM)*.

PIREP. (See PILOT WEATHER REPORT).

POINT OUT. (See RADAR POINT OUT).

POLAR TRACK STRUCTURE. A system of organized routes between Iceland and Alaska which overlie Canadian MNPS Airspace.

POSITION REPORT. A report over a known location as transmitted by an aircraft to ATC. *(Refer to AIM)*.

POSITION SYMBOL. A computer-generated indication shown on a radar display to indicate the mode of tracking.

POSITIVE CONTROL. The separation of all air traffic within designated airspace by air traffic control.

PRACTICE INSTRUMENT APPROACH. An instrument approach procedure conducted by a VFR or an IFR aircraft for the purpose of pilot training or proficiency demonstrations.

PREARRANGED COORDINATION. A standardized procedure which permits an air traffic controller to enter the airspace assigned to another air traffic controller without verbal coordination. The procedures are defined in a facility directive which ensures standard separation between aircraft.

PRECIPITATION. Any or all forms of water particles (rain, sleet, hail, or snow) that fall from the atmosphere and reach the surface.

PRECISION APPROACH. (See PRECISION APPROACH PROCEDURE).

PRECISION APPROACH PROCEDURE. A standard instrument approach procedure in which an electronic glideslope/glidepath is provided; e.g., ILS/MLS and PAR. *(See INSTRUMENT LANDING SYSTEM)*. *(See MICROWAVE LANDING SYSTEM)*. *(See PRECISION APPROACH RADAR)*.

PRECISION APPROACH RADAR. Radar equipment in some ATC facilities operated by the FAA and/or the military services at joint-use civil/military locations and separate military installations to detect and display azimuth, elevation, and range of aircraft on the final approach course to a runway. This equipment may be used to monitor certain nonradar approaches, but is primarily used to conduct a precision instrument approach (PAR) wherein the controller issues guidance instructions to the pilot based on the aircraft's position in relation to the final approach course (azimuth), the glidepath (elevation), and the distance (range) from the touchdown point on the runway as displayed on the radar scope. *(See GLIDEPATH)*. *(See PAR)*. *(Refer to AIM)*. The abbreviation "PAR" is also used to denote preferential arrival routes in ARTCC computers. *(See PREFERENTIAL ROUTES)*. *(See ICAO term PRECISION APPROACH RADAR)*.

PRECISION APPROACH RADAR [ICAO]. Primary radar equipment used to determine the position of an aircraft during final approach, in terms of lateral and vertical deviations relative to a nominal approach path, and in range relative to touchdown.

Note: Precision approach radars are designed to enable pilots of aircraft to be given guidance by radio communication during the final stages of the approach to land.

PRECISION RUNWAY MONITOR. Provides air traffic controllers with high precision secondary surveillance data for aircraft on final approach to closely spaced parallel runways. High resolution color monitoring displays (FMA) are required to present surveillance track data to controllers along with detailed maps depicting approaches and no transgression zone.

PREFERENTIAL ROUTES. Preferential routes (PDRs, PARs, and PDARs) are adapted in ARTCC computers to accomplish inter/intrafacility controller coordination and to assure that flight data is posted at the proper control positions. Locations having a need for these specific inbound and outbound routes normally publish such routes in local facility bulletins, and their use by pilots minimizes flight plan route amendments. When the workload or traffic situation permits, controllers normally provide radar vectors or assign requested routes to minimize circuitous routing. Preferential routes are usually confined to one ARTCCs area and are referred to by the following names or acronyms:

1. Preferential Departure Route (PDR). A specific departure route from an airport or terminal area to an en route point where there is no further need for flow control. It may be included in a Standard Instrument Departure (SID) or a Preferred IFR Route.

2. Preferential Arrival Route (PAR). A specific arrival route from an appropriate en route point to an airport or terminal area. It may be included in a Standard Terminal Arrival (STAR) or a Preferred IFR Route. The abbreviation "PAR" is used primarily within the ARTCC and should not be confused with the abbreviation for Precision Approach Radar.

3. Preferential Departure and Arrival Route (PDAR). A route between two terminals which are within or immediately adjacent to one ARTCCs area. PDARs are not synonymous with Preferred IFR Routes but may be listed as such as they do accomplish essentially the same purpose.

(See PREFERRED IFR ROUTES). *(See NAS STAGE A)*.

PREFERRED IFR ROUTES. Routes established between busier airports to increase system efficiency and capacity. They normally extend through one or more ARTCC areas and are designed to achieve balanced traffic flows among high density terminals. IFR clearances are issued on the basis of these routes except when severe weather avoidance procedures or other factors dictate otherwise. Preferred IFR Routes are listed in the Airport/Facility Directory. If a flight is planned to or from an area having such routes but the departure or arrival point is not listed in the Airport/Facility Directory, pilots may use that part of a Preferred IFR Route which is appropriate for the departure or arrival point that is listed. Preferred IFR Routes are correlated with SIDs and STARs and may be defined by airways, jet routes, direct routes between NAVAIDs, Waypoints, NAVAID radials/DME, or any combinations thereof. *(See STANDARD INSTRUMENT DEPARTURE). (See STANDARD TERMINAL ARRIVAL). (See PREFERENTIAL ROUTES). (See CENTER'S AREA). (Refer to AIRPORT/FACILITY DIRECTORY). (Refer to NOTICES TO AIRMEN PUBLICATION).*

PREFLIGHT PILOT BRIEFING. (See PILOT BRIEFING).

PREVAILING VISIBILITY. (See VISIBILITY).

PRM. (See PRECISION RUNWAY MONITOR).

PROCEDURE TURN. The maneuver prescribed when it is necessary to reverse direction to establish an aircraft on the intermediate approach segment or final approach course. The outbound course, direction of turn, distance within which the turn must be completed, and minimum altitude are specified in the procedure. However, unless otherwise restricted, the point at which the turn may be commenced and the type and rate of turn are left to the discretion of the pilot. *See ICAO term PROCEDURE TURN).*

PROCEDURE TURN [ICAO]. A maneuver in which a turn is made away from a designated track followed by a turn in the opposite direction to permit the aircraft to intercept and proceed along the reciprocal of the designated track.

Note 1: Procedure turns are designated "left" or "right" according to the direction of the initial turn.

Note 2: Procedure turns may be designated as being made either in level flight or while descending, according to the circumstances of each individual approach procedure.

PROCEDURE TURN INBOUND. That point of a procedure turn maneuver where course reversal has been completed and an aircraft is established inbound on the intermediate approach segment or final approach course. A report of "procedure turn inbound" is normally used by ATC as a position report for separation purposes. *(See FINAL APPROACH COURSE). (See PROCEDURE TURN). (See SEGMENTS OF AN INSTRUMENT APPROACH PROCEDURE).*

PROFILE DESCENT. An uninterrupted descent (except where level flight is required for speed adjustment; e.g., 250 knots at 10,000 feet MSL) from cruising altitude/level to interception of a glideslope or to a minimum altitude specified for the initial or intermediate approach segment of a nonprecision instrument approach. The profile descent normally terminates at the approach gate or where the glideslope or other appropriate minimum altitude is intercepted.

PROGRAMMABLE INDICATOR DATA PROCESSOR. The PIDP is a modification to the AN/TPX-42 interrogator system currently installed in fixed RAPCONs. The PIDP detects, tracks, and predicts secondary radar aircraft targets. These are displayed by means of computer-generated symbols and alphanumeric characters depicting flight identification, aircraft altitude, ground speed, and flight plan data. Although primary radar targets are not tracked, they are displayed coincident with the secondary radar targets as well as with the other symbols and alphanumerics. The system has the capability of interfacing with ARTCCs.

PROGRESS REPORT. (See POSITION REPORT).

PROGRESSIVE TAXI. Precise taxi instructions given to a pilot unfamiliar with the airport or issued in stages as the aircraft proceeds along the taxi route.

PROHIBITED AREA. (See SPECIAL USE AIRSPACE). *(See ICAO term PROHIBITED AREA).*

PROHIBITED AREA [ICAO]. An airspace of defined dimensions, above the land areas or territorial waters of a State, within which the flight of aircraft is prohibited.

PROPOSED BOUNDARY CROSSING TIME. Each center has a PBCT parameter for each internal airport. Proposed internal flight plans are transmitted to the adjacent center if the flight time along the proposed route from the departure airport to the center boundary is less than or equal to the value of PBCT or if airport adaptation specifies transmission regardless of PBCT.

PROPOSED DEPARTURE TIME. The time a scheduled flight will depart the gate (scheduled operators) or the actual runway off time for nonscheduled operators. For EDCT purposes, the ATCSCC adjusts the "P" time for scheduled operators to reflect the runway offtimes.

PROTECTED AIRSPACE. The airspace on either side of an oceanic route/track that is equal to one-half the lateral separation minimum except where reduction of protected airspace has been authorized.

PT. (See PROCEDURE TURN).

PTS. (See POLAR TRACK STRUCTURE).

PUBLISHED ROUTE. A route for which an IFR altitude has been established and published; e.g., Federal Airways, Jet Routes, Area Navigation Routes, Specified Direct Routes.

QUEUING. (See STAGING/QUEUING).

LOW. (See QUOTA FLOW CONTROL).

QNE. The barometric pressure used for the standard altimeter setting (29.92 inches Hg.).

QNH. The barometric pressure as reported by a particular station.

QUADRANT. A quarter part of a circle, centered on a NAVAID, oriented clockwise from magnetic north as follows: NE quadrant 000-089, SE quadrant 090-179, SW quadrant 180-269, NW quadrant 270-359.

QUICK LOOK. A feature of NAS Stage A and ARTS which provides the controller the capability to display full data blocks of tracked aircraft from other control positions.

QUOTA FLOW CONTROL. A flow control procedure by which the Central Flow Control Function (CFCF) restricts traffic to the ARTC Center area having an impacted airport, thereby avoiding sector/area saturation. *(See AIR TRAFFIC CONTROL SYSTEM COMMAND CENTER). (Refer to AIRPORT/FACILITY DIRECTORY).*

RADAR. A device which, by measuring the time interval between transmission and reception of radio pulses and correlating the angular orientation of the radiated antenna beam or beams in azimuth and/or elevation, provides information on range, azimuth, and/or elevation of objects in the path of the transmitted pulses.

1. *Primary Radar.* A radar system in which a minute portion of a radio pulse transmitted from a site is reflected by an object and then received back at that site for processing and display at an air traffic control facility.

2. *Secondary Radar/Radar Beacon (ATCRBS).* A radar system in which the object to be detected is fitted with cooperative equipment in the form of a radio receiver/transmitter (transponder). Radar pulses transmitted from the searching transmitter/receiver (interrogator) site are received in the cooperative equipment and used to trigger a distinctive transmission from the transponder. This reply transmission, rather than a reflected signal, is then received back at the transmitter/receiver site for processing and display at an air traffic control facility. *(See TRANSPONDER). (See INTERROGATOR). (Refer to AIM). (See ICAO term RADAR). (See ICAO term PRIMARY RADAR). (See ICAO term SECONDARY RADAR).*

RADAR (ICAO). A radio detection device which provides information on range, azimuth and/or elevation of objects.

1. Primary Radar. Radar system which uses reflected radio signals.

2. Secondary Radar. Radar system wherein a radio signal transmitted from a radar station initiates the transmission of a radio signal from another station.

RADAR ADVISORY. The provision of advice and information based on radar observations. *(See ADVISORY SERVICE).*

RADAR ALTIMETER. (See RADIO ALTIMETER).

RADAR APPROACH. An instrument approach procedure which utilizes Precision Approach Radar (PAR) or Airport Surveillance Radar (ASR). *(See SURVEILLANCE APPROACH). (See AIRPORT SURVEILLANCE RADAR). (See PRECISION APPROACH RADAR). (See INSTRUMENT APPROACH PROCEDURE). (Refer to AIM). (See ICAO term RADAR APPROACH).*

RADAR APPROACH [ICAO]. An approach, executed by an aircraft, under the direction of a radar controller.

RADAR APPROACH CONTROL FACILITY. A terminal ATC facility that uses radar and nonradar capabilities to provide approach control services to aircraft arriving, departing, or transiting airspace controlled by the facility. *(See APPROACH CONTROL SERVICE).*

Provides radar ATC services to aircraft operating in the vicinity of one or more civil and]or military airports in a terminal area. The facility may provide services of a ground controlled approach (GCA); i.e., ASR and PAR approaches. A radar approach control facility may be operated by FAA, USAF, US Army, USN, USMC, or jointly by FAA and a military service. Specific facility nomenclatures are used for administrative purposes only and are related to the physical location of the facility and the operating service generally as follows:

> Army Radar Approach Control (ARAC) (Army).
>
> Radar Air Traffic Control Facility (RATCF) (Navy/FAA).
>
> Radar Approach Control (RAPCON) (Air Force/FAA).
>
> Terminal Radar Approach Control (TRACON) (FAA).
>
> Tower/Airport Traffic Control Tower (ATCT) (FAA). (Only those towers delegated approach control authority.).

RADAR ARRIVAL. An aircraft arriving at an airport served by a radar facility and in radar contact with the facility. *(See NONRADAR).*

RADAR BEACON. (See RADAR).

RADAR CONTACT.

1. Used by ATC to inform an aircraft that it is identified on the radar display and radar flight following will be provided until radar identification is terminated. Radar service may also be provided within the limits of necessity and capability. When a pilot is informed of "radar contact," he automatically discontinues reporting over compulsory reporting points. *(See RADAR FLIGHT FOLLOWING). (See RADAR CONTACT LOST). (See RADAR SERVICE). (See RADAR SERVICE TERMINATED). (Refer to AIM).*

2. The term used to inform the controller that the aircraft is identified and approval is granted for the aircraft to enter the receiving controllers airspace. *(See ICAO term RADAR CONTACT).*

RADAR CONTACT LOST. Used by ATC to inform a pilot that radar data used to determine the aircraft's position is no longer being received, or is no longer reliable and radar service is no longer being provided. The loss may be attributed to several factors including the aircraft merging with weather or ground clutter, the aircraft operating below radar line of sight coverage, the aircraft entering an area of poor radar return, failure of the aircraft transponder, or failure of the ground radar equipment. (See Clutter) (See Radar Contact). *(See CLUTTER). (See RADAR CONTACT).*

RADAR CLUTTER [ICAO]. The visual indication on a radar display of unwanted signals.

RADAR CONTACT [ICAO]. The situation which exists when the radar blip or radar position symbol of a particular aircraft is seen and identified on a radar display.

RADAR ENVIRONMENT. An area in which radar service may be provided. *(See RADAR CONTACT). (See RADAR SERVICE). (See ADDITIONAL SERVICES). (See TRAFFIC ADVISORIES).*

RADAR FLIGHT FOLLOWING. The observation of the progress of radar identified aircraft, whose primary navigation is being provided by the pilot, wherein the controller retains and correlates the aircraft identity with the appropriate target or target symbol displayed on the radar scope. *(See RADAR CONTACT). (See RADAR SERVICE). (Refer to AIM).*

RADAR IDENTIFICATION. The process of ascertaining that an observed radar target is the radar return from a particular aircraft. *(See RADAR CONTACT). (See RADAR SERVICE). (See ICAO term RADAR IDENTIFICATION).*

RADAR IDENTIFICATION [ICAO]. The process of correlating a particular radar blip or radar position symbol with a specific aircraft.

RADAR IDENTIFIED AIRCRAFT. Ar aircraft, the position of which has been correlated with an observed target or symbol on the radar display. *(See RADAR CONTACT). (See RADAR CONTACT LOST).*

RADAR MONITORING. (See RADAR SERVICE).

RADAR NAVIGATIONAL GUIDANCE. (See RADAR SERVICE).

RADAR POINT OUT. Ar action taken by a controller to transfer the radar identification of an aircraft to another controller if the aircraft will or may enter the airspace or protected airspace of another controller and radio communications will not be transferred.

RADAR REQUIRED. A term displayed on charts and approach plates and included in FDC Notams to alert pilots that segments of either an instrument approach procedure or a route are not navigable because of either the absence or unusability of a NAVAID. The pilot can expect to be provided radar navigational guidance while transiting segments labeled with this term. *(See RADAR ROUTE). (See RADAR SERVICE).*

RADAR ROUTE. A flight path or route over which an aircraft is vectored. Navigational guidance and altitude assignments are provided by ATC. *(See FLIGHT PATH). (See ROUTE).*

RADAR SEPARATION. (See RADAR SERVICE).

RADAR SERVICE. A term which encompasses one or more of the following services based on the use of radar which can be provided by a controller to a pilot of a radar identified aircraft.

1. Radar Monitoring. The radar flight-following of aircraft, whose primary navigation is being performed by the pilot, to observe and note deviations from its authorized flight path, airway, or route. When being applied specifically to radar monitoring of instrument approaches; i.e., with precision approach radar (PAR) or radar monitoring of simultaneous ILS/MLS approaches, it includes advice and instructions whenever an aircraft nears or exceeds the prescribed PAR safety limit or simultaneous ILS/ MLS no transgression zone. *(See ADDITIONAL SERVICES). (See TRAFFIC ADVISORIES).*

2. Radar Navigational Guidance. Vectoring aircraft to provide course guidance.

3. Radar Separation. Radar spacing of aircraft in accordance with established minima. (See ICAO term RADAR SERVICE).

RADAR SERVICE [ICAO]. Term used to indicate a service provided directly by means of radar.

1. *Radar Monitoring.* The use of radar for the purpose of providing aircraft with information and advice relative to significant deviations from nominal flight path.

2. *Radar Separation.* The separation used when aircraft position information is derived from radar sources.

RADAR SERVICE TERMINATED. Used by ATC to inform a pilot that he will no longer be provided any of the services that could be received while in radar contact. Radar service is automatically terminated, and the pilot is not advised in the following cases:

1. An aircraft cancels its IFR flight plan, except within Class B airspace, Class C airspace, a TRSA, or where Basic Radar service is provided.

2. An aircraft conducting an instrument, visual, or contact approach has landed or has been instructed to change to advisory frequency.

3. An arriving VFR aircraft, receiving radar service to a tower-controlled airport within Class B airspace, Class C airspace, a TRSA, or where sequencing service is provided, has landed; or to all other airports, is instructed to change to tower or advisory frequency.

4. An aircraft completes a radar approach.

RADAR SURVEILLANCE. The radar observation of a given geographical area for the purpose of performing some radar function.

RADAR TRAFFIC ADVISORIES. Advisories issued to alert pilots to known or observed radar traffic which may affect the intended route of flight of their aircraft. *(See TRAFFIC ADVISORIES)*.

RADAR TRAFFIC INFORMATION SERVICE. (See TRAFFIC ADVISORIES).

RADAR VECTORING [ICAO]. Provision of navigational guidance to aircraft in the form of specific headings, based on the use of radar.

RADAR WEATHER ECHO INTENSITY LEVELS. Existing radar systems cannot detect turbulence. However, there is a direct correlation between the degree of turbulence and other weather features associated with thunderstorms and the radar weather echo intensity. The National Weather Service has categorized radar weather echo intensity for precipitation into six levels. These levels are sometimes expressed during communications as "VIP LEVEL" 1 through 6 (derived from the component of the radar that produces the information-Video Integrator and Processor). The following list gives the "VIP LEVELS" in relation to the precipitation intensity within a thunderstorm:

Level 1. WEAK
Level 2. MODERATE
Level 3. STRONG
Level 4. VERY STRONG
Level 5. INTENSE
Level 6. EXTREME

(See AC00-45).

RADIAL. A magnetic bearing extending from a VOR/VORTAC/TACAN navigation facility.

RADIO.

1. A device used for communication.
2. Used to refer to a flight service station; e.g., "Seattle Radio" is used to call Seattle FSS.

RADIO ALTIMETER. Aircraft equipment which makes use of the reflection of radio waves from the ground to determine the height of the aircraft above the surface.

RADIO BEACON. (See NONDIRECTIONAL BEACON).

RADIO DETECTION AND RANGING. (See RADAR).

RADIO MAGNETIC INDICATOR. An aircraft navigational instrument coupled with a gyro compass or similar compass that indicates the direction of a selected NAVAID and indicates bearing with respect to the heading of the aircraft.

RAMP. (See APRON).

RANDOM ALTITUDE. An altitude inappropriate for direction of flight and/or not in accordance with paragraph 4–60.

RANDOM ROUTE. Any route not established or charted/published or not otherwise available to all users.

RC. (See ROAD RECONNAISSANCE).

RCAG. (See REMOTE COMMUNICATIONS AIR/GROUND FACILITY).

RCC. (See RESCUE COORDINATION CENTER).

RCO. (See REMOTE COMMUNICATIONS OUTLET).

RCR. (See RUNWAY CONDITION READING).

READ BACK. Repeat my message back to me.

RECEIVING CONTROLLER. A controller/facility receiving control of an aircraft from another controller/facility.

RECEIVING FACILITY. (See RECEIVING CONTROLLER).

REDUCE SPEED TO (SPEED). (See SPEED ADJUSTMENT).

REIL. (See RUNWAY END IDENTIFIER LIGHTS).

RELEASE TIME. A departure time restriction issued to a pilot by ATC (either directly or through an authorized relay) when necessary to separate a departing aircraft from other traffic. *(See ICAO term RELEASE TIME)*.

RELEASE TIME [ICAO]. Time prior to which an aircraft should be given further clearance or prior to which it should not proceed in case of radio failure.

REMOTE COMMUNICATIONS AIR/GROUND FACILITY. An unmanned VHF/UHF transmitter/receiver facility which is used to expand ARTCC air/ground communications coverage and to facilitate direct contact between pilots and controllers. RCAG facilities are sometimes not equipped with emergency frequencies 121.5 mHz and 243.0 mHz. *(Refer to AIM)*.

REMOTE COMMUNICATIONS OUTLET. An unmanned communications facility remotely controlled by air traffic personnel. RCO's serve FSS's. RTR's serve terminal ATC facilities. An RCO or RTR may be UHF or VHF and will extend the communication range of the air traffic facility. There are several classes of RCO's and RTR's. The class is determined by the number of transmitters or receivers. Classes A through G are used primarily for air/ground purposes. RCO and RTR class O facilities are nonprotected outlets subject to undetected and prolonged outages. RCO (O's) and RTR (O's) were established for the express purpose of providing ground-to-ground communications between air traffic control specialists and pilots located at a satellite airport for delivering en route clearances, issuing departure authorizations, and acknowledging instrument flight rules cancellations or departure/landing times. As a secondary function, they may be used for advisory purposes whenever the aircraft is below the coverage of the primary air/ground frequency.

REMOTE TRANSMITTER/RECEIVER. (See REMOTE COMMUNICATIONS OUTLET).

REPORT. Used to instruct pilots to advise ATC of specified information; e.g., "Report passing Hamilton VOR."

REPORTING POINT. A geographical location in relation to which the position of an aircraft is reported. *(See COMPULSORY REPORTING POINTS). (Refer to AIM). (See ICAO term REPORTING POINT).*

REPORTING POINT [ICAO]. A specified geographical location in relation to which the position of an aircraft can be reported.

REQUEST FULL ROUTE CLEARANCE. Used by pilots to request that the entire route of flight be read verbatim in an ATC clearance. Such request should be made to preclude receiving an ATC clearance based on the original filed flight plan when a filed IFR flight plan has been revised by the pilot, company, or operations prior to departure.

RESCUE COORDINATION CENTER search and rescue (SAR) facility equipped and manned to coordinate and control SAR operations in an area designated by the SAR plan. The U.S. Coast Guard and the U.S. Air Force have responsibility for the operation of RCCs. *(See ICAO term RESCUE CO-ORDINATION CENTRE).*

RESCUE CO-ORDINATION CENTRE [ICAO]. A unit responsible for promoting efficient organization of search and rescue service and for coordinating the conduct of search and rescue operations within a search and rescue region.

RESTRICTED AREA. (See SPECIAL USE AIRSPACE). *(See ICAO term RESTRICTED AREA).*

RESTRICTED AREA [ICAO]. An airspace of defined dimensions, above the land areas or territorial waters of a State, within which the flight of aircraft is restricted in accordance with certain specified conditions.

RESUME OWN NAVIGATION. Used by ATC to advise a pilot to resume his own navigational responsibility. It is issued after completion of a radar vector or when radar contact is lost while the aircraft is being radar vectored. *(See RADAR CONTACT LOST). (See RADAR SERVICE TERMINATED).*

RMI. (See RADIO MAGNETIC INDICATOR).

RNAV. (See AREA NAVIGATION).

RNAV [ICAO]. (See ICAO Term AREA NAVIGATION).

RNAV APPROACH. An instrument approach procedure which relies on aircraft area navigation equipment for navigational guidance. *(See INSTRUMENT APPROACH PROCEDURE). (See AREA NAVIGATION).*

ROAD RECONNAISSANCE. Military activity requiring navigation along roads, railroads, and rivers. Reconnaissance route/route segments are seldom along a straight line and normally require a lateral route width of 10 NM to 30 NM and an altitude range of 500 feet to 10,000 feet AGL.

ROGER. I have received all of your last transmission. It should not be used to answer a question requiring a yes or a no answer. *(See AFFIRMATIVE). (See NEGATIVE).*

ROLLOUT RVR. (See VISIBILITY).

ROUTE. A defined path, consisting of one or more courses in a horizontal plane, which aircraft traverse over the surface of the earth. *(See AIRWAY). (See JET ROUTE). (See PUBLISHED ROUTE). (See UNPUBLISHED ROUTE).*

ROUTE SEGMENT. As used in Air Traffic Control, a part of a route that can be defined by two navigational fixes, two NAVAIDs, or a fix and a NAVAID. *(See FIX). (See ROUTE). (See ICAO term ROUTE SEGMENT).*

ROUTE SEGMENT [ICAO]. A portion of a route to be flown, as defined by two consecutive significant points specified in a flight plan.

RSA. (See RUNWAY SAFETY AREA).

RTR. (See REMOTE TRANSMITTER/RECEIVER).

RUNWAY. A defined rectangular area on a land airport prepared for the landing and takeoff run of aircraft along its length. Runways are normally numbered in relation to their magnetic direction rounded off to the nearest 10 degrees; e.g., Runway 01, Runway 25. *(See PARALLEL RUNWAYS). (See ICAO term RUNWAY).*

RUNWAY [ICAO]. A defined rectangular area on a land aerodrome prepared for the landing and takeoff of aircraft.

RUNWAY CENTERLINE LIGHTING. (See AIRPORT LIGHTING).

RUNWAY CONDITION READING. Numerical decelerometer readings relayed by air traffic controllers at USAF and certain civil bases for use by the pilot in determining runway braking action. These readings are routinely relayed only to USAF and Air National Guard Aircraft. *(See BRAKING ACTION).*

RUNWAY END IDENTIFIER LIGHTS. (See AIRPORT LIGHTING).

RUNWAY GRADIENT. The average slope, measured in percent, between two ends or points on a runway. Runway gradient is depicted on Government aerodrome sketches when total runway gradient exceeds 0.3%.

RUNWAY HEADING. The magnetic direction that corresponds with the runway centerline extended, not the painted runway number. When cleared "to fly or maintain runway heading," pilots are expected to fly or maintain the heading that corresponds with the extended centerline of the departure runway. Drift correction shall not be applied; e.g., Runway 4, actual magnetic heading of the runway centerline 044, fly 044.

RUNWAY IN USE/ACTIVE RUNWAY/DUTY RUNWAY. Any runway or runways currently being used for takeoff or landing. When multiple runways are used, they are all considered active runways. In the metering sense, a selectable adapted item which specifies the landing runway configuration or direction of traffic flow. The adapted optimum flight plan from each transition fix to the vertex is determined by the runway configuration for arrival metering processing purposes.

RUNWAY LIGHTS. (See AIRPORT LIGHTING).

RUNWAY MARKINGS. (See AIRPORT MARKING AIDS).

RUNWAY OVERRUN. In military aviation exclusively, a stabilized or paved area beyond the end of a runway, of the same width as the runway plus shoulders, centered on the extended runway centerline.

RUNWAY PROFILE DESCENT. An instrument flight rules (IFR) air traffic control arrival procedure to a runway published for pilot use in graphic and/or textual form and may be associated with a STAR. Runway Profile Descents provide routing and may depict crossing altitudes, speed restrictions, and headings to be flown from the en route structure to the point where the pilot will receive clearance for and execute an instrument approach procedure. A Runway Profile Descent may apply to more than one runway if so stated on the chart. *(Refer to AIM).*

RUNWAY SAFETY AREA. A defined surface surrounding the runway prepared, or suitable, for reducing the risk of damage to airplanes in the event of an undershoot, overshoot, or excursion from the runway. The dimensions of the RSA vary and can be determined by using the criteria contained within Advisory Circular 150/5300-13, Chapter 3. Figure 3-1 in Advisory Circular 150/5300-13 depicts the RSA. The design standards dictate that the RSA shall be:

1. Cleared, graded, and have no potentially hazardous ruts, humps, depressions, or other surface variations;

2. Drained by grading or storm sewers to prevent water accumulation;

3. Capable, under dry conditions, of supporting snow removal equipment, aircraft rescue and firefighting equipment, and the occasional passage of aircraft without causing structural damage to the aircraft; and,

4. Free of objects, except for objects that need to be located in the runway safety area because of their function. These objects shall be constructed on low impact resistant supports (frangible mounted structures) to the lowest practical height with the frangible point no higher than 3 inches above grade.

(Refer to AC 150/5300-13, Chap. 3.).

RUNWAY USE PROGRAM. A noise abatement runway selection plan designed to enhance noise abatement efforts with regard to airport communities for arriving and departing aircraft. These plans are developed into runway use programs and apply to all turbojet aircraft 12,500 pounds or heavier; turbojet aircraft less than 12,500 pounds are included only if the airport proprietor determines that the aircraft creates a noise problem. Runway use programs are coordinated with FAA offices, and safety criteria used in these programs are developed by the Office of Flight Operations. Runway use programs are administered by the Air Traffic Service as "Formal" or "Informal" programs.

1. Formal Runway Use Program. An approved noise abatement program which is defined and acknowledged in a Letter of Understanding between Flight Operations, Air Traffic Service, the airport proprietor, and the users. Once established, participation in the program is mandatory for aircraft operators and pilots as provided for in FAR Part 91.129.

2. Informal Runway Use Program. An approved noise abatement program which does not require a Letter of Understanding, and participation in the program is voluntary for aircraft operators/pilots.

RUNWAY VISIBILITY VALUE. See VISIBILITY).

RUNWAY VISUAL RANGE. (See VISIBILITY).

SAFETY ALERT. A safety alert issued by ATC to aircraft under their control if ATC is aware the aircraft is at an altitude which, in the controller's judgment, places the aircraft in unsafe proximity to terrain, obstructions, or other aircraft. The controller may discontinue the issuance of further alerts if the pilot advises he is taking action to correct the situation or has the other aircraft in sight.

1. Terrain/Obstruction Alert. A safety alert issued by ATC to aircraft under their control if ATC is aware the aircraft is at an altitude which, in the controller's judgment, places the aircraft in unsafe proximity to terrain/obstructions; e.g., "Low Altitude Alert, check your altitude immediately."

2. Aircraft Conflict Alert. A safety alert issued by ATC to aircraft under their control if ATC is aware of an aircraft that is not under their control at an altitude which, in the controller's judgment, places both aircraft in unsafe proximity to each other. With the alert, ATC will offer the pilot an alternate course of action when feasible; e.g., "Traffic Alert, advise you turn right heading zero niner zero or climb to eight thousand immediately."

The issuance of a safety alert is contingent upon the capability of the controller to have an awareness of an unsafe condition. The course of action provided will be predicated on other traffic under ATC control. Once the alert is issued, it is solely the pilots prerogative to determine what course of action, if any, he will take.

SAIL BACK. A maneuver during high wind conditions (usually with power off) where float plane movement is controlled by water rudders/opening and closing cabin doors.

SAME DIRECTION AIRCRAFT. Aircraft are operating in the same direction when:

1. They are following the same track in the same direction; or

2. Their tracks are parallel and the aircraft are flying in the same direction; or

3. Their tracks intersect at an angle of less than 45 degrees.

SAR. (See SEARCH AND RESCUE).

SAY AGAIN. Used to request a repeat of the last transmission. Usually specifies transmission or portion thereof not understood or received; e.g., "Say again all after ABRAM VOR."

SAY ALTITUDE. Used by ATC to ascertain an aircraft's specific altitude/flight level. When the aircraft is climbing or descending, the pilot should state the indicated altitude rounded to the nearest 100 feet.

SAY HEADING. Used by ATC to request an aircraft heading. The pilot should state the actual heading of the aircraft.

SDF. (See SIMPLIFIED DIRECTIONAL FACILITY).

SEA LANE. A designated portion of water outlined by visual surface markers for and intended to be used by aircraft designed to operate on water.

SEARCH AND RESCUE. A service which seeks missing aircraft and assists those found to be in need of assistance. It is a cooperative effort using the facilities and services of available Federal, state and local agencies. The U.S. Coast Guard is responsible for coordination of search and rescue for the Maritime Region, and the U.S. Air Force is responsible for search and rescue for the Inland Region. Information pertinent to search and rescue should be passed through any air traffic facility or be transmitted directly to the Rescue Coordination Center by telephone. *(See FLIGHT SERVICE STATION). (See RESCUE COORDINATION CENTER). (Refer to AIM).*

SEARCH AND RESCUE FACILITY. A facility responsible for maintaining and operating a search and rescue (SAR) service to render aid to persons and property in distress. It is any SAR unit, station, NET, or other operational activity which can be usefully employed during an SAR Mission; e.g., a Civil Air Patrol Wing, or a Coast Guard Station. *(See SEARCH AND RESCUE).*

SECTIONAL AERONAUTICAL CHARTS. (See AERONAUTICAL CHART).

SECTOR LIST DROP INTERVAL. A parameter number of minutes after the meter fix time when arrival aircraft will be deleted from the arrival sector list.

SEE AND AVOID. A visual procedure wherein pilots of aircraft flying in visual meteorological conditions (VMC), regardless of type of flight plan, are charged with the responsibility to observe the presence of other aircraft and to maneuver their aircraft as required to avoid the other

aircraft. Right-of-way rules are contained in FAR Part 91. *(See INSTRUMENT FLIGHT RULES). (See VISUAL FLIGHT RULES). (See VISUAL METEOROLOGICAL CONDITIONS). (See INSTRUMENT METEOROLOGICAL CONDITIONS).*

SEGMENTED CIRCLE. A system of visual indicators designed to provide traffic pattern information at airports without operating control towers. *(Refer to AIM).*

SEGMENTS OF AN INSTRUMENT APPROACH PROCEDURE. An instrument approach procedure may have as many as four separate segments depending on how the approach procedure is structured.

1. Initial Approach. The segment between the initial approach fix and the intermediate fix or the point where the aircraft is established on the intermediate course or final approach course. *(See ICAO term INITIAL APPROACH SEGMENT).*

2. Intermediate Approach. The segment between the intermediate fix or point and the final approach fix. *(See ICAO term INTERMEDIATE APPROACH SEGMENT).*

3. Final Approach. The segment between the final approach fix or point and the runway, airport, or missed approach point. *(See ICAO term FINAL APPROACH SEGMENT).*

4. Missed Approach. The segment between the missed approach point or the point of arrival at decision height and the missed approach fix at the prescribed altitude. *(Refer to FAR Part 97). (See ICAO term MISSED APPROACH PROCEDURE).*

SELECTED GROUND DELAYS. A traffic management procedure whereby selected flights are issued ground delays to better regulate traffic flows over a particular fix or area.

SEPARATION. In air traffic control, the spacing of aircraft to achieve their safe and orderly movement in flight and while landing and taking off. *(See SEPARATION MINIMA). (See ICAO term SEPARATION).*

SEPARATION [ICAO]. Spacing between aircraft, levels or tracks.

SEPARATION MINIMA. The minimum longitudinal, lateral, or vertical distances by which aircraft are spaced through the application of air traffic control procedures. *(See SEPARATION).*

SERVICE. A generic term that designates functions or assistance available from or rendered by air traffic control. For example, Class C service would denote the ATC services provided within a Class C airspace area.

SEVERE WEATHER AVOIDANCE PLAN. An approved plan to minimize the affect of severe weather on traffic flows in impacted terminal and/or ARTCC areas. SWAP is normally implemented to provide the least disruption to the ATC system when flight through portions of airspace is difficult or impossible due to severe weather.

SEVERE WEATHER FORECAST ALERTS. Preliminary messages issued in order to alert users that a Severe Weather Watch Bulletin (WW) is being issued. These messages define areas of possible severe thunderstorms or tornado activity. The messages are unscheduled and issued as required by the National Severe Storm Forecast Center at Kansas City, Missouri. *(See SIGMET). (See CONVECTIVE SIGMET). (See CWA). (See AIRMET).*

SFA. (See SINGLE FREQUENCY APPROACH).

SFO. (See SIMULATED FLAMEOUT).

SHF. (See SUPER HIGH FREQUENCY).

SHORT RANGE CLEARANCE. A clearance issued to a departing IFR flight which authorizes IFR flight to a specific fix short of the destination while air traffic control facilities are coordinating and obtaining the complete clearance.

SHORT TAKEOFF AND LANDING AIRCRAFT. An aircraft which, at some weight within its approved operating weight, is capable of operating from a STOL runway in compliance with the applicable STOL characteristics, airworthiness, operations, noise, and pollution standards. *(See VERTICAL TAKEOFF AND LANDING AIRCRAFT).*

SIAP. (See STANDARD INSTRUMENT APPROACH PROCEDURE).

SIDESTEP MANEUVER. A visual maneuver accomplished by a pilot at the completion of an instrument approach to permit a straight-in landing on a parallel runway not more than 1,200 feet to either side of the runway to which the instrument approach was conducted. *(Refer to AIM).*

SIGMET. A weather advisory issued concerning weather significant to the safety of all aircraft. SIGMET advisories cover severe and extreme turbulence, severe icing, and widespread dust or sandstorms that reduce visibility to less than 3 miles. *(See AWW). (See CONVECTIVE SIGMET). (See CWA). (See AIRMET). (Refer to AIM). (See ICAO term SIGMET INFORMATION).*

SIGMET INFORMATION [ICAO]. Information issued by a meteorological watch office concerning the occurrence or expected occurrence of specified en-route weather phenomena which may affect the safety of aircraft operations.

SIGNIFICANT METEOROLOGICAL INFORMATION. (See SIGMET).

SIGNIFICANT POINT. A point, whether a named intersection, a NAVAID, a fix derived from a NAVAID(s), or geographical coordinate expressed in degrees of latitude and longitude, which is established for the purpose of providing separation, as a reporting point, or to delineate a route of flight.

SIMPLIFIED DIRECTIONAL FACILITY. A NAVAID used for nonprecision instrument approaches. The final approach course is similar to that of an ILS localizer except that the SDF course may be offset from the runway, generally not more than 3 degrees, and the course may be wider than the localizer, resulting in a lower degree of accuracy. *(Refer to AIM).*

SIMULATED FLAMEOUT. A practice approach by a jet aircraft (normally military) at idle thrust to a runway. The approach may start at a relatively high altitude over a runway (high key) and may continue on a relatively high and wide downwind leg with a high rate of descent and a continuous turn to final. It terminates in a landing or low approach. The purpose of this approach is to simulate a flameout. *(See FLAMEOUT).*

SIMULTANEOUS ILS APPROACHES. An approach system permitting simultaneous ILS/MLS approaches to airports having parallel runways separated by at least 4,300 feet between centerlines. Integral parts of a total system are ILS/MLS, radar, communications, ATC procedures, and appropriate airborne equipment. *(See PARALLEL RUNWAYS). (Refer to AIM).*

SIMULTANEOUS MLS APPROACHES. (See SIMULTANEOUS ILS APPROACHES).

SIMULTANEOUS OPERATIONS ON INTERSECTING RUNWAYS. Operations which include simultaneous takeoffs and landings and/or simultaneous landings when a landing aircraft is able and is instructed by the controller to hold short of the intersecting runway or designated hold short point. Pilots are expected to promptly inform the controller if the hold short clearance cannot be accepted. *(See PARALLEL RUNWAYS) (Refer to AIM).*

SINGLE DIRECTION ROUTES. Preferred IFR Routes which are sometimes depicted on high altitude en route charts and which are normally flown in one direction only. *(See PREFERRED IFR ROUTES) (Refer to AIRPORT/FACILITY DIRECTORY).*

SINGLE FREQUENCY APPROACH. A service provided under a letter of agreement to military single-piloted turbojet aircraft which permits use of a single UHF frequency during approach for landing. Pilots will not normally be required to change frequency from the beginning of the approach to touchdown except that pilots conducting an en route descent are required to change frequency when control is transferred from the air route traffic control center to the terminal facility. The abbreviation "SFA" in the DOD FLIP IFR Supplement under "Communications" indicates this service is available at an aerodrome.

SINGLE-PILOTED AIRCRAFT. A military turbojet aircraft possessing one set of flight controls, tandem cockpits, or two sets of flight controls but operated by one pilot is considered single-piloted by ATC when determining the appropriate air traffic service to be applied. *(See SINGLE FREQUENCY APPROACH).*

SLASH. A radar beacon reply displayed as an elongated target.

SLDI. (See SECTOR LIST DROP INTERVAL).

SLOT TIME. (See METER FIX TIME/SLOT TIME).

SLOW TAXI. To taxi a float plane at low power or low RPM.

SN. (See SYSTEM STRATEGIC NAVIGATION).

SPEAK SLOWER. Used in verbal communications as a request to reduce speech rate.

SPECIAL EMERGENCY. A condition of air piracy or other hostile act by a person(s) aboard an aircraft which threatens the safety of the aircraft or its passengers.

SPECIAL INSTRUMENT APPROACH PROCEDURE. (See INSTRUMENT APPROACH PROCEDURE).

SPECIAL USE AIRSPACE. Airspace of defined dimensions identified by an area on the surface of the earth wherein activities must be confined because of their nature and/or wherein limitations may be imposed upon aircraft operations that are not a part of those activities. Types of special use airspace are:

1. Alert Area. Airspace which may contain a high volume of pilot training activities or an unusual type of aerial activity, neither of which is hazardous to aircraft. Alert Areas are depicted on aeronautical charts for the information of nonparticipating pilots. All activities within an Alert Area are conducted in accordance with Federal Aviation Regulations, and pilots of participating aircraft as well as pilots transiting the area are equally responsible for collision avoidance.

2. Controlled Firing Area. Airspace wherein activities are conducted under conditions so controlled as to eliminate hazards to nonparticipating aircraft and to ensure the safety of persons and property on the ground.

3. Military Operations Area (MOA). An MOA is an airspace assignment of defined vertical and lateral dimensions established outside Class A airspace to separate/segregate certain military activities from IFR traffic and to identify for VFR traffic where these activities are conducted. *(Refer to AIM)*.

4. Prohibited Area. Designated airspace within which the flight of aircraft is prohibited. *(Refer to En Route Charts, AIM)*.

5. Restricted Area. Airspace designated under Part 73, within which the flight of aircraft, while not wholly prohibited, is subject to restriction. Most restricted areas are designated joint use and IFR/ VFR operations in the area may be authorized by the controlling ATC facility when it is not being utilized by the using agency. Restricted areas are depicted on en route charts. Where joint use is authorized, the name of the ATC controlling facility is also shown. *(Refer to Part 73)*. *(Refer to AIM)*.

6. Warning Area. Airspace which may contain hazards to nonparticipating aircraft in international airspace.

SPECIAL VFR CONDITIONS. Meteorological conditions that are less than those required for basic VFR flight in Class B, C, D, or E surface areas and in which some aircraft are permitted flight under visual flight rules. *(See SPECIAL VFR OPERATIONS)*. *(Refer to FAR Part 91)*.

SPECIAL VFR FLIGHT [ICAO]. A VFR flight cleared by air traffic control to operate within Class B, C, D, and E surface areas in meteorological conditions below VMC.

SPECIAL VFR OPERATIONS. Aircraft operating in accordance with clearances within Class B, C, D, and E surface areas in weather conditions less than the basic VFR weather minima. Such operations must be requested by the pilot and approved by ATC. *(See SPECIAL VFR CONDITIONS)*. *(See ICAO term SPECIAL VFR FLIGHT)*.

SPEED. (See AIRSPEED). *(See GROUND SPEED)*.

SPEED ADJUSTMENT. An ATC procedure used to request pilots to adjust aircraft speed to a specific value for the purpose of providing desired spacing. Pilots are expected to maintain a speed of plus or minus 10 knots or 0.02 mach number of the specified speed.

Examples of speed adjustments are:

1. "Increase/reduce speed to mach point (number)."
2. "Increase/reduce speed to (speed in knots)" or "Increase/reduce speed (number of knots) knots."

SPEED BRAKES. Moveable aerodynamic devices on aircraft that reduce airspeed during descent and landing.

SPEED SEGMENTS. Portions of the arrival route between the transition point and the vertex along the optimum flight path for which speeds and altitudes are specified. There is one set of arrival speed segments adapted from each transition point to each vertex. Each set may contain up to six segments.

SQUAWK (Mode, Code, Function). Activate specific modes/codes/functions on the aircraft transponder; e.g., "Squawk three/alpha, two one zero five, low." *(See TRANSPONDER)*.

STAGING/QUEUING. The placement, integration, and segregation of departure aircraft in designated movement areas of an airport by departure fix, EDCT, and/or restriction.

STANDARD INSTRUMENT APPROACH PROCEDURE. (See INSTRUMENT APPROACH PROCEDURE).

STANDARD INSTRUMENT DEPARTURE. A preplanned instrument flight rule (IFR) air traffic control departure procedure printed for pilot use in graphic and/or textual form. SIDs provide transition from the terminal to the appropriate en route structure. *(See IFR TAKEOFF MINIMUMS AND DEPARTURE PROCEDURES)*. *(Refer to AIM)*.

STANDARD INSTRUMENT DEPARTURE CHARTS. (See AERONAUTICAL CHART).

STANDARD RATE TURN. A turn of three degrees per second.

STANDARD TERMINAL ARRIVAL. A preplanned instrument flight rule (IFR) air traffic control arrival procedure published for pilot use in graphic and/or textual form. STAR's provide transition from the en route structure to an outer fix or an instrument approach fix/arrival waypoint in the terminal area.

STANDARD TERMINAL ARRIVAL CHARTS. (See AERONAUTICAL CHART).

STAND BY. Means the controller or pilot must pause for a few seconds, usually to attend to other duties of a higher priority. Also means to wait as in "stand by for clearance." The caller should reestablish contact if a delay is lengthy. "Stand by" is not an approval or denial.

STAR. (See STANDARD TERMINAL ARRIVAL).

STATE AIRCRAFT. Aircraft used in military, customs and police service, in the exclusive service of any government, or of any political subdivision, thereof including the government of any state, territory, or possession of the United States or the District of Columbia, but not including any government-owned aircraft engaged in carrying persons or property for commercial purposes.

STATIC RESTRICTIONS. Those restrictions that are usually not subject to change, fixed, in place, and/ or published.

STATIONARY RESERVATIONS. Altitude reservations which encompass activities in a fixed area. Stationary reservations may include activities, such as special tests of weapons systems or equipment, certain U.S. Navy carrier, fleet, and anti-submarine operations, rocket, missile and drone operations, and certain aerial refueling or similar operations.

STEPDOWN FIX. A fix permitting additional descent within a segment of an instrument approach procedure by identifying a point at which a controlling obstacle has been safely overflown.

STEP TAXI. To taxi a float plane at full power or high RPM.

STEP TURN. A maneuver used to put a float plane in a planing configuration prior to entering an active sea lane for takeoff. The STEP TURN maneuver should only be used upon pilot request.

STEREO ROUTE. A routinely used route of flight established by users and ARTCCs identified by a coded name; e.g., ALPHA 2. These routes minimize flight plan handling and communications.

STOL AIRCRAFT. (See SHORT TAKEOFF AND LANDING AIRCRAFT).

STOP ALTITUDE SQUAWK. Used by ATC to inform an aircraft to turn-off the automatic altitude reporting feature of its transponder. It is issued when the verbally reported altitude varies 300 feet or more from the automatic altitude report. *(See ALTITUDE READOUT). (See TRANSPONDER)*.

STOP AND GO. A procedure wherein an aircraft will land, make a complete stop on the runway, and then commence a takeoff from that point. *(See LOW APPROACH). (See OPTION APPROACH)*.

STOP BURST. (See STOP STREAM).

STOP BUZZER. (See STOP STREAM).

STOPOVER FLIGHT PLAN. A flight plan format which permits in a single submission the filing of a sequence of flight plans through interim full-stop destinations to a final destination.

STOP SQUAWK (Mode or Code). Used by ATC to tell the pilot to turn specified functions of the aircraft transponder off. *(See STOP ALTITUDE SQUAWK). (See TRANSPONDER)*.

STOP STREAM. Used by ATC to request a pilot to suspend electronic countermeasure activity. *(See JAMMING)*.

STOPWAY. An area beyond the takeoff runway no less wide than the runway and centered upon the extended centerline of the runway, able to support the airplane during an aborted takeoff, without causing structural damage to the airplane, and designated by the airport authorities for use in decelerating the airplane during an aborted takeoff.

STRAIGHT-IN APPROACH-IFR. An instrument approach wherein final approach is begun without first having executed a procedure turn, not necessarily completed with a straight-in landing or made to straight-in landing minimums. *(See STRAIGHT-IN LANDING). (See LANDING MINIMUMS). (See STRAIGHT-IN APPROACH-VFR)*.

STRAIGHT-IN APPROACH-VFR. Entry into the traffic pattern by interception of the extended runway centerline (final approach course) without executing any other portion of the traffic pattern. *(See TRAFFIC PATTERN)*.

STRAIGHT-IN LANDING. A landing made on a runway aligned within 30' of the final approach course following completion of an instrument approach. *(See STRAIGHT-IN APPROACH-IFR)*.

STRAIGHT-IN LANDING MINIMUMS. (See LANDING MINIMUMS).

STRAIGHT-IN MINIMUMS. (See STRAIGHT-IN LANDING MINIMUMS).

SUBSTITUTIONS. Users are permitted to exchange CTAs. Normally, the airline dispatcher will contact the ATCSCC with this request. The ATCSCC shall forward approved substitutions to the TMU's who will notify the appropriate terminals. Permissible swapping must not change the traffic load for any given hour of an EQF program.

SUBSTITUTE ROUTE. A route assigned to pilots when any part of an airway or route is unusable because of NAVAID status. These routes consist of:

1. Substitute routes which are shown on U.S. Government charts.

2. Routes defined by ATC as specific NAVAID radials or courses.

3. Routes defined by ATC as direct to or between NAVAIDs.

SUNSET AND SUNRISE. The mean solar times of sunset and sunrise as published in the Nautical Almanac, converted to local standard time for the locality concerned. Within Alaska, the end of evening civil twilight and the beginning of morning civil twilight, as defined for each locality.

SUPER HIGH FREQUENCY. The frequency band between 3 and 30 gigahertz (gHz). The elevation and azimuth stations of the microwave landing system operate from 5031 mHz to 5091 mHz in this spectrum.

SUPPLEMENTAL WEATHER SERVICE LOCATION. Airport facilities staffed with contract personnel who take weather observations and provide current local weather to pilots via telephone or radio. (All other services are provided by the parent FSS).

SUPPS. Refers to ICAO Document 7030 Regional Supplementary Procedures. SUPPS contain procedures for each ICAO Region which are unique to that Region and are not covered in the worldwide provisions identified in the ICAO Air Navigation Plan. Procedures contained in AIM Chapter 8 are based in part on those published in SUPPS.

SURFACE AREA. The airspace contained by the lateral boundary of the Class B, C, D, or E airspace designated for an airport that begins at the surface and extends upward.

SURPIC. A description of surface vessels In the area of a Search and Rescue incident Including their predicted positions and their characteristics. *(See AIM Paragraph 10-73, In-Flight Contingencies).*

SURVEILLANCE APPROACH. An instrument approach wherein the air traffic controller issues instructions, for pilot compliance, based on aircraft position in relation to the Final approach course (azimuth), and the distance (range) from the end of the runway as displayed on the controller's radar scope. The controller will provide recommended altitudes on final approach if requested by the pilot. *(Refer to AIM).*

SWAP. (See SEVERE WEATHER AVOIDANCE PLAN).

SWSL. (See SUPPLEMENTAL WEATHER SERVICE LOCATION).

SYSTEM STRATEGIC NAVIGATION. Military activity accomplished by navigating along a preplanned route using internal aircraft systems to maintain a desired track. This activity normally requires a lateral route width of 10

NM and altitude range of 1,000 feet to 6,000 feet AGL with some route segments that permit terrain following.

TACAN. (See TACTICAL AIR NAVIGATION).

TACAN-ONLY AIRCRAFT. An aircraft, normally military, possessing TACAN with DME but no VOR navigational system capability. Clearances must specify TACAN or VORTAC fixes and approaches.

TACTICAL AIR NAVIGATION. An ultra-high frequency electronic rho-theta air navigation aid which provides suitably equipped aircraft a continuous indication of bearing and distance to the TACAN station. *(See VORTAC). (Refer to AIM).*

TAILWIND. Any wind more than 90 degrees to the longitudinal axis of the runway. The magnetic direction of the runway shall be used as the basis for determining the longitudinal axis.

TAKEOFF AREA. (See LANDING AREA).

TAKEOFF DISTANCE AVAILABLE [ICAO]. The length of the takeoff run available plus the length of the clearway, if provided.

TAKEOFF RUN AVAILABLE [ICAO]. The length of runway declared available and suitable for the ground run of an aeroplane takeoff.

TARGET. The indication shown on a radar display resulting from a primary radar return or a radar beacon reply. *(See RADAR). (See TARGET SYMBOL). (See ICAO term TARGET).*

TARGET [ICAO]. In radar:

1. Generally, any discrete object which reflects or retransmits energy back to the radar equipment.

2. Specifically, an object of radar search or surveillance.

TARGET RESOLUTION. A process to ensure that correlated radar targets do not touch. Target resolution shall be applied as follows:

1. Between the edges of two primary targets or the edges of the ASR–9 primary target symbol.

2. Between the end of the beacon control slash and the edge of a primary target.

3. Between the ends of two beacon control slashes.. MANDATORY TRAFFIC ADVISORIES AND SAFETY ALERTS SHALL BE ISSUED WHEN THIS PROCEDURE IS USED.

Note: The procedure shall not be provided utilizing mosaic radar systems.

TARGET SYMBOL. A computer-generated indication shown on a radar display resulting from a primary radar return or a radar beacon reply.

TAXI. The movement of an airplane under its own power on the surface of an airport (FAR Part 135.100-Note). Also, it describes the surface movement of helicopters equipped with wheels. *(See AIR TAXI). (See HOVER TAXI). (Refer to AIM). (Refer to FAR Part 135.100).*

TAXI INTO POSITION AND HOLD. Used by ATC to inform a pilot to taxi onto the departure runway in takeoff position and hold. It is not authorization for takeoff. It is used when takeoff clearance cannot immediately be issued because of traffic or other reasons. *(See CLEARED FOR TAKEOFF)*.

TAXI PATTERNS. Patterns established to illustrate the desired flow of ground traffic for the different runways or airport areas available for use.

TCAS. (See TRAFFIC ALERT AND COLLISION AVOIDANCE SYSTEM).

TCH. (See THRESHOLD CROSSING HEIGHT).

TCLT. (See TENTATIVE CALCULATED LANDING TIME).

TDZE. (See TOUCHDOWN ZONE ELEVATION).

TELEPHONE INFORMATION BRIEFING SERVICE. A continuous telephone recording of meteorological and/ or aeronautical information. *(Refer to AIM)*.

TENTATIVE CALCULATED LANDING TIME. A projected time calculated for adapted vertex for each arrival aircraft based upon runway configuration, airport acceptance rate, airport arrival delay period, and other metered arrival aircraft. This time is either the VTA of the aircraft or the TCLT/ACLT of the previous aircraft plus the AAI, whichever is later. This time will be updated in response to an aircraft's progress and its current relationship to other arrivals.

TERMINAL AREA. A general term used to describe airspace in which approach control service or airport traffic control service is provided.

TERMINAL AREA FACILITY. A facility providing air traffic control service for arriving and departing IFR, VFR, Special VFR, and on occasion en route aircraft. *(See APPROACH CONTROL FACILITY)*. *(See TOWER)*.

TERMINAL VFR RADAR SERVICE. A national program instituted to extend the terminal radar services provided instrument flight rules (IFR) aircraft to visual flight rules (VFR) aircraft. The program is divided into four types service referred to as basic radar service, terminal radar service area (TRSA) service, Class B service and Class C service. The type of service provided at a particular location is contained in the Airport] Facility Directory.

1. Basic Radar Service: These services are provided for VFR aircraft by all commissioned terminal radar facilities. Basic radar service includes safety alerts, traffic advisories, limited radar vectoring when requested by the pilot, and sequencing at locations where procedures have been established for this purpose and/or when covered by a letter of agreement. The purpose of this service is to adjust the flow of arriving IFR and VFR aircraft into the traffIc pattern in a safe and orderly manner and to provide traffic advisories to departing VFR aircraft.

2. TRSA Service: This service provides, in addition to basic radar service, sequencing of all IFR and participating VFR aircraft to the primary airport and separation between all participating VFR aircraft. The purpose of this service is to provide separation between all participating VFR aircraft and all IFR aircraft operating within the area defined as a TRSA.

3. Class C Service: This service provides, in addition to basic radar service, approved separation between IFR and VFR aircraft, and sequencing of VFR aircraft, and sequencing of VFR arrivals to the primary airport.

4. Class B Service: This service provides, in addition to basic radar service, approved separation of aircraft based on IFR, VFR, and/or weight, and sequencing of VFR arrivals to the primary airport(s).

(See CONTROLLED AIRSPACE). *(See TERMINAL RADAR SERVICE AREA)*. *(Refer to AIM)*. *(Refer to AIRPORT/FACILITY DIRECTORY)*.

TERMINAL RADAR SERVICE AREA. Airspace surrounding designated airports wherein ATC provides radar vectoring, sequencing, and separation on a full-time basis for all IFR and participating VFR aircraft. Service provided in a TRSA is called Stage III Service. The AIM contains an explanation of TRSA. TRSAs are depicted on VFR aeronautical charts. Pilot participation is urged but is not mandatory. *(See TERMINAL RADAR PROGRAM)*. *(Refer to AIM)*. *(Refer to AIRPORT/FACILITY DIRECTORY)*.

TERMINAL-VERY HIGH FREQUENCY OMNIDIRECTIONAL RANGE STATION. A very high frequency terminal omnirange station located on or near an airport and used as an approach aid. *(See NAVIGATIONAL AID)*. *(See VOR)*.

TERRAIN FOLLOWING. The flight of a military aircraft maintaining a constant AGL altitude above the terrain or the highest obstruction. The altitude of the aircraft will constantly change with the varying terrain and/ or obstruction.

TETRAHEDRON. A device normally located on uncontrolled airports and used as a landing direction indicator. The small end of a tetrahedron points in the direction of landing. At controlled airports, the tetrahedron, if installed, should be disregarded because tower instructions supersede the indicator. *(See SEGMENTED CIRCLE)*. *(Refer to AIM)*.

TF. (See TERRAIN FOLLOWING).

THAT IS CORRECT. The understanding you have is right.

360 OVERHEAD. (See OVERHEAD APPROACH).

THRESHOLD. The beginning of that portion of the runway usable for landing. *(See AIRPORT LIGHTING)*. *(See DISPLACED THRESHOLD)*.

THRESHOLD CROSSING HEIGHT. The theoretical height above the runway threshold at which the aircraft's glideslope antenna would be if the aircraft maintains the trajectory established by the mean ILS glideslope or MLS glidepath. *(See GLIDESLOPE). (See THRESHOLD).*

THRESHOLD LIGHTS. (See AIRPORT LIGHTING).

TIBS. (See TELEPHONE INFORMATION BRIEFING SERVICE).

TIME GROUP. Four digits representing the hour and minutes from the 24-hour clock. Time groups without time zone indicators are understood to be UTC (Coordinated Universal Time); e.g., "0205." The term "Zulu" is used when ATC procedures require a reference to UTC. A time zone designator is used to indicate local time; e.g., "0205M." The end and the beginning of the day are shown by "2400" and "0000," respectively.

TMPA. (See TRAFFIC MANAGEMENT PROGRAM ALERT).

TMU. (See TRAFFIC MANAGEMENT UNIT).

TODA [ICAO]. (See ICAO Term TAKE-OFF DISTANCE AVAILABLE).

TORA [ICAO]. (See ICAO Term TAKEOFF RUN AVAILABLE).

TORCHING. The burning of fuel at the end of an exhaust pipe or stack of a reciprocating aircraft engine, the result of an excessive richness in the fuel air mixture.

TOTAL ESTIMATED ELAPSED TIME [ICAO]. For IFR flights, the estimated time required from take-off to arrive over that designated point, defined by reference to navigation aids, from which it is intended that an instrument approach procedure will be commenced, or, if no navigation aid is associated with the destination aerodrome, to arrive over the destination aerodrome. For VFR flights, the estimated time required from takeoff to arrive over the destination aerodrome. *(See ESTIMATED ELAPSED TIME).*

TOUCH-AND-GO. An operation by an aircraft that lands and departs on a runway without stopping or exiting the runway.

TOUCH-AND-GO LANDING. (See TOUCH-AND-GO).

TOUCHDOWN.

1. The point at which an aircraft first makes contact with the landing surface.

2. Concerning a precision radar approach (PAR), it is the point where the glide path intercepts the landing surface.

(See ICAO term TOUCHDOWN).

TOUCHDOWN [ICAO]. The point where the nominal glide path intercepts the runway.

Note: Touchdown as defined above is only a datum and is not necessarily the actual point at which the aircraft will touch the runway.

TOUCHDOWN RVR. (See VISIBILITY).

TOUCHDOWN ZONE. The first 3,000 feet of the runway beginning at the threshold. The area is used for determination of Touchdown Zone Elevation in the development of straight-in landing minimums for instrument approaches. *(See ICAO term TOUCHDOWN ZONE).*

TOUCHDOWN ZONE [ICAO]. The portion of a runway, beyond the threshold, where it is intended landing aircraft first contact the runway.

TOUCHDOWN ZONE ELEVATION. The highest elevation in the first 3,000 feet of the landing surface. TDZE is indicated on the instrument approach procedure chart when straight-in landing minimums are authorized. (See TOUCHDOWN ZONE).

TOUCHDOWN ZONE LIGHTING. (See AIRPORT LIGHTING).

TOWER. A terminal facility that uses air/ground communications, visual signaling, and other devices to provide ATC services to aircraft operating in the vicinity of an airport or on the movement area. Authorizes aircraft to land or takeoff at the airport controlled by the tower or to transit the Class D airspace area regardless of flight plan or weather conditions (IFR or VFR). A tower may also provide approach control services (radar or nonradar). *(See AIRPORT TRAFFIC CONTROL SERVICE). (See APPROACH CONTROL FACILITY). (See APPROACH CONTROL SERVICE). (See MOVEMENT AREA). (See TOWER EN ROUTE CONTROL SERVICE). (Refer to AIM). (See ICAO term AERODROME CONTROL TOWER).*

TOWER EN ROUTE CONTROL SERVICE. The control of IFR en route traffic within delegated airspace between two or more adjacent approach control facilities. This service is designed to expedite traffic and reduce control and pilot communication requirements.

TOWER TO TOWER. (See TOWER EN ROUTE CONTROL SERVICE).

TPX–42. A numeric beacon decoder equipment/system. It is designed to be added to terminal radar systems for beacon decoding. It provides rapid target identification, reinforcement of the primary radar target, and altitude information from Mode C. *(See AUTOMATED RADAR TERMINAL SYSTEMS). (See TRANSPONDER).*

TRACK. The actual flight path of an aircraft over the surface of the earth. *(See COURSE). (See ROUTE). (See FLIGHT PATH). (See ICAO term TRACK).*

TRACK [ICAO]. The projection on the earth's surface of the path of an aircraft, the direction of which path at any point is usually expressed in degrees from North (True, Magnetic, or Grid).

TRAFFIC.

1. A term used by a controller to transfer radar identification of an aircraft to another controller for the purpose of coordinating separation action. Traffic is normally issued: (a) in response to a handoff or point out, (b) in anticipation of a handoff or point out, or (c) in conjunction with a request for control of an aircraft.

2. A term used by ATC to refer to one or more aircraft.

TRAFFIC ADVISORIES. Advisories issued to alert pilots to other known or observed air traffic which may be in such proximity to the position or intended route of flight of their aircraft to warrant their attention. Such advisories may be based on:

1. Visual observation.
2. Observation of radar identified and nonidentified aircraft targets on an ATC radar display, or
3. Verbal reports from pilots or other facilities.

The word "traffic" followed by additional information, if known, is used to provide such advisories; e.g., "Traffic, 2 o'clock, one zero miles, southbound, eight thousand."

Traffic advisory service will be provided to the -tent possible depending on higher priority duties of the controller or other limitations; e.g., radar limitations, volume of traffic, frequency congestion, or controller workload. Radar/nonradar traffic advisories do not relieve the pilot of his responsibility to see and avoid other aircraft. Pilots are cautioned that there are many times when the controller is not able to give traffic advisories concerning all traffic in the aircraft's proximity; in other words, when a pilot requests or is receiving traffic advisories, he should not assume that all traffic will be issued. (Refer to AIM).

(Identification), TRAFFIC ALERT. ADVISE YOU TURN LEFT/RIGHT (specific heading if appropriate), AND/OR CLIMB/DESCEND (specific altitude if appropriate) IMMEDIATELY.(See SAFETY ALERT).

TRAFFIC ALERT AND COLLISION AVOIDANCE SYSTEM. An airborne collision avoidance system based on radar beacon signals which operates independent of ground-based equipment. TCAS-I generates traffic advisories only. TCAS-II generates traffic advisories, and resolution (collision avoidance) advisories in the vertical plane.

TRAFFIC INFORMATION. (See TRAFFIC ADVISORIES).

TRAFFIC IN SIGHT. Used by pilots to inform a controller that previously issued traffic is in sight. *(See NEGATIVE CONTACT). (See TRAFFIC ADVISORIES).*

TRAFFIC MANAGEMENT PROGRAM ALERT. A term used in a Notice to Airmen (NOTAM) issued in conjunction with a special traffic management program to alert pilots to the existence of the program and to refer them to either the Notices to Airmen publication or a special traffic management program advisory message for program details. The contraction TMPA is used in NOTAM text.

TRAFFIC MANAGEMENT UNIT. The entity in ARTCCs and designated terminals responsible for direct involvement in the active management of facility traffic. Usually under the direct supervision of an assistant manager for traffic management.

TRAFFIC NO FACTOR. Indicates that the traffic described in a previously issued traffic advisory is no factor.

TRAFFIC NO LONGER OBSERVED. Indicates that the traffic described in a previously issued traffic advisory is no longer depicted on radar, but may still be a factor.

TRAFFIC PATTERN. The traffic flow that is prescribed for aircraft landing at, taxiing on, or taking off from an airport. The components of a typical traffic pattern are upwind leg, crosswind leg, downwind leg, base leg, and final approach.

1. Upwind Leg. A flight path parallel to the landing runway in the direction of landing.
2. Crosswind Leg. A flight path at right. angles to the landing runway off its upwind end.
3. Downwind Leg. A flight path parallel to the landing runway in the direction opposite to landing. The downwind leg normally extends between the crosswind leg and the base leg.
4. Base Leg. A flight path at right angles to the landing runway off its approach end. The base leg normally extends from the downwind leg to the intersection of the extended runway centerline.
5. Final Approach. A flight path in the direction of landing along the extended runway centerline. The final approach normally extends from the base leg to the runway. An aircraft making a straight-in approach VFR is also considered to be on final approach.

(See STRAIGHT-IN APPROACH-VFR). (See TAXI PATTERNS). (Refer to AIM). (Refer to FAR Part 91). (See ICAO term AERODROME TRAFFIC CIRCUIT).

TRANSCRIBED WEATHER BROADCAST. A continuous recording of meteorological and aeronautical information that is broadcast on L/MF and VOR facilities for pilots. *(Refer to AIM).*

TRANSFER OF CONTROL. That action whereby the responsibility for the separation of an aircraft is transferred from one controller to another. *(See ICAO term TRANSFER OF CONTROL).*

TRANSFER OF CONTROL [ICAO]. Transfer of responsibility for providing air traffic control service.

TRANSFERRING CONTROLLER. A controller/facility transferring control of an aircraft to another controller/facility. *(See ICAO term TRANSFERRING UNIT/CONTROLLER).*

TRANSFERRING FACILITY. (See TRANSFERRING CONTROLLER).

TRANSFERRING UNIT/CONTROLLER [ICAO]. Air traffic control unit/air traffic controller in the process of transferring the responsibility for providing air traffic control service to an aircraft to the next air traffic control unit/air traffic controller along the route of flight.

Note: See definition of accepting unit/controller.

TRANSITION.

1. The general term that describes the change from one phase of flight or flight condition to another; e.g., transition from en route flight to the approach or transition from instrument flight to visual flight.

2. A published procedure (SID Transition) used to connect the basic SID to one of several en route airways/jet routes, or a published procedure (STAR Transition) used to connect one of several en route airways/jet routes to the basic STAR.

(Refer to SID/STAR Charts).

TRANSITIONAL AIRSPACE. That portion of controlled airspace wherein aircraft change from one phase of flight or flight condition to another.

TRANSITION POINT. A point at an adapted number of miles from the vertex at which an arrival aircraft would normally commence descent from its en route altitude. This is the first fix adapted on the arrival speed segments.

TRANSMISSOMETER. An apparatus used to determine visibility by measuring the transmission of light through the atmosphere. It is the measurement source for determining runway visual range (RVR) and runway visibility value (RVV). *(See VISIBILITY).*

TRANSMITTING IN THE BLIND. A transmission from one station to other stations in circumstances where two-way communication cannot be established, but where it is believed that the called stations may be able to receive the transmission.

TRANSPONDER. The airborne radar beacon receiver] transmitter portion of the Air Traffic Control Radar Beacon System (ATCRBS) which automatically receives radio signals from interrogators on the ground, and selectively replies with a specific reply pulse or pulse group only to those interrogations being received on the mode to which it is set to respond. *(See INTERROGATOR). (Refer to AIM). (See ICAO term TRANSPONDER).*

TRANSPONDER [ICAO]. A receiver/transmitter which will generate a reply signal upon proper interrogation; the interrogation and reply being on different frequencies.

TRANSPONDER CODES. (See CODES).

TRSA. (See TERMINAL RADAR SERVICE AREA).

TURBOJET AIRCRAFT. A aircraft having a jet engine in which the energy of the jet operates a turbine which in turn operates the air compressor.

TURBOPROP AIRCRAFT. An aircraft having a jet engine in which the energy of the jet operates a turbine which drives the propeller.

TWEB. (See TRANSCRIBED WEATHER BROADCAST).

TVOR. (See TERMINAL-VERY HIGH FREQUENCY OMNIDIRECTIONAL RANGE STATION).

TWO-WAY RADIO COMMUNICATIONS FAILURE. (See LOST COMMUNICATIONS).

UDF. (See DIRECTION FINDER).

UHF. (See ULTRAHIGH FREQUENCY).

ULTRAHIGH FREQUENCY. The frequency band between 900 and 3,000 mHz. The bank of radio frequencies used for military air/ground voice communications. In some instances this may go as low as 225 mHz and still be referred to as UHF.

ULTRALIGHT VEHICLE. An aeronautical vehicle operated for sport or recreational purposes which does not require FAA registration, an airworthiness certificate, nor pilot certification. They are primarily single occupant vehicles, although some two-place vehicles are authorized for training purposes. Operation of an ultralight vehicle in certain airspace requires authorization from ATC. *(See FAR Part 103).*

UNABLE. Indicates inability to comply with a specific instruction, request, or clearance.

UNDER THE HOOD. Indicates that the pilot is using a hood to restrict visibility outside the cockpit while simulating instrument flight. An appropriately rated pilot is required in the other control seat while this operation is being conducted. *(Refer to FAR Part 91).*

UNICOM. A nongovernment communication facility which may provide airport information at certain airports. Locations and frequencies of UNICOMs are shown on aeronautical charts and publications. *(See AIRPORT/FACILITY DIRECTORY). (Refer to AIM).*

UNPUBLISHED ROUTE. A route for which no minimum altitude is published or charted for pilot use. It may include a direct route between NAVAIDS, a radial, a radar vector, or a final approach course beyond the segments of an instrument approach procedure. *(See PUBLISHED ROUTE). (See ROUTE).*

UPWIND LEG. (See TRAFFIC PATTERN).

URGENCY. A condition of being concerned about safety and of requiring timely but not immediate assistance; a potential distress condition. *(See ICAO term URGENCY).*

URGENCY [ICAO]. A condition concerning the safety of an aircraft or other vehicle, or of person on board or in sight, but which does not require immediate assistance.

USAFIB. (See ARMY AVIATION FLIGHT INFORMATION BULLETIN).

UVDF. (See DIRECTION FINDER).

VASI. (See VISUAL APPROACH SLOPE INDICATOR).

VDF. (See DIRECTION FINDER).

VDP. (See VISUAL DESCENT POINT).

VECTOR. A heading issued to an aircraft to provide navigational guidance by radar. *(See ICAO term RADAR VECTORING).*

VERIFY. Request confirmation of information; e.g., "verify assigned altitude."

VERIFY SPECIFIC DIRECTION OF TAKEOFF (OR TURNS AFTER TAKEOFF). Used by ATC to ascertain an aircraft's direction of takeoff and/or direction of turn after takeoff. It is normally used for IFR departures from an airport not having a control tower. When direct communication with the pilot is not possible, the request and information may be relayed through an FSS, dispatcher, or by other means. *(See IFR TAKEOFF MINIMUMS AND DEPARTURE PROCEDURES).*

VERTEX. The last fix adapted on the arrival speed segments. Normally, it will be the outer marker of the runway in use. However, it may be the actual threshold or other suitable common point on the approach path for the particular runway configuration.

VERTEX TIME OF ARRIVAL. A calculated time of aircraft arrival over the adapted vertex for the runway configuration in use. The time is calculated via the optimum flight path using adapted speed segments.

VERTICAL SEPARATION. Separation established by assignment of different altitudes or flight levels. *(See SEPARATION). (See ICAO term VERTICAL SEPARATION).*

VERTICAL SEPARATION [ICAO]. Separation between aircraft expressed in units of vertical distance.

VERTICAL TAKEOFF AND LANDING AIRCRAFT. Aircraft capable of vertical climbs and/or descents and of using very short runways or small areas for takeoff and landings. These aircraft include, but are not limited to, helicopters. *(See SHORT TAKEOFF AND LANDING AIRCRAFT).*

VERY HIGH FREQUENCY. The frequency band between 30 and 300 mHz. Portions of this band, 10 to 118 mHz, are used for certain NAVAIDS; 118 t 136 mHz are used for civil air/ground voice communications. Other frequencies in this band are used for purposes not related to air traffic control.

VERY HIGH FREQUENCY OMNIDIRECTIONAL RANGE STATION. (See VOR).

VERY LOW FREQUENCY. The frequency band between 3 and 30 kHz.

VFR. (See VISUAL FLIGHT RULES).

VFR AIRCRAFT. Are aircraft conducting flight in accordance with visual flight rules. *(See VISUAL FLIGHT RULES).*

VFR CONDITIONS. Weather conditions equal to or better than the minimum for flight under visual flight rules. The term may be used as an ATC clearance] instruction only when:

1. An IFR aircraft requests a climb/descent in **VFR** conditions.

2. The clearance will result in noise abatement benefits where part of the IFR departure route does not conform to an FAA approved noise abatement route or altitude.

3. A pilot has requested a practice instrument approach and is not on an IFR flight plan. All pilots receiving this authorization must comply with the VFR visibility and distance from cloud criteria in FAR Part 91. Use of the term does not relieve controllers of their responsibility to separate aircraft in Class B and Class C airspace or TRSAs as required by FAA Order 7110.65. When used as an ATC clearance] instruction, the term may be abbreviated "VFR;" e.g., "MAINTAIN VFR," "CLIMB/DESCEND VFR," etc.

VFR FLIGHT. (See VFR AIRCRAFT).

VFR MILITARY TRAINING ROUTES. Routes used by the Department of Defense and associated Reserve and Air Guard units for the purpose of conducting low-altitude navigation and tactical training under VFR below 10,000 feet MSL at airspeeds in excess of 250 knots IAS.

VFR NOT RECOMMENDED. An advisory provided by a flight service station to a pilot during a preflight or inflight weather briefing that flight under visual flight rules is not recommended. To be given when the current and/or forecast weather conditions are at or below VFR minimums. It does not abrogate the pilot's authority to make his own decision.

VFR-ON-TOP. ATC authorization for an IFR aircraft to operate in VFR conditions at any appropriate VFR altitude (as specified in FAR and as restricted by ATC). A pilot receiving this authorization must comply with the VFR visibility, distance from cloud criteria, and the minimum IFR altitudes specified in FAR Part 91. The use of this term does not relieve controllers of their responsibility to separate aircraft in Class B and Class C airspace or TRSA's as required by FAA Order 7110.65.

VFR TERMINAL AREA CHARTS. (See AERONAUTICAL CHART).

VHF. (See VERY HIGH FREQUENCY).

VHF OMNIDIRECTIONAL RANGE/TACTICAL AIR NAVIGATION. (See VORTAC).

VIDEO MAP. An electronically displayed map on the radar display that may depict data such as airports, heliports, runway centerline extensions, hospital emergency landing areas, NAVAIDs and fixes, reporting points, airway/route centerlines, boundaries, handoff points, special use tracks, obstructions, prominent geographic features, map alignment indicators, range accuracy marks, minimum vectoring altitudes.

VISIBILITY. The ability, as determined by atmospheric conditions and expressed in units of distance, to see and identify prominent unlighted objects by day and prominent lighted objects by night. Visibility is reported as statute miles, hundreds of feet or meters. *(Refer to FAR Part 91). (See AIM).*

1. Flight Visibility. The average forward horizontal distance, from the cockpit of an aircraft in flight, at which prominent unlighted objects may be seen and identified by day and prominent lighted objects may be seen and identified by night.

2. Ground Visibility. Prevailing horizontal visibility near the earth's surface as reported by the United States National Weather Service or an accredited observer.

3. Prevailing Visibility. The greatest horizontal visibility equaled or exceeded throughout at least half the horizon circle which need not necessarily be continuous.

4. Runway Visibility Value (RVV). The visibility determined for a particular runway by a transmissometer. A meter provides a continuous indication of the visibility (reported in miles or fractions of miles) for the runway. RVV is used in lieu of prevailing visibility in determining minimums for a particular runway.

5. Runway Visual Range (RVR). An instrumentally derived value, based on standard calibrations, that represents the horizontal distance a pilot will see down the runway from the approach end. It is based on the sighting of either high intensity runway lights or on the visual contrast of other targets whichever yields the greater visual range. RVR, in contrast to prevailing or runway visibility, is based on what a pilot in a moving aircraft should see looking down the runway. RVR is horizontal visual range, not slant visual range. It is based on the measurement of a transmissometer made near the touchdown point of the instrument runway and is reported in hundreds of feet. RVR is used in lieu of RVV and/or prevailing visibility in determining minimums for a particular runway.

   a. Touchdown RVR. The RVR visibility readout values obtained from RVR equipment serving the runway touchdown zone.

   b. Mid-RVR. The RVR readout values obtained from RVR equipment located midfield of the runway.

   c. Rollout RVR. The RVR readout values obtained from RVR equipment located nearest the rollout end of the runway.

(See ICAO term VISIBILITY). (See ICAO term FLIGHT VISIBILITY). (See ICAO term GROUND VISIBILITY). (See ICAO term RUNWAY VISUAL RANGE).

VISIBILITY [ICAO]. The ability, as determined by atmospheric conditions and expressed in units of distance, to see and identify prominent unlighted objects by day and prominent lighted objects by night.

1. *Flight Visibility.* The visibility forward from the cockpit of an aircraft in flight.

2. *Ground Visibility.* The visibility at an aerodrome as reported by an accredited observer.

3. *Runway Visual Range [RVR].* The range over which the pilot of an aircraft on the centre line of a runway can see the runway surface markings or the lights delineating the runway or identifying its centre line.

VISUAL APPROACH. An approach wherein an aircraft on an IFR flight plan, operating in VFR conditions under the control of an air traffic control facility and having an air traffic control authorization, may proceed to the airport of destination in VFR conditions. *(See ICAO term VISUAL APPROACH).*

VISUAL APPROACH [ICAO]. An approach by an IFR flight when either part or all of an instrument approach procedure is not completed and the approach is executed in visual reference to terrain.

VISUAL APPROACH SLOPE INDICATOR. (See AIRPORT LIGHTING).

VISUAL DESCENT POINT. A defined point on the final approach course of a nonprecision straight-in approach procedure from which normal descent from the MDA to the runway touchdown point may be commenced, provided the approach threshold of that runway, or approach lights, or other markings identifiable with the approach end of that runway are clearly visible to the pilot.

VISUAL FLIGHT RULES. Rules that govern the procedures for conducting flight under visual conditions. The term "VFR" is also used in the United States to indicate weather conditions that are equal to or greater than minimum VFR requirements. In addition, it is used by pilots and controllers to indicate type of flight plan. *(See INSTRUMENT FLIGHT RULES). (See INSTRUMENT METEOROLOGICAL CONDITIONS). (See VISUAL METEOROLOGICAL CONDITIONS). (Refer to FAR Part 91). (Refer to AIM).*

VISUAL HOLDING. The holding of aircraft at selected, prominent geographical fixes which can be easily recognized from the air. *(See HOLDING FIX).*

VISUAL METEOROLOGICAL CONDITIONS. Meteorological conditions expressed in terms of visibility, distance from cloud, and ceiling equal to or better than specified minima. *(See INSTRUMENT FLIGHT RULES). (See INSTRUMENT METEOROLOGICAL CONDITIONS). (See VISUAL FLIGHT RULES).*

VISUAL SEPARATION. A means employed by ATC to separate aircraft in terminal areas. There are two ways to effect this separation:

1. The tower controller sees the aircraft involved and issues instructions, as necessary, to ensure that the aircraft avoid each other.

2. A pilot sees the other aircraft involved and upon instructions from the controller provides his own separation by maneuvering his aircraft as necessary to avoid it This may involve following another aircraft or keeping it in sight until it is no longer a factor.

(See and Avoid). (Refer to FAR Part 91).

VLF. (See VERY LOW FREQUENCY).

VMC. (See VISUAL METEOROLOGICAL CONDITIONS).

VOR. A ground-based electronic navigation aid transmitting very high frequency navigation signals, 360 degrees in azimuth, oriented from magnetic north. Used as the basis for navigation in the National Airspace System. The VOR periodically identifies itself by Morse Code and may have an additional voice identification feature. Voice features may be used by ATC or FSS for transmitting instructions/information to pilots. *(See NAVIGATIONAL AID). (Refer to AIM).*

VORTAC. A navigation aid providing VOR azimuth, TACAN azimuth, and TACAN distance measuring equipment (DME) at one site. *(See DISTANCE MEASURING EQUIPMENT). (See NAVIGATIONAL AID). (See TACAN). (See VOR). (Refer to AIM).*

VORTICES. Circular patterns of air created by the movement of an airfoil through the air when generating lift. As an airfoil moves through the atmosphere in sustained flight, an area of area of low pressure is created above it. The air flowing from the high pressure area to the low pressure area around and about the tips of the airfoil tends to roll up into two rapidly rotating vortices, cylindrical in shape. These vortices are the most predominant parts of aircraft wake turbulence and their rotational force is dependent upon the wing loading, gross weight, and speed of the generating aircraft. The vortices from medium to heavy aircraft can be of extremely high velocity and hazardous to smaller aircraft. *(See AIRCRAFT CLASSES). (See WAKE TURBULENCE). (Refer to AIM).*

VOR TEST SIGNAL. (See VOT).

VOT. A ground facility which emits a test signal to check VOR receiver accuracy. Some VOTs are available to the user while airborne, and others are limited to ground use only. *(Refer to FAR Part 91). (See AIM). (See AIRPORT/FACILITY DIRECTORY).*

VR. (See VFR MILITARY TRAINING ROUTES).

VTA. (See VERTEX TIME OF ARRIVAL).

VTOL AIRCRAFT. (See VERTICAL TAKEOFF AND LANDING AIRCRAFT).

WA. (See AIRMET). *(See WEATHER ADVISORY).*

WAKE TURBULENCE. Phenomena resulting from the passage of an aircraft through the atmosphere. The term includes vortices, thrust stream turbulence, jet blast, jet wash, propeller wash, and rotor wash both on the ground and in the air. *(See AIRCRAFT CLASSES). (See JET BLAST). (See VORTICES). (Refer to AIM).*

WARNING AREA. (See SPECIAL USE AIRSPACE).

WAYPOINT. A predetermined geographical position used for route/instrument approach definition, or progress reporting purposes, that is defined relative to a VORTAC station or in terms of latitude/longitude coordinates.

WEATHER ADVISORY. In aviation weather forecast practice, an expression of hazardous weather conditions not predicted in the area forecast, as they affect the operation of air traffic and as prepared by the NWS. *(See SIGMET). (See AIRMET).*

WHEN ABLE. When used in conjunction with ATC instructions, gives the pilot the latitude to delay compliance until a condition or event has been reconciled. Unlike "pilot discretion," when instructions are prefaced "when able," the pilot is expected to seek the first opportunity to comply. Once a maneuver has been initiated, the pilot is expected to continue until the specifications of the instructions have been met. "When able," should not be used when expeditious compliance is required.

WILCO. I have received your message, understand it, and will comply with it.

WIND SHEAR. A change in wind speed and/or wind direction in a short distance resulting in a tearing or shearing effect. It can exist in a horizontal or vertical direction and occasionally in both.

WING TIP VORTICES. (See VORTICES).

WORDS TWICE.

1. As a request: "Communication is difficult. Please say every phrase twice."

2. As information: "Since communications are difficult, every phrase in this message will be spoken twice."

WORLD AERONAUTICAL CHARTS. (See AERONAUTICAL CHART).

WS. (See SIGMET). *(See WEATHER ADVISORY).*

WST. (See CONVECTIVE SIGMET). *(See ETHER ADVISORY).*

Pronounceable acronyms will be in **BOLD** caps; all others are spoken as individual letters (e.g., FAA).

ADF. Automatic direction finder; a receiver with an associated indicator which points to the transmitting station.

AERODYNAMICS. The study of the forces acting on bodies moving through the air.

ADVECTION. Horizontal movement of air.

A/FD. Airport/Facility Directory.

AGL. Above Ground Level.

AGONIC LINE. The line of zero magnetic variation.

AILERONS. Movable control surfaces at the outer trailing edge of each wing. They control the airplane in rolling around the longitudinal axis of the airplane.

AIM. Airman's Information Manual.

3 AIRFOIL. A shape designed to develop lift by accelerating airflow over its surface.

AIRMET. A broadcast of weather hazardous to light aircraft.

AIRPORT ADVISORY AREA. An area within 10 miles of an airport with a Flight Service Station.

AIRPORT FACILITY DIRECTORY (A/FD). A government publication containing information on all airport including radio frequencies and navigational aids available.

AIRSPEED INDICATOR. An instrument which measures the pressure difference between the pitot and static inputs and is calibrated in speed units.

ALTIMETER. An instrument which indicates altitude by measuring changes in atmospheric pressure.

ALTIMETER SETTING. A value received from a ground station to which the altimeter setting window must be adjusted to correct for pressure variations.

AMMETER. A meter which indicates the output of the generator or alternator in amperes, the unit of electric current.

AMPHIBIAN. An airplane able to land and takeoff on both land and water. Airplanes with boat hulls (and retractable wheels) and float planes (with retractable wheels) are amphibians.

ANGLE OF ATTACK. The angle between the chord line and the relative wind; the pilot's best means of controlling lift development.

ANGLE OF INCIDENCE. The fixed angle at which the wing is attached to the fuselage; the angle between the chord line and the longitudinal axis.

ARM. The distance a weight is located from a fulcrum or datum point.

ATA. Actual Time of Arrival: To be filled in on your flight log and compared with your estimates to determine how the actual flight is progressing.

ATC. Air Traffic Control.

ATE. Actual Time Enroute.

ATIS. Automatic Terminal Information Service. A recorded broadcast of non-control information at busy airports.

ATTITUDE. The position of the airplane's nose or wings in relation to the natural horizon.

AXIS OF CONTROL. An imaginary line around which the pilot controls the airplane.

BLEED AIR. Compressed air "bled" from the turbocharger to operate pressurization cabin heating and de-icing systems.

CALIBRATED AIRSPEED. The reading of the airspeed indicator corrected for installation or position error.

CAMBER. The convexity or curvature of an airfoil from its chord.

CARBURETOR. A device which mixes a metered amount of fuel with airflow atomizing it for combustion.

CDI. Course Deviation Indicator; the "needle" on a VOR display that tells you if you are on the desired radial.

CENTER OF GRAVITY. That part of a body (an airplane, in this case) about which all forces are balanced.

CENTER OF LIFT. The single point on the wing where all lifting forces are desolved (concentrated).

CERTIFICATE OF AIRWORTHINESS. A certificate awarded at the time of manufacture which is kept current by compliance with maintenance and inspection requirements.

CHORD LINE. An imaginary line from the leading edge to the trailing edge of an airfoil.

CLASS C AIRSPACE. Airport Radar Service Area: an area where pilots must maintain two-way communication with the controlling agency, and where radar service is available to VFR pilots.

COEFFICIENT OF LIFT. A complex element of the lift formula which includes angle of attack as one component.

COMPRESSOR DISCHARGE TEMPERATURE GAUGE. An instrument which monitors the temperature of the air being discharged from the compressor into the intake manifold of a turbocharged engine.

CONTROLLABLE PITCH PROPELLER. A propeller with two (or more) blades, joined at the hub and capable of having the blade angle changed in flight by a governor to maintain a constant engine speed.

CONTROLLED AIRPORT. An airport with an operating control tower.

CONTROL YOKE. The control the pilot uses to pitch and roll the airplane; older airplanes used a "stick" and this term continues in use today.

CONVECTION. Vertical movement of air.

CORIOLIS FORCE. A force generated by the rotation of the earth that deflects the gradient wind to the right in the Northern Hemisphere.

COURSE. A line connecting two points on a planned flight.

COWLING. The smooth metal or fiberglass enclosure surrounding the engine. The cowling streamlines the engine compartment and directs cooling air over the engine.

CROSSWIND COMPONENT. That portion of the total wind which tends to drift the airplane sideways.

CTAF. Common Traffic Advisory Frequency. A frequency used at uncontrolled airports by all airplanes operating at that airport. Also, a frequency to be used at a controlled airport when the tower is not in operation.

CYLINDER HEAD TEMPERATURE GAUGE. An instrument which monitors the temperature of the cylinder head itself. It is a better guide to general engine overheating than is the oil temperature gauge.

DENSITY. Weight per unit volume. A cubic foot of air that weighs two pounds is more dense than a cubic foot of air that weighs one pound.

DETONATION. The explosive burning of the fuel/air mixture in the cylinder, as opposed to smooth burning. Detonation can result in destructive forces in a matter of seconds.

DEVIATION. A compass error caused by magnetic influences within the airplane which varies with magnetic heading.

DEW POINT. The temperature at which an air mass becomes saturated with moisture.

DISPLACED THRESHOLD. A threshold moved down the runway so that landing aircraft will clear obstructions in the approach path.

DME. Distance Measuring Equipment. DME operates in the UHF range and is limited to line-of-sight. It measures slant range between an airplane and a VORTAC or VOR-DME.

DUPLEX. Transmitting on one frequency while receiving on another.

EFAS. En route Flight Advisory Service (Flight Watch) a weather-only position at a flight service station.

ELEVATOR. A hinged surface at the rear of the horizontal stabilizer with which the pilot controls the airplane around the lateral (pitch) axis.

ELT. Emergency Locator Transmitter: a VHF/UHF transmitter designed to be turned on by impact and to transmit a signal to searchers.

EMPENNAGE. The horizontal stabilizer, elevator rudder, and vertical fin or any combination thereof to control the airplane in pitch and bank.

ETA. Estimated Time of Arrival.

ETE. Estimated Time Enroute.

EXHAUST GAS TEMPERATURE GAUGE. An instrument used for proper leaning of the mixture. If the mixture contains too much fuel or too much air, the exhaust gas temperature will be lower than peak (Use the manufacturer's recommended EGT setting).

FA. An area weather forecast.

FAR. Federal Aviation Regulations.

FD. A wind and temperatures aloft forecast.

FIXED PITCH PROPELLER. A propeller which is forged from one solid piece of metal or laminated from several plies of wood with a fixed pitch or blade angle.

FLAPS. Hinged surfaces at the trailing edge of the wing which are deflected symmetrically to lower the stalling speed and allow for a steeper angle of descent while on a landing approach.

FLIGHT FOLLOWING. A workload-permitting service which ATC radar facilities provide to VFR pilots.

FLIGHT SERVICE STATION (FSS). Air traffic facilities which provide pilot briefing enroute communications, and many other services to pilots.

FLIGHT WATCH. Another name of Enroute Flight Advisory Service, a weather-information-only service of the Flight Service Station.

FRONT. Where two air masses with different properties meet.

FT. A terminal weather forecast.

FUEL INJECTION. An induction system which delivers a metered amount of fuel to each cylinder.

FUSELAGE. The main body of the airplane to which the wings and empennage are attached. Passenger and crew seating is in the fuselage.

G. The force of gravity-one times the weight of an object.

GPO. Government Printing Office.

GPS. Global Positioning System.

GRADIENT WIND, GRADIENT FORCE. The wind (and the force that drives it) caused solely by pressure differences.

GREAT CIRCLE. An imaginary circle on the face of the earth cut by a plane which passes through the center of the earth. All meridians are Great Circles, and the equator is a Great Circle.

GROUND CONTROLLER. An air traffic control specialist in a control tower who controls operations on the ramps and taxiways of a controlled airport.

GROUND EFFECT. A reduction in induced drag experienced when the wing is within one-half the wing span of the ground.

GYROSCOPIC PRECESSION. A slow movement of the axis of a spinning body. Noticeable in gyroscopic heading indicators as a drift away from agreement with the magnetic compass.

HEADING. The direction in which the airplane is pointing. When correcting for wind drift the heading will differ from the course by several degrees.

HEADWIND COMPONENT. That portion of the reported wind which opposes the forward motion of the airplane.

HOMING. Navigating to a non-directional beacon by simply keeping the ADF needle pointed directly to the nose of the airplane.

HORIZONTAL SITUATION INDICATOR (HSI). An instrument which incorporates a heading indicator and an omni-indicator to show the pilot the airplane's position in relation to a VOR radial as seen from a point above the airplane.

HORIZONTAL STABILIZER. An airfoil-shaped surface at the rear of the airplane which develops a negative lift force to balance (stabilize) the airplane's pitch attitude.

INDICATED AIRSPEED. What the airspeed indicator reads, uncorrected for position and installation error. See calibrated airspeed.

INDUCED DRAG. Drag which is the inevitable result of lift generation. Induced drag increases with increased angle of attack and is greatest at the low speeds which require large angles of attack.

INTERNATIONAL STANDARD ATMOSPHERE (ISA). *See* standard day.

INVERSION. When warm air overlies cold air; the reverse of a stable condition.

ISOBARS. Lines of equal barometric pressure on a weather map.

ISOGONIC LINES. Lines of equal magnetic variation.

KHz. Kilohertz (thousands of cycles per second); a measure of radio frequency.

KNOT. One nautical mile per hour. It is redundant to say "90 knots per hour."

KOLLSMAN WINDOW. The altimeter setting window.

LANDING GEAR. The two main wheels and the nose-wheel (or tailwheel).

LOADMETER. An ammeter which is calibrated to indicate the electrical load on the alternator in amperes.

LONGITUDINAL AXIS. An imaginary line from the nose to the tail of the airplane.

LATERAL AXIS. A line drawn from wing tip to wing tip.

LORAN-C. A long-range navigation system using very low frequency transmissions.

MAGNETIC BEARING. The direction to or from a transmitting station measured in relation to magnetic north.

MAGNETIC COMPASS. A direction-indicating device that reacts to the earth's magnetic field.

MAGNETIC NORTH. The direction to the magnetic North pole, located in Northern Canada.

MAGNETO. A self powered source of ignition using fixed magnets.

MANIFOLD. A pipe with several lateral outlets. In an airplane, the intake manifold delivers the fuel/air mixture to the cylinders and the exhaust manifold collects the exhaust from the cylinders and pipes it overboard or through a turbocharger.

MANIFOLD PRESSURE. An indirect measure of power output obtained by measuring the pressure of the air in the intake manifold. The higher the pressure, the greater the power output of the engine.

MAYDAY. The voice equivalent of SOS; used to declare an emergency.

MERIDIANS. Lines of longitude. They run from pole to pole and are all the same length each degree of latitude measured along a line of longitude equals 60 nautical miles.

MHz. Megahertz (millions of cycles per second); a measure of radio frequency.

MODE A. The "location only' mode of a transponder.

MODE C. The "ALT" position on the transponder function switch. If an encoding altimeter is installed, Mode C will transmit your altitude to the ground radar facility.

MOMENT. The product of a distance times a weighs used in loading calculations.

NAUTICAL MILE. One minute of latitude; 6,080 feet (rounded off to 6,000 feet for convenience).

NAVAID. Short for navigational aid.

NDB. Non-Directional Beacon used for navigation with an automatic direction finder.

NORTHERLY TURNING ERROR. An error in the magnetic compass induced by the vertical component of the earth's magnetic field.

NTSB. National Transportation Safety Board.

NWS. National Weather Service, the source of all government weather information.

OBS. Omni-Bearing Selector; Used in VOR navigation to select radials.

OCCLUSION. A type of weather front formed when a cold front overtakes a warm front.

OMNIDIRECTIONAL. Visible or usable in all directions.

OROGRAPHIC. Induced by the presence of mountains.

OVERRUN. A stabilized area of pavement not used for normal operations at the end of a runway.

P-FACTOR. A force which causes a left-turning tendency at low speed and high power in airplanes with propellers which turn clockwise.

PARALLELS. Lines of latitude, which are parallel from the equator to the poles.

PARASITE DRAG. Drag that does not contribute to lift generation; drag caused by landing gear struts, cooling intakes, antennas, rivet heads, etc.

PILOTAGE. navigation from point to point by ground reference.

PIREPs. Pilot reports of inflight weather.

PITCH AXIS. An imaginary line drawn from wing tip to wing tip: also, lateral axis.

PITOT-STATIC SYSTEM. A pressure-measuring system that provides input to the airspeed indicator altimeter, and vertical speed indicator.

PITOT TUBE. A forward facing tube or aperture that measures ram air pressure and delivers that pressure to the airspeed indicator.

POSITION LIGHTS. The red, green, and white lights required for night flight.

RADIAL. A line FROM a VOR station. Radials used as airways are printed in blue on sectional charts.

REGION OF REVERSED COMMAND. That area in the power/airspeed relationship where it takes more power to go more slowly, and less power to increase speed.

RELATIVE BEARING. The direction to a transmitting station measured clockwise from the nose of the airplane.

RELATIVE WIND. Wind caused by motion. A moving body experiences relative wind in calm air.

RICH MIXTURE. One with more than one part of fuel to fifteen of air.

RMI. Radio Magnetic Indicator; a combination heading indicator, VOR indicator and ADF indicator.

RNAV. Area Navigation. A random-route method of navigation using VORTACs and VOR-DMEs.

ROLL AXIS. An imaginary line from nose to tail also, longitudinal axis.

RUDDER. A hinged surface at the rear of the vertical fin with which the pilot controls the airplane around the yaw axis.

SA. An hourly weather sequence report.

SIGMET. A broadcast of weather hazardous to all aircraft.

SIMPLEXING. Communication where one person must complete a transmission before the other person can begin; transmitting and receiving on the same frequency.

STALL. Loss of lift caused by exceeding the critical angle of attack and destroying the smooth flow of air over an airfoil.

STANDARD DAY. Sea level altitude, a temperature of 15'C or 59'F and a barometric pressure of 29.92" Hg (1013.2 mb).

STATIC. At rest or in equilibrium; not dynamic or moving.

STATIC SOURCE. A point on the airplane where no air pressure is exerted as a result of movement through the air; a reference input for the airspeed indicator; the source of air pressure change information for the altimeter and vertical speed indicator.

STATUTE MILE. A 5,280-foot mile.

STRUTS: supports. The main landing gear and nosewheel have struts to absorb the shock of landing. Wing sets are braced to the fuselage to support the wing and help absorb any wing movement in relation to the fuselage when landing or in turbulence. Low wing airplanes and some high wing airplanes have no external bracing.

TACHOMETER. An instrument which reads revolutions per minute. Used on bicycles and automobiles as well as airplanes.

TCA. Terminal Control Area; an airspace division which requires a clearance from Air Traffic Control for entry.

THRESHOLD. The beginning of the landing surface at the approach end of a runway.

TO-FROM INDICATOR. Used in VOR navigation to tell the pilot whether the selected radial is the direction TO or FROM the transmitter; also, ambiguity indicator.

TORQUE. A twisting force; used as a term of convenience in flight instruction to incorporate several forces which combine to create a left-turning tendency.

TOWER CONTROLLER. An air traffic control specialist in a control tower who controls operations on the active runway and in the airport traffic area. (Also "local controller.")

TRACK. The actual path over the ground followed by an airplane.

TRAILING EDGE. The sharp edge of the wing; flaps and ailerons are hinged at the trailing edge of the wing.

TRANSPONDER. A UHF transmitter which replies to coded inquiries from ground radar stations, giving your position and possibly your altitude for identification and traffic separation purposes.

TRIM TABS. Small adjustable tabs on control surfaces (elevator, rudder and ailerons) used by the pilot to relieve control forces. Typically, the tab moves opposite to desired control surface movement deflecting the elevator trim tab downward causes the elevator to move upward.

TRSA. Terminal Radar Service Area; An area where radar service is available to VFR pilots on a voluntary basis; outlined in black on sectional charts.

TRUE AIRSPEED. Indicated airspeed corrected for temperature and pressure altitude.

TRUE AIRSPEED INDICATOR. An airspeed indicator which allows the pilot to set temperature and altitude values and read true airspeed directly.

TRUE NORTH POLE. The northern extremity of the earth's axis; where all of the lines of longitude meet.

TRUE WIND. The actual movement of air over the earth's surface.

TURBOCHARGED. An engine with intake air compressed by a turbine-driven compressor.

TWEB. A transcribed weather broadcast.

UNCONTROLLED AIRPORT. An airport without a control tower or an airport with a tower outside of the towels hours of operation.

UNICOM. An acronym for Universal Communications. Also, Aeronautical Advisory Service, a radio service operated by individuals at airports to provide services to pilots. Not used for air traffic control purposes.

UHF. Ultrahigh Frequency range, 300 MHz to 3,000 MHz. Used for DME and some radar equipment.

VARIATION. The angular difference between measurements in relation to true north and magnetic north Variation is independent of aircraft heading.

VASI. Visual Approach Slope Indicator; A means of providing approach slope guidance to VFR pilots.

VECTOR. A heading to steer, received from a controller.

VENTURI. A tube with a restriction which accelerates air and reduces pressure; venturis are used in carburetors and are used on older airplanes to deliver vacuum to power flight instruments.

VERTICAL AXIS. An imaginary line through the center of gravity which intersects the lateral and longitudinal axes; also, yaw axis.

VERTICAL FIN. A fixed vertical airfoil at the rear of the airplane which stabilizes the airplane in the vertical axis.

VERTICAL SPEED INDICATOR. An instrument which indicates rate of change in altitude by measuring rate of change of air pressure.

VFR. Visual Flight Rules.

VHF. Very High Frequency range. 30 MHz to 300 MHz Range limited to line-of-sight.

VHF/DF. Very High Frequency Direction Finding; a service available at some Flight Service Stations to orient lost pilots. No equipment other than a transmitter and a receiver is required in order to use this service.

VORTEX. A mass of air having a whirling or circular motion Plural. Vortices.

VOR. VHF Omni-directional Range. The basis for the airways system.

VOR-DME. The civilian equivalent of a VORTAC, with both navigation and distance measuring signals under the control of the FAA.

VORTAC. A VOR co-located with a military TACAN (tactical aid to navigations) station. Civilians use the navigational signal from the VOR and the distance information from the TACAN.

VOT. A special transmitter located at major airports to test VOR receivers for accuracy.

WIND CORRECTION ANGLE. The angular difference between course and heading.

WIND DRIFT. The sideways motion over the ground caused by a crosswind.

WIND TRIANGLE. A graphic means of computing wind correction angle and groundspeed.

YAW AXIS. A vertical line through the center of gravity; the pilot uses rudder to control the airplane around the yaw axis.

YAW AXIS. A vertical line through the center of gravity which intersects the longitudinal and lateral axes.

ZULU TIME. Time in relation to the time at Greenwich, England or Greenwich Mean Time.

Phonetic Alphabet

A	ALFA	R	ROMEO
B	BRAVO	S	SIERRA
C	CHARLIE	T	TANGO
D	DELTA	U	UNIFORM
E	ECHO	V	VICTOR
F	FOXTROT	W	WHISKEY
G	GOLF	X	X-RAY
H	HOTEL	Y	YANKEE
I	INDIA	Z	ZULU
J	JULIETT		
K	KILO	1	WUN
L	LIMA	2	TWO
M	MIKE	3	THREE
N	NOVEMBER	4	FOWER
O	OSCAR	5	FIFE
P	PAPA	6	SIX
Q	QUEBEC (Kay-beck)	7	SEVEN
		8	EIGHT
		9	NINER

The new formats for hourly weather reports and terminal forecasts are intended to bring the United States more closely into agreement with international practice; however, because the US has not fully shifted to metric measurements there have been some accommodations. Also, because the number of automatic weather observing stations will increase dramatically in the next few years the report format takes their limitations into account.

Hourly Sequences

METAR KPIT 1955Z 22015G25KT 3/4SM R22L/ 2700FT TSRA OVC010CB 18/16 A2992

That is an hourly sequence for the Pittsburgh airport. Let's take it one element at a time. This is a regularly scheduled report; a special report would begin with SPECI.

The station identifier will not change, except that the letter K will be added in some cases to meet ICAO requirements.

Time

The time of the report is given in Coordinated Universal Time, as indicated by the Z.

Wind

The first group is wind; the first three digits report the wind direction in relation to true north to the nearest ten degrees (or VRB when the wind is less than 6 knots) , and the next two digits report the speed. KT means knots, of course, and the letter G reports that during the ten-minute period prior to the report a gust has exceeded the mean speed by 10 knots or more; the ten- minute mean is relevant because that is how automated weather stations measure the wind.

If during the ten minutes prior to the report the wind direction has shifted more than 60 degrees and the mean wind is greater than 3 knots, the extreme directions will be given with the letter V: 280V350.

Visibility

The prevailing visibility is given in statute miles, and to prevent any confusion SM is appended. This is the first instance in which the international metric standard has been changed for use in the United States.

Runway Visual Range

Where this value is measured and available, the group lists first the runway number and second the visibility in feet. In the example, the runway visual range for runway 22L is 2,700 feet.

Present Weather

This group consists of abbreviations taken from the table below, modified as necessary. In the example, the present weather is thunderstorm and rain. Note that UP is used when the type of precipitation is unknown; this is because the automatic stations derive information from the scattering of a light source. If the type of precipitation is not confirmed to be rain from water collecting in a container or snow because of temperature, it has to be coded as UP. Almost all of the other descriptors require subjective input by an observer.

Cloud Amount

SKC (sky clear) is a new abbreviation to US pilots. When clouds cover 1/8 or 2/8 of the sky, FEW will be used. SCT will be used for 3/8 to 4/8 sky coverage. No ceiling designators will be used; the first BKN or OVC layer is the ceiling. Note that there are no longer such things as "thin" layers. The three digits indicate the height of the layer in hundreds of feet, as did the old format. The example indicates an overcast sky with bases at 1,000 feet and cumulonimbus clouds.

Cloud types are ignored with the exception of convective clouds— cumulonimbus (CB) and towering cumulonimbus (TCU). More than one layer can be coded. Automatic sites will send CLR to indicate no clouds below 12,000 feet.

Weather Phenomena	
Precipitation	DZ = drizzle RA = rain SN = snow SG = snow grains IC = diamond dust PE = ice pellets GR = hail GS = small hail/snow pellets UP = unknown
Obscuration	BR = mist FG = fog FU = smoke VA = volcanic ash SA = sand HZ = haze PY = spray DU = widespread dust
Other	SQ = squall SS = sandstorm DS = duststorm FC = funnel cloud/tornado/waterspout PO = well developed dust/sand whirls
Qualifiers	
Intensity	- = Light + = Heavy no sign = moderate
Proximity	VC = within 5-10 miles of the airport
Descriptor	MI = shallow BC = patches DR = drifting TS = thunderstorm BL = blowing SH = showers FZ = supercooled/freezing

Table C-1. METAR/TAF abbreviations

When the sky is obscured, the cloud group will be VVnnn; vertical visibility of 400 feet would be VV004. If the base of the clouds is on the ground, the group will be VV///.

Temperature/Dew Point

This is the only measurement where the metric standard prevailed; temperature and dew point are reported in degrees Celsius. A minus temperature is prefaced with an M. If you read a weather report from Phoenix in July and the temperature is given as 40, you will appreciate the difference.

Altimeter Setting

No more worry about confusing inches of mercury with millibars. The altimeter setting is given in inches (no decimal) and the A means altimeter. All four digits will be reported.

Remarks

Remarks are prefaced with RMK. AOA tells you that an automated observation has been augmented by a human observer, and the type of information included in this section makes that obvious. Visibility from a tower would be included in remarks, as would wind shear (abbreviated WS with LDG for landing and TKOF for takeoff, with runway number), relevant recent weather with the time of occurrence, and such obviously objective items as tornadoes, waterspouts, lightning, etc.

Terminal Forecasts

TAF KPIT 091720Z 1818 22020KT 3SM -SHRA
BKN020 FM20 PROB40 2022
TEMPO 0407 BECMG 1315

The TAF tells you that this forecast is in the new format; once again we will take it one element at a time.

Date/Time

The date/time group is the date and time of issuance in UTC: 1720Z on the 9th day of the month.

Valid Period

This is a forecast, after all. In this case the valid period is from 1800Z on the 9th until 1800Z on the tenth.

Wind

The wind is forecast using the METAR format.

Visibility

Same as the METAR format except that if the visibility is expected to be greater than six miles the group will be P6SM.

Forecast Weather

See the METAR table; the same abbreviations will be used in terminal forecasts.

Cloud Amount

Same as the METAR format.

Forecast Details

FM20 means from 2000Z; remember that the valid period began at 1800Z. PROB40 gives you the odds—a 40 percent probability. 2022 tells you that the probability of change will exist between 2000Z and 2200Z.

TEMPO is used when the change will occur over a brief period of time (less than one hour); 0407 means that the temporary change is expected to occur between 0400Z and 0700Z.

BECMG is a forecast gradual change. 1315 means that the change is expected to occur between 1300Z and 1500Z.

NSW (no significant weather) is used to identify periods when not much is going on, weatherwise. This could be the lull between the storms.

LEGEND

This Directory is an alphabetical listing of data on record with the FAA on all airports that are open to the public, associated terminal control facilities, air route traffic control centers and radio aids to navigation within the conterminous United States, Puerto Rico and the Virgin Islands. Airports are listed alphabetically by associated city name and cross referenced by airport name. Facilities associated with an airport, but with a different name, are listed individually under their own name, as well as under the airport with which they are associated.

The listing of an airport in this directory merely indicates the airport operator's willingness to accommodate transient aircraft, and does not represent that the facility conforms with any Federal or local standards, or that it has been approved for use on the part of the general public.

The information on obstructions is taken from reports submitted to the FAA. It has not been verified in all cases. Pilots are cautioned that objects not indicated in this tabulation (or on charts) may exist which can create a hazard to flight operation.

Detailed specifics concerning services and facilities tabulated within this directory are contained in Airman's Information Manual, Basic Flight Information and ATC Procedures.

The legend items that follow explain in detail the contents of this Directory and are keyed to the circled numbers on the sample on the preceding page.

① CITY/AIRPORT NAME

Airports and facilities in this directory are listed alphabetically by associated city and state. Where the city name is different from the airport name the city name will appear on the line above the airport name. Airports with the same associated city name will be listed alphabetically by airport name and will be separated by a dashed rule line. All others will be separated by a solid rule line.

② NOTAM SERVICE

All public use landing areas are provided NOTAM "D" (distant dissemination) and NOTAM "L" (local dissemination) service. Airport NOTAM file identifier is shown following the associated FSS data for individual airports, e.g. "NOTAM FILE IAD". See AIM, Basic Flight Information and ATC Procedures for detailed description of NOTAM's.

③ LOCATION IDENTIFIER

A three or four character code assigned to airports. These identifiers are used by ATC in lieu of the airport name in flight plans, flight strips and other written records and computer operations.

④ AIRPORT LOCATION

Airport location is expressed as distance and direction from the center of the associated city in nautical miles and cardinal points, i.e., 4 NE.

⑤ TIME CONVERSION

Hours of operation of all facilities are expressed in Coordinated Universal Time (UTC) and shown as "Z" time. The directory indicates the number of hours to be subtracted from UTC to obtain local standard time and local daylight saving time UTC-5(-4DT). The symbol ‡ indicates that during periods of Daylight Saving Time effective hours will be one hour earlier than shown. In those areas where daylight saving time is not observed that (-4DT) and ‡ will not be shown. All states observe daylight savings time except Arizona and that portion of Indiana in the Eastern Time Zone and Puerto Rico and the Virgin Islands.

⑥ GEOGRAPHIC POSITION OF AIRPORT

Positions are shown in degrees, minutes and hundredths of a minute.

⑦ CHARTS

The Sectional Chart and Low and High Altitude Enroute Chart and panel on which the airport or facility is located. Helicopter Chart locations will be indicated as, i.e., COPTER.

⑧ INSTRUMENT APPROACH PROCEDURES

IAP indicates an airport for which a prescribed (Public Use) FAA Instrument Approach Procedure has been published.

⑨ ELEVATION

Elevation is given in feet above mean sea level and is the highest point on the landing surface. When elevation is sea level it will be indicated as (00). When elevation is below sea level a minus (-) sign will precede the figure.

⑩ ROTATING LIGHT BEACON

B indicates rotating beacon is available. Rotating beacons operate dusk to dawn unless otherwise indicated in AIRPORT REMARKS.

⑪ SERVICING

S1: Minor airframe repairs.
S2: Minor airframe and minor powerplant repairs.
S3: Major airframe and minor powerplant repairs.
S4: Major airframe and major powerplant repairs.

4

DIRECTORY LEGEND

⑫ FUEL

CODE	FUEL	CODE	FUEL
80	Grade 80 gasoline (Red)	B	Jet B—Wide-cut turbine fuel, freeze point-50° C.
100	Grade 100 gasoline (Green)		
100LL	100LL gasoline (low lead) (Blue)	B+	Jet B—Wide-cut turbine fuel with icing inhibitor, freeze point-50° C.
115	Grade 115 gasoline		
A	Jet A—Kerosene freeze point-40° C.	MOGAS	Automobile gasoline which is to be used as aircraft fuel.
A1	Jet A-1—Kerosene freeze point-50°C.		
A1+	Jet A-1—Kerosene with icing inhibitor, freeze point-50° C.		

NOTE: Automobile Gasoline. Certain automobile gasoline may be used in specific aircraft engines if a FAA supplemental type cetificate has been obtained. Automobile gasoline which is to be used in aircraft engines will be identified as "MOGAS", however, the grade/type and other octane rating will not be published.

Data shown on fuel availability represents the most recent information the publisher has been able to acquire. Because of a variety of factors, the fuel listed may not always be obtainable by transient civil pilots. Confirmation of availability of fuel should be made directly with fuel dispensers at locations where refueling is planned.

⑬ OXYGEN

OX 1 High Pressure
OX 2 Low Pressure
OX 3 High Pressure—Replacement Bottles
OX 4 Low Pressure—Replacement Bottles

⑭ TRAFFIC PATTERN ALTITUDE

Traffic Pattern Altitude (TPA)—The first figure shown is TPA above mean sea level. The second figure in parentheses is TPA above airport elevation.

⑮ AIRPORT OF ENTRY, LANDING RIGHTS, AND CUSTOMS USER FEE AIRPORTS

U.S. CUSTOMS USER FEE AIRPORT—Private Aircraft operators are frequently required to pay the costs associated with customs processing.
AOE—Airport of Entry—A customs Airport of Entry where permission from U.S. Customs is not required, however, at least one hour advance notice of arrival must be furnished.
LRA—Landing Rights Airport—Application for permission to land must be submitted in advance to U.S. Customs. At least one hour advance notice of arrival must be furnished.
NOTE: Advance notice of arrival at both an AOE and LRA airport may be included in the flight plan when filed in Canada or Mexico, where Flight Notification Service (ADCUS) is available the airport remark will indicate this service. This notice will also be treated as an application for permission to land in the case of an LRA. Although advance notice of arrival may be relayed to Customs through Mexico, Canadian, and U.S. Communications facilities by flight plan, the aircraft operator is solely responsible for insuring that Customs receives the notification. (See Customs, Immigration and Naturalization, Public Health and Agriculture Department requirements in the International Flight Information Manual for further details.)

⑯ CERTIFICATED AIRPORT (FAR 139)

Airports serving Department of Transportation certified carriers and certified under FAR, Part 139, are indicated by the ARFF index; i.e., ARFF Index A, which relates to the availability of crash, fire, rescue equipment.

FAR-PART 139 CERTIFICATED AIRPORTS
INDICES AND AIRCRAFT RESCUE AND FIRE FIGHTING EQUIPMENT REQUIREMENTS

Airport Index	Required No. Vehicles	Aircraft Length	Scheduled Departures	Agent + Water for Foam '
A	1	<90'	≥1	500#DC or HALON 1211 or 450#DC + 100 gal H$_2$O
B	1 or 2	≥90', <126'	≥5	Index A + 1500 gal H$_2$O
		≥126', <159'	<5	
C	2 or 3	≥126', <159'	≥5	Index A + 3000 gal H$_2$O
		≥159', <200'	<5	
D	3	≥159', <200'	≥5	Index A + 4000 gal H$_2$O
		>200'	<5	
E	3	≥200'	≥5	Index A + 6000 gal H$_2$O

> Greater Than; < Less Than; ≥ Equal or Greater Than; ≤ Equal or Less Than; H$_2$O—Water;
DC—Dry Chemical.

NOTE: The listing of ARFF index does not necessarily assure coverage for non-air carrier operations or at other than prescribed times for air carrier. ARFF Index Ltd.—indicates ARFF coverage may or may not be available, for information contact airport manager prior to flight.

⑰ FAA INSPECTION

All airports not inspected by FAA will be identified by the note: Not insp. This indicates that the airport information has been provided by the owner or operator of the field.

⑱ RUNWAY DATA

Runway information is shown on two lines. That information common to the entire runway is shown on the first line while information concerning the runway ends are shown on the second or following line. Lengthy information will be placed in the Airport Remarks.

Runway direction, surface, length, width, weight bearing capacity, lighting, gradient and appropriate remarks are shown for each runway. Direction, length, width, lighting and remarks are shown for sealanes. The full dimensions of helipads are shown, i.e., 50X150.

RUNWAY SURFACE AND LENGTH

Runway lengths prefixed by the letter "H" indicate that the runways are hard surfaced (concrete, asphalt). If the runway length is not prefixed, the surface is sod, clay, etc. The runway surface composition is indicated in parentheses after runway length as follows:

(AFSC)—Aggregate friction seal coat	(GRVD)—Grooved	(TURF)—Turf
(ASPH)—Asphalt	(GRVL)—Gravel, or cinders	(TRTD)—Treated
(CONC)—Concrete	(PFC)—Porous friction courses	(WC)—Wire combed
(DIRT)—Dirt	(RFSC)—Rubberized friction seal coat	

RUNWAY WEIGHT BEARING CAPACITY

Runway strength data shown in this publication is derived from available information and is a realistic estimate of capability at an average level of activity. It is not intended as a maximum allowable weight or as an operating limitation. Many airport pavements are capable of supporting limited operations with gross weights of 25-50% in excess of the published figures. Permissible operating weights, insofar as runway strengths are concerned, are a matter of agreement between the owner and user. When desiring to operate into any airport at weights in excess of those published in the publication, users should contact the airport management for permission. Add 000 to figure following S, D, DT, DDT and MAX for gross weight capacity:

    S—Runway weight bearing capacity for aircraft with single-wheel type landing gear, (DC-3), etc.

    D—Runway weight bearing capacity for aircraft with dual-wheel type landing gear, (DC-6), etc.

    DT—Runway weight bearing capacity for aircraft with dual-tandem type landing gear, (707), etc.

    DDT—Runway weight bearing capacity for aircraft with double dual-tandem type landing gear, (747), etc.

Quadricycle and dual-tandem are considered virtually equal for runway weight bearing consideration, as are single-tandem and dual-wheel.

Omission of weight bearing capacity indicates information unknown.

RUNWAY LIGHTING

Lights are in operation sunset to sunrise. Lighting available by prior arrangement only or operating part of the night only and/or pilot controlled and with specific operating hours are indicated under airport remarks. Since obstructions are usually lighted, obstruction lighting is not included in this code. Unlighted obstructions on or surrounding an airport will be noted in airport remarks. Runway lights nonstandard (NSTD) are systems for which the light fixtures are not FAA approved L-800 series: color, intensity, or spacing does not meet FAA standards. Nonstandard runway lights, VASI, or any other system not listed below will be shown in airport remarks.

Temporary, emergency or limited runway edge lighting such as flares, smudge pots, lanterns or portable runway lights will also be shown in airport remarks.

Types of lighting are shown with the runway or runway end they serve.

NSTD—Light system fails to meet FAA standards.	SALS—Short Approach Lighting System.
LIRL—Low Intensity Runway Lights	SALSF—Short Approach Lighting System with Sequenced Flashing Lights.
MIRL—Medium Intensity Runway Lights	
HIRL—High Intensity Runway Lights	SSALS—Simplified Short Approach Lighting System.
RAIL—Runway Alignment Indicator Lights	SSALF—Simplified Short Approach Lighting System with Sequenced Flashing Lights.
REIL—Runway End Identifier Lights	
CL—Centerline Lights	SSALR—Simplified Short Approach Lighting System with Runway Alignment Indicator Lights.
TDZ—Touchdown Zone Lights	
ODALS—Omni Directional Approach Lighting System.	ALSAF—High Intensity Approach Lighting System with Sequenced Flashing Lights
AF OVRN—Air Force Overrun 1000' Standard Approach Lighting System.	
LDIN—Lead-In Lighting System.	ALSF1—High Intensity Approach Lighting System with Sequenced Flashing Lights, Category I, Configuration.
MALS—Medium Intensity Approach Lighting System.	
MALSF—Medium Intensity Approach Lighting System with Sequenced Flashing Lights.	ALSF2—High Intensity Approach Lighting System with Sequenced Flashing Lights, Category II, Configuration.
MALSR—Medium Intensity Approach Lighting System with Runway Alignment Indicator Lights.	VASI—Visual Approach Slope Indicator System.

NOTE: Civil ALSF-2 may be operated as SSALR during favorable weather conditions.

VISUAL GLIDESLOPE INDICATORS

APAP—A system of panels, which may or may not be lighted, used for alignment of approach path.

PNIL	APAP on left side of runway
PNIR	APAP on right side of runway

PAPI—Precision Approach Path Indicator

P2L	2-identical light units placed on left side of runway
P2R	2-identical light units placed on right side of runway
P4L	4-identical light units placed on left side of runway
P4R	4-identical light units placed on right side of runway

PVASI—Pulsating/steady burning visual approach slope indicator, normally a single light unit projecting two colors.

PSIL·	PVASI on left side of runway
PSIR·	PVASI on right side of runway

SAVASI—Simplified Abbreviated Visual Approach Slope Indicator

S2L	2-box SAVASI on left side of runway
S2R	2-box SAVASI on right side of runway

TRCV—Tri-color visual approach slope indicator, normally a single light unit projecting three colors.

TRIL	TRCV on left side of runway
TRIR	TRCV on right side of runway

VASI—Visual Approach Slope Indicator

V2L	2-box VASI on left side of runway
V2R	2-box VASI on right side of runway
V4L	4-box VASI on left side of runway
V4R	4-box VASI on right side of runway
V6L	6-box VASI on left side of runway
V6R	6-box VASI on right side of runway
V12	12-box VASI on both sides of runway
V16	16-box VASI on both sides of runway

NOTE: Approach slope angle and threshold crossing height will be shown when available; i.e., –GA 3.5° TCH 37'.

PILOT CONTROL OF AIRPORT LIGHTING

Key Mike	Function
7 times within 5 seconds	Highest intensity available
5 times within 5 seconds	Medium or lower intensity (Lower REIL or REIL-Off)
3 times within 5 seconds	Lowest intensity available (Lower REIL or REIL-Off)

Available systems will be indicated in the Airport Remarks, as follows:

ACTIVATE MALSR Rwy 07, HIRL Rwy 07-25-122.8 (or CTAF).
or
ACTIVATE MIRL Rwy 18-36-122.8 (or CTAF).
or
ACTIVATE VASI and REIL, Rwy 07-122.8 (or CTAF).

Where the airport is not served by an instrument approach procedure and/or has an independent type system of different specification installed by the airport sponsor, descriptions of the type lights, method of control, and operating frequency will be explained in clear text. See AIM, "Basic Flight Information and ATC Procedures," for detailed description of pilot control of airport lighting.

RUNWAY GRADIENT

Runway gradient will be shown only when it is 0.3 percent or more. When available the direction of slope upward will be indicated, i.e., 0.5% up NW.

RUNWAY END DATA

Lighting systems such as VASI, MALSR, REIL; obstructions; displaced thresholds will be shown on the specific runway end. "Rgt tfc"—Right traffic indicates right turns should be made on landing and takeoff for specified runway end.

RUNWAY DECLARED DISTANCE INFORMATION

TORA—Take-off Run Available
TODA—Take-off Distance Available
ASDA—Accelerate-Stop Distance Available
LDA—Landing Distance Available

⑲ AIRPORT REMARKS

Landing Fee indicates landing charges for private or non-revenue producing aircraft, in addition, fees may be charged for planes that remain over a couple of hours and buy no services, or at major airline terminals for all aircraft.

Remarks—Data is confined to operational items affecting the status and usability of the airport.

Parachute Jumping.—See "PARACHUTE" tabulation for details.

Unless otherwise stated, remarks including runway ends refer to the runway's approach end.

⑳ WEATHER DATA SOURCES

ASOS—Automated Surface Observing System. Reports the same as an AWOS-3 plus precipitation identification and intensity, and freezing rain occurrence (future enhancement).

AWOS—Automated Weather Observing System

AWOS-A—reports altimeter setting.

AWOS-1—reports altimeter setting, wind data and usually temperature, dewpoint and density altitude.

AWOS-2—reports the same as AWOS-1 plus visibility.

AWOS-3—reports the same as AWOS-1 plus visibility and cloud/ceiling data.

See AIM, Basic Flight Information and ATC Procedures for detailed description of AWOS.

HIWAS—See RADIO AIDS TO NAVIGATION

LAWRS—Limited Aviation Weather Reporting Station where observers report cloud height, weather, obstructions to vision, temperature and dewpoint (in most cases), surface wind, altimeter and pertinent remarks.

LLWAS—indicates a Low Lev Wind Shear Alert System consisting of a center field and several field perimeter anemometers.

SAWRS—identifies airports that have a Supplemental Aviation Weather Reporting Station available to pilots for current weather information.

SWSL—Supplemental Weather Service Location providing current local weather information via radio and telephone.

㉑ COMMUNICATIONS

Communications will be listed in sequence in the order shown below:

Common Traffic Advisory Frequency (CTAF), Automatic Terminal Information Service (ATIS) and Aeronautical Advisory Stations (UNICOM) along with their frequency is shown, where available, on the line following the heading "COMMUNICATIONS." When the CTAF and UNICOM is the same frequency, the frequency will be shown as CTAF/UNICOM freq.

Flight Service Station (FSS) information. The associated FSS will be shown followed by the identifier and information concerning availability of telephone service, e.g., Direct Line (DL), Local Call (LC-384-2341), Toll free call, dial (TF 800–852-7036 or TF 1-800–227-7160), Long Distance (LD 202-426-8800 or LD 1-202-555-1212) etc. The airport NOTAM file identifier will be shown as "NOTAM FILE IAD." Where the FSS is located on the field it will be indicated as "on arpt" following the identifier. Frequencies available will follow. The FSS telephone number will follow along with any significant operational information. FSS's whose name is not the same as the airport on which located will also be listed in the normal alphabetical name listing for the state in which located. Remote Communications Outlet (RCO) providing service to the airport followed by the frequency and name of the Controlling FSS.

FSS's provide information on airport conditions, radio aids and other facilities, and process flight plans. Local Airport Advisory Service is provided on the CTAF by FSS's located at non-tower airports or airports where the tower is not in operation.

(See AIM, Par. 157/158 Traffic Advisory Practices at airports where a tower is not in operation or AC 90 - 42C.)

Aviation weather briefing service is provided by FSS specialists. Flight and weather briefing services are also available by calling the telephone numbers listed.

Remote Communications Outlet (RCO)—An unmanned air/ground communications facility, remotely controlled and providing UHF or VHF communications capability to extend the service range of an FSS.

Civil Communications Frequencies—Civil communications frequencies used in the FSS air/ground system are now operated simplex on 122.0, 122.2, 122.3, 122.4, 122.6, 123.6; emergency 121.5; plus receive-only on 122.05, 122.1, 122.15, and 123.6.

a. 122.0 is assigned as the Enroute Flight Advisory Service channel at selected FSS's.

b. 122.2 is assigned to most FSS's as a common enroute simplex freq.

c. 123.6 is assigned as the airport advisory channel at non-tower FSS locations, however, it is still in commission at some FSS's collocated with towers to provide part time Local Airport Advisory Service.

d. 122.1 is the primary receive-only frequency at VOR's. 122.05, 122.15 and 123.6 are assigned at selected VOR's meeting certain criteria.

e. Some FSS's are assigned 50 kHz channels for simplex operation in the 122-123 MHz band (e.g. 122.35). Pilots using the FSS A/G system should refer to this directory or appropriate charts to determine frequencies available at the FSS or remoted facility through which they wish to communicate.

Part time FSS hours of operation are shown in remarks under facility name.

Emergency frequency 121.5 is available at all Flight Service Stations, Towers, Approach Control and RADAR facilities, unless indicated as not available.

Frequencies published followed by the letter "T" or "R", indicate that the facility will only transmit or receive respectively on that frequency. All radio aids to navigation frequencies are transmit only.

TERMINAL SERVICES

CTAF—A program designed to get all vehicles and aircraft at uncontrolled airports on a common frequency.

ATIS—A continuous broadcast of recorded non-control information in selected areas of high activity.

UNICOM—A non-government air/ground radio communications facility utilized to provide general airport advisory service.

APP CON—Approach Control. The symbol ® indicates radar approach control.

TOWER—Control tower

GND CON—Ground Control

DEP CON—Departure Control. The symbol ® indicates radar departure control.

CLNC DEL—Clearance Delivery.

PRE TAXI CLNC—Pre taxi clearance

VFR ADVSY SVC—VFR Advisory Service. Service provided by Non-Radar Approach Control.

Advisory Service for VFR aircraft (upon a workload basis) ctc APP CON.

STAGE II SVC—Radar Advisory and Sequencing Service for VFR aircraft

STAGE III SVC—Radar Sequencing and Separation Service for participating VFR Aircraft within a Terminal Radar Service Area (TRSA)

ARSA—Airport Radar Service Area

TCA—Radar Sequencing and Separation Service for all aircraft in a Terminal Control Area (TCA)

TOWER, APP CON and DEP CON RADIO CALL will be the same as the airport name unless indicated otherwise.

㉒ RADIO AIDS TO NAVIGATION

The Airport Facility Directory lists by facility name all Radio Aids to Navigation, except Military TACANS, that appear on National Ocean Service Visual or IFR Aeronautical Charts and those upon which the FAA has approved an Instrument Approach Procedure. All VOR, VORTAC ILS and MLS equipment in the National Airspace System has an automatic monitoring and shutdown feature in the event of malfunction. Unmonitored, as used in this publication for any navigational aid, means that FSS or tower personnel cannot observe the malfunction or shutdown signal. The NAVAID NOTAM file identifier will be shown as "NOTAM FILE IAD" and will be listed on the Radio Aids to Navigation line. When two or more NAVAIDS are listed and the NOTAM file identifier is different than shown on the Radio Aids to Navigation line, then it will be shown with the NAVAID listing. NOTAM file identifiers for ILS's and their components (e.g., NDB (LOM) are the same as the identifiers for the associated airports and are not repeated. Hazardous Inflight Weather Advisory Service (HIWAS) will be shown where this service is broadcast over selected VOR's.

NAVAID information is tabulated as indicated in the following sample:

		TWEB	TACAN/DME Channel		Geographical Position				Site Elevation	

NAME (L) ABVORTAC 117.55   ■ ABE   Chan 122(Y)   N40°43.60' W75°27.30'   180°   4.1 NM to fld.   1110/8E. HIWAS.

Class   Frequency   Identifier   Bearing and distance   Magnetic Variation   Hazardous Inflight

facility to center of airport   Weather Advisory Service

VOR unusable 020°-060° beyond 26 NM below 3500'

Restriction within the normal altitude/range of the navigational aid (See primary alphabetical listing for restrictions on VORTAC and VOR/DME).

Note: Those DME channel numbers with a (Y) suffix require TACAN to be placed in the "Y" mode to receive distance information.

HIWAS—Hazardous Inflight Weather Advisory Service is a continuous broadcast of inflight weather advisories including summarized SIGMETs, convective SIGMETs, AIRMETs and urgent PIREPs. HIWAS is presently broadcast over selected VOR's and will be implemented throughout the conterminous U.S.

ASR/PAR—Indicates that Surveillance (ASR) or Precision (PAR) radar instrument approach minimums are published in U.S. Government Instrument Approach Procedures.

RADIO CLASS DESIGNATIONS

VOR/DME/TACAN Standard Service Volume (SSV) Classifications

SSV Class	Altitudes	Distance (NM)
(T) Terminal	1000' to 12,000'	25
(L) Low Altitude	1000' to 18,000'	40
(H) High Altitude	1000' to 14,500'	40
	14,500' to 18,000'	100
	18,000' to 45,000'	130
	45,000' to 60,000'	100

NOTE: Additionally, (H) facilities provide (L) and (T) service volume and (L) facilities provide (T) service. Altitudes are with respect to the station's site elevation. Coverage is not available in a cone of airspace directly above the facility.

The term VOR is, operationally, a general term covering the VHF omnidirectional bearing type of facility without regard to the fact that the power, the frequency protected service volume, the equipment configuration, and operational requirements may vary between facilities at different locations.

AB _____   Automatic Weather Broadcast (also shown with ■ following frequency.)

DF _____   Direction Finding Service.

DME _____   UHF standard (TACAN compatible) distance measuring equipment.

DME(Y) _____   UHF standard (TACAN compatible) distance measuring equipment that require TACAN to be placed in the "Y" mode to receive DME.

Index

Airport/Facility Directory Excerpts: Ellensburg, Everett, Olympia, Seattle

ELLENSBURG N47°01.46' W120°27.51'   NOTAM FILE ELN.   **SEATTLE** H-1B, L-1C, 9A
(H) VORTAC 117.9 ELN   Chan 126   259° 3.0 NM to Bowers Fld. 1766/21E.
  VORTAC unusable:
    090°–158° byd 10 NM
    158°–163° byd 27 NM
    163°–268° byd 33 NM
  VOR portion unusable:
    300°–040° byd 25 NM
    040°–080° byd 34 NM
  RCO 122.2 (SEATTLE FSS)

ELLENSBURG
BOWERS FLD (ELN) 2 N UTC–8(–7DT) N47°01.98' W120°31.84'   **SEATTLE** H-1B, L-1C,-9A
  1760 B S4 FUEL 100, JET A TPA—2594(834)   IAP
  RWY 07-25: H5550X150 (ASPH) S-28 0.9% up E
  RWY 25: P-line.
  RWY 11-29: H4301X150 (ASPH) S-35, D-57, DT-100 MIRL
  RWY 29: REIL. VASI(V2L)—GA 3.0° TCH 48'.
  AIRPORT REMARKS: Attended Mon–Sat 1600–0100Z‡, Sun 1700–0000Z‡. Approach lgts Rwy 29 NSTD. ACTIVATE MIRL Rwy 11–29–123.0.
  COMMUNICATIONS: CTAF/UNICOM: 123.0
    SEATTLE FSS (SEA) TF 1–800–WX–BRIEF. NOTAM FILE ELN.
    ELLENSBURG RCO 122.2 (SEATTLE FSS)
  RADIO AIDS TO NAVIGATION: NOTAM FILE ELN.
    ELLENSBURG (H) VORTAC 117.9 ELN   Chan 126 N47°01.46' W120°27.51' 259° 3.0 NM to fld.
    1766/21E.

EVERETT
SNOHOMISH CO (PAINE FLD) (PAE) 6 SW UTC–8(–7DT) N47°54.46' W122°16.90'   **SEATTLE** H-1A, L-1D
  606 B S4 FUEL 80, 100LL, JET A OX 1 TPA—See Remarks LRA ARFF Index A   IAP
  RWY 16R-34L: H9010X150 (ASPH-PFC) S-100, D-200, DT-350, DDT-830 HIRL
  RWY 16R: MALSR. RWY 34L: ODALS. VASI(V6L) Upper—GA 3.25° TCH 86, Lower—GA 3.0° TCH 51'. Trees.
  RWY 11-29: H4514X75 (ASPH) S-30 MIRL
  RWY 11: VASI(V2L)—GA 3.25° TCH 60'. Thld dsplcd 799'. Trees.
  RWY 29: VASI(V2R)—GA 4.0° TCH 57'. Trees.
  RWY 16L-34R: H3000X75 (ASPH) S-12.5 MIRL
  RWY 16L: REIL. Pole. RWY 34R: REIL. Pole.
  AIRPORT REMARKS: Attended Nov–Apr 1500–0500Z‡, May–Oct 1600–0500Z‡. For AVGAS after hours call 206-353-6600, for 24 hour credit card fuel call 206-743-9123. Arpt CLOSED to air carrier acft with more than 30 passenger seats 0500–1500Z‡ except PPR ctc arpt manager 206-353-2110/1606. For additional ARFF capability ctc arpt manager 206-353-2110/1606. Rwy 11–29 and Rwy 16L–34R CLOSED 0500–1500Z‡. Aircraft over 250 horsepower use Rwy 16R–34L. Personnel and equipment working adjacent Rwy 16R–34L and Twy A 1500–0700Z‡. Twy A clsd B747 acft N of A2. Twy A-2 restricted to 12,500 lbs. Numerous lgtd cranes up to 270' AGL within 2 NM radius of arpt. Landing fee for acft over 30,000 lbs GWT. Helipad H1: 100 X 100 (ASPH) on arpt. Heavy operation of military helicopters Thur and Fri nights and on first weekend of each month. Avoid overflights of Boeing ramp NE corner of arpt. Flocks of large and small birds in vicinity of arpt. The following areas are not visible from the twr: Twy Alpha the S 800' of the twy and including the Alpha 8 intersection and from hold lines E to Alpha twy; Twy Bravo at the intersection of the outer terminal ramp; Taxilane Echo from the SE corner of the W hangers to Twy Alpha; Twy Golf from Golf 1 to Golf 4 intersection. When twr clsd ACTIVATE HIRL Rwy 16R–34L, MALSR Rwy 16R and ODALS Rwy 34L—CTAF. Noise sensitive arpt, for noise abatement procedures and tfc procedures call arpt manager 206-353-2110 or ctc FBO. If access to Boeing ramp required, ctc Boeing flight dispatch 206-655-3421 for approval during normal duty hours. TPA-1606 (1000) for light acft, 2006 (1400) for heavy acft. NOTE: See SPECIAL NOTICE—Simultaneous Operations on Intersecting Runways.
  WEATHER DATA SOURCES: LAWRS
  COMMUNICATIONS: CTAF 121.3 ATIS 128.65 (206)355-9797. UNICOM: 122.95
    SEATTLE FSS (SEA) TF 1–800–WX–BRIEF. NOTAM FILE PAE.
    PAINE RCO 122.55 (SEATTLE FSS)
  Ⓡ SEATTLE CENTER APP/DEP CON 128.5
    PAINE TOWER 121.3 (acft arrival W of centerline or departure Rwy 16R–34L) 120.2 (acft arrival E of centerline or departure Rwy 16L–34R) (1500–0500Z‡) GND CON 121.8
  AIRSPACE: CLASS D svc effective 1500–0500Z‡ other times CLASS G.
  RADIO AIDS TO NAVIGATION: NOTAM FILE PAE.
    PAINE (L) VORW/DME 110.6 PAE   Chan 43 N47°55.19' W122°16.67' at fld. 670/20E.
    RITTS NDB (LOM) 396 PA N48°03.17' W122°17.33' 156° 8.7 NM to fld.
    ILS 109.3 I-PAE   Rwy 16R LOM RITTS NDB. Localizer back course unusable.
  COMM/NAVAID REMARKS: Emerg frequency 121.5 not avbl at twr.

OLYMPIA
AERO PLAZA (WA44) 5 SE UTC–8(–7DT) N46°59.56' W122°49.66'   **SEATTLE**
  213
  RWY 07-25: 2015X116 (TURF)
  RWY 07: Trees. RWY 25: Trees.
  AIRPORT REMARKS: Unattended.
  COMMUNICATIONS: CTAF 122.9
    SEATTLE FSS (SEA) TF 1–800–WX–BRIEF. NOTAM FILE SEA.

OLYMPIA (OLM) 4 S UTC–8(–7DT) N46°58.24' W122°54.17'   **SEATTLE** H-1A, L-1C
  206 B S4 FUEL 80, 100, 100LL, JET A OX 1, 2 LRA ARFF Index Ltd   IAP
  RWY 17-35: H5419X150 (ASPH) S-55, D-69, DT-117 MIRL
  RWY 17: MALSR. Thld dsplcd 427'. Road. RWY 35: VASI(V4L)—GA 3.0° TCH 50'. Trees. Rgt tfc.
  RWY 08-26: H5001X150 (ASPH) S-30
  RWY 08: Ground. Rgt tfc. RWY 26: Tree.
  AIRPORT REMARKS: Attended Apr–Sep 1600Z‡–sunset. For svc after hours call 206-754-4043 or 206-786-8333. PPR for unscheduled air carrier ops with more than 30 passenger seats call arpt manager 206-586-6164. Rwy 08–26 and Taxiways F, G, C, E and D not avbl for air carrier ops with more than 30 passenger seats. NSTD hold short lgts intersection Twy E and Rwy 17. During hours twr clsd ACTIVATE MALSR Rwy 17 and VASI Rwy 35—CTAF. NOTE: See SPECIAL NOTICE—Simultaneous Operations on Intersecting Runways.
  COMMUNICATIONS: CTAF 124.4 UNICOM 122.95
    SEATTLE FSS (SEA) TF 1–800–WX–BRIEF. NOTAM FILE OLM:
  Ⓡ SEATTLE APP/DEP CON 121.1
    TOWER 124.4 (1600–0400Z‡) GND CON 121.6
  AIRSPACE: CLASS D svc effective 1600–0400Z‡ other times CLASS E.
  RADIO AIDS TO NAVIGATION: NOTAM FILE OLM.
    (H) VORTACW 113.4 OLM   Chan 81 N46°58.30' W122°54.11' at fld. 200/19E.
    VOR portion unusable:
      043°–082° blo 17,500'   333°–358° byd 25 NM blo 6,000'
      143°–183° byd 20 NM blo 6,000'   358°–043° byd 20 NM blo 6,000'
      333°–358° byd 10 NM blo 4,000'   358°–043° byd 20 NM blo 7,000'
      DME unusable:
      223°–258° byd 20 NM blo 4,100'   358°–043° byd 10 NM blo 6,000'
      258°–283° byd 20 NM blo 4,100'   358°–043° byd 20 NM blo 7,000'
    ILS 111.9 I-OLM   Rwy 17 Unmonitored during hours twr closed. BC unusable.
  COMM/NAVAID REMARKS: Emerg frequency 121.5 not avbl at twr.

Ⓡ SEATTLE CENTER   H-1, L-1 (KZSE)
  Beacon Hill – 135.525 120.3 120.3
  Cottonwood – 120.05 118.05
  Fort Lawton – 128.5
  Horton – 134.65 125.8 121.4
  Klamath Falls – 127.6 124.85
  Lakeside – 123.95
  Lakeview – 134.9 127.6
  Larch Mountain – 132.45 128.3 128.3 126.6 126.6
  Marlin – 126.1
  Medford – 135.15 124.85 121.4
  Mohler – 128.45
  Mullan Pass – 128.45
  Neah Bay – 125.1 125.1
  Pendleton – 135.45 132.6
  Redmond – 135.45 128.15
  Scappoose – 124.2 128.15
  Spokane – 134.75 123.95 120.05
  Stampede Pass – 134.95 134.95
  The Dalles – 135.45 119.65
  Whidbey Island – 134.95 134.95 125.1 125.1
  Yakima – 135.525 134.75 132.6 120.3 120.3 118.05

Sectional Chart Legend Excerpt

CONTROL TOWER FREQUENCIES ON SEATTLE SECTIONAL CHART

Airports which have control towers are indicated on this chart by the letters CT followed by the primary VHF local control frequency. Selected transmitting frequencies for each control tower are tabulated in the adjoining spaces, the low or medium transmitting frequency is listed first followed by a VHF local control frequency, and the primary VHF and UHF military frequencies, when these frequencies are available. An asterisk (*) follows the part-time tower frequency remoted to the collocated full-time FSS for use as Local Airport Advisory (LAA) during hours tower is closed. Hours shown are local time. Ground control frequencies listed are the primary ground control frequencies.

Automatic Terminal Information Service (ATIS) frequencies, shown on the face of the chart are primary arrival VHF/UHF frequencies. All ATIS frequencies are listed below. ATIS operational hours may differ from control tower operational hours.

ASR and/or PAR indicates Radar Instrument Approach available.
"MON-FRI" indicates Monday thru Friday.

CONTROL TOWER	OPERATES	TWR FREQ	GND CON	ATIS	ASR/PAR
ABBOTSFORD BC	0700-2300	119.4 295.0 121.0	121.8	119.8	
BELLINGHAM INTL NF	CONTINUOUS	124.9 385.6	127.4 385.6	134.45	
BOEING FIELD/ KING CO INTL	CONTINUOUS	118.3 126.6 257.8	121.9	127.75	
COEUR D'ALENE	0900-1500 SAT-SUN OCSL MON-FRI	119.1 308.9	121.8		
FAIRCHILD AFB	CONTINUOUS	126.2 289.6	275.8		
FELTS	0600-2200	132.5* 241.0	121.7	120.55	
GRANT CO	0630-2300	118.1 (EAST) 128.0 (WEST) 257.8	121.9	119.05	
GRAY AAF	0800-2400 MON-FRI EXCL HOL	126.2 241.0	121.9 229.5	124.65 248.2	ASR/PAR
LEWISTON-NEZ PERCE CO	0600-2200	119.4 318.8	121.9		
McCHORD AFB	CONTINUOUS	124.8 259.3	121.65 275.8	109.6 270.1	
McNARY	0700-2100	119.1 257.2	121.9	124.55	
OLYMPIA	0800-2000	124.4 233.2	121.6		
PENDLETON NF	0700-1900	118.8 257.8	121.9 257.8		
PORTLAND HILLSBORO	0600-2200	119.3* 239.3	121.7	127.65	
PORTLAND INTL	CONTINUOUS	118.7 257.8	121.9 348.6	128.35 269.9	
PORTLAND TROUTDALE	0700-2200	120.5 254.3	121.8		
RENTON	0700-2200	124.7 256.9	121.6	126.95	

(cont. next column)

Control Tower Frequencies, continued

SEATTLE-TACOMA INTL	CONTINUOUS	119.9 239.3	121.7	118.0
SNOHOMISH CO (PAINE FIELD)	0700-2100	120.2 (ARR E OF CNTRLN OR DEP RWY 16L/34R) 121.3 (ARR W OF CNTRLN OR DEP RWY 16R/34L) 287.9	121.8 339.8	128.65
SPOKANE INTL	CONTINUOUS	118.3 257.8	121.9 348.6	127.8 269.9
TACOMA NARROWS	0800-2000	118.5 241.2	121.8	124.05
TRI CITIES	0600-2200	118.2 323.3	121.8	125.65
VICTORIA BC	0600-2400	119.1 (OUTER) 119.7 (INNER) 239.6	121.9 361.4	118.8
WALLA WALLA REGIONAL	0600-2200	118.5 289.4	121.7	
NAS WHIDBEY ISLAND (AULT)	0730-2400	127.9 340.2	121.75 336.4	134.15 280.3	ASR/PAR
YAKIMA AIR TERMINAL	0600-2200	118.4 257.8	121.9	125.25
YAKIMA FIRING CENTER AAF	0700-1630 MON-FRI	126.2 241.0		

CLASS B, CLASS C, TRSA AND SELECTED RADAR APPROACH CONTROL FREQUENCIES

SEATTLE CLASS B	RWY 16/34 119.2 284.7 (341°-075°)	RWY 16/34 120.1 290.9 (199°-300°)
	RWY 16 119.2 284.7 (076°-160°)	RWY 16 125.9 290.9 (301°-340°)
	RWY 34 125.9 290.9 (076°-160°)	RWY 34 120.4 395.0 (301°-340°)
	RWY 16/34 126.5 391.9 (161°-198°)	
FAIRCHILD AFB/ SPOKANE CLASS C	124.3 384.9 (205°-025°)	
	124.7 263.0 (026°-204°)	
PORTLAND CLASS C	118.1 284.6 (100°-279°) 133.0 360.8 (280°-099°)	
WHIDBEY ISLAND CLASS C	118.2 286.0 (WEST) 120.7 270.8 (EAST)	